A Matter of Fate

A MATTER OF FATE

The Concept of Fate in the Arab World as Reflected in Modern Arabic Literature

Dalya Cohen-Mor

OXFORD
UNIVERSITY PRESS
2001

OXFORD
UNIVERSITY PRESS

Oxford New York
Athens Auckland Bangkok Bogotá Buenos Aires Calcutta
Cape Town Chennai Dar es Salaam Delhi Florence Hong Kong Istanbul
Karachi Kuala Lumpur Madrid Melbourne Mexico City Mumbai Nairobi
Paris São Paulo Shanghai Singapore Taipei Tokyo Toronto Warsaw

and associated companies in
Berlin Ibadan

Published by Oxford University Press, Inc.
198 Madison Avenue, New York, New York 10016

Library of Congress Cataloging-in-Publication Data
Cohen-Mor, Dalya.
A matter of fate : the concept of fate in the Arab world
as reflected in modern Arabic literature / Dalya Cohen-Mor.
p. cm.
Includes translations of sixteen Arabic stories into English.
Includes bibliographical references and index.
ISBN 0-19-513398-6
1. Fate and fatalism in literature. 2. Arabic literature—20th
century—History and criticism. 3. Fate and fatalism—Religious
aspects—Islam. I. Title.
PJ7519.F37C64 2000
892.7'09382—dc21 99-30401

1 3 5 7 9 8 6 4 2

Printed in the United States of America
on acid-free paper

In memory of my son, Amit Cohen, whose life ended abruptly after twenty springs. The courage and dignity with which he faced his destiny constitute his personal moral victory.

ת נ צ ב ה

ACKNOWLEDGMENTS

I thank all the individual authors, as well as their publishers and agents, for permission to include the stories selected from their writings. All translations of full-length stories, except "Fate" by Samīra ʿAzzām, are the product of my own work.

This work was written with the kind assistance of several colleagues and institutes. I acknowledge with gratitude their valuable contributions. I thank Professor M. Woidich, chairman of the Department of Arabic and Islamic Studies at the University of Amsterdam, for welcoming me to his department for a three-year period, during which time I taught modern Arabic literature and began this research. I thank Professor Barbara Stowasser, director of the Center for Contemporary Arab Studies at Georgetown University; Professor Gerald M. Mara, associate dean for research at the Graduate School of Arts and Sciences; and Professor Karin Ryding of the Department of Arabic for granting me a two-year affiliation as a visiting researcher. Additional sources for this study were obtained during a summer stay as a CASA III fellow at the American University in Cairo. I thank Professor Gerald E. Lampe, director of the Center for Arabic Study Abroad at the Johns Hopkins University School of Advanced International Studies, for the opportunity to participate in the program. I thank Professor El Said M. Badawi, director of the Arabic Language Institute at the American University in Cairo; Dr. Zeinab M. Ibrahim, CASA executive director; and Dr. Hussein Hamouda of the Department of Arabic at Cairo University for their assistance in clarifying linguistic and bibliographical items. Professor Andras Hamori of the Department of Near Eastern Studies at Princeton University made useful remarks on several issues. Professor Stefan Wild of the Orientalisches Seminar at the University of Bonn offered critical comments and suggestions. Mrs. Beverly Colman served as editor. Her insightful reading and practical advice were of great help in refining the entire manuscript and shaping it into its present form. The responsibility for any views expressed in this work rests entirely with me.

Throughout this research, I benefited greatly from the sources available at the Library of Congress. My thanks are due to the staff of the African and Middle Eastern Reading Room for their efforts in locating the various texts needed for this work.

My greatest debt is to my husband, Michael Cohen, who helped to bring this project to fruition. His boundless support during the long and arduous process of putting pen to paper made this endeavor possible.

CONTENTS

KEY TO THE TRANSLITERATION

Consonants

ء	ʾ [1]	ز	z	ق	q
ب	b	س	s	ك	k
ت	t	ش	sh	ل	l
ث	th	ص	ṣ	م	m
ج	j	ض	ḍ	ن	n
ح	ḥ	ط	ṭ	ه	h
خ	kh	ظ	ẓ	و	w
د	d	ع	ʿ	ي	y
ذ	dh	غ	gh	ة	in pause: -a
ر	r	ف	f		in construct: -at

[1] except when initial

Short Vowels		Long Vowels		Diphthongs	
ـَ	a	ـَا ـَى	ā	ـَوْ	aw
ـُ	u	ـُو	ū	ـَيْ	ay
ـِ	i	ـِي	ī		

Note on the Transliteration

Arabic names and terms have been transliterated, except when they have a generally accepted Anglicized form. Occasionally, the form used in scholarly literature is preferred to the Anglicized form. In quotations from the Qur'ān and poetry, case endings and verb endings are fully represented. In quotations from prose, these endings have been dropped, except before suffixes. Elision is not used for the sake of clarity and simplification. Proverbs are occasionally shown with all word endings to indicate the rhyme. Phrases from colloquial Abrabic are shown the way they sound. For ease of reading, titles of literary works are given first in English translation and then in transliteration.

LIST OF TRANSLATED STORIES

INTRODUCTION

The Arabs and the World

The West has often regarded the Arab world with suspicion mixed with awe. On the one hand, the Arab nations have preserved the special features of their culture and have been critical of the Western way of life, its institutions, and ideas. On the other hand, Arab culture has been poorly understood in the West and conceived mostly in stereotypical terms. The tendency of the Arab world to exercise a certain degree of separatism has also prevented a clear perception of its people. Yet the Arabs have had a dramatic influence on human history: they produced a world religion—Islam—which has become the second largest monotheistic religion, and at the height of the Islamic empire they made important contributions to civilization in every field of human endeavor. However, after the fall of Baghdad in 1258, and especially during the Ottoman age, the Arab world underwent a process of intellectual lethargy, resulting in its decline. The reversal of fortune culminated in a period of European domination that began in the early nineteenth century and lasted until well after the middle of the twentieth century.

Major developments following the liberation of Arab lands, including the discovery of vast reserves of petroleum under Arab sands, the Arab-Israeli conflict, and the resurgence of Islamic fundamentalism, along with the significance of these events for global peace, stability, and prosperity, have focused increased attention on the Arab world and generated international concern with its affairs. The West feels an urgent need to know the forces that shape the Arabs' worldview and motivate their actions and reactions. In cross-cultural communication, especially between nations that sometimes find themselves at loggerheads, literature can be an invaluable aid.

The Idea of Fate

The idea of fate has always had a special appeal in religious, mystical, and philosophical thinking. There are several compelling reasons for this fascination, the most obvious of which is that human life is short and human efforts are frequently futile. As a species endowed with the capacity for thought, people want to find some kind of explanation, purpose, or meaning for their lives. The idea that a superior power—fate—shapes the course of their lives and determines what becomes of them helps people to interpret their experiences and adjust themselves to their circumstances. Arising out of a state of anxiety and bewilderment, it thus fulfills a basic human need for order and harmony.

Despite the inherent appeal of the idea of fate, the concept is not simple, and it is fraught with problems. The controversy at the heart of the matter relates to the role of free will in developing human civilization. Throughout the ages, philosophers, theologians, jurists, historians, psychologists, sociologists, biologists, and other scholars have struggled with the issue of free will versus fate and predestination. An ongoing dilemma, it raises thorny points: Are people masters of their actions, or are they puppets in the hands of fate? Does one's life evolve like the turning of pages in a book, or is it directly related to one's own doings? The implications are significant: If people are not masters of their actions, then they can be neither morally nor legally responsible for them. Furthermore, if one's future is predetermined, then of what use is hard work?

Although the notion of fate may be as old as religion, some religions have come to be more intimately connected with this issue than others. Among the great world faiths, Islam is closely associated with a belief in fate and divine decree. For Muslims, the doctrine of predestination is found in the Qur'ān and in the traditions of the prophet Muḥammad, but pre-Islamic Arab beliefs are known to have influenced these sources. At various stages in the history of Islam, there have been attempts to reinterpret the doctrine of predestination and reconcile it with a theory of free will. On the whole, the issue of predestination has been a prominent topic in Islamic thought since the seventh century, when the Arabs emerged from Arabia carrying the banner of Islam, with the goal of uniting humanity in the monotheistic worship of Allah and submission to His will. The expression of the belief in fate is found in every domain of Arab life, including religious festivals, folklore, literature, and ordinary speech.

Aim and Relevance of This Book

This book explores the belief in fate in the Arab world as it is reflected in modern Arabic literature, with particular emphasis on poetry, fiction, drama, and proverbial lore. The primary goal in this exploratory work is to examine the origin, evolution, and various manifestations of this belief, including its effect on the individual in everyday life. An additional objective is to use the insights gained through the analysis of literary texts to shed light on the dynamics of Arab society and its culture. The underlying assumption of this work is that the belief in fate provides a key to understanding the Arabs' outlook on life, their social psychology, and traditional value orientations.

The thesis of this book is that, despite the significant changes in Arab thought from the birth of Islam through the modern era, the belief in fate has retained its vitality and continues to function as a viable cultural force. In the modern era, the influences of nationalism, socialism, Marxism, Darwinism, Freudianism, existentialism, and other developments in science and philosophy have introduced new ideas about human destiny, such as biological determinism, psychological determinism, socioeconomic determinism, and the notion of pure chance. These modern ideas have challenged the belief in fate and reduced its scope somewhat but failed to replace it. Thus the traditional concept of fate has not disappeared, even though new views of human destiny have become prevalent, at least in certain circles.

It is contended in this book that the belief in fate is still powerful in the Arab world, even in a partly modernized society, and can be isolated as a variable that influences human behavior. Admittedly, the belief in fate can be found in other societies, such as those of Latin America and the Far East, and also in other religions, such as Judaism and Christianity. However, in the case of Arab culture the concept has much deeper roots and wider ramifications. Although a deterministic view of human existence had varying levels of importance in the Judeo-Christian heritage, both Judaism and Christianity in the West, through the various stages of their development, have departed from their original determinism and emphasized the role of human free will in the affairs of everyday life, especially in respect to success in rationalized economic activity. Contrary to this transformation, in Islam God's will is still regarded as an inexorable law, exercising absolute control over the course of events and determining the major aspects of human fate.[1]

Additional features characterize the belief in fate in the Arab world and endow this concept with a heuristic value to interpret modern Arabic literature. To begin with, the belief in fate in the Arab world has strong ideological underpinnings. There is a traceable historical evolution of the concept from pre-Islamic times through the Islamic era to the contemporary period. Rooted in the pre-Islamic conception of time (*dahr*) as the source of whatever happened to people, fate in Islam was attributed to God and assimilated into a doctrine of predestination that in the modern period finds various reinterpretations, the most radical of which is expressed in the teaching of the fundamentalist movement.

Another distinctive feature of the belief in fate in the Arab world derives from the fact that Islam is both a religion and a social, economic, and cultural system. As a total way of life, Islam embraces all the realms of activity of the individual and the community. It is generally recognized that value orientations that can be directly traced back to religion are deeply internalized and extremely effective in directing social behavior. Often identified as factors that hinder development in Arab society, these traditional value orientations include fatalism, absolutism, conformity, preoccupation with the past, compliance rather than rebellion, and charity rather than justice.[2] The common denominator in all these value orientations is the implicit notion of God's will and the duty, enjoined by piety, to submit to the divine decree.

As most Arab societies are authoritarian and display centralized power systems, the belief in fate dominates social behavior and thought patterns to a greater degree than in freer forms of social organization. Moreover, it is continually reinforced through the education system, religious institutions, the mass media, and other agencies of socialization. Its organic incorporation into the fabric of society gives rise to certain roles, attitudes, and motives that influence the individual in everyday life. Ultimately, these sentiments find their expression in works of literature. Writers commonly draw on the life experiences of the people who surround them, and their beliefs, conscious and unconscious, become fodder for the writers' creative work. The form and content of literary works both reflect and affect the social reality. Hence the concept of fate has an undeniable heuristic value in interpreting modern Arabic literature and Arab intellectual discourse.

Lastly, a treatment of the belief in fate is particularly relevant at this specific historical juncture because of its potential implications for the future of Arab society. Many intellectuals in the Arab world, frustrated with the lack of development and social change, blame the ills of their societies on the fatalistic value orientation, which they see as an impediment to progress. In addition, the ongoing struggle between the fundamentalists and the modernists for the direction of Arab society is inextricably connected with their respective interpretations of the concept of fate.

Defining Basic Terms

In this book, the expression *modern Arabic literature* refers to the literature of the nineteenth and twentieth centuries. Arab scholars usually consider their modern literature to have begun with Napoleon's invasion of Egypt in 1798, thus acknowledging the impact of the West on the process of literary revival. The expression *classical Arabic literature* refers to the literature of the medieval period, beginning with the pre-Islamic era and ending with the close of the Middle Ages. The intervening centuries, when practically no Arabic literature of outstanding merit was written, are called the Age of Depression.[3] Modern Arabic literature is distinguished from its classical parent in several respects, notably the introduction of new genres such as the novel, the short story, and the drama, and new forms of poetry such as free verse and the prose poem.

For the sake of clarity, it is necessary to explain how the terms *fate, fatalism, predestination,* and *determinism* are used in this book. *Fate* has several shades of meaning. The general sense is "what in the course of events will become, or has become, of a person or thing." *Fate* is also "a power regarded as predetermining events unalterably," and respectively, "an individual's appointed lot." *Destiny* is treated as synonymous with *fate* and used interchangeably with it. In the Islamic context, *fate* denotes the belief that everything in people's lives and in the world happens according to a set pattern, which, determined by God's will, is beyond human control. *Fatalism* is the belief that all things are subject to fate or inevitable predestination; it implies submission to an omnipotent and arbitrary sovereign power. *Predestination* refers to the doctrine that God has foreordained all the events that occur in the world, including the fate of each and every individual. There is a degree of overlap between *fate, fatalism,* and *predestination* in the Arab-Muslim context in the sense that they all share the idea of predetermination by God.[4] *Determinism* is the doctrine that every event, action, or decision is the inevitable result of earlier causes, such as physical, psychological, or environmental conditions, which are independent of the human will. In other words, *determinism* is the belief that people's lives are determined for them from without, by something other than themselves, and that they are dependent on that other, whatever it may be. These terms contrast with the notion of *free will,* which implies that human beings are endowed with the capacity for choice of action or for decision among alternatives.[5]

Organization

This book is organized around the various manifestations of the idea of fate in modern Arabic literature. Each chapter deals with one of these manifestations as a subtheme to the overarching theme of fate. The chapters are then each followed by two short stories, accompanied by critical analysis. The purpose of the stories is to supplement the examples cited in the body of each chapter and to provide the reader with a basis for further discussion.

The first chapter explores the concept of fate in the religious context—the Qur'ān and the Ḥadīth—with attention to Islamic philosophy and Islamic mysticism (Ṣūfism). The second chapter puts this concept in the historical context, tracing the pre-Islamic roots of the belief in fate and its place in the poetry and system of ideas of the pagan Arabs. The succeeding chapters present modern views of the forces that shape human destiny, seen in the context of the dramatic changes in Arab sociopolitical reality and the spread of Western ideas. The final chapter constitutes an effort to draw the main conclusions of the study. This effort is not limited to the integration of the various subthemes to paint an overall picture of literary orientations and their respective interpretations of human fate; it is also aimed at using the insights gained to evaluate currents of thought and potential developments in Arab society.

The various manifestations of the idea of fate, represented by the chapters' headings, were not chosen arbitrarily but rather out of a careful examination of the major themes in modern Arabic literature. These themes often center on the decisive influence of religion, tradition, gender, character, and socioeconomic factors on the struggle of the individual for self-fulfillment. In essence, then, these themes delineate the dynamic interaction between human destiny and objective reality.

Underlying Assumptions and Methodological Considerations

This book explores a specific aspect of Arab culture—the belief in fate—through the medium of literature. Several assumptions underlie this exploration and provide the basis for a transition from the worlds of fiction and narrative discourses to statements on culture and society, and vice versa.

The first assumption is that literature is the most faithful and authentic mirror of a living reality. As such, literary texts, aside from being works of art, are also social documents. As the Syrian novelist and sociologist Halim Barakat states: "Poems, stories, novels, plays, paintings, graphics and songs constitute historical sources of knowledge about society as well as aesthetic objects to be appreciated in their own right."[6] This is particularly true for a closed society not readily accessible through other means of investigation. Moreover, this is crucial for understanding a deep-seated value orientation that is also exceptionally multifaceted and complex.

The second assumption pertains to the reciprocal relationship between literature and society. While literature is affected by the conditions of the society in which it is generated, it also has its own impact on society: "A work of art both reflects and shapes reality at the same time."[7] In this respect, the Bible and the Qur'ān, regarded as models of literary excellence, have had a profound effect on the consciousness of generations of people. Great literary works arise from the depth of human existence and communicate people's earnest needs and concerns. In their powerful depiction of oppressive situations and the search for ideals, great literary works can inspire people toward critical thinking and revolutionary action that may lead to social and political transformation. In this manner, literature can leave an imprint on the value system of a society and influence the course of its development. Given that literary works are strongly anchored in collective life and express shared experiences, they can serve as a tool with which to probe the nature, role, and impact of core beliefs in a particular society.

The third assumption is that literature has a certain predictive value. This is based on the fact that literature penetrates the most intimate facets of human life to reveal the dynamic interplay between the frustrations and aspirations of the individual and the community. The literary resolution of conflicts depicted on the moral, social, and political levels may be indicative of events to come. Thus literary works can serve as a window through which early signs of changes in society can be observed long before they gain force and are transformed into a reality. As literary texts contain the grammar of discourse of a particular society, they offer keen insights into the past, present, and potential future of that society. Hence the contribution of literature to the study of peoples, their societies, and cultures is as vital as that of other disciplines: "Literature is a way of exploring human behavior like science and philosophy. Great novels depict reality in its innermost essence and in its totality. The novels of Naguib Mahfouz, for instance, portray Egyptian life and society more comprehensively and accurately than the works of all the social scientists put together."[8] Inasmuch as the social sciences are concerned with predictions of likely trends of development, literature can be an indispensable aid.

The decision to use literary works to gain an understanding of Arab society was also stimulated by the fact that contemporary studies of the Arab world tend to exclude literature as a source of information. This exclusion has resulted in an incomplete picture of the Arab world, whose portrayal often lacks the full human dimension. The Palestinian scholar Edward Said criticizes this tendency and affirms the relevance of literature to social and cultural studies:

> One of the striking aspects of the new American social-science attention to the Orient is its singular avoidance of literature. You can read through reams of expert writing on the modern Near East and never encounter a single reference to literature. What seem to matter far more to the regional expert are "facts," of which a literary text is perhaps a disturber. The net effect of this remarkable omission in the modern American awareness of the Arab or Islamic Orient is to keep the region and its people conceptually emasculated, reduced to "attitudes," "trends," statistics: in short dehumanized. Since an Arab poet or novelist—and there are many—writes of his experiences, of his values, of his humanity . . . he effectively disrupts the various patterns (images, clichés, abstractions) by which the Orient is represented. A literary text speaks more or less directly of a living reality.[9]

This study is guided by the desire to base the investigation on the most authentic material from which to draw conclusions. The literary text, therefore, is viewed throughout this study as the best documentary evidence of the culture and distinctive features of Arab society.

An ongoing debate on the study of the Arab world has some bearing on this work. As discussed by Fred Halliday in his article " 'Orientalism' and Its Critics,"[10] the debate pits the traditional approach, represented by Bernard Lewis, against the postmodernist approach, represented by Edward Said. Bernard Lewis relies on the social sciences for the study of the Arab world. Edward Said, rejecting the traditional Western discourse on the Orient as a discourse of domination, seeks to apply literary-critical methodology and to offer an analysis specific to the peoples of the Middle East. Halliday suggests a bridge between these two positions as the soundest and most enlightened approach. This work follows Halliday's suggestion in that it draws on literature yet does not ignore the multidisciplinary constructs provided by the social sciences. In this manner, a balanced methodological framework has been developed to evaluate an important and intriguing aspect of Arab culture—the concept of fate.

Altogether, the methodology that guides this work can be delineated as analytical, critical, and integrative. It is analytical in the sense that it attempts to explain a specific concept rather than merely describe it; critical in the sense that it examines all facts and theoretical aspects in the cultural, social, and historical contexts; and integrative in the sense that besides literary works it draws on other sources—religious and philosophical writings, social and anthropological studies, lexicography, and folklore—to present an accurate portrait of the concept under discussion. This multidimensional framework is designed to yield a broad, dynamic, and objective perspective.

Interpretative Tools and Literary Approaches

The main tool of this study is literary analysis and interpretation: searching for the probable meaning of the literary text, discussing thematic aspects and componential characteristics, and offering relevant commentary. This being the case, the end of the literary work had to be seen as an authentic vision of reality and the formal aspects of art—conventions and techniques—treated as means to this end.[11] In the process of analysis, the critical thought was guided by a conviction that "evaluation—seeing things for what they are, seeing them in their importance—is not a matter of caprice, custom, or affectation, but . . . can emerge from intelligently conceived premises and aims."[12] The principal aim in this study, which subserved all others and inspired the critical analysis throughout, has been to put into action "the quality of sincerity, the desire to discern the truth, to see some point in what one is doing or thinking, and to keep penetrating until the answer is found."[13]

Of all the critical approaches to literature, this book relies primarily on the psychological one. This choice was dictated by the topic of the study—

the concept of fate—which is directly related to the field of psychology. Originating in basic human fears and uncertainties, this concept provides the individual with an indispensable coping mechanism, which, when combined with religious underpinnings, becomes a potent cultural force. As the psychological approach is concerned with understanding the psychical life of the individual—the deep mental, emotional, and motivational forces that shape personality and influence conduct—it is uniquely suited for this study. The application of the psychological approach here is further justified by the fact that the belief in fate is manifested in certain attitudes and norms of behavior. Finally, the psychological approach is the ideal tool with which to interpret the language of dreams, symbols, archetypes, and other forms of subliminal communication.

It is self-evident that no interpretative technique can fathom fully that which is at the heart of a literary work. Any approach to literary criticism can result in oversimplification, and each approach has its limitations. The insights provided by the psychological frame of reference are therefore balanced with relevant considerations of the cultural, social, and historical contexts, as well as with biographical details. Thus the literary works were carefully examined against the background of their creation. Each text was analyzed systematically, first for its direct, explicit message, and second for its symbolic, deeper meaning.

When reading through this work, one must bear in mind that even the most meticulous analysis cannot exhaust the diverse interpretative possibilities of a literary text or offer a conclusive account of it. This is all the more so in dealing with symbols, the complex and ambiguous nature of which allows for more than one meaning. At the same time, it is necessary to remember that the writer of this work did have to come to some conclusions. Although at times these conclusions appear emphatic, they do not rule out other points of view. Rather, the series of comments and observations are intended as plausible explanations. Naturally, the reader is encouraged to delve independently into the literary text in search of other solutions.

Rationale and Criteria for the Stories

The body of each chapter in this book is replete with citations from literary texts to illustrate specific points made in the discussion. While these citations present a compelling picture, they are inevitably limited in focus and scope. It is indisputable that there is no substitute for a work of art in its entirety. In an effort to satisfy the needs of the reader who wishes to acquire a deeper knowledge of the subject, each chapter is supplemented with two of full-length stories. These stories may also render the book more accessible to the reader who has a limited background in Arabic literature. For students, teachers, and scholars, the stories provide useful material for study and research. To keep the volume of the book within reasonable bounds, turning to the realm of the short story was logical. The medium of the short story is well suited for the task at hand not only because of its brevity but also because of its concentrated focus on a single theme.

Selecting stories to fit the needs of the specific topic covered in each chapter was an exacting task. The difficulty lay not in the absence of appropriate examples but rather in the large number of excellent works from which to choose. Several criteria were employed in selecting the stories. First, it was thought desirable to offer stories which have not been translated into English before. Thus the material presented here is largely original and fresh. Second, an attempt was made to include writers, both male and female, from different parts of the Arab world. Egypt, which stands at the center of Arab cultural life both quantitatively and qualitatively, has consequently a larger representation. Third, the stories were evaluated for their literary merit and artistic quality. An effort was made to display a variety of styles, from traditional to modern and from realistic to surrealistic, and a variety of techniques, including stream of consciousness and interior monologue. Fourth, the original publication date of the stories was taken into account in order to introduce examples from older as well as from more recent writings. With this aim in mind, it was possible to cover a broad literary period, from the mid-1920s well into the last quarter of the twentieth century.

While these objective criteria guided the choice of stories for this work, the ultimate decision was also influenced by personal taste—an unavoidable factor in such a process.

A Matter of Fate

1

GOD'S WILL

The Principle of the Prime Mover

> We are but chessmen, destined it is plain,
> That great chess player, Heaven, to entertain;
>   It moves us on life's chess-board to and fro,
> And then in death's box shuts [us] up again.
>
> —Omar Khayyam[1]

The Doctrine of Predestination

The primary basis of Islam is the Qur'ān, revealed to the prophet Muḥammed by God through his angel Gabriel. The second major source of religious law and moral guidance is the Ḥadīth, the corpus of traditions of the sayings and doings of Muḥammed. The idea that God's will determines all things and that they are entirely beyond human control is explicitly stated in the Qur'ān: "God has created you and your handiwork!" (37:96). This unequivocal verse is supported by numerous others: "If God afflicts you with evil, none can remove it but He; and if He blesses you with good fortune, know that He has power over all things" (6:17); "Praise the Name of your Lord the Most High, who has created all things and proportioned them; who has ordained their destinies and guided them" (87:2). The divine decree is based on divine omnipotence, for God is the almighty creator and sole governor of the universe: "God has sovereignty over the heavens and the earth. He creates what He will. He gives daughters to whom He will and sons to whom he pleases. To some He gives both sons and daughters, and He makes sterile whom He will. Omniscient is God, and mighty" (42:49–50). God is the supreme authority; His decrees are absolute and inescapable. Nothing can have an effect on God's will (*irāda*) or His command (*amr*): "And the command of God is a decree determined" (33:38); "It is He who ordains life and death. If He decrees a thing, He need only say: 'Be,' and it is" (40:68); "We command but once: Our will is done in the twinkling of an eye" (54:50). Human beings are utterly impotent in the face of God's infinite power and cannot do anything unless God wills it: "If God wills to guide a man, He opens his bosom to Islam. But if He pleases to confound him, He makes his bosom small and narrow as though he were climbing up to the sky" (6:125); "This is but an admonition to all men: to those among you who have the will to be upright. Yet you cannot will, except by the will of God, Lord of the Universe" (81:27–29).

Time and again, the verses of the Qur'ān proclaim God's unlimited sovereignty over His creation. Nothing escapes God, His will, or His power. God has foreknowledge of everything: "He has the keys of all that is hidden: none knows them but He. He has knowledge of all that land and sea contain: every leaf that falls is known to Him" (6:59). The divine omniscience extends to the smallest action of the smallest created thing: "Not an atom's weight in the heavens or the earth escapes Him; nor is there anything smaller or greater but is recorded in a glorious book" (34: 3). Human weakness and total dependence on God are manifested especially in the term of life (*ajal*) and sustenance (*rizq*), which are both predetermined: "God reprieves no soul when its term expires" (63:11); "Never did We destroy a population that had not a term decreed and assigned beforehand. Neither can a people anticipate its term, nor delay it" (15:4–5); "There is not a creature on earth but God provides its sustenance. He knows its dwelling and its resting-place. All is recorded in a glorious book" (11:6).

The idea of predestination is reinforced by the frequent mention of events "being written" or "being in a book" before they happen: "Say: 'Nothing will happen to us except what God has decreed [written] for us' " (9:51); "No misfortune can happen on earth or in your souls but is recorded in a decree before We bring it into existence" (57:22). Such verses imply that all events on earth occur in conformity with a divine design originating in the distant past. According to orthodox belief, this permanent writing, inscribed on a "preserved tablet" (*lawḥ maḥfūẓ*) and safely kept in heaven by the guardian angel, contains all the decisions of the divine will. These decisions form "the archetypes of all things, past, present, and future," by which the whole of creation is ordered and regulated.[2] The preserved tablet occurs only once in the the Qur'ān (85:22), where it relates to the Qur'ān as being written thereon. The preserved tablet on which human actions are written is described as the "clear prototype" (*imām mubīn*): "Verily, it is We who will quicken the dead, and write down the works which they have sent on before them, and the traces which they have left behind them: and everything have We set down in the clear Book of our decrees" (36:12).[3]

The canonical collections of traditions of the sayings and doings of Muḥammad—the Ḥadīth—support the doctrine of predestination. A recurrent idea is that everything that transpires in the world was recorded in the distant past. At times this is said to be the immediate work of God and at times this is ascribed to a pen writing on a preserved tablet.[4] The following tradition states: "God wrote down the decrees regarding the created world fifty thousand years before He created the heavens and the earth while His throne was on the water."[5] Another tradition relates: "The first thing God created was the Pen. He said to it: Write. It asked: Lord, what shall I write? He answered: Write the destinies of all things till the advent of the Hour."[6] Such traditions depict the course of both the world and human life as having been fixed by God before the creation. They reflect the fundamental thought of the powerlessness of human beings, whose actions are regarded merely as the replica of what had been recorded long before on the preserved tablet.[7]

Belief in predestination is presented as one of the most important articles of faith. According to a famous tradition, one does not qualify as a true believer unless one professes it: "And if you should spend in the path of God an amount larger than mount Uḥud, He would not accept it from you, unless you believe in the decree and acknowledge that what reaches you could not possibly have missed you, and what misses you could not possibly have reached you. And if you should die in a different conviction, you would go to hell."[8]

Another common idea that runs through the Ḥadīth and emphasizes the predetermined nature of human life is that God assigns an angel to write down the fate of each individual while still an embryo in the womb. This conception is expressed in the following tradition:

> When the embryo has passed two and forty days in the womb, God sends an angel, who gives it a form and creates his hearing, sight, skin, flesh and bones. This having been done, the angel asks: O Lord, shall this be male or female? Then the Lord decrees what He pleaseth, and the angel writes it down. Then he asks: O Lord, what shall be his term [of life]? Then the Lord will say what He pleaseth, and the angel will write it down. Thereupon the latter will go away with the scroll in his hand, and nothing will be added to or subtracted from the decree.[9]

A parallel tradition specifies the four main points which constitute a person's foreordained fate:

> As for any one of you, his generation in the womb of his mother is effected in the course of forty days, after which, for the same length of time, he exists there in the form of coagulated blood, and then, for the same time, as a mass of flesh; afterwards the Angel is commissioned to breathe the living spirit into him, and is charged, in four words, to write down his allotment of good, his moral conduct, his term of life, and whether he is to be one of the miserable or one of the blessed. Therefore, by him beside whom there is no God, any one of you may even conduct himself as do those destined for Paradise, until there is only an ell

> between him and it; and yet the registered decree shall prevent him, so that he shall conduct himself as do those destined for Hell, and accordingly enter therein: and any one of you may even conduct himself as do those destined for Hell, until the distance between him and it is only an ell; and yet the registered decree shall prevent him, so that he shall conduct himself as do those destined for Paradise, and accordingly enter therein.[10]

This tradition implies that the final acts serve as the criteria for a person's eternal fate—hell or paradise. In other traditions, this principle is summed up in the sentence: "Works must be judged from the concluding acts only."[11] According to A. J. Wensinck, the Ḥadīth literature has not preserved a single report in which free will is advocated. Thus, to all appearances, the main attitude of Islam is in favor of predestination.[12]

The Arabic expression for fate is *al-qaḍā' wa-al-qadar*, a binary term in which the first word, *qaḍā'*, denotes "God's eternal decision or decree" concerning all existing things, and the second, *qadar*, denotes "destiny, predestination."[13] Although the relationship between these words is understood in different ways, the most common interpretation is that *qadar* is the divine application of *qaḍā'* in time. As a set phrase, it is often used to designate the absolute nature of the divine decree, both in eternity and in its contingent realizations.[14] The noun form *qadar* derives from the root *qdr*, which means primarily "to measure, estimate" and then "to assign specifically by measure," as though God measured out his decrees.[15] In its literal sense, *qadar* occurs in several places in the Qur'ān: "And there is not a thing but with Us are the stores thereof. And We send it not down save in appointed measure [*qadar maʿlūm*]" (15:21); "Verily thy Lord doth provide sustenance in abundance for whom He pleaseth, and He provideth in a just measure [*yaqdiru*]" (17:30). Hence in its technical sense, *qadar* (and the cognate *qadr*) signifies the divine decree inasmuch as it sets the fixed limits for each thing, or the measure of its being: "God will surely bring about what He decrees. God has set a measure for all things" (65:3).[16]

The preceding verses and traditions would seem to indicate that the doctrine of predestination prevails in Islam, were it not for the existence of numerous other Qur'ānic verses that lend support to free will. For one thing, the idea of the Last Judgment, of reward (paradise) and punishment (hell), which is so central to the Qur'ān and Islamic dogma, would be meaningless without an underlying assumption of human responsibility. For another, Muḥammad's admonitions and repeated appeals to people to repent presuppose that they have the ability to respond. Above all, the notion of God's justice stands supreme: "God will wrong none by an atom's weight. A good deed He will repay twofold. Of His own bounty He will bestow a rich recompense" (4:40); "Then, on that Day, not a soul will be wronged in the least, and ye shall but be repaid the meeds of your past Deeds" (36:54).[17]

The contradiction arising between these distinct sets of verses generated much controversy within Islam. As Wensinck notes: "The advocates of predestination, as well as those of free will, could claim a scriptural basis for their view."[18] With the growth of Islamic theology and philosophy during the first centuries of the Muslim era, the opposing views came to be represented by three sects: the Jabrites (advocates of predestination), the Qadarites (advocates of free will), and the orthodox, generally called Ashʿarites (who followed the middle path between these positions).[19] Muḥammad Badr al-Dīn ʿAlawī discusses the differences among these sects. As he states, the Jabrites denied free agency in human beings and attributed their actions entirely to God. They took their name from *jabr*, which means necessity or compulsion, as they were convinced that human beings are inevitably compelled to act as they do, by force of God's eternal and immutable decree. The direct opponents of the Jabrites were the Qadarites, who asserted human power to act freely and independently, without necessity but with choice (*ikhtiyār*). Curiously, they were given the name Qadarites despite (or perhaps because of) the fact that they denied God's absolute *qadar*, that is, predetermination of events. The Qadarites are considered rationalists (Muʿtazilites) in their religious thinking and goals. In between these two extremes were the Ashʿarites, who derived their name from their leader Abū al-Ḥasan al-Ashʿarī (d. 935). They argued that human actions are created by God, who brings them into being, but they are employed through the agency of people. This is called "acquisition" (*kasb*), which means a person's joining or linking the action with individual power and will; the person has no effect on the action itself, except serving as a locus (*maḥall*) for it.[20]

Thus the Ashʿarites could reconcile the notion of predestination with free will. Basing their view on the Qur'ānic verse "God will not burden any soul beyond its power. It shall enjoy the good which it hath acquired, and shall bear the evil for the acquirement of which it labored" (2:286), they maintained that people "acquire" responsibility for their actions, although the actions are willed and created by God.[21] Eventually, this middle position came to be regarded as orthodoxy.[22]

The compromise reached on the theological level, however, had little effect on popular belief. The conceptions underlying deterministic views were deeply rooted among the common people. In addition, there was a mythological tradition favorable to fatalism. According to this tradition, after creating Adam, God took his entire posterity, in the form of swarms of ants, and assigned them to two classes, the blessed and the damned, into the right and left sides of Adam's body. Subsequently, the fate of each embryo is outlined by a special angel appointed by God. According to an idea borrowed from India, one's fate is "written on the forehead."[23] This ancient and widespread tradition was a contributing factor in the failure of contrary doctrines to find support among the masses, who persisted in the belief in unalterable predestination. In particular a person's *ajal*—term of life or date of death—was regarded as predetermined. If it was one's destiny to die on a certain day, one would die then, no matter what one did.[24] In this connection, Carra de Vaux remarks: "The willingness to believe that death cannot come except at a fixed time and place is a source of great courage in battle; for where is the danger in recklessness? If it is not written that one is to die, he will suffer no harm; and, if it is written, then nothing can save him." De Vaux notes that orthodox theology disapproved of this attitude. The Caliph Omar (d. 644) is reported to have said: "He who is in the fire should resign himself to the will of God; but he who is not yet in the fire need not throw himself into it." Still, de Vaux affirms that "resignation" or "abandonment" to God is the form of fatalism admitted by the teaching of Islam: "The very name of Islām expresses this sentiment: *islām* means 'the action of giving up oneself, of surrendering' (i.e., to God)."[25]

De Vaux's comments bear upon a controversial subject—the heroism of the first Muslim forces. Edward E. Salisbury, in his important compilation of original sources on the history of the Islamic doctrine of predestination and free will, criticizes the tendency to simplify this issue. He prefers to ascribe the heroic achievements of the early followers of Muḥammad equally as much to "an awakened consciousness of power in their own wills, as to the persuasion of a favoring divine predestination, or to a self-abandonment to absolute divine decrees." Salisbury concludes his work with a pertinent question: How did it come about that the doctrine of predestination, despite its being only one side of the teaching of the Qur'ān and the traditions on God's relation to human conduct and destiny, and despite all efforts of theologians and philosophers to reconcile it with a theory of free will, should have finally prevailed, as it did, in the beliefs and practices of the Muslim world? His reply highlights the influence of despotic rulers who limited the popular mind to ideas consistent with bondage to the power of the palace. No doctrine of free will could flourish under the reign of absolute princes; in such a situation, the tendency was compelling to magnify the doctrine of divine decrees.[26]

Ignaz Goldziher analyzes the political motive behind the rulers' espousal of the dogma of predestination, even when they did not care much for points of theology. Predestination served not only to legitimize their rule but also to calm the people in the face of injustice or tyranny. The Umayyads (661–750), for example, were well aware that their dynasty was not recognized by the pious, who regarded them as murderers, usurpers of power, and enemies of the family of the Prophet. To control the masses and keep them from rioting against the dynasty, no belief was more useful than predestination: "It is God's eternal decree that these men must rule; all their actions are inevitable and destined by God." The pious could not rebel against God's will. Not surprisingly, at the caliphal court there were poets, such as al-Farazdaq (d. 728) and Jarīr (d. 738), who glorified the Umayyad caliphs as men whose authority was foreordained in God's eternal decree.[27]

The religious leadership, who sought to secure their privileged position, also endorsed the dogma of predestination. The dominance of this school of thought was further facilitated by pre-Islamic Arabic poetry, which abounds in references to human impotence in the face of time–fate (*dahr*).

The Notion of the Muḥarrik

Besides the ninety-nine most beautiful names of God derived from the Qur'ān (*al-asmā' al-ḥusnā*), an additional attribute was ascribed to Allah during the flowering of Islamic theology and philosophy. The territorial conquests of the first centuries of the Muslim era brought the Arabs into contact with diverse philosophical traditions, notably those of Greece. Through intellectual inquiry and translations, the ideas and writings of prominent Greek philosophers such as Pythagoras, Plato, and Aristotle became known to Muslim thinkers and served to inform and influence their work.[28] Among the pivotal notions adopted was the principle of the first or prime mover. Introduced by Aristotle (384–322 B.C.E) in his *Metaphysics*, it was subsequently developed by philosophers and theologians in all the three great monotheistic traditions—Judaism, Christianity, and Islam. Aristotle argued that everything that moves receives its motion from something else. It is impossible to go back infinitely in the series of movers and things moved. Therefore, there must be a prime, unmoved mover, which he identified with God. Thus the prime mover came to designate the eternal originator of all motion and existence in the universe. Aristotle's God, however, neither created the world, which emanated from Him as a necessary effect of His existence, nor guided and directed it. Timeless and impassible, He did not take notice of mundane events, did not reveal himself in history, and would not judge the world at the end of time.[29]

Muslim thinkers who sought to establish God's existence by logic and shed light on God's essence through reason took their cue from Aristotle in embracing the notion of the prime mover—*al-muḥarrik*. Al-Kindī (803–73), the first Muslim philosopher of Arab origin, presented the cosmological proof: the universe, being a network of causes and effects, needs a first cause to escape infinite regress. The first cause, or causeless cause, is God, whose power brings the universe into existence.[30] The Turkish-born al-Fārābī (870–950) employed the proof from motion, from efficient causation, and from contingency to argue the existence of God. Avicenna (Ibn Sīnā, 980–1037), of Persian extraction, maintained that the chain of causation must have its beginning in the first causeless cause—namely,

God—who is the supremely necessary being. The Andalusian Averroës (Ibn Rushd, 1126–98), considered the greatest commentator on Aristotle, concluded that God's priority over the world consists solely in His being its first cause from all eternity.[31] In the main, the philosophers' theory of causation led to a closed and thoroughly deterministic view of reality.

Ṣūfism, the mysticism developed by ascetic believers in early Islam, upheld the notion of God as the one and only agent behind all phenomena, which, as the outward expression of reality, veil the essence of the Divine. However, the mystics differed fundamentally from the philosophers. The philosophers relied on rational knowledge to arrive at the realization of God's essence, whereas the mystics relied on intuitive knowledge. The philosophers emphasized the mind, the mystics the heart. In matters of doctrine, the philosophers rejected creation ex nihilo and the idea of bodily resurrection in the hereafter, whereas the mystics affirmed both and insisted on God's knowledge not only of universals or things in general but of the particulars as well.[32]

Al-Ghazzālī (1058–1111), the authoritative theologian of Islam who is credited with reconciling orthodox Islam with Ṣūfism, insisted that there could be no metaphysics on a basis of pure thought and attacked the philosophers for their tendency to turn the faith of the common people into a system of rationally proven articles. For him, faith was based on direct personal experience and ecstatic revelation. He preached fear of God and the horrors of hell to the pious and stressed the notion of *tawakkul*—complete trust in God. As he explained: "Since God is the sole cause of all that exists or can exist, and all His acts are the result of His perfect goodness and wisdom, and all things depend on His power, then the servant can in perfect trust give up his will to the Divine Will and abandon himself to God, trusting in Him to provide for all his needs."[33] Likewise, al-Ghazzālī commended love of God as a necessary virtue and defended popular practices. His teachings gave spiritual, emotional, and mystical dimensions to Islamic religious life and thus rescued it from the constraints of both rationalism and literalism.[34]

Belief in predestination forms an integral part of Ṣūfī thought.[35] In this connection, it is related that the philosopher Avicenna was asked to explain the meaning of the Ṣūfī saying "To make known the secret of predestination is an act of heresy." He answered as follows: "This is an extremely recondite problem, and one which cannot be put on paper save in the language of cypher, a matter which may not be made known except as a hidden mystery: to disclose it in full would work much mischief to the people at large. The fundamental text in this connection is the saying of the Prophet: 'Predestination is the secret of God: do ye not disclose God's secret.' "[36] For Avicenna, the secret of predestination is logically constructed on three propositions: "First, the fact of an ordered universe, then the doctrine that men's actions will be rewarded and punished, and finally the belief that the soul will be restored after death."[37] With this speculation, Avicenna attempts to provide a moral rationale for predestination: human beings are forbidden to ask questions about this divine domain because doing so will disturb the existing order of the universe, which is carefully regulated by God. For human beings, the main consolation of predestination is to be found in the concept of reward and punishment as it relates to the degree to which the soul achieves perfection and thereby closeness to God, or alternatively remains imperfect and consequently remote from God.[38]

The notion of the Muḥarrik—the prime mover—occurs frequently in Ṣūfī writings, particularly in connection with analogies of the shadow play to earthly life and the relation of God to human beings. For example, the great Andalusian mystical poet and prose writer Muḥyī al-Dīn Ibn al-ʿArabī (1165–1240), in his celebrated treatise *The Meccan Revelations (Al-Futūḥāt al-makkiyya)*, describes the shadow play as a parable produced by God to reveal his role as the Muḥarrik to His creatures. In this parable, the first figure to appear represents Adam, and the screen is the veil that hides the foreordained future or the divine secret. The master of the show conveys his message through the visual images to the spectators, who are under the illusion that what they see and hear is performed by the figures. In reality, the play is run from behind the screen by the hidden master, who symbolizes the sole mover of creation.[39] The major Egyptian Ṣūfī poet ʿUmar Ibn al-Fāriḍ (1182–1235), in his long poem "The Greater Ode" ("Al-Tā'iyya al-kubrā"), makes a similar reference to the shadow play. He describes how the showman, positioned behind the screen, displays his figures in various actions and leads the audience to believe that they act on their own. But when the screen is removed, he alone is seen to be the real actor. In this analogy, which guides human beings to the truth of things, "the showman is the soul, the shadowy figures are the phenomena of sensation, the screen is the body: remove it and the soul is one with God."[40] On the whole, the principle of the prime mover was compatible with the Islamic doctrine of predestination and the idea of God's will as propelling everything that transpires in the universe.

Related Religious Festivals

Some of the major festivals of Islam are closely connected with the belief in predestination. The holy Laylat al-Barā'a, or the Night of the Fifteenth of Shaʿbān (the eighth month of the Muslim calendar), which precedes the fast of Ramaḍān by a short interval, has retained features characteristic of a New Year's festival. According to popular belief, on this night the heavenly tree of life on whose leaves are written the names of the living is shaken. The leaves which fall down indicate those who are to die in the coming year.[41] Edward William Lane points out that in Egypt Muslims hold this night in great reverence as the time when the fate of every person is confirmed for the following year:

> The Sidr (or lote tree) of Paradise, which is more commonly called Shegeret el-Muntahā (or the Tree of the Extremity), probably for several reasons, but chiefly (as is generally supposed) because it is said to be at the extremity or on the most elevated spot in Paradise, is believed to have as many leaves as there are living human beings in the world; and the leaves are said to be inscribed with the names of all those beings, each leaf bearing the name of one person, and those of his father and mother. The tree, we are taught, is shaken on the night above mentioned, a little after sunset; and when a person is destined to die in the ensuing year, his leaf, upon which his name is written, falls on this occasion. If he be to die very soon, his leaf is almost wholly withered, a very small portion only remaining green. If he be to die later in the year, a larger portion remains green. According to the time he has yet to live, so is the proportion of the part of the leaf yet green. This, therefore, is a very awful night to the serious and considerate Muslims, who accordingly observe it with solemnity and earnest prayer.[42]

The prayer recited by Muslims, which Lane cites, affirms the doctrine of predestination and God's sovereignty to reverse one's fate:

> O God, if thou hast recorded me in thy abode, upon the "Original of the Book," miserable, or unfortunate, or scanted in my sustenance, cancel, O God, of thy goodness, my misery, and misfortune, and scanty allowance of sustenance, and confirm me in thy abode, upon the Original of the Book, as happy, and provided for, and directed to good: for thou hast said (and thy saying is true) in thy Book revealed by the tongue of thy commissioned Prophet, "God will cancel what he pleaseth, and confirm; and with him is the Original of the Book."[43]

According to orthodox belief, God never revokes what He has decreed, but prayer and supplication (*duʿāʾ*) can make things easier to bear. The historian al-Jabartī, for example, in his chronicle of the first seven months of the French occupation of Egypt in 1798, relates that on learning of the French invasion, all the al-Azhar shaykhs and other religious leaders convened with the common people at the mosques and engaged in profuse invocations and supplications. He comments: "Although the prayers did not undo the French invasion, which was a foreordained fate and could not be reversed through supplication, they brought about kindness."[44] When people gather together to invoke God's name and ask for His forgiveness, their spiritual efforts and the union of their hearts induce acts of kindness toward each other, and that is what makes the pious practice meritorious.[45] Ṭāhā Ḥusayn, in his novel *The Tree of Misery (Shajarat al-bu'ṣ,* 1944), further elaborates on the purpose of supplication: "The truly faithful is he who does not ask God to recall His decree, for God's decree is not recalled. Rather, he should ask for His gentleness in applying His decree."[46] Thus when the wife of Khālid, the hero of the novel, is struck with mental illness, Khālid appeals to God, repeatedly uttering two supplications often made by shaykhs in the countryside: "God, be kind to us in your application of destiny. God, we ask you not to recall your decree, but to be gentle in applying it."[47] In al-Ghazzālī's teachings, the procurement of God's mercy and the removal of an affliction through supplication do not imply the revocation of the divine decree, for even such a matter—the removal of an affliction—is a part of predestination.[48] The doctrine of the Ṣūfīs recognizes the prophets' right of intercession (*shafāʿa*) to mitigate the divine decree.[49]

Unlike the celebration of Laylat al-Barā'a, which exhibits regional variations in practice and ritual, the blessed Laylat al-Qadr (the Night of Power, or of the Divine Decree) is uniformly observed throughout the Arab world. It falls in the month of Ramaḍān (the ninth month of the Muslim calendar), which is passed in fasting every day from sunrise to sunset. Lane provides a detailed account of this special night, venerated by all Muslims worldwide:

> Some few pious persons spend the last ten days and nights of Ramaḍān in the mosque of the Ḥasaneyn or that of the Seyyideh Zeyneb. One of these nights, generally supposed to be the 27th of the month (that is, the night preceding the 27th day), is called "Leylet el-Ḳadr" (the Night of Power, or of the Divine Decree). On this night the Ḳur'ān is said to have been sent down to Mohammad. It is affirmed to be "better than a thousand months"; and the angels are believed to descend and to be occupied in conveying blessings to the faithful from the commencement of it until daybreak. Moreover, the gates of heaven being then opened, prayer is held to be certain of success. Salt water, it is said, suddenly becomes sweet on this night; and hence some devout persons, not knowing which of the last ten days of Ramaḍān is the Leylet el-Ḳadr, observe all those nights with great solemnity, and keep before them a vessel of salt water, which they occasionally taste, to try if it become sweet, so that they may be certain of the night.[50]

A period of atonement and forgiveness, Ramaḍān constitutes a festival in which the conduct of Muslims is closely examined by their creator. A sustained effort of fasting, prayer, and spiritual contemplation is deemed essential in order to present themselves to God in the best light possible and to plead with Him for mercy. Thus their days will be fortunate and their fate not altered for the worse.

The Concept of Fate in Everyday Life

In view of the importance of doctrine of predestination in the beliefs and practices of the Arab Muslim world, it is inevitably reflected in the conduct and mentality of the people. Edward William Lane, who lived in Cairo for extended periods of time during which he penetrated the inner life of the Egyptians and obtained firsthand information about their manners and customs, observes:

> Influenced by their belief in predestination, the men display, in times of distressing uncertainty, an exemplary patience, and, after any afflicting event, a remarkable degree of resignation and fortitude, approaching nearly to apathy, generally exhibiting their sorrow only by a sigh and the exclamation of "Allah Kereem" ("God is bountiful!"). . . . When [the Muslim] sees his end approaching, his resignation is still conspicuous; he exclaims, "Verily to God we belong, and verily to Him we return!"[51]

Lane notes that unlike Christians, who tend to blame themselves for every unhappy event they think they have brought on themselves or might have avoided, the Muslim enjoys a rare peace of mind in all the vicissitudes of life. This state of spiritual resilience is also emphasized by Arab scholars, who claim that the Muslim psyche is endowed with a unique sense of repose, derived from submission to God's will. The Muslim's "tranquil soul" (*al-nafs al-muṭma'inna,* Qur'ān 89:27) contrasts sharply with the Westerner's soul, which is riddled with endless anxieties and phobias.

Another manifestation of the belief in predestination is the invocation of God's name on almost every occasion, public or private, holy or mundane. While these invocations also serve as a demonstration of piety, they reveal the constant presence of God in people's minds. Lane elaborates:

> The Muslims frequently swear by God (but not irreverently), and also by the Prophet. . . . When one is told anything that excites his surprise and disbelief, he generally exclaims, "Wa-llāh?" or "Wa-llāhi?" (by God?); and the other replies, "Wa-llāhi!" As on ordinary occasions before eating and drinking, so also on taking medicine, commencing a writing or any important undertaking, and before many a trifling act, it is their habit to say, "In the name of God, the Compassionate, the Merciful"; and after the act, "Praise be to God."[52]

Lane further remarks that the belief in predestination does not prevent people from taking steps to obtain an object they desire, nor does it make them careless of avoiding danger. However, it engenders reliance on God:

> The same belief in predestination renders the Muslim utterly devoid of presumption with regard to his future actions or to any future events.

> He never speaks of anything that he intends to do, or of any circumstance which he expects and hopes may come to pass, without adding, "If it be the will of God"; and in like manner, in speaking of a past event of which he is not certain, he generally prefaces or concludes what he says with the expression, "God is all-knowing" (or "God is most knowing").[53]

The lexicographer Moshe Piamenta has collected common formulae, idioms, and expressions used in everyday Arabic speech. His data show that these formulae, both standard and dialect-based, are largely inspired by religion and in most instances include the name of God explicitly or implicitly. They encompass every area of social interaction and affective communication, from wishes to congratulations to greetings to condolences. The major themes running through them are human anxiety and security in God and human attitude toward God's will and God's decree.[54] For example, when frustrated, overcome, or defeated, one proclaims: "God decrees, and whatever He wills He does," "God is sufficient for me!" "Most excellent is He in whom I trust," or "There is no power but in God." Similarly, someone who undertakes an activity or relates an incident or hears news accompanies it with exclamations such as "In the name of God," "God is great," or "Praise be to God." Any mention of the future—of the fulfillment of an action, the occurrence of an event, or the execution of a thought or plan—includes the conditional clause *in shā'a allāh* ("If God wills"), abbreviated colloquially to *inshāllah*.[55] Piamenta concludes that these formulae constitute popular Islamic constructions of "reality" and "danger," elicited by socioemotional situations and shared by all speakers of Arabic.[56]

According to various studies, the belief in fate exercises a dual—both positive and negative—influence on the Arabs.[57] On the one hand, it endows people with composure in the face of adversity, with stoic resignation to whatever happens, and with calm acceptance of their station and circumstances, which make life's trials and tribulations easier to bear.[58] On the other hand, the belief in fate inhibits normal ambition and motivation: "It engenders an attitude of passivity and of disinclination to undertake efforts to change or improve things. It especially discourages long-range efforts which require advance planning, because any such activity might come dangerously close to rebelling against Allah and His will as manifested in the existing order of things."[59] Given that everything in life is already predetermined, a person has no choice but "to go through the course of events which have been written down for him in God's Book to the smallest detail. Not even in everyday life can a man do anything either to hasten or otherwise influence events. . . . It does not pay and is not even possible to try to do anything to procure an advantage."[60] Fatalism has been observed to foster a defeatist attitude to life, marked by unquestioning obedience to authority, surrender to one's lot, refusal to accept personal responsibility, and reluctance to revolt: "Man may follow the law of Allah, but must, nonetheless, submit to his own destiny; an absolute determinism blights all spontaneity of action, leaving room at best for fanaticism."[61] Thus the loss of the self in God's will can be a cause of inactivity and stagnation as well as a source of stability and strength.

In the nineteenth century, following several military defeats of the Ottoman Empire at the hands of European powers, Muslim thinkers could not fail to recognize the pitfalls inherent in a fatalistic outlook. With the Muslim world in a general state of apathy and decline, the great teachers of Islam considered the popular belief in fate a cultural liability and an impediment to progress.[62] Jamāl al-Dīn al-Afghānī (1839–97), one of the most prominent Muslim reformers, taught that Islam means activity and not passive resignation to whatever happens, as happening by God's will, and that people are responsible before God for all their actions, including the welfare of their community. Along with his followers, he repeatedly quoted a Qur'ānic verse which, for them, summed up the whole: "God changes not what is in a people, until they change what is in themselves" (13:10). Al-Afghānī explained that the genuine Islamic doctrine of predestination implies that all events in the universe occur by sequence of cause and effect, and God is the first cause that initiated the chain. Human actions are free, but God has provided, through reason and the prophets, an indication as to how they should be performed. To believe in predestination is to believe that God will be with a person who acts rightly. This belief should therefore stimulate people to activity rather than lead them to passivity.[63] Like al-Afghānī, his Egyptian disciple Muḥammad ʿAbduh (1849–1905) also spoke out forcefully in rejection of fatalism and in defense of free will.

Contemporary Arab intellectuals continue to address this topic. In *The Crisis in Arab Thought (Azmat al-fikr al-ʿarabī)*, the Palestinian scholar Isḥāq Mūsā al-Ḥusaynī discusses the major problems that confront the Arab world today. In examining Arab ways of thinking in general, he finds five basic shortcomings: absence of a sense of direction, a tendency toward improvisation, lack of logical reasoning, lack of ideological freedom and self-criticism, and an obsession with the past. Al-Ḥusaynī believes that these faults are ultimately responsible for the low level of social and economic development in Arab countries. The source of the first shortcoming, he writes, is the popular belief in fate. The widespread conviction in the total predestination of the course of events and of all one's comings and goings results in complete dependence on God and lack of planning, which, in turn, lead to uncertainty and the absence of a sense of direction. Al-Ḥusaynī concludes that the crisis facing the Arab world at present is in essence a crisis in thought, and all the other dilemmas arise from it.[64]

The Syrian novelist and sociologist Halim Barakat has examined socio-economic, cultural, and personality forces that hinder development in Arab society. He identifies fatalism as one of the main cultural obstacles to change. He sees religion as the direct source, but not necessarily the only source, of this value orientation:

> Man is seen as a passive and predestined creature. He is virtuous inasmuch as he accepts his condition. Acceptance, resignation, contentment rather than rejection, rebellion and dissatisfaction are seen as positive values. Events are understood as the expression of the will of God. An Arab's position vis-à-vis challenges is typically one of nonconfrontation, denial and justification. He accepts his poverty and whatever births are likely to occur in the family, "for heaven has ordered and earth has to abide, and the creator has written and planned, and the created has to be contented with his lot." . . . Proverbs to the same effect are common in Arab society. The tendency is to sit and wait for justice to be brought about.[65]

The social scientist Sania Hamady argues that the fatalistic attitude of the Arabs stems not so much from religion as from the "nefarious influence of political subjugation, economic poverty, and social tyranny." She cites "landlordism and sheikhcraft" as the two primary institutions that keep the people in bondage to fatalism: "Sheikhcraft holds the people in the chains of superstition and defends poverty and ignorance. It teaches them to accept the political and social systems, under which they happen to be, and to reconcile themselves to their lowly position while religion supplies them with the necessary spiritual consolation." Economic hardships enhance the appeal of the fatalistic outlook: "The average Arab has been leading a deprived and miserable life for ages. His fatalistic attitude is the result of a subsistence economy where people live in material want until death."[66] This state of affairs suggests a vicious circle: the harsher the reality, the deeper the belief in fate. Hence people's beliefs cannot be reformed unless their environment is reformed. The difficulty with this argument pertains to the rich Arab countries, such as Saudi Arabia and the Gulf oil states: their populations are small and enjoy considerable wealth, yet the belief in fate is as rife among them as among the large and poor populations of Egypt and Sudan.

Among the various anthropological studies conducted in the Arab world are Hilma Granqvist's *Birth and Childhood among the Arabs* and Hamed Ammar's *Growing Up in an Egyptian Village*. Granqvist, a Finnish social scientist, has examined the value orientations of a village community in Palestine. Her observations indicate a thoroughly fatalistic view of life: "In small things as in great, man is absolutely subject to Fate:

qisma, naṣīb."[67] She supports her conclusions with numerous anecdotes, proverbs, and colloquial expressions. The Egyptian sociologist Hamed Ammar has examined the attitudes of the peasant population of Silwa, a village in the province of Aswan. He finds the belief in fate to be an important psychological mechanism in the personality of the individual in this community. He quotes the social psychologist Abram Kardiner to the effect that "such a mechanism is a tendency to shift personal responsibility on to others or on to supernatural forces. The prevalence of such a tendency is a cultural mode of displacing dependency on parent-surrogates, and thus escaping blame and punishment."[68] Ammar also mentions the large number of statements the villagers made in praise of contentment, asceticism, and submission to fate.[69]

Halim Barakat rejects the literal interpretation given to fatalistic utterances by scholars such as Ammar and Granqvist. Instead, he argues that verbal expressions of fatalism do not always imply submission, resignation, or refusal to accept personal responsibility: "Statements indicating fatalism need to be interpreted in their social context or in reference to the particular occasions on which they are repeated."[70] Moreover, Arabic poetry and proverbial lore abound in sayings that assert human free will and responsibility, as, for example, "Hope without effort is a tree without fruit" and "Only he who goes to the market will buy and sell." Barakat cautions against overgeneralization and advocates an analytical approach in evaluating fatalistic phrases: "Proverbs or expressions indicating fatalism serve as mechanisms of adjustment to specific situations and should not be interpreted in absolute terms or at face value. They may have the opposite meaning. In order to grasp their real rather than their ostensible meaning, we must explain them in terms of the actual functions they serve in particular circumstances. They need to be examined as psychological mechanisms for dealing with human reality."[71]

On the political level, the concept of fate—like *jihād*, holy war—has been manipulated by Arab regimes for control and legitimation. The recent history of the Middle East illustrates this phenomenon. The late Egyptian president Gamal Abdel Nasser, for example, resorted to Islam to explain Egypt's unexpected military defeat in the Six-Day War of June 1967. In speeches, he labeled it "Egypt's fate," "God's will," and "a destiny from which there could be no escape."[72]

Nasser's invocation of the belief in predestination to justify the humiliating defeat was echoed by other authorities in the Arab world. In *Self-Criticism after the Defeat (Al-Naqd al-dhātī baʿda al-hazīma)*, the Syrian intellectual Ṣādiq Jalāl al-ʿAẓm examines Arab behavior before and after the Six-Day War. He finds a classic example of Arab fatalism and of the desire to escape personal responsibility in the statement of the mufti of the Jordanian kingdom to the newspaper *al-Dustūr*: "The Jews do not possess the ability, strength, or courage that are needed to do what they have done. We know them better than anyone else. But God wished to impose them as a punishment on us because we have neglected our religion."[73] Al-ʿAẓm refers to a similar display of attitude in the book *The Pillars of the Disaster (Aʿmidat al-nakba)*, which appeared in Beirut immediately after the war. In it, the author Ṣalāḥ al-Dīn al-Munajjid declares: "The Arabs have forsaken their belief in God, and therefore God has forsaken them."[74] For al-ʿAẓm, the very term selected by the Arabs to delineate their defeat in Palestine—*al-nakba* ("the disaster")—indicates their unwillingness to accept responsibility: "When a person is stricken by a disaster, he is not considered responsible for it, and even if he is, his responsibility is very small compared to the horror and scope of the disaster. That is why we have become accustomed to ascribing disasters to fate, time, and nature—namely, to factors which we do not control and for which we cannot possibly be called to account."[75]

As a phenomenon in itself, the tendency to regard a national calamity as a collective punishment from God to His congregation for having strayed from the straight path is common to religious dogma in all the three great monotheistic faiths—Judaism, Christianity, and Islam. In Judaism, for example, the destruction of the Temple and the exile of the Israelites from their land was seen as the result of the wrongful conduct of the people, who had invoked God's wrath by abandoning His commandments. In Catholicism, diseases and plagues were viewed as God's punishment for the sinful behavior of humankind. This tendency, however, appears to be more prominent in Islam because of the belief in fate and divine decree. A typical example can be found in *My Life (Ḥayātī*, 1950), the autobiography of the Egyptian scholar Aḥmad Amīn (1886–1954). As a child growing up under the British occupation of his country, he saw the fear and despair that possessed the Egyptians at the sight of British soldiers. He remembers the view of his father, a teacher at al-Azhar:

> My father rarely spoke of politics and when he did, his philosophy was that of most of the people: that this was God's destiny and His revenge of His servants. Because Egyptians wronged one another, and because their rulers wronged them and disobeyed God's commands and prohibitions, God gave the English power over them to torment them badly. This calamity would not be taken away from them until the Egyptians became upright and just, and abode by the commands of religion.[76]

Amīn relates that when he became a little older, he once asked his father: "Are these English people obedient to God that He makes them victorious over us and powerful in our country?" His father rebuked him and did not answer.[77]

A similar view is expressed in Najīb Maḥfūẓ's novel *Love in the Rain (Al-Ḥubb taḥta al-maṭar*, 1973). ʿAshmāwī, the shoeshine man who works in the coffee shop al-Inshirāḥ, offers his explanation for the Egyptian defeat in the Six-Day War: "Why did what happened happen? Because we have neglected our religion and morals." ʿAshmāwī is confident that ultimately God will grant the Arabs victory over their Jewish enemies: "In the end, God will make us victorious." His customer, Ḥusnī Ḥijāzī, immediately corrects him: "Say, *if God wills,* we'll be victorious." Realizing his mistake, ʿAshmāwī quickly amends: "Everything is subject to God's will."[78]

The Concept of Fate in Arabic Literature

In classical Arabic literature, which was essentially an Islamic literature, authors generally conveyed the orthodox view on fate in their writings. Even in the most famous collection of popular narrative, *The Arabian Nights,* where chance and coincidence play a large role, people are shown to follow God's will, as, for instance, in the tales of "The Rich Man Who Became Poor and Then Rich Again" and "The Man Who Stole the Golden Plate from Which He Had Eaten with the Dogs."[79] Further, throughout the collection there are repeated statements to the effect that one or other event happened according to God's decree (*qaḍāʾ*), or as it was decreed (*maqdūr* or *muqaddar*).[80] For example, in the tale of "Ḥasan of Baṣrah" it is said that Ḥasan and his wife traveled night and day through the desert, "and God decreed them safety. So they were safe, and arrived at the city of El-Baṣrah." In the tale of the "The Porter and the Ladies of Baghdad," the third mendicant begins his account by declaring: "My story is not like those of my two companions, but more wonderful; the course of fate and destiny brought upon them events against which they could not guard." He admits that in his case, he himself provoked fate. But a little later, he describes how "his foot slipped, as God had decreed."[81]

The Egyptian literary scholar M. M. Badawi states that "on the whole, the orthodox position on Fate was maintained in classical Islamic Arabic literature, using the word literature in the narrow sense of imaginative creative writing."[82] Examining modern Arabic literature, Badawi looks at selected works by four Egyptian authors: the playwright Tawfīq al-Ḥakīm (1898–1987), the short-story writer Maḥmūd Ṭahīr Lāshīn (1894–1954), the poet Ṣalāḥ ʿAbd al-Ṣabūr (1931–81), and the novelist Najīb Maḥfūẓ (b. 1912). His analysis yields mixed results. In some cases, there is a clear rejection of the notion of fate, as, for example, in the poem "The People of My Country" ("Al-Nās fī bilādī") by Ṣalāḥ ʿAbd al-Ṣabūr. In others, such as the novel *The Thief and the Dogs (Al-Liṣṣ wa-al-kilāb,* 1961) by Najīb Maḥfūẓ, fate still plays a part, though "not to the exclusion of other, equally important human factors, be they psychological, ideological, and political or economic." Badawi concludes that "the role of Fate, therefore, has been considerably reduced, but it has not disappeared altogether from modern Egyptian literature."[83] Despite the plausibility of his conclusion, Badawi's discussion does not consider the fact that literary works can also serve as a vehicle for the writer's didactic intentions and wishful thoughts. Such works reflect not the way things are but the way things ought to be. Hence they do not paint an accurate picture of the prevailing literary or social climate. Nevertheless, the Egyptian cultural scene is of paramount significance, for Egypt has always been in the forefront of Arabic literary activity and its output is both influential and familiar throughout the Arab world.

The field of drama has special relevance to the topic under discussion. It has often been observed that classical Arabic literature, despite its unique accomplishments, did not cultivate the dramatic art. As one of the scholars remarks: "It is a strange feature of Arabic literature (otherwise so rich, developed even to the point of degeneration) that the art of the drama has never advanced beyond the very crudest beginnings."[84] Among the various explanations offered for the absence of Arabic drama is the belief in fate. The European orientalist Georg Jacob, who has compiled the most important bibliographies on Oriental shadow theater, argues that "the Muhammadan view of life, with its autocratic idea of God and fate, has absolutely no comprehension of individual conflict, of rebellion against the 'eternal mover,' the Muḥarrik, or of any combat between will and duty, and has therefore no comprehension of the dramatic."[85] Of all the forms of folk dramatic art that existed in the medieval Arab world, the most important was the shadow play or *khayāl al-ẓill*, which, though not originated by the Arabs, was to a certain extent developed by them.[86]

Believed to have been introduced from the Far East, possibly China or India, the shadow play involved using flat, translucent figures cut out of leather in front of a linen screen. Placing a candle or lamp behind the figures cast shadows that were visible to the audience. The hidden master manipulated the figures by means of pins or sticks attached to them, as he delivered the dialogue and songs with the help of one or more assistants.[87] In Egypt, the shadow play was popular not only with laypeople but also among theologians, who saw a parallel between the shadow-play master who moved all the figures and God as the sole mover of creation.[88] It is reported that in 1171 the sultan Saladin invited his vizier, the noted man of learning al-Qāḍī al-Fāḍil, to attend a shadow play. After some hesitation, the vizier agreed to watch the show. When asked at the end of the performance what he thought of it, he answered that "he found it most edifying, for it showed people and states coming and going but when it was all over and the screen was removed the one mover behind them all was revealed."[89]

Usually performed in the streets and market places and occasionally also in the palaces of sultans and emirs, the shadow play entertained even the rich and educated, but in the main it served as an amusement for the common people. Jacob M. Landau classifies the different types of this early theater: "Puppet shows fall naturally into three categories: marionette plays, hand-puppet plays, and shadow plays. . . . The common denominator is the puppet's lack of existence or possibility of action outside the will of the hidden manipulator of the strings. The puppet's unsteady steps between the ceiling and the floor are a powerful reminder of our own precarious existence between heaven and earth. . . . More generally, puppet shows symbolize the ultimate futility of human life, while shadow plays, in particular, stress the phantom-like aspect of our life's course."[90] The puppet show known as *karagöz* was brought into Egypt by the Turks. Considered to be aesthetically on a lower level than the shadow play, it bore a close resemblance to the traditional Punch and Judy show.[91]

An analogy between the shadow play and transitory human life was drawn by the Andalusian scholar Ibn Ḥazm in *A Philosophy of Character and Conduct (Kitāb al-akhlāq wa-al-siyar)*. Ibn Ḥazm compares this world to a shadow play in which images are mounted on a rapidly revolving wooden wheel. One group of images disappears as another appears, in much the same way as one generation follows another in this world.[92] Shmuel Moreh notes that "this is the earliest attempt to be found in Arabic to see a philosophical significance in the shadow play. Later, scholars and poets, mainly among the Ṣūfis, further developed this idea and added the principle of the *muḥarrik* (the Aristotelian *primus motor*)."[93] An example of the mystical interpretation of the shadow play is provided by al-Ghazzālī in his *Revival of the Religious Sciences (Iḥyā' 'ulūm al-dīn)*. Al-Ghazzālī describes another staging technique in which the presenter pulls the strings of puppets made of rags and leads the audience to believe that the puppets are moving on their own. This situation is analogous with people's belief that they themselves determine their movements, whereas in reality God determines them, just as the presenter determines those of the puppets.[94]

The medieval poet Aḥmad al-Bayrūtī further elaborates on the shadow play and its allegorical meaning. In two notable verses, he mentions that the presenter had two boxes: he would take his figures from the first, where they were arranged in order of appearance, and place them in the second after they had been displayed. This procedure leads al-Bayrūtī to see a moral lesson in the shadow play: the boxes signify the human cycle of life and death, and the world is a stage, with God as the Muḥarrik.[95] As he writes:

> I see this Universe as a shadow play;
> Its Mover is the much-forgiving Lord.
> The right-hand box is Eve's womb;
> The left-hand box is the grave.[96]

Not all scholars and poets strove to emphasize the didactic intention of the shadow play. Those Muslim philosophers who were to a certain degree nonconformist introduced cynicism and skepticism into the perceived analogy between the puppet show variety and human life. This can be seen in the following quatrain by the Persian Omar Khayyam (1048–1131):

> We all are Puppets of the Sky, we run
> As wills the Player till the Game is done,
>   And when the Player wearies of the Sport,
> He throws us into Darkness One by One.

And again:

> We are no other than a moving row
> Of Magic Shadow-shapes that come and go
>   Round with the Sun-illumin'd Lantern held
> In Midnight by the Master of the Show.[97]

It is generally accepted that real dramatic art, in the Western sense of the word, is a late development in the Arabic literary tradition. Borrowed from Europe in about the middle of the nineteenth century, the drama underwent a long and arduous process of acculturation before gaining acceptability and reaching maturity. While an explanation linking the absence of drama in classical Arabic literature to the belief in fate is plausible, it is, of course, hypothetical and may well be muted by other theories.[98] Moreh argues that the problem is not why drama was absent, but why it was present without developing into a high art. Drawing on a wide range of early sources, he shows that the medieval Arab world was far richer in theatrical culture than has been recognized. He rejects the view that holds Islam to be the main reason for the lack of Arabic drama, stating that there is nothing about the essence of Islam to prevent dramatic development of Islamic or even non-Islamic themes.[99]

The genres of the novel and the short story are also young arts in Arabic literature. Adopted from the West in the late nineteenth century, they have since come into their own, achieving a high level of sophistication and popularity. While traditional themes have gradually been replaced by ones more relevant to the contemporary scene, and conventional techniques have been relinquished in favor of innovative and experimental approaches, certain old notions—the belief in fate being a case in point—still persist. For example, in Ṭāhā Ḥusayn's novel *The Call of the Curlew (Duʿāʾ al-karawān*, 1934), the young village girl, Hanādī, is killed by her uncle for bringing shame on the family by engaging in premarital sex. The victim's sister, Āmina, decides to take revenge on the man, an agricultural engineer, who seduced Hanādī while she was employed in his household. She devises an elaborate scheme and goes to excessive lengths to trap him, only to discover belatedly that she has fallen in love with him and he with her. When he proposes to her, she refuses, saying: "We are condemned to unhappiness." Unable to understand, he presses for an explanation, but she merely repeats: "It is our destiny; it has already been fulfilled in an unfavorable way for us." When she finally reveals her true identity and the real reason for working her way into his service, the engineer recognizes their predicament and remorsefully suggests: "Let us bear our misfortune together until God accomplishes the matter which has already been decreed."[100] Significantly, neither Āmina nor the engineer questions their own roles in the chain of events. Rather, they are inclined to ascribe the entire situation to fate, which allows them to reconcile their relationship with the emotional conflict that it provokes.

A similar crime of honor is depicted in the novel *News from the Meneisi Farm (Akhbār ʿizbat al-Manīsī,* 1971) by Yūsuf al-Qaʿīd. Set in the country estate of Ḥājj al-Manīsī, the work presents the tragedy of Ṣābirīn, the night watchman's daughter who has been seduced and made pregnant by Ṣafwat, the son of the estate owner. Although the scandal is kept secret by her parents and Ṣābirīn undergoes an abortion, she is eventually killed by her brother al-Zanātī to preserve the family's honor. Throughout this ordeal, the girl says to her mother: "It is the ordained mother. I'm not to be blamed." The mother says to her agitated son: "It is the ordained for Ṣābirīn, our fate." And the father says to the farm's chief clerk: "It is the ordained and destined; what could she have done about it?"[101] It should be noted that owing to the grave consequences that seduction, rape, and illegitimate pregnancy have for the girl's future and the family's honor, these misfortunes are instinctively attributed to fate and divine decree. At a deeper level, the novel expresses the mood of frustration and defeat which pervaded Egypt after the 1967 war.[102]

The concept of fate occurs frequently in Fatḥī Ghānim's novel *The Man Who Lost His Shadow (Al-Rajul alladhī faqad ẓillahu,* 1962). The work—a quartet consisting of four monologues by four characters, two women and two men, each telling the story from her or his point of view—begins with Mabrūka's monologue. As a peasant girl of ten, she arrives in Cairo to work in the house of a wealthy and aristocratic family. Over a decade of service with her old and exceedingly pious mistress, she manages to save a small amount of money. When the mistress becomes terminally ill, Mabrūka realizes that she must take possession of her money now, or else risk losing it:

> I was suddenly afraid for the money I had entrusted to her. Who would know to give it to me when she was dead? So I lied to her, said that a man had come from my village bringing news that my mother was ill and needed it.
>
> "Mabrūka—you aren't going to give all this money to your mother?"
>
> "What else can I do? It's God's will."
>
> So I got the money back.[103]

This incident reveals the shrewdness of the peasant girl, who cleverly manipulates the belief in fate to obtain her wish from her religiously minded mistress. Further references to fate occur in the monologue of the hero, an ambitious Cairene journalist named Yūsuf Ḥāmid. As he recounts, after Mabrūka's mistress dies, Mabrūka is sent to work for his father, a retired schoolteacher. The aging widower becomes infatuated with the youthful maid and has an affair with her. When Mabrūka becomes pregnant, she pressures him to marry her and he gives in. But Yūsuf is unable to reconcile himself to the fact that his father has married a servant. The self-indulgent father explains his conduct: "Kismet! . . . It's what God has decreed." Pondering the unexpected turn of events in his life, especially his spectacular success in the face of others' devastating downfall, Yūsuf wonders: "Is this God's will and to be accepted? . . . Thinking about life drives a man mad. Life is irrational."[104] Thus, while one character in the novel questions the notion of fate, several others from different backgrounds—peasant, aristocratic, and educated—are motivated by this belief, at times employing it to defend or advance their personal desires.

The theme of fatalism, on both the individual and the collective levels, figures prominently in the novel *It is Happening in Egypt Now (Yaḥduth fī Miṣr al-ān*, 1977) by Yūsuf al-Qaʿīd. Set in the village of al-Ḍahriyya in the Delta, the work revolves around the wrongful death of al-Dabīsh ʿArāʾis, a poor day laborer, at the hands of the police. The cause of this outburst of violence is the unfair distribution of food aid from the United States, which the corrupt local authorities have restricted to families with pregnant mothers. Frustrated that his wife is not pregnant, al-Dabīsh rebukes her: "From the day I married you, you've always been pregnant. I never needed your pregnancy. I'm not a civil servant who gets a pay increase with each child. The present government has even stopped giving child benefit altogether. But today you should have been pregnant. What can we do? It's fate."[105] When al-Dabīsh attempts to defy his fate and sends his wife, feigning pregnancy, to obtain her share of basic foodstuffs, he is caught and punished. The incident, which takes place on the eve of President Nixon's visit to the area in 1974, causes great embarrassment to the local authorities—the district police officer, the doctor, and the head of the village council—and they conspire to cover it up. At first they spread rumors that al-Dabīsh escaped from prison and was found dead. Later they claim that no official papers can be found to confirm his existence: he is therefore a fictitious figure and not a real person. Despite the peasants' knowledge of the crime which has been committed and their indignation at the injustice which they constantly suffer at the hands of their corrupt authorities, they do not join forces and do not rise up against their oppressors. Rather, when the news of al-Dabīsh's death reaches them, they accept it in submission and resignation:

> Some of them slapped their palms together in despair. The usual words uttered under such circumstances were said, "There is no power and no strength save in God." The veins in the neck of the most agitated person among those assembled bulged out and their blue knots became engorged as he spoke:
>
> "God will take revenge on the evildoers."
>
> Another man added:
>
> "Their day will come. That day is near."
>
> The rest of the reactions centered around the notion that what happened was al-Dabīsh's fate. The imam of the mosque said that one's fate is irrevocably fixed and recorded in the preserved tablet, quoting the proverb "What is written on the forehead must be seen by the eye." The peasants realized that the assembly came to an end when a man who received a religious education in his youth exclaimed:
>
> "It's fate and divine decree."
>
> Then, looking up at the sky, he concluded:
>
> "It's God's will."[106]

Not only are the peasants unable to unite and take action but they are mostly apathetic, servile, and weak. These facts serve their oppressors well. When the three conspirators get together to work out the details of their scheme, the district police officer, who resides elsewhere, inquires whether there are subversive elements in the village that might expose them. The doctor readily informs him:

> You are in rural Egypt of 1974. Political activity—none. Objective evaluation of facts—none. Banding together—none. Joint positions—none. Social consciousness—none. The government is the government and the people are the people. The twenty thousand inhabitants of this village have a familiar slogan. This is what God the Sublime has said in His glorious Book, and He is the most truthful: "Obey God, and the Prophet, and your rulers." We are the rulers to whom the Qur'ān referred. Surely, I don't have to tell you about the religious feelings in the countryside of Egypt.[107]

The novel's title itself, *It Is Happening in Egypt Now*, conveys a powerful message. Al-Qaʿīd suggests that the state of affairs depicted in the novel is not limited to a certain time frame but is continuous, extending from the past to the present.[108] He sees no hope for the peasants to escape their harsh condition as long as they are unable to transcend their traditional values and attitudes—most notably fatalism, compliance, and divisiveness—in order to develop the social consciousness necessary to change their lot.

References to fate also abound in the novel *Houses behind the Trees (Buyūt warā' al-ashjār*, 1993) by Muḥammad al-Bisāṭī. In this work, when Musʿad the butcher goes to ask for Saʿdiyya's hand, her brother carefully informs him that she has been engaged before: "Two years ago we made a contract of marriage. Just a contract. We were all ready for the wedding. Everything is a matter of destiny."[109] With this statement, the brother manages to avoid mentioning the scandal of having broken the engagement upon learning that her fiancé earned his living as a pimp. Later, when Musʿad asks Saʿdiyya why she agreed to marry him, for she is young and pretty whereas he is old and already once divorced, she answers evasively: "Destiny and fate."[110] In fact, Saʿdiyya is well aware that, as a homeless person and a girl who lost her virginity, she was not in a position to refuse him. After Musʿad catches her with another man in her bedroom, he faces a crisis in which personal emotions, public opinion, and fatalism play a decisive role. His ill-fated struggle for revenge ends with his own death.

The Arabic short story, like the novel, displays the various aspects of the belief in fate reviewed earlier in this chapter. In "God's World" ("Dunyā Allāh") by Najīb Maḥfūẓ,[111] the poor and elderly ʿAmm Ibrāhīm harbors a lifelong wish to see the sea. To achieve this end, he steals the salaries of the clerks at the office where he works and travels with a prostitute to Alexandria, where he enjoys a short period of bliss. When the police finally seize him, the detective is curious to know what motivated the old man to commit such a foolish crime:

> "Can you tell me what made you do all that at your age!" he asked.
> "God . . ." he muttered with a smile, and then raised his finger up to the sky.
> The word escaped from him like a sigh.[112]

In this instance, the reference to God's will is an excuse—a mechanism for shifting personal responsibility and thus escaping blame and punishment.

In "An Open Wound" ("Jurḥ maftūḥ") by Idwār al-Kharrāṭ,[113] a village woman is found beaten and raped. As her guardian (who alternately assumes the roles of brother and husband) tries to comprehend how the tragedy came to pass, the following conversation, possibly an interior monologue, takes place:

> She was a virgin and she has fallen. Where was her son?
> "It was fate and it was written. There was no way round it."
> "How? How could it have happened?"
> "Who would have believed it?"
> "She was alone, my sister, my darling."
> "It was God's will and His command."
> "She couldn't have done a thing."
> "My sister, my child."

"What's the use of talking now? It was God's will."
"How did she come to be here on her own?"
"Our sister, our love. We were with her, our hearts were with her."[114]

At a deeper level, several details in the story suggest that the woman represents Egypt. Because the story was written two years after the devastating blow of the Six-Day War, when the Arab world was still undergoing tremors of shock, it is most likely that the rape signifies the Arab defeat. Al-Kharrāṭ's depiction of Egypt as a raped woman whose fate was foreordained resonates with Nasser's own rationalization of the debacle. Thus the reference to God's will is used as a means to justify the calamity that befell the nation as well as the individual.

In "The Wagon and the Man" ("Al-ʿAraba wa-al-rajul") by the Lebanese writer ʿAbdallāh ʿAbd,[115] the poor porter, Maḥmūd, whose donkey has died, finds himself pulling the wagon, which constitutes his livelihood, all by himself. The heavily loaded wagon proves too difficult to haul when he has to go up a steep street. As several carefully placed household items begin to roll off the back of the wagon and smash to bits, Maḥmūd thinks to himself: "Despite every precaution, there is a superior power that frustrates our efforts every now and then. We cannot escape our fate." The story, however, ends on an affirmative note. Nearly at breaking point, Maḥmūd still perseveres: "He realized that man has a greater ability to withstand pain as long as he stands on his feet and keeps moving forward."[116]

Finally, in "The Assassination of Light at the River's Flow" ("Ightiyāl al-ḍawʾ ʿinda majrā al-nahr") by the Saudi woman writer Khayriyya al-Saqqāf,[117] the heroine, Rahā, is beaten and jailed because she refuses to consent to an arranged marriage. In defying her parents, she derives courage from the idea of God's will and divine decree: "Oh, how great you are, Allah! You made my heart, my feelings! No one can own another's heart, you decreed it so! Even if my room is a locked jail, even if my parents are my jailors and my terror, my heart is still alive."[118] Here, in contrast to the traditional implications of submission and resignation, the reference to God's will serves as a mechanism for self-assertion and rebellion.[119]

Poetry, the literary medium of the Arabs par excellence, is a rich source of statements concerning the power of fate. This theme can be traced in numerous verses from classical to modern poetry. Some verses from classical poetry, which convey the inevitability of fate, have retained their popularity to this day. A famous line by the medieval poet al-Mutanabbī runs:

Not every human desire can be fulfilled.
Winds may blow opposite to sailors' wishes.[120]

In the same vein, two widely quoted lines by an unknown poet declare:

> We trod the steps appointed for us; and he whose steps are appointed must tread them.
> He whose death is decreed to take place in one land will not die in any land but that.[121]

And again:

> Firm resolution cannot prevent the vicissitudes of time,
> Nor undo what fate decrees.[122]

In a love poem entitled "The Ruins" ("Al-Aṭlāl"), the romantic poet Ibrāhīm Nājī (1898–1953) expresses human impotence in the face of fate:

> O my beloved, everything is by decree.
> We can't help it if we are doomed to misery.
> Perhaps our fates will bring us together
> One day after we have despaired of meeting.
> And if a friend does not recognize a friend,
> And we meet as strangers,
> And each of us goes his own way,
> Don't say that is what we wanted. Say that is what destiny intended.[123]

The Mahjar poet Gibran Khalil Gibran (1883–1931), in his philosophical poem "The Processions" ("Al-Mawākib"), offers a similar conclusion:

> Had I the days in hand to string,
> Only in forest they'd be strewn,
> But circumstances drive us on
> In narrow paths by Kismet hewn.
>
> For Fate has ways we cannot change,
> While weakness prays upon our Will;
> We bolster with excuse the self,
> And help that Fate ourselves to kill.[124]

The Syrian poet Nizār Qabbānī (1923–98) condemns this attitude. In his poem "Bread, Hashish and Moonlight" ("Khubz wa-ḥashīsh wa-qamar"), Qabbānī reflects on the sources of the Arab predicament. He labels the belief in fate "an opium" of the masses:

> What does heaven have
> For lazy poor people

Who become dead when the moon lives?
They shake the tombs of saints
Hoping the tombs of saints will give them rice and children.
They spread out elegant soft carpets
And amuse themselves with an opium we call fate
And destiny
In my country, in the country of the simple.[125]

All the preceding examples from the main domains of creative writing—fiction and poetry—have been presented to illustrate the persistence of the concept of fate into modern Arabic literature. Admittedly, alongside these examples are others that assert human free will. The much-recited poem "Life's Will" ("Irādat al-ḥayāh"), by the Tunisian poet Abū al-Qāsim al-Shābbī (1909–34), reads:

When people choose
To live by life's will,
Fate can do nothing but give in;
The night discards its veil,
All shackles are undone.

Whoever never felt
Life celebrating him
Must vanish like the mist;
Whoever never felt
Sweeping through him
The glow of life
Succumbs to nothingness.

This I was told by the secret
Voice of All-Being:
Wind roared in the mountains,
Roared through valleys, under trees:
"My goal, once I have set it,
And put aside all caution,
I must pursue to the end.
Whoever shrinks from scaling the mountain
Lives out his life in potholes."

Then it was earth I questioned:
"Mother, do you detest mankind?"
And earth responded:
"I bless people with high ambition,
Who do not flinch at danger.

I curse people out of step with time,
People content to lie like stone.
No horizon nurtures a dead bird.
A bee will choose to kiss a living flower.

If my mothering heart
Were not so tender,
The dead would have no hiding place
In those graves yonder."[126]

Written while Tunisia was still under French colonial rule, which lasted for three-quarters of a century (1881–1956), the poem's didactic intention in seeking to awaken the people to revolt and radical change cannot be discounted. As a poet, Abū al-Qāsim al-Shābbī was also strongly influenced by the novel ideas of the romantic school of Arab-American writers (the Emigrants), who were known for their opposition to the traditional values and attitudes that dominate Arab society.[127]

Arabic proverbial lore abounds in references to the power of fate. For example: "All precautions are in vain when man faces his destiny" (*lā yanfaʿ ḥadhar min qadar*); "No amount of wisdom can help one escape one's fate" (*idhā jā'a al-qadar ghashiya al-baṣar*); "God's hand is above all hands" (*wa-mā min yad illā yad Allāhi fawquhā*); "What God will no frost can kill" (*lā rādda li-mā arāda Allāh*); "What is destined will be fulfilled" (*al-maktūb ʿalā al-jabīn lā budda an tarāhu al-ʿayn*; literally, "What is written on the forehead must be seen by the eye"). Colloquial lore has similar sayings on the subject: "There can be no flight from fate" (*il-maktūb ma-minnū-sh mahrūb*, Egyptian); "Whatever fate is allotted to you will befall you" (*illi min naṣībak yiṣībak*, Levantine); "Everything is a matter of fate" (*kull shee' qisma w-naṣīb*, Egyptian). In these popular sayings, fate is variously described as *qadar*, *naṣīb*, *qisma*, and *maktūb* (what is "written," i.e., preordained). It should be noted that proverbial lore is multifaceted and also includes contradictory statements. For example: "You reap what you sow" (*ka-mā tazraʿ taḥṣad*); "A man's livelihood depends on good planning" (*al-tadbīr niṣf al-maʿīsha*); "He who tries hard will find his reward" (*man jadda wajada*).

The present discussion has shown that the belief in fate, however questioned and reinterpreted, is still an integral part of Arabic writing and thought. Deeply embedded in the consciousness of the people, it continues to function as a viable cultural force. The following chapter traces the pre-Islamic roots of this belief to place it in the historical context.

The belief in fate retained its vitality even as new perspectives on human life began to be conceived and propagated. While the belief in fate has prevailed as a literary theme, further examination of modern Arabic literature reveals a growing awareness of alternative theories of human destiny. These modern views, influenced by Western ideas and changes in Arab social reality, appear in certain circles, especially among the educated elite. The role of these views and the extent to which they manage to challenge the traditional concept of fate form the subject matter of the succeeding chapters.

Maḥmūd Ṭāhir Lāshīn
The Village Tale

Maḥmūd Ṭāhir Lāshīn (1894–1954) was born into a middle-class family in Cairo. He completed his secondary education in 1912 and then attended the College of Engineering in Cairo, graduating in 1917. From 1918 until his retirement in 1953, he was employed by the government in the Department of Public Works. Lāshīn was a prominent member of the literary group known as the Modern School, which played an important role in developing the Egyptian short story. As a fiction writer, he penned mostly short stories, which appeared in three volumes: *The Irony of the Flute (Sukhriyyat al-nāy*, 1926), *It Is Told That (Yuḥkā anna*, 1929), and *The Flying Veil (Al-Niqāb al-ṭā'ir*, 1940). His style is realistic, and his themes are drawn from Egyptian life.

"The Village Tale" ("Ḥādith al-qarya") appears in the collection *It Is Told That*. The story depicts the blind belief in fate that prevails among simple village communities.

My friend invited me to accompany him on a visit to his village. We were to spend Friday in the heart of the country, while he attended to some business affairs. So we went, and there we found beauty and joy. But that beauty, which captivates the city man when he encounters the infinity of the countryside, and that joy, which pervades his entire being when he sees nature glowing everywhere, were tempered for me by a certain sadness. The sadness was evoked by the sight of the half-naked peasants who were bent over the land, which they worked with hoes or sickles. They appeared exhausted and drenched with sweat in the blaze of the heat. I felt no less sadness at the sight of the peasant women who squatted submissively next to their reed and mud huts. When we walked along the narrow winding alleys and looked at the women, they blended into each other and veiled themselves from us with their shabby rags, as dusty as the ground itself. That same heartache overtook me when I saw the little children, half-naked like their fathers and covered with dust like their mothers, roaming with the goats and the chickens between the palm trees and over the mounds of earth and around the stagnant pond nearby.

I began to confide my sadness to my friend, but he did not sympathize. Instead, he began to explain to me that this was the most suitable way of life for such people, who were quite oblivious to the misery in their lives. He went on to offer firsthand accounts of his experiences with them to prove that their naive appearance hid the treachery of jackals and the cunning of foxes. Then he proceeded to ridicule my poetic sensibilities and naivety.

As the evening approached and the twilight poured its sad, solemn splendor over the fields, my poetic sensibilities—as my friend referred to them—overwhelmed me and I became depressed. We were walking through a dusty path between rows of stalks of maize. The light was fading, and silence enveloped us and everything around us. Nothing could be heard except for the plodding fall of the hooves of the returning bulls and the peasants' greetings, which they offered in weary voices as they dragged themselves along. We were silent, and I thought about the people passing by. What joyful talk would they exchange with their wives? Were they really oblivious to the misery in their lives? What made them happy, and where did they turn for consolation?

I was unable to find answers to my questions, and I had no desire to ask my friend. We were heading toward the place of prayer. When we arrived, the twilight had vanished and darkness prevailed everywhere. The place of prayer was a courtyard by the canal bridge. It was covered with a woven reed matting and marked off by a low brick wall that reached half the height of the people seated alongside. When the peasants wished to congregate, that was where they went. They also prayed there and spent part of the night chatting among themselves.

They rose to greet us and remained standing until we signaled them to sit down again. After my friend had finished questioning and instructing someone in matters related to his business, silence fell, disturbed only by exclamations of greetings now and then. I whispered to my friend that we might have interrupted their talk. He replied in English, "And what could they possibly be talking about?" Then one of them suggested sending for Shaykh Muḥsin, and a messenger rushed to get him. We learned that the man sent for was the village legal official,[128] who was the best person to converse with people like us. Everyone remained silent until the awaited guest arrived, preceded by the messenger holding a lamp. The glowing wick in the lamp revealed clearly that the shaykh had cut his mustache but spared his beard, and that both his turban and his robe were red.

Undoubtedly, the shaykh knew the reason he had been sent for. No sooner had he settled down and the introductions been completed than he embarked on a long, rambling speech. He began by stating that he had met with the village mayor and the government deputy, illuminating for them the way to investigate the case of ʿAbd al-Samīʿ. Halfway through, he said that he had attended lectures at al-Azhar for several years. And at the end he said that Muḥammad ʿAlī Pasha had established a factory for calico. Then he shifted in his seat, bristling with self-importance, and the audience glanced at us as if to say: "Can you give a speech like that?"

The crescent moon had passed through part of its journey across the sky, casting pale rays that the calm water received as a loving mother would receive a sick child. A piper by a fire in the distance began to play melancholy tunes on his flute. I was caught up in the surrounding magic and for a long while became oblivious to those around me, until my friend shook me. To my surprise, I found the shaykh abandoning himself to the exegesis of Qur'ānic verses. He was manipulating them aggressively, shedding their spirituality and applying his interpretation as balm on the hearts of his listeners.

This became increasingly difficult for me to bear. My friend sensed my agitation and whispered to me that it was pointless to interrupt. But I did not take his advice. I politely argued with the hero of the circle, and he disputed with me stubbornly and resorted to myths, which my friend laughed at in secret though he remained outwardly neutral. Then I lost control and began to refute his lies and destroy his fabrications. I found an opening in the debate that enabled me to address the condition of the peasants. I referred frankly to their wretched circumstances and harsh way of life, and reminded them about their children, and wives, and huts. I suggested ways in which they could improve their lot, if they wanted to. Then I spoke at length about free will and action, and how they could work miracles if they *felt* their existence and resolved to justify that existence.

I spoke passionately, believing, as I mentioned their vulnerabilities, that my speech would be readily accepted. But whenever I paused to gauge the effect of my words, I found the people staring open-mouthed in stupid amazement, now at me, now at their teacher, as if yearning for an explanation. During my heated outburst, I noticed two men, their heads close together, whispering to each other without paying any attention to me. Then a voice within me said: "You fool. You are wearing out your lungs for nothing. They will never understand you because you are an outsider, an intruder!"

I yielded and interrupted my speech. As soon as I stopped, one of the whispering men cried out:

"Well now, our master, did the mayor testify for ʿAbd al-Samīʿ or against him?"

Everyone began to shout remarks on this subject, and I ceased to exist along with my speech. I realized that my friend was embarrassed on my account, and we avoided looking at each other for some time. The shaykh remained silent until everyone had calmed down. Then he whispered, "I ask God for forgiveness," and proceeded to declare grandly:

"Misfortunes descend upon us yet we don't cry. We don't cry because the eyes are petrified, and the eyes are petrified because of a hard heart. A hard heart comes from a profusion of sins, and a profusion of sins is caused by an immoderate hope. Such a hope stems from the love of the material world, which, in turn, derives from the will. That is, the will of man—the created one—is everything, and the will of the Creator, glory and praise be to Him, is nothing."

He let his eyes wander about his listeners, and they lowered their heads and sucked in the corners of their mouths in anguish and distress. Gazing at me, my friend muttered softly:

"This is their man. You assailed their minds, so they didn't understand you. As for him, he speaks to their hearts, and you can see what effect it has."

By now the crescent moon had reached the end of its journey. As it drew near the lighted fire, it turned red, as though aflame. It was an exhilarating and enthralling sight, but my ears were glued to the speaker, who began to refute what I had said.

"This gentleman, folks, has led us to a good topic, which is the notion of will, in the sense that if a person wants something, all he has to do is say 'Be!' and it will be."

I shuddered at this bitter mockery and foolish advice. I bit my lips to control myself and withhold the obscenities that I wanted to hurl at this bearded, misguided man. Just then my friend squeezed my leg and whispered to me:

"I see that we are about to witness a scene the like of which we may never experience again in our lives. Calm down and listen!"

So I listened, and there was the shaykh, shouting at those around him: "Which of you wouldn't like to be a village mayor?"

A thin peasant with glossy eyes pushed away the mosquitoes from his face and exclaimed: "Everyone! Even a pasha would!"[129]

All those who understood the error laughed at the remark, except for Shaykh Muḥsin, who rectified the situation by saying:

"No, no, we made a mistake. The gentleman makes action conditional upon will. Let's assume at once that ʿAbd al-Samīʿ did just that. And how disastrous it turned out to be!"

Voices: "May God be kind to him! May God help him!"

The man with the glossy eyes sat upright and raised his hands to the sky in a humble prayer:

"O God, preserve us from the evil of our hearts and the evil of the devil. O Lord. . . ."

In truth, with this prayer he was dismissing from his mind the vision of a foul trick he had been plotting against the owner of the field next to his.

The shaykh began to tell us the story of ʿAbd al-Samīʿ. As he spoke, the croaking of frogs in a remote corner accompanied his story like an orchestra.

"This ʿAbd al-Samīʿ was, no offense, a cobbler. He patched out a living from the shoes he patched. (He laughed at his joke and then laughter rang out from every corner.[130]) But he was not content with what God had allotted to him and wanted (and here he clapped his hands once to emphasize the word) *to raise* himself to a place that was not ordained for him in eternity."

A voice: "The ancients said, 'Greed debases the greedy.' "

"God tempted him—and God is the best of schemers[131]—sending him the assistant prosecutor, one of those young men who have traded their share in the next world for a share in this one. He appointed ʿAbd al-Samīʿ to be his personal doorman in the district capital. He welcomed him into his home and showered him with material comforts, so ʿAbd al-Samīʿ became a city dweller. He began to wear a jacket and a fez and walked around proudly, although God the Sublime has said: 'Do not walk proudly on the earth. You cannot cleave the earth, nor can you rival the mountains in stature.' "[132]

Mingled voices uttered: "Glory be to Him who said this!" and sighs followed in rapid succession. Some people turned to us with eyes that sparkled in admiration at the eloquence of this speech, others bowed their heads until their faces almost touched the ground. The rest exchanged glances and pushed the mosquitoes away from their noses.

The shaykh gathered up the edges of his robe, adjusted his turban, and stuck his hand into his beard in a way that indicated that he was about to reach a critical point in the story. Silence reigned for a moment, during which the melancholy tunes of the flute could be heard in the distance.

"This job and such favors were not intended for ʿAbd al-Samīʿ—may God forgive me for what I'm about to say—but for his wife. Despite her poverty, she was very beautiful, as you know. The assistant prosecutor had often seen her at the public fountain beside her husband, who would sit there to patch shoes. He suggested that ʿAbd al-Samīʿ bring her along with him to the district capital. Under this arrangement, ʿAbd al-Samīʿ could keep an eye on his wife and she could do the housework for the assistant prosecutor, who was a bachelor. And he got what he wanted. As for ʿAbd al-Samīʿ, did he really derive benefit from his efforts? Absolutely not. After a while, God set the devil on him!"

"God preserve us!"

"And he became beset with anxiety!"

"God protect us!"

"And he could no longer find rest or peace of mind!"

The shaykh left his listeners to vent their emotions in different ways. He reached for a round earthen pitcher containing water and began to slurp from it with the loudest and most irritating noise possible. As the peasant closest to him rushed to return the pitcher to its place, the shaykh took a large handkerchief from his pocket—a quarter of it would have sufficed as a large handkerchief—and, after belching and asking God for forgiveness, wiped his mouth, mumbling praise to God. He then placed the handkerchief back in his pocket, stroked his beard for a long while, and went on to say:

"And how could ʿAbd al-Samīʿ find peace of mind when events took an unexpected turn? I'm afraid I've prolonged my speech, gentlemen! (This remark was directed at us, and we replied to it as best as we could.) The poor cobbler's wife who used to sing at festivals of saints and accept charity—my goodness, my goodness—became a mistress who orders and forbids, and she had no one to order about except her husband. (Voices of anguish, and amazement, and anger.) Whenever he rebuked her, she would rush to her master crying and wailing, and he would rush to rebuke the husband and accuse him of being a peasant who doesn't know a woman's worth."

Voices: "There is no power and no strength save in God!"

"The poor man had often complained to me about his situation, and I advised him to leave what was not his and return to the life he was cut out for. But he was like a drowning man. Things continued this way until the true nature of the situation became crystal clear, and ʿAbd al-Samīʿ began to experience the scorching flame of jealousy. He became absent-minded, constantly gloomy, and unable to rest, whether asleep or awake. Nevertheless, he couldn't extricate himself from this hell. First, because it was difficult for him to give up the easy life that came his way. Second, because the devil was playing with his mind. Whenever he tried to take matters firmly in hand, the Devil would whisper to him that he really was just a peasant and that city life was as he saw it, and then his nerves would calm down and he would give in."

Voices: "God damn city life and the day we ever heard about it!"

"The situation persisted this way until that horrible night when the assistant prosecutor asked ʿAbd al-Samīʿ to deliver a letter to the mayor here and to bring him the reply, not at once, but on the following morning."

At this point, one of the listeners suddenly said, "How strange!" It sounded like joking, and the rest of the people burst into abrupt laughter.

Lowering his voice until it became deep and impressive, the shaykh informed his eager listeners that what they were about to hear was confidential information, which the investigators had passed on to him because of his standing with them and their trust in him. He asked the people to keep it a secret among themselves, and heads nodded in compliance and admiration. At that moment, one man wanted to fix the lamp, which had been placed in the center of the circle. Squadrons of mosquitoes were hovering around it and attacking its sides in frenzied maneuvers. But the others rebuked him for his lack of propriety when the teacher was speaking.

"ʿAbd al-Samīʿ made his way along the railroad track. He was pondering his situation, and his heart was filled with doubt. The moon lighted his way, and as he went along he came upon an iron bar on the ground between the rails. It was as long as a man's arm—I've seen it with my own eyes. He picked it up, and as soon as he felt how heavy it was he was seized with the desire to go back. The poor man confirms that he tried to overcome this desire but that he could not. It was as if a hidden force from God the Sublime was pulling him back. In the end, he went back and found the house in darkness. He cautiously opened the doors, one by one, until he came to his master's bedroom, and there he saw—God forbid—he saw his master in . . . the husband's place with his own wife!"

Everybody reacted with expressions of revulsion and disgust, and with numerous entreaties to God. Shaykh Muḥsin availed himself of the opportunity that this tumult provided to welcome us again, and it was as if he were saying: "Am I not an eloquent speaker?" After silence was restored, he continued:

"When he entered, they were asleep. He couldn't restrain himself, so he pounced on them with the iron bar and bashed their heads in. They died instantly."

Voices of cheering and approval rang out.

"That wasn't enough for him, however, because the desire for revenge raged inside him. So he continued to hit them until he smashed their heads so hard that the investigators found pieces of brain—of brain, God forbid—clinging to the wall."

This time voices of approval as well as of disgust rang out simultaneously. Then there was silence, during which the croaking of the frogs could be heard above all else because the sound of the flute had died away.

"But the strangest thing is that after he had quenched his thirst for revenge, he made himself tea and stayed up all night, drinking and smoking next to the bodies."

Staring open-mouthed, my friend said: "How horrible!"

In my amazement, I said: "I wish I'd been there!"

The peasants' voices reverberated with expressions of shock.

"At dawn, ʿAbd al-Samīʿ took the iron bar and went to the police station. There he confessed everything that had happened."

The shaykh took the water pitcher and slurped from it just as he had done before. Then he said:

"And so, my sons, life is a matter of worship, not of free will. And the best path is God's path."

He prepared to leave on the pretext that the mayor and many of the notables were expecting him. The peasants approached him, reassured and contented. They kissed his hand and thanked God for the divine grace that protected them from disgrace.

We—my friend and I—preferred to stay. So they left the lamp for us and were pleased to follow their teacher in the darkness.

Comments

The harsh living conditions of the peasants in the countryside throw the narrator, an educated visitor from the city, into emotional turmoil. His sensibilities are offended at the sight of the squalor and poverty of these people, who toil like ants, in close proximity to the earth. An idealist and a romantic, he does not understand the peasants' submissiveness and doubts their ability to be content with their lot. The peasants' religious mode of existence becomes apparent through the arrival of the shaykh, who is brought by a messenger holding a lamp. The shaykh and the lamp represent the peasants' world order, which consists of the religious institution and the light of the Qur'ān.

The confrontation between progress and backwardness, knowledge and ignorance, reveals the tension existing between two fabrics of the same society: one that is guided by reason, and one that is bound by religious dogma. The shaykh, who recites Qur'ānic verses to his audience to explain the real lesson behind the tragedy of ʿAbd al-Samīʿ, is understood by the peasants. He makes sense to them, and his ideological and moral authority are accepted. The narrator's arguments are not heard by the peasants. His philosophy of developing self-awareness, exercising free choice, and striving for self-betterment is alien to their rough and narrow world. The conflict that unfolds is therefore not resolved, and the dividing line between religious belief and fate on the one hand, and rational thought and free will on the other, is all the more accentuated.

The story of ʿAbd al-Samīʿ dramatizes the futility of rebellion and highlights the strife between rural and urban values as well as between tradition and modernity. The shaykh manipulates the personal tragedy of ʿAbd al-Samīʿ to warn his audience that it does not pay to take one's fate into one's own hands and change one's preordained place. He presents the chain of events that occurred in this case as the ultimate proof of the fallacy of human will: ʿAbd al-Samīʿ loses his self-respect as a man when he becomes subservient to his wife, who in turn becomes the mistress of the assistant prosecutor. In the involvement of the latter, there is another lesson to learn: ʿAbd al-Samīʿ was tempted by material gains offered by a government official. The government is an extension of the city and of secular thought—two inherently corruptive elements. Thus the shaykh exploits the story of ʿAbd al-Samīʿ to enhance the authority of the religious institution, secure his own position of power, and instill obedience and conformity in his flock.

The assistant prosecutor exemplifies the religious dogma of sin and punishment. He has violated the sanctity of the marriage of ʿAbd al-Samīʿ and his wife, and he has committed adultery. Therefore, he, as well as the adulterous wife, must be punished. ʿAbd al-Samīʿ serves as a tool in the hands of fate to carry out their punishment. In other words, both the sinners and the killer are made to play out their respective roles as preordained for them.

The climax of the narrator's visit is antithetical to his idealistic stand: instead of swaying the audience to his side with his reasoning on free will, he realizes that the wretched circumstances of the peasants predispose them to the fatalistic outlook propagated by the shaykh. After all, of what use is his logic to their day-to-day life? Reluctantly, he recognizes that the belief in fate offers the peasants precisely what they need most: comfort and reassurance in the face of an unbearable and inescapable reality.

While the complex design of the narrative, which contains a story within a story, leaves it both closed and open-ended, some conclusions are self-evident. The depiction of the shaykh as a charlatan and of the peasants as inherently superstitious and ignorant explains why the belief in fate is so rife in village communities. This belief is castigated as a debilitating force that puts obstacles in the way of change and progress. The peasants' docile acceptance of God's will as interpreted for them by their shaykh exposes them to exploitation and contributes to the perpetuation of their harsh social and economic situation.

"The Village Tale" is regarded by many critics as the first manifestation of a mature and sophisticated Arabic short story. The Egyptian literary scholar Sabry Hafez has called it "a momentous story, not only because it constitutes the real birth of the coherent, indigenous, realistic Arabic short story, but also because it focuses its attention on the crossroads at which modern Egypt stood, where the conflict between rural and urban values, between modernism and traditional religious thought, between occidental and oriental cultures, was at its height." Hafez has written a detailed analysis of this story, using the sociological approach to literature and poststructuralist theory. He discusses several aspects, such as prefatory devices, the dialectics of *fabula* and *sjuzhet*, the polyphony of discourses, and intertextuality. His analysis elucidates the conflict between the different social groups represented in the story and the issues dividing them, including ideology, religion, and fatalism. In his final conclusion, Hafez points out that the dispute depicted in a story written in 1929 is still relevant to the contemporary scene: "The conflict between the story's two characters and opposing discourses is still being waged, sixty years after its publication, between the Islamic descendants of Sheikh Muḥsin and the secular progeny of the narrator. It remains unsolved today and it will probably continue for many years to come to be the major debate in the Arab world."[133]

Mubārak Rabīʿ
Our Lord Qadr

Mubārak Rabīʿ was born in 1935 in Banmaʿāshū, a Moroccan village near Casablanca. He received his elementary and secondary education in Casablanca, after which he studied psychology and philosophy at Muḥammad V University in Rabat. He has a keen interest in child psychology and pedagogy and has worked as a schoolteacher, university lecturer, and radio host on cultural programs. Regarded as one of the leading writers of Morocco, he has published several novels and collections of short stories. His fiction is written in a realistic style and deals mainly with the changes in contemporary Moroccan society, the issues of liberation, modernity, and cultural diversity, and commitment to Arab causes. He has won literary prizes for his novels *The Good Folk (Al-Ṭayyibūn*, 1972), which depicts the alienation of the peasants following their transfer to the city, and *Comrades in Arms and the Moon (Rifqat al-silāḥ wa-al-qamar*, 1976), which is set on the Syrian front during the Arab-Israeli war of 1973.

"Our Lord Qadr" ("Sayyidunā Qadr") is the title story of a collection published in 1969. The story revolves around the Night of the Divine Decree (Laylat al-Qadr) as it affects a servant girl afflicted with baldness.

Wasn't it her right to rest now, after she had completed all her chores? In fact, she had done not only her work but also other people's work. Shouldn't she be left in peace after kneading bread, washing dishes, and scrubbing the kitchen floor as well as the stairs and the windows for the third or fourth time in one day? Miftāḥa realized that if she didn't take a break right away, that woman—that fat black European cow—would surely return to think of new work for her to do.

"Miftāḥa, may God cut your chest open, wash the floor."

And sometimes Miftāḥa would answer truthfully: "I just did it, Lalla Masʿūda."

"May your luck turn black. And the dough?"

"I kneaded it."

"May a train run you over like kneaded dough. And the upstairs bathroom? And the downstairs one?"

"Including the bathrooms and the stairs. I did the ironing, and I found the missing black sock. I threw away the mice from the trap. I made fresh bait. I stitched. . . ."

"May your tongue be twisted. Busy rubbing your bald head, ha?"

Alas, at this point she could only give in. Experience had taught her that every exchange with Masʿūda—or, more precisely, every rebuke from her—inevitably ended with the mention of this head. So Miftāḥa would remain silent while Lalla Masʿūda walked around her, masterfully describing the bald head, eyes searching for more work for her companion. Soon enough, the European cow (as Miftāḥa secretly referred to her) would bellow:

"Wash the floor again!"

And, at the door, she would unfailingly add:

"May you be washed out of this world."

Once again Miftāḥa would bend over the floor. She had often wondered why none of this ever happened to any other servant in the household. Masʿūda herself was only a servant, just like her, or rather, worse than her. Wasn't she dark-skinned and old? Could Miftāḥa's baldness be the reason? This was certainly the case, and she knew that she was guilty of this offense. Then she would give in. Not that the stuff growing on Masʿūda's head was an improvement over baldness, mind you. It was curly and as coarse as its owner, who never stopped snapping orders—orders directed only at Miftāḥa, no one else. Once, as Miftāḥa followed Masʿūda's movements while the latter searched for additional work for her, she imagined that Masʿūda would order her to wash the sky. But Masʿūda's eyes completed their survey to settle on her. She approached Miftāḥa and stretched out her hand toward her ear. A violent fear seized Miftāḥa, certain that Masʿūda intended to pinch her. She jumped with pain as Masʿūda's hand drew back, having plucked out a few short hairs that seemed odd on the edge of the smooth head. Smiling viciously, Masʿūda said:

"What do you need these for?"

Then the smile vanished and the cow grumbled again:

"Damn you. Wash yourself!"

With a shattered voice and eyes filled with pain, Miftāḥa answered:

"I washed myself just an hour ago."

"May you be washed dead. Do you hear me! And come back to me at once—I'll be waiting."

Miftāḥa would vanish into the servants' bathroom to wash up again until Masʿūda found some more work for her to do.

Wasn't it her right to grab this opportunity to escape to freedom before Masʿūda returned? Most of the household had already retired for the night. The master had gone to the mosque to celebrate the Night of the Divine Decree. The Night of the Divine Decree was Miftāḥa's awaited night. She sneaked out of the wide basement kitchen and crossed the adjacent storeroom. Then she climbed the stairs to the first floor, concealing herself by the pillars and the walls, draping herself in every shadow. She passed the second floor, where there was only the mistress's bedroom, from which a pale light filtered out. And then she was up on the flat roof, with the door securely closed behind her. Masʿūda could search endlessly for her, but she would never find her! And in the morning—it would be just like any other morning.

She was filled with joy at her good luck. Had the master celebrated the Night of the Divine Decree at home, the rooms would have been packed with guests and visitors, and she would have been overwhelmed with work. Now, however, she was free on the spacious roof. The sky was pitch black, and the stars sparkled serenely. The biting cold of February stung her face like needles, making her shiver. Miftāḥa touched her head and adjusted the scarf covering it. Her hands felt a few little hairs near her ears. Perhaps the miracle was already happening. It would surely happen if nothing disturbed her. Our Lord Qadr would not break his promise. So she would await his arrival, along with all the other anguished, wakeful souls in other places. She would request many things from Our Lord Qadr—health, and ample food, and beauty, and marriage . . . oh, and hair. That was the most important thing. Hair, first of all, Our Lord Qadr. She would not foolishly waste her prayers on anything but hair. The hair comes first and foremost, and she should not forget that. Baldness is repulsive, and a girl without hair is a laughingstock. Be noble and merciful, Our Lord Qadr.

Miftāḥa looked right and left, searching for a hiding place on the roof, which was scattered with chimneys. She chose a chimney from which smoke was still gushing out. She huddled by its side, away from the biting wind. The heat flowed in her joints, and a pleasant stupor filled her. She rested her head against the chimney wall and soon became lost in thought. Would her hair grow all at once, she wondered, assuming that Our Lord Qadr took pity on her? In that case, she might come down from the roof with long tresses hanging below her waist. Everyone would be stunned, but then, that would be enough to stun her as well. Masʿūda would assail her with curses and perhaps even blows—from jealousy, of course. But at that point, she would be able to leave the house, for she would be a girl *with hair*. Every household would want her, just as every household had wanted her sister. Her sister. Oh, her sister was really lucky. When she sat down to comb her hair, it looked as if two thick sheaves of wheat hung at her sides. Pitch black, it was. Undoubtedly, the master's son, at whose house her sister had worked as a maid, had married her because of her hair. Miftāḥa wondered what color her new hair would be. Let it be pitch black, just like her sister's. That would do. That would suit her fair complexion and her round face. What would they say, if she came down with a head full of pitch-black hair? Masʿūda would reach over to see whether the hair was genuine. She would try to pluck out some of it, muttering: "You, baldy! You. . . ."

As for her great master, as soon as he heard the news, he would send for her. Perhaps he would bound down the stairs in his rush to the kitchen to see the miracle. He would mumble about the glory of God, his hand playing with his pearly prayer beads. As for her young master—he would marry her. She would smile shyly at him as he reached out his hand to her. . . . Suddenly, she woke from her reverie.

"You, baldy, you're dreaming!"

Startled, Miftāḥa realized that she had dozed off. She decided to leave her place by the chimney. The heat might cause her to doze off again, and then she might miss the opportunity to witness the night of Our Lord Qadr. Could it actually have happened while she was asleep? She looked around, wondering. The night was still dark, the stars were dancing in the sky, and the lights of the city glittered within sight. Again she rebuked herself for sleeping. If she fell asleep again, she would not benefit at all from her night. She should remain awake until the end of the night, until Our Lord Qadr arrived, bringing happiness and joy to all those for whom it was decreed. She cried out to herself:

"You, baldy, if you fall asleep. . . ."

She paced up and down the roof to avoid falling asleep. Before long her vigor had returned, despite the biting cold. She was filled with joy at the spectacle she was relishing by herself, in freedom. She was waiting for hope. Excited, she began to hum an old song:

> Your hair, Zayn, is as long as your shape
> It has the fragrance of rose and musk and lavender
> Your hair, Zayn. . . .

She spent many long hours in that state, pacing up and down the roof, until the lights of the city faded. Suddenly a glaring light shone from the east. How wonderful it was! How frightening! A light of a thousand colors, of no color, of the color of safety and tranquility and peace. Miftāḥa looked on as the light gradually drew near. It seemed to her that its approach was not continuous, as if it paused sometimes. And why not? It paused to collect the requests of the anguished, wakeful souls. Tears welled in her eyes and flowed profusely down her cheeks. She thought the light would pass her before she found the right words. What should she say? How should she say it? Our Lord Qadr . . . Our Lord Qadr. . . . The light seemed to stand still. Quick! He was listening! Mixed images flashed through her mind: Masʿūda snapping orders, her sister combing her hair, a handsome gentleman smiling. No! No! And she screamed:

"Hair! Hair, Our Lord Qadr. Pitch dark, just like my sister's!"

It seemed to her that the light was smiling and that a reassuring hand was stroking her shoulder. It was as if a heart full of tenderness was embracing her and a handkerchief of mercy was holding back her tears. A sense of peace and safety permeated her being. The light seemed to produce blazing, magical rays. It frightened her at first, but then a pleasant stupor began to emanate from the blaze into the pores of her head.

The blaze began to move away, retreating to the east, but the stupor continued to intensify. It seemed to her that it came from little hairs struggling to rise to the surface of her smooth head, to cover her baldness. That answered one of her previous questions: the hair, then, would not grow all at once; it would grow slowly, slowly. She made every effort to expose her head as much as possible to the rays of the blaze, which looked like a terrible fire in the far east of the city. From time to time, black ghosts came between her and the blaze, concealing its piercing rays. They must be the anguished, wakeful souls, exposing themselves, just as she was, to the merciful rays. A thousand thanks, Our Lord Qadr!

The ghosts kept moving between her and the blaze every now and then. Whenever they concealed the rays, she felt as though a bucket of ice water had been poured over her. The intervals between the disappearance of the rays and their return became shorter. She was about to shout at those ghosts—although she knew they could not hear her at such a distance—when she heard voices from among them call out:

"Have mercy on this poor girl! Have mercy on her and burn Masʿūda!"

And Miftāḥa cried from the bottom of her heart:

"Thank you, Our Lord Qadr. Don't burn her. Don't, don't. . . ."

She opened her eyes and found herself staring at a frightening, angry ghost that stood swaying between her and the blazing morning sun. Startled, she jumped up.

"Oh, Lalla Masʿūda!"

"May your tongue be twisted! Sleeping on the roof until noon while we search for you!"

Miftāḥa rushed toward the lower part of the house, trying to avoid physical harm.

Her face was grave, as though she were thinking about something far away.

Comments

This story focuses on the important tradition of the Night of the Divine Decree (Laylat al-Qadr). Highly venerated as the night when the Qurʾān was first revealed to the prophet Muḥammad, it is celebrated during the night between the twenty-sixth and twenty-seventh of Ramaḍān. A common belief holds that on this night a light appears to a chosen few, who thereby acquire fulfillment of a wish.

Miftāḥa is in dire need of a miracle to change her life. Alopecia, the medical term for her baldness, is rarely curable. Seldom congenital, it is seen in young women who are under severe psychological stress. Baldness, apart from the social stigma attached to it, has another symbolic connotation: it signifies Miftāḥa's wholly impoverished state. The hair, which is vital for her acceptance as a female in society, is gone, plucked from her head by the same arbitrary fate that made her a servant without any rights or future prospects. As the youngest and lowliest among the servants, she is tyrannized by Masʿūda, the oppressive housekeeper who takes delight in reminding her of her pathetic condition.

Like most wealthy Arab households, the one in which Miftāḥa serves is headed by a man. The master is unseen, yet his domination is the most important factor in organizing the status of the women in the household. Only the master's absence and the resultant loosening of discipline provide Miftāḥa the opportunity to partake of the blessings brought about by witnessing this special night.

Miftāḥa, who is at the very bottom of the social ladder, yearns to have her sister's luck in capturing the affection of her master's son—or of any other male—and getting him to marry her. But how can she achieve this without hair? Thus she lives in a vicious circle: her baldness leads to social isolation and rejection, which in turn aggravate the emotional stress that causes her baldness. Yet to survive as a female, she must gain, through hair and marriage, acceptance into society.

In the absence of any viable avenue or option for action, Miftāḥa's only key to redemption is religion. Significantly, the name Miftāḥa is the feminine form of *miftāḥ*, which means "key." In Arabic proverbial lore, a much-quoted saying runs: "Patience is the key to relief" (*al-ṣabr miftāḥ al-faraj*). The religious faith that Miftāḥa nurtures is her point of strength. For one thing, she has hope: God may have mercy on her. For another, in religion she has the same rights as anyone else: the Night of the Divine Decree is her night as much as her master's. This gives her confidence and a framework within which to conceive her redemption.

What has Miftāḥa seen on the Night of the Divine Decree? The author leaves it deliberately vague. It may have been the sunrise, which she has mistaken for the divine light, or it may have been a dream or a vision. Whatever the case may be, it induced in her a deep mystical experience and a sense of peace. As a result, it is possible that it will alter her life: in some instances, relief from psychological pressure can result in hair regeneration. Such a fortuitous event would not only rescue this poor servant girl but also reaffirm the belief in the Night of the Divine Decree for future generations.

The author presents the Night of the Divine Decree sensitively yet somewhat skeptically. He acknowledges the significance of religion as a ray of hope for poor people in their most desperate moments. At the same time, he questions the validity of religion as the cure for social and physical ills. Miftāḥa puts her faith in a miracle and does all the right things: she prays and is kindly in asking the Lord not to burn Masʿūda. She thinks her wish has been granted—and then everything goes back to the way it was, and she is left bald and defenseless to face the abusive housekeeper, obeying her orders and dodging her blows.[134]

2
THE WHEEL OF TIME
The Agent of Corrosion

> Time is the most malicious of companions.
> —Al-Mutanabbī[1]

The Pre-Islamic Worldview

The Arab conception of time has its origins in the pre-Islamic age. As illustrated by many passages in their poetry, the pre-Islamic Arabs regarded time as the source of whatever happened to people in the course of their lives. They thus equated it with fate, though they did not engage in worshiping it.[2] Viewed predominantly as an impersonal force with irresistible and arbitrary action, time was believed to control human existence and to bring people their prosperity and above all their adversity:

> Time in the abstract was popularly imagined to be the cause of all earthly happiness and especially of all earthly misery. . . . The poets are continually alluding to the action of Time (*dahr, zamān*), for which they often substitute "the days," or "the nights." Time is represented as bringing misfortune, causing perpetual change, as biting, wearing down, shooting arrows that never miss the mark, hurling stones and so forth. In such cases we are often obliged to render "time" by "fate," which is not quite correct, since time is here conceived as the determining factor, not as being itself determined by some other power, least of all by a conscious agent. But it must be admitted that the Arabs themselves do not always clearly distinguish the power of Time from that of Destiny pure and simple.[3]

There is a sharp contrast between the theistic predestinarian views of the Qur'ān and the pre-Islamic notion of time–fate. This conflict is reflected in the verses of the Qur'ān, in which the deities and heathen beliefs of the pagan Arabs are denounced: "And they say: 'What is there but our life in this world? We shall die and we live, and nothing but Time [*dahr*] can destroy us.' But of that they have no knowledge: they merely conjecture" (45:24); "Say: 'It is God Who gives you life, then gives you death; then He will gather you together for the Day of Judgment about which there is no doubt': but most men do not understand" (45:26). The dispute here revolves not only around an erroneous assumption concerning the cause of human death, but also around a general outlook that rejects the idea of the Last Judgment and the hereafter.[4] The pre-Islamic view of life was largely based on the ideal of manliness (*muruwwa*) and its related virtues, especially courage, loyalty, honor, and generosity, as practiced by the desert Arabs. Religion occupied a peripheral place:

> The warrior of Central Arabia glories in his high courage and the bravery of his companions; it does not occur to him to be grateful to higher powers for his successes—though he does not completely exclude the recognition of their domination. Only the thought of the necessity of death, the result of day-to-day experience which he cannot shut out from his mind, stirs up in him grim thoughts of the *Manāyā* or *Manūna*, that is, the powers of Fate, which, operating blindly and without consciousness of their goal, yet with inevitability, are able to bring to naught all the plans of mortals; good fortune increases his egoism and heightens his self-confidence, but is not in the least suited to lead him to religion.[5]

Theodor Nöldeke points out that the word *manīya* (derived from the verb *manā*, "to count," which denotes the apportioning carried out by destiny) has gained the meaning of "doom of death," "destruction." Both *manīya* and its plural *manāyā* are favorite expressions with the poets: "Manīya appears in poetry as driving man into the grave, piercing him with an arrow, handing to him the cup of death, lying in ambush for him, receiving him as a guest (when he is about to die), and so forth. Not infrequently the possessive suffix is added, 'when my Manīya overtakes me,' 'his Manīya has come upon him,' and the like."[6] These personifications, dramatizing the dual idea of individual death and fate in general, convey the ultimate unity of human destiny.

The pre-Islamic notion of time–fate is better understood when seen in the context of a rugged desert environment and a nomadic way of life. The hardships encountered under such living conditions are closely connected with the passage of time:

> Then the poet, looking at the abandoned camp-sites, could only see the elements of tragedy, of irrevocable change, of the permanent dissolution

> of a once happy existence. The pre-Islamic man's whole life yielded to the element of change as inherent in the very nature of desert life: springs drying up, pastures becoming arid, loved ones departing, youth withering away. It was the poet's wonder and bewilderment at the realization that everything was subject to change and ruin that colored his long and insistent grief as he stood on the deserted ruins of the camp, where only the traces of life and love remain, where the wind has almost swept away all that was left of a once happy tribe.[7]

It has been argued that a fatalistic attitude was appropriate to nomadic life and actually assisted in enduring harsh circumstances. This theory is consistent with the fact that in the Arabian deserts the regularities of nature encountered in other lands are replaced by haphazard occurrences. A person who tried to take precautions against all possible dangers would become extremely tense and nervous, but a willingness to accept whatever happened fatalistically reduced anxiety and thus served as an adaptive mechanism and an aid to survival.[8] W. Montgomery Watt notes that in the system of ideas prevalent in Arabia before Islam not every act of the individual was regarded as determined by fate; only certain aspects of life were thus fixed. The main points in which human life was held to be predestined were a person's term (*ajal*) or date of death—whether one chose to participate in a battle or to stay away from it, one would die if one's term had come; a person's happiness or misery; and a person's sustenance (*rizq*)—a critical matter in regions where food was often scarce.[9]

Although not devoid of positive attributes and at times gentle, time for the pre-Islamic Arabs was mostly the relentless force of fate—the agent of change, decay, and death. The poets, who dwelled on human frailty, engaged in bitter complaints against time's oppression and in exhortations to seek love, wine, and adventure as means to escape it. Ultimately, the censure of time (*dhamm al-dahr*) became "a topos of Arabic poetry signifying the braving of destiny—often through the pursuit of pleasure or passion."[10] L. E. Goodman observes that the emotive thrust of the references to time's power is not metaphysical but elegiac or grieving, like "the outcry in which Job . . . curses his day or the lament in which Jeremiah . . . wishes he had never been born."[11] This sentiment is expressed by the sixth-century poet Yazīd Ibn al-Khadhdhāq:

> I lie as though Time had shot my shape with darts unawares,
> winged sure to pierce me, unfeathered, sent from no bow-string.
> What man can hope for a guard against the Daughters of Time?
> What spells avail to defeat the fated onset of Doom?
> They closed my eyes—but it was not sleep that held them from sight:
> One who stood by—"He's gone, the son of al-Khadhdhāq!"[12]

The corrosive effect of time is depicted in a myriad of colorful images that reflect the nomadic experience of life and the concrete reality of Arabia: "Time is a thief (*khallās*) who snatches away friends and relatives, an injurer (*ḍarrār*) or a disturber (*rayyāb*) who afflicts (or disturbs, *rāba*) with misfortune and death. In its shifting, it acts treacherously to young men in the bloom of life and to old men broken by age. It consumes man like a camel that drinks repeatedly without moderation; it never becomes fat in spite of rich pasture."[13] Time knows no boundaries: it has "sharp teeth" that sink deep and "hands" that reach everywhere; it is a "traitorous desert demon" (*ghūl*) devouring human beings; it is "slyer than a fox"; it unites friends, only to separate them again, "turning as a waterwheel."[14] No one can escape the ravages of time, whose vicissitudes alter the condition of every existing thing. Yet time itself does not change and is eternal and infinite: "Is Time (*dahr*) anything but today and yesterday and tomorrow? Thus Time (*zamān*) goes and comes among us, giving us another night and another day. We do not remain, but Time does not disappear."[15]

Judging by their poetry, the pre-Islamic Arabs knew little of real piety and their attitude to life was mainly hedonistic.[16] In addition to the pleasures of romance and wine, they favored the activities of gambling and hunting and those of poetical and oratorical display. Beyond these joys, there loomed only the harrowing sight of the grave:

> Roast meat and wine: the swinging ride
> On a camel sure and tried,
> Which her master speeds amain
> O'er low dale and level plain:
> Women marble-white and fair
> Trailing gold-fringed raiment rare:
> Opulence, luxurious ease,
> With the lute's soft melodies—
> Such delights hath our brief span;
> Time is Change, Time's fool is Man.
> Wealth or want, great store or small,
> All is one since Death's are all.[17]

The poem conveys a melancholic recognition of death as the grand leveler and time's impartial executioner.

The Islamic Transformation

With the advent of Islam, a fundamental change was introduced into the old Arab conception of time. The monotheistic religious revelation centered on God's omnipotence, reiterating the message that the control of human life is in the hands of God, not of time. The Qur'ān makes many references to the factor of time, often in connection with the phenomena of nature, whose magnitude and regularity are presented as evidence of God's infinite power and majesty. Here time is reduced to one of the various elements that are under God's direct rule and absolute command: "He causes the night to pass into the day and the day to pass into the night. He has forced the sun and the moon into His service, each running for an appointed term" (35:13). Time, like other natural phenomena, has been ordered in such a way that it contributes to the maintenance of human life and to the comfort and benefit of people. The alternation of day and night, for example, has been created to facilitate an orderly life based on the rotation of work and rest: "He it is who has ordained the night for you to rest in and given the day its light for you to see with" (10:67); "It was He that gave the sun his brightness and the moon her light, ordaining her phases that you may learn to compute the seasons and the years (10:5).[18] Above all, the promise of an afterlife disarmed time of its most dreaded weapon—death. As a result, new poetic motifs began to appear, which depicted the night, for example, as a time of communal prayer and hope rather than of despair and loneliness.[19]

The poets' inspiration for the redemptive potential of the night is derived in large part from the Qur'ān, which enjoins: "And celebrate the name of thy Lord morning and evening. And part of the night prostrate thyself to Him; and glorify Him a long night through" (76:25–26). The testimony of time throughout the ages is that it searches out and destroys everything material. The Qur'ān teaches that the only defense human beings have against the tyranny of never-resting time is faith, good works, and persistence: "By (the Token of) Time (through the Ages), verily Man is in loss, except such as have Faith and do righteous deeds, and (join together) in the mutual teaching of Truth, and of Patience and Constancy" (103:1–3). If human beings merely run a race against time, they are bound to lose. It is the spiritual part of human beings that conquers time and attains peace amid the stress of outer life.[20]

Despite the Qur'ān's denunciation of the deification of time by the pagan Arabs, the Ḥadīth literature includes a tradition which attempts to identify God with time (*dahr*). Muḥammad is reported to have said: "God said: Man insults Me in blaming *dahr*; I am *dahr*; in My hand is the command, and I cause the alternation of day and night." That the attempt met with opposition and the identification was felt to be inappropriate can be deduced from the existence of another version, which read *anā al-dahra* for *anā al-dahru* and translated it: "I am eternal."[21] In consequence of this tradition, Muslim theologians have had to struggle with the problem whether or not *dahr*, time or fate, is one of God's fair names.[22]

In his critical survey *Free Will and Predestination in Early Islam*, W. Montgomery Watt suggests that some of the canonical traditions of Islam contain pre-Islamic ideas in Islamic dress, especially what was previously attributed to time–fate came to be ascribed explicitly or implicitly to God.[23]

His findings are supported by a literary study of Arab fatalism in the poetry of the pre-Islamic era, the early Islamic period, and the age of the Abbasids, which was conducted by the Swedish scholar Helmer Ringgren. In this detailed work, entitled *Studies in Arabian Fatalism*, Ringgren argues that in theory, fatalism, strictly defined as the belief that human destiny is determined by an impersonal fate, precludes any belief in God as the author of destiny, but in practice the theistic and fatalistic ideas of destiny often occur together. In the poetry of pre-Islamic Arabia, the fatalistic attitude was predominant and the religious attitude to human destiny was relatively weak. Muḥammad changed this situation. His approach was thoroughly religious and focused on God's unlimited power: "The subsequent evolution led to a gradual intermingling of the two conceptions, resulting in the rigid determinism which is characteristic of later Islam and which is commonly denoted as 'fatalism,' although it is God and not impersonal Fate that is regarded as the determiner of destiny."[24]

Ringgren quotes extensively from poetry to show that God and fate (*dahr* or *qaḍāʾ*) have merged into each other in a way that makes it extremely difficult to distinguish between them. He also draws on the popular tales and verses of *The Arabian Nights*, which he regards as representative of the sentiments of the common people. The following lines illustrate the close relation between God and fate:

> Take all things easy; for all worldly things (*umūr*)
> in Allah's hand are ruled by Destiny (*bikaffi-llāhi maqādīruhā*);
> Ne'er shall befall thee aught of things forbidden,
> nor what is bidden (*maʾmūr*) e'er shall fail to thee.[25]

A striking example of the juxtaposition of time–fate and God can be found in the elegy of Ibn al-Muʿtazz on the deceased caliph al-Muʿtaḍid bi-Allāh:

> O Time (*dahr*) thou didst not leave me a single one; thou art a bad father, who devours his own children!
> I beg the pardon of God! All this is God's predestination. I am content with Allah as the one eternal Lord.[26]

In view of the inevitability of fate, one has to resign and bear patiently:

> O thou who fearest Fate (*dahr*), confiding fare,
> trust all to Him who built the world, and wait:
> What Fate saith "Be" perforce must be (*al-muqaddar kāʾin*), my lord!
> And safe art thou from th'undecreed of Fate (*alladhī mā quddira*).[27]

The same advice is expressed in these verses:

Turn thee from grief nor care a jot,
commit thy deeds to Fate and Lot (*qaḍāʾ*)!
Enjoy the Present passing well
and let the Past be clean forgot;
For what so haply seemeth worse
shall work thy weal as Allah wot:
Allah shall do whate'er He wills (*shāʾa*)
and in His will oppose Him not.[28]

In a subsequent work, Ringgren reiterates his conclusion that the religious interpretation of destiny has contributed to, rather than hindered, the development of Islamic fatalism, and the many instances of its occurrence in folklore and literature show how deeply rooted this attitude has become in the consciousness of the people.[29]

The historical background helps to explain why in the Islamic period the word *time (dahr)* continued to be used by poets and prose writers in the pre-Islamic way. Even the dramatic changes that took place in Arabia, including urbanization, the diminishing importance of desert life, and the migration of poets to the towns, were inconsequential with respect to the image of time: "If the camp-sites, or at least their pre-Islamic concept, were gone, the nostalgia for the departed loved ones remained, and so did the anguish at the passing away of youth and its joys."[30] The verses of the eighth-century poet Abū al-ʿAtāhiya provide a typical example:

What ails me, World, that every place perforce
I lodge thee in, it galleth me to stay?
And, O Time, how do I behold thee run
To spoil me? Thine own gift thou tak'st away!
O Time! inconstant, mutable art thou,
And o'er the realm of ruin is thy sway.[31]

The poetry of al-Mutanabbī (915–65) in particular is known for its personifications of time: "Time [*al-dahr*] is the most malicious of companions"; "Time [*al-dahr*] has shot me with misfortunes until my heart is in an envelope of shafts"; "I exchange thrusts with a cavalry whose horsemen are the fates [*al-dahr*]"; "I do not suppose that Time's vicissitudes [*banāt al-dahr*, literally, "the daughters of Time"] will leave me. . . . Blame the nights [*al-layālī*] which have destroyed my wealth with tenuous circumstances, and excuse me, and do not blame me." [32] Occasionally, there are instances in which man is depicted as the master of time–fate but usually only through hyperbole in a panegyric, as, for example, when al-Mutanabbī addresses his patron, Sayf al-Dawla.[33]

The quatrains of Abū al-ʿAlāʾ al-Maʿarrī (973–1057), a poet and philosopher, contain cynical references to the relation of time to human beings:

The voiceless, countless Army of our Time
Invades the darkest and the brightest clime—
    The human soul, under its burning feet
Still groans, and Time, alas! is in his prime.[34]

Although al-Maʿarrī was a firm monotheist, he rejected the dogmas of Islam, and his belief in God consisted mainly in the conviction that all things are governed by inexorable fate, whose omnipotence no one can escape. [35] His unorthodox views are expressed in a critical and mocking tone:

The pillars of this earth are four,
  Which lend to human life a base;
  God shaped two vessels, Time and Space,
The world and all its folk to store.

That which Time holds, in ignorance
  It holds—why vent on it our spite?
  Man is no cave-bound eremite,
But still an eager spy on Chance.

He trembles to be laid asleep,
  Tho' worn and old and weary grown.
  We laugh and weep by Fate alone,
Time moves us not to laugh or weep;

Yet we accuse it innocent,
  Which, could it speak, might us accuse,
  Our best and worst, at will to choose,
United in a sinful bent.[36]

In the domain of prose writing, a biographer says that time (*zamān*) and the days (*al-ayyām*) took al-Ghazzālī away. [37] In the *Assemblies (maqāmāt)* of al-Hamadhānī (967–1008), the complaints of the rogue hero Abū al-Fatḥ al-Iskandarī against time's duplicity once again evoke the pre-Islamic image of time as an enemy and the cause of human misery.[38]

Contemporary Interpretations

The old image of time, along with the accompanying motifs of grief and lament, has persisted into the modern period. In the neoclassical stage of poetry, for example, adherence to past poetic models was also expressed by adopting old attitudes.[39] This tendency is reflected in the poem "Life's

Complaint" ("Shakwā al-ḥayāh") by the neoclassical poet Ismāʿīl Ṣabrī (1854–1923):

> Many an hour has pained me with its touch and distressed me with its cruel hand.
> I have searched ceaselessly for a moment of peace but found none.
> Many a time I have suffered bitterly through an oppressive hour, until I began to complain about it to the next.
> Then this hour delivered me to another, while I remained in anguish and bitterness.
> Woe to you, poor man! Are you complaining about the frying pan to the fire?
> Beware of the hours! And woe to him who trusts in merciless tyrants.
> If you find among the hours one whose quiver is free of agony,
> Then enjoy yourself like a wise man whose present does not make him forget his past.
> And rejoice as a drunk rejoices on a mountain top overlooking an abyss.
> For this hour, despite its smiles and jests, is surely treacherous, deceitful, and assailing.
> Its embrace is strangulation and its kiss is like the bite of a vicious snake.
> Such is life, so tell those who are wounded by the passage of the hour and the moment:
> O you who complain about time, listen, perhaps the hour of death will deliver you from all pain and sorrow![40]

In a similar vein, the Mahjar poet Gibran Khalil Gibran (1883–1931), in his major poem "The Processions" ("Al-Mawākib"), makes gloomy references to time. In memorable verses, he depicts the world as a tavern owned by time:

> This world is but a winery,
> Its host and master Father Time,
> Who caters only to those steep'd
> In dreams discordant, without rhyme.

Human beings are merely puppets in the careless hands of time:

> The good in man should freely flow,
> As evil lives beyond the grave;
> While Time with fingers moves the pawns
> Awhile, then breaks the knight and knave.

Even science and knowledge cannot liberate human beings from the tyranny of time:

Learning follows various roads.
  We note the start but not the end,
For Time and Fate must rule the course,
  While we see not beyond the bend.[41]

Thus time and fate form the boundaries of human existence. People may seek escape in learning, but they cannot cast off their mortal mold.

Despite the tenacious persistence of the hostile image of time into modern Arabic literature, the concept has nevertheless undergone a distinct modification, acquiring a more positive and balanced interpretation. The Palestinian woman poet and critic Salma Khadra Jayyusi points out that the historic events that have shaken the Arab world since the end of World War II—including the loss of Palestine, the Egyptian, Algerian, and Iraqi revolutions, the Six-Day War, and the Lebanese civil war—have led to a radical change in the outlook on time. She detects an optimistic perspective in avant-garde Arabic poetry of the 1950s:

> In contemporary Arabic poetry, the interpretation of time has changed drastically. . . . It is no more an element of disintegration by which the very essence of life is consumed. An attitude like this towards the immediate past, for example, would be dangerous, for it would mean finalizing its main issues—accepting the loss of all the precious elements that constitute the Arab nations' struggle for a dignified existence after 1948, the loss of Palestine, of honor, of freedom. There could be no finality, therefore, in the poet's attitude towards his past. Life cannot, any more, lose its substance; what has been lost must be replaced, what has disintegrated must be made whole again. Life is not a rigid machine that can be destroyed forever. It *must* contain the possibility of rebirth, otherwise the whole nation is doomed.[42]

Jayyusi notes that by focusing on the change of the seasons, for example, the poets of the 1950s established a theme of hope for the future. They also derived inspiration from revival and fertility myths, such as those of Adonis, Tammuz, and the phoenix, thereby expressing their faith that "winter *will* give birth to spring, and death will eventually produce life and resurrection."[43] These sentiments are eloquently articulated by the Iraqi poet Badr Shākir al-Sayyāb (1926–64) in the poem "Rain Song" ("Unshūdat al-maṭar"), which concludes:

"Rain . . .
Drip, drop, the rain . . .
Drip, drop."
In every drop of rain
A red or yellow color buds from the seeds of flowers.
Every tear wept by the hungry and naked people

And every spilt drop of slaves' blood
Is a smile aimed at a new dawn,
A nipple turning rosy in an infant's lips
In the young world of tomorrow, bringer of life.
And still the rain pours down.[44]

The Syrian poet Adonis (ʿAlī Aḥmad Saʿīd), in "Resurrection and Ashes" ("Al-Baʿth wa-al-ramād"), uses the legendary phoenix to symbolize the ongoing process of life, death, and rebirth:

Phoenix, O phoenix
O bird of yearning and burning
O little feather walking with no companion
Dragging darkness and light.
Traveler, your footsteps are as old as a flower
Your glance is a moment of rapture, your look a mine.
Traveler, your Time is the morrow you created
Your Time is the morrow—the eternal Presence in the morrow
Of a promise:
By it you become a creator, you become a clay
In you heaven and earth unite.[45]

In the poem "Presence" ("Al-Ḥuḍūr"), Adonis expresses his commitment to change and renewal and his rejection of ideas that are relics of the distant past:

The door I open on the world
ignites the present
under battling clouds
that track each other
over oceans spined with waves,
over mountains, forests, rocks.

From roots and ashes I create
a country for the night
and watch it grow.
Fields fountain into song.
Flaring out of thunder, lightning
burns the mummies of the centuries.[46]

For Adonis, the endless struggle with time signifies the challenge of creative vision and dynamic response.

Modern Arabic prose manifests both the old and the new images of time. Among the leading fiction writers of today, the Nobel Prize laureate Najīb Maḥfūẓ is known for his concern with the issue of time. A fundamental thought that runs through his work is how time affects the individual, human memory, and society. As Mursi Saad El Din remarks: "Time is a constant theme in all his novels and a constant preoccupation of his characters. Maḥfūẓ's works are typically laced with sentences—such as 'Time is a terrible companion,' 'What has time done to my friend? It has imposed a hideous mask on his face'—that suggest almost a *horror temporis*."[47] In *Wedding Song (Afrāḥ al-qubba,* 1981), for example, the effects of time on the individual are studied closely and recorded faithfully. The reader can see: "How time works changes, transforming love into hate, beauty into ugliness, loyalty into treachery, idealism into debauchery. . . . Like all the novels of Maḥfūẓ, *Wedding Song* may thus be regarded in part as a history of time and its impact on character. Avoiding such obvious information as the age of the protagonists, Maḥfūẓ gives us instead an evocation of what has happened to their features, their bodies, the look in their eyes, the despair in their hearts."[48] In his most recent work, *Echoes of an Autobiography (Aṣdā' al-sīra al-dhātiyya,* 1995), which contains reflective commentary on events and situations in his life, Maḥfūẓ offers an insight into the mystery of time: "Time deserves to imagine that it is more powerful than any destructive force. However, it accomplishes its goals silently."[49]

While Maḥfūẓ views the relation between human beings and time as tragic on the individual level, he sees it in a more optimistic light on the social level.[50] As he has stated on several occasions, time is the driving force of human advancement: "Time represents the evolutionary spirit of man; it perpetuates the human experience of life. Therefore, while it may mean extinction to the individual, it means eternity for the species."[51] Maḥfūẓ maintains that in the unceasing struggle between the quest for progress and the corrosive effect of time, the existence of society as a whole is unaffected: "My contemplation of time and death has taught me to regard them with the eye of collective man and not [that of] the individual. To the individual they are calamitous, but to collective man a mere illusion. . . . What can death do to human society? Nothing. At any moment you will find society bustling with millions [of lives]."[52]

Of all Maḥfūẓ's works, the most acclaimed is *The Trilogy (Al-Thulāthiyya,* 1956–57), a monumental three-part novel that chronicles the history of three generations of a Cairene family, as well as Egyptian life and society, from the end of World War I to the end of World War II. Sasson Somekh, in his critical study of Maḥfūẓ's novels, comments on the significance of time in this imaginative work. The novel traces the process of change that takes place in Egypt during this period: the rapid rejection of age-old social norms, the slow emancipation of women, the spread of education, the growing influence of Western culture, and the renunciation of religion among the urban middle class. Maḥfūẓ depicts the "changing rhythm" of Egyptian life in great detail, providing a painstaking account of the transformation that time produces in people's appearance, their livelihood, habits, amusements, beliefs, houses, dress, and even furniture.[53] Here, then, time—the great destroyer as well as the great healer—is the true hero of the novel.

A similar theme is portrayed in the novel *The Man Who Lost His Shadow (Al-Rajul alladhī faqad ẓillahu*, 1962) by Fatḥī Ghānim. Time as the factor controlling human destiny is represented by the alarm clock which Mabrūka's old and pious mistress always carries around with her.[54] In this novel, it is time that ultimately defeats Muḥammad Nājī, the influential editor-in-chief of *al-Ayyām*, as well as his master, the corrupt capitalist Shuhdī Pasha. Time displaces the great king and his ministers and ushers in the Egyptian revolution. Eventually, time will also bring down the new rising star, the opportunist Yūsuf Ḥāmid. It is interesting to note that the novel consists of master–servant relationships, with recurrent allusions to a puppet show. Mabrūka is a servant employed in an aristocratic household. When her old mistress dies, she is passed on to a new master, Yūsuf Ḥāmid's widowed father. The mighty king, the important ministers, and the prominent journalist are all Shuhdī Pasha's puppets, and he runs the show from the privacy of his office. When Muḥammad Nājī decides to promote Yūsuf as his assistant, he hopes he will gain a new ally in his struggles with his master. But Yūsuf Ḥāmid soon turns into another puppet in Shuhdī Pasha's army. In this game, however, the true and ultimate manipulator, as hidden and invisible as the puppet-show master, is time. Time stands above Shuhdī Pasha and everyone else—rich and poor, strong and weak—to wield its power as the inescapable and final equalizer.

The Ship (Al-Safīna, 1970), by the Palestinian novelist Jabrā Ibrāhīm Jabrā, provides yet another example of the tyranny of time. In a series of monologues by four characters, each of whom relates the events from his or her viewpoint, a gloomy picture of reality is painted. The author shows the characters, seemingly on a week's cruise in the Mediterranean, to be in a state of desperate escape from different things and for different reasons. Wadīʿ ʿAssāf, a Palestinian living in exile and haunted by memories of his lost homeland, tries to shake off his past in a life of debauchery and decadence. In a conversation with a fellow passenger, ʿIṣām Salmān, he acknowledges that time is the enemy:

> Our creative attempts are merely tranquilizers, a kind of weeping. Yet nothing in life can take the place of large flowing tears. Time, in any case, is a horrible thing. In its unabating tide it robs everything of vigor and newness. In the end, it leaves you nothing of any worth. Time has trampled down everything I see and left it faded and dull. If I were a painter, I'd paint it. Do you know how? One huge black smudge on a canvas. In two or three places I would spot it with red paint. Time is

> the enemy. Live if you wish; stay alive as long as you can. But you'll have nothing else: a big black smudge filling the fabric of your life, with a red spot here and there; the trivia that come your way whether you want them or not, without your ever being able to achieve that great relentless experience which is the product of choice and will.[55]

In the novella *The Sinners* (*Al-Ḥarām*, 1959) by Yūsuf Idrīs, however, time has healing powers. When Linda, the daughter of the Copt Masīḥa Effendi, disappears and he learns that she has gone off to marry the Muslim Aḥmad Sulṭān, he is heartbroken: "He severed all ties with Linda and her husband, and swore that he, his sons, and his wife would never acknowledge her, see her, or speak of her again. But the passage of the days—ah, those days—soon made him forgive and forget. He replied to the many letters Linda sent him every week with a single communication, grave and tersely worded but beginning with the salutation, 'Our dear daughter Linda.' "[56]

A similar point of view is expressed in *The Days* (*Al-Ayyām*, 1929) the autobiography of Ṭāhā Ḥusayn. The author describes how, when still a young boy, he experienced the double tragedy of the death of his little sister and of his older and highly talented brother: "Then the day came, whereupon the lad really tasted pain, and thereafter knew that the pains he had suffered previously and on account of which he had hated life were nothing at all; he also realized that Time is able to pain people and afflict them and yet at the same time endear life to them and make its course run smooth for them."[57]

Arabic proverbial lore abounds in both negative and positive references to the action of time. For example: "Every man is formed by his days" (*al-insān ibn yawmihi*); "Harsher than fate [time]" (*ajfā min al-dahr*); "Mankind is the prey of fate [the days]" (*al-anām farā'is al-ayyām*); "No drug can erase the mark of time" (*wa-hal yuṣliḥ al-ʿaṭṭār mā afsada al-dahr*); "Time is the best of all mentors" (*niʿma al-mu'addibu al-dahr*); "He who challenges his destiny [the days, time] will be vanquished every time" (*man ghālaba al-ayyām ghuliba; man sābaqa al-dahr ʿathara*).

These examples show the multifaceted role of time in human life. The uniqueness of this theme in Arabic literature lies in the fact that the inexorable course of time serves as a symbol for the inevitability of fate. As a dynamic force with supreme presence, time is imagined to have absolute control over all events, including the unfolding of history and human destiny. Time is conceived in abstract terms as well as in concrete details; it possesses opposite, irreconcilable attributes; it is both colossal and minute. Hence time has a dual portrayal: on the one hand, it is represented as impersonal and oblivious to people and, on the other, as intimately involved in their lives and closely connected with their fate.

Najīb Maḥfūẓ
An Old Picture

Najīb Maḥfūẓ was born into a middle-class family in Cairo in 1911. He studied philosophy at Cairo University and received his B.A. in 1934. Although he began writing early on, he had to look elsewhere for a living. At first he held a secretarial post at Cairo University and then entered the civil service. From 1939 until his retirement in 1971, he worked in various government departments, including the Ministry of Religious Endowments, the Ministry for National Guidance, and the Ministry of Culture. Since 1971, he has been writing a weekly column for Cairo's leading newspaper, *al-Ahrām*.

Maḥfūẓ is recognized as the foremost novelist of the Arab world. His literary output is formidable. Since his first publication in 1939, he has written thirty-five novels and fourteen volumes of short stories. Many of his novels and short stories have been made into films.

As a novelist, Maḥfūẓ excels at painting on a wide canvas to create a portrait of an era. He employs a myriad of characters and subplots to develop his theme and pays great attention to detail. His stories are almost all set in Cairo—the city where he has lived all his life. The subject matter encompasses the petite bourgeoisie and their endless quest for material security, the developments in Egyptian society and its intellectual history, and the individual's search for meaning and identity. Maḥfūẓ's style has evolved from realism into allegory and symbolism and subsequently into a synthesis of these distinct modes.

Maḥfūẓ is best known for *The Trilogy*, a novel in three parts (*Bayn al-qaṣrayn, Al-Sukkariyya*, and *Qaṣr al-shawq*) published in 1956 and 1957, for which he won the Egyptian State Prize. In 1988, he achieved the distinction of being the first Arab author to receive the Nobel Prize for literature.

"An Old Picture" ("Ṣūra qadīma") appears in the collection *God's World (Dunyā Allāh*, 1963). The story presents the author's philosophy of time in a nutshell: fifteen pages as compared with the approximately fifteen hundred pages of *The Trilogy*. The story depicts the effects of time on the lives of a group of high school graduates over a period of three decades.

An idea flashed through Ḥusayn's mind and promised to solve his predicament. It occurred when his gaze fell upon the old school picture. He was having difficulty conjuring up a subject for the magazine, as must happen to any journalist required to come up with something new every day. Suddenly he had an idea. The picture had been hanging in the sitting room for more than thirty years. It made no statement. In fact, it was scarcely visible. Now, however, the time had come for it to suggest something.

Ḥusayn's attention was riveted on the picture, almost faded with time, of the final class of the Humanities Department of Giza High School in 1928. Why not write an investigative report on these young men? School and life—1928 to 1960. It was basically a good idea. He wondered whether he could obtain the necessary information for an interesting article. How many years had passed without his casting so much as a glance at the picture? How many features represented in the picture had irretrievably vanished? Take that fez, for example, and those Englishmen and Frenchmen they had as teachers!

Usually, merely glancing at a face was a sufficient reminder of a person, even if he could not recall his name and knew nothing about his fate. He had no contact with any of these people today, not even with this intriguing fellow who had long been his neighbor in the apartment building where they had lived.

He examined the faces, beginning with the upper row. The first two meant nothing to him, so he skipped them, pausing before a boy who had been a football hero in school. He had died in a match between Giza and another school—an unforgettable incident. In the picture he looked self-assured and conceited, the corners of his mouth twisted into a suggestion of a smile. Today he was nothing but bones! Ḥusayn's eyes traveled from one person to another until his gaze was arrested by a long thin face. He remembered this boy standing atop a ladder belonging to the school secretary, giving a fiery speech that urged the students to strike in protest against the Declaration of 28 February.[58] At his side was an elegantly handsome face that indicated wealth and privilege. The boy's family name, al-Māwardī, instantly came to mind, and he wrote it in his notebook. Ḥusayn was confident that he could find him easily, especially as he had been a shining star in political life for the last ten years. He would be the first important person in the article.

Ḥusayn glanced over the faces one by one—many of them failed to stir any memory—until he came across a face not easily forgotten. The boy personified scholastic skill in all its glory. He was at the head of his class, of every class—of the entire school in fact. Al-Ūrfalī was his name. He remembered it both because of the boy's talent and because the name was unusual. After enjoying some prestige in law school, he had been appointed to the public prosecutor's office at a time when such an appointment was considered extremely important. He could easily find him by inquiring at the Ministry of Justice. He would be the second important person in the article. Yes, al-Ūrfalī after al-Māwardī.

Another face challenged Ḥusayn with a memory marred by violence. It involved a schoolyard fight between this boy and his friend, but he could not remember the reason for the fight. Ḥusayn continued to examine the faces, which were as silent as stone, until he arrived at an intriguing one—that of his old neighbor, Ḥāmid Zahrān, currently the director of the Step Pyramid Company. He smiled coldly. This was the boy of the century! He remembered distinctly that Ḥāmid Zahrān had left Giza High School after failing the baccalaureate examination and that he had joined the Ministry of Defense with a mere secondary school diploma. Ḥusayn's contact with him had ended only ten years before, when he left Abū Khūdha Alley after God granted him success in journalism. He had received news of Ḥāmid's resignation from the government to work as a secretary for the director of the Step Pyramid Company. Then he had heard that Ḥāmid had been promoted to director at a monthly salary of five hundred Egyptian pounds! What an extraordinary person he was, whether in his amazing success or in his total insignificance. Nevertheless, he would be a valuable and meaningful element in what Ḥusayn hoped would turn into an interesting article. This article would present his objective analysis and observations rather than the personal accounts of obscure people, for the really interesting point was the social significance of these people, not their individual lives. In any event, he would postpone the final report on the picture until he had collected all the material.

ʿAbbās al-Māwardī's circle of acquaintances was in al-Azhar Square. On learning that he was at his country estate in Qalyūb, Ḥusayn proceeded to request a meeting. At the appointed time, he walked along a path lined with flowerpots on either side, which led to the ground-floor reception room. The two-story house was an architectural treasure set in a garden of approximately two acres overflowing with mango, orange, and lemon trees, as well as vine trellises. There were countless squares, triangles, and circles of flowers and greenery, and several brooks. The mansion rose magnificently amid a vast expanse of fields stretching toward the horizon. It was a haven of peace, tranquility, and harmony. In the distance he could see bodies bent over, virtually lost among the plants and the open space. ʿAbbās al-Māwardī received him wearing a long, flowing gown. He had a full, rosy face, with shiny, well-groomed hair on a big, round head. His large figure looked like a statue wrapped in a sheet before being unveiled! He looked at Ḥusayn with a smile that bespoke cautious surprise and curiosity, and proceeded to greet him:

"Welcome, Mr. Ḥusayn Manṣūr."

They shook hands and sat down.

"I follow your articles with admiration. It reminds me of our school days, though we haven't met since we graduated from Giza High School."

Smiling, Ḥusayn said: "We met once briefly in Parliament. It was in 1950 or 1951."

ʿAbbās raised his eyebrows: "Really?"

For a long while the two reminisced about school. Finally, Ḥusayn told ʿAbbās the reason for his visit.

"Wouldn't it be better if you left me out altogether?" ʿAbbās asked hopefully.

Ḥusayn rejoined: "I disagree. This investigation might be the first step toward the study of an entire generation. I will not publish one word about you without your consent. I promise. It might not be necessary to mention any names at all."

He did not object, but neither was he enthusiastic. His face revealed nothing, so Ḥusayn Manṣūr began to wonder anxiously what might be troubling him. Could it be that his presence and the memories it provoked were painful to ʿAbbās? Whatever the current state of his financial affairs,[59] in the past he had indisputably been a millionaire and a rising political star. He had won elections as an unopposed candidate owing to his family's high social status, and it was rumored that he had been nominated for a cabinet post at the end of 1950.

"I live here permanently. That's why I've sent my son, who is a student, to his aunt in Cairo. I almost never leave the estate, except on rare occasions."

ʿAbbās relaxed a little and began to talk freely. He said that he farmed his land himself, using the latest agricultural machinery, and that he was keenly interested in raising cattle and fowl. He had set up a large library for his free time and rode horses as a hobby and sport. He had retired into a small kingdom where he was able to ignore the outside world. He wished that he could spend his entire life within the confines of this estate and never have to leave.

At that point, Ḥusayn asked him about the peasants.

"I, too, am a peasant at heart, and so was my father. I have no trouble dealing with them. They're good people."

Ḥusayn began wondering again, but he wisely avoided the subject.

"Didn't you nominate yourself to the National Union?"

"I suggested it to a number of people, but I'm quite content as I am!" ʿAbbās replied emphatically.

Ḥusayn imagined this kind of life, which combined nature with civilization and was blessed with every fortune. A life lived in perfect seclusion, imbued with pride and glory, invigorated with earthly and intellectual delights, enchanted with the night and the moon and his own American bar and the local café. . . .

"What about the friends of the past?"

"Which ones? Those who are special spend weekends with me. As for the rest, I know nothing about them."

ʿAbbās refused to talk about current affairs, and Ḥusayn did not insist.

"Don't you ever want to go to the movies, for example?"

"I have a private movie theater. I don't miss a thing!"

Then Ḥusayn showed him the old school picture, hoping that he might recognize someone. ʿAbbās examined it with a smile. Pointing to one face, he said: "ʿAlī Sulaymān. He was hit by a bullet in the chest at the time of Ṣidqī.[60] Because of this, he was appointed to the diplomatic corps after graduation. He left eventually, during the purge."

Ḥusayn pointed to Ḥāmid Zahrān's face, but ʿAbbās shook his head. So he said: "Ḥāmid Zahrān, the director of the Step Pyramid Company. He makes five hundred Egyptian pounds a month!"

ʿAbbās raised his eyebrows: "Really?"

He said nothing more, though a puzzled look clouded his eyes, and Ḥusayn ended the conversation.

At the Ministry of Justice, Ḥusayn discovered the whereabouts of the former head of the class, Mr. Ibrāhīm al-Ūrfalī, currently a judge at the criminal court. Ḥusayn waited for him outside the court building until he emerged, followed by the doorman, who rushed to call a taxi. Ḥusayn approached with a smile. The judge stared at him in surprise but soon recognized him and extended his hand in greeting. He understood the gist of what Ḥusayn wanted and kindly invited him to lunch. The taxi took them to Māhir Street where they entered his home. It was respectable, but modest, which surprised Ḥusayn Manṣūr. However, when al-Ūrfalī's eight children, not far apart in age, gathered with them around the dinner table, he ceased to be surprised.

"Your articles really attract attention!"

Ḥusayn thanked him, stealing a glance at al-Ūrfalī's thin body and shining, weary eyes. At school he had been extremely popular and well known because of his talent. Today no one outside the Court of Justice knew his name!

After Ḥusayn had discussed his project in some detail, al-Ūrfalī hastened to say: "My work has nothing to do with the press. When I was a chief prosecutor, investigating a well-known case, the press tried to push me into the spotlight, but I refused. Fame means nothing to a judge. As for the accused, either they are innocent, in which case we must protect them, or they are guilty, in which case we shouldn't give them publicity."

Ḥusayn replied reassuringly: "Don't worry about publicity. I'm merely studying school and life. If you like, I can refer to you by your initials only. I may be able to avoid any reference to your identity."

"That would be better. But what exactly is it that you want?"

Ḥusayn observed him with a journalist's curiosity. They were drinking coffee alone in the living room. There was no sign of the children, except for the occasional noise that penetrated the closed door.

"I'd like to hear your views of our generation and the present one, the most important cases you've presided over, and your thoughts on your work and on life."

Al-Ūrfalī began to expound his views slowly and somewhat timidly. He was partial to the older generation, though he preferred the philosophy of the young. He seemed content with his job, and proud of it, despite the constant effort it required. Then he began to discuss the strange cases over which he had presided.

"You were always the best in our class."

Al-Ūrfalī pondered a while, then said: "I was also the best in the entire country in our baccalaureate year."

"Despite everything, I see a strange serenity in your face."

"Despite what?"

Gently, Ḥusayn replied: "A man who sentences others to death. . . ."

Al-Ūrfalī cut him short: "As long as my conscience is clear, I know no fear."

"But truly, your serenity is unusual."

The other laughed loudly. "Consider me a Ṣūfī, if you wish."

A look of surprise came into Ḥusayn's eyes, and he leaned forward in anticipation of more on the subject, but al-Ūrfalī seemed to regret what he had said and refused to continue.

"Your work must be extremely difficult."

"Life is consumed between the papers of one case and another."

It was quite obvious that he was exhausted from work, just as he had been as a student. A noble solitude, a constant struggle, eight children, and Ṣūfism.

"Nevertheless, employees of the Court of Justice will go to paradise."

"Paradise is ours!" Al-Ūrfalī repeated after him, smiling.

Then Ḥusayn showed him the school picture. The other looked at it carefully. Pointing to Ḥāmid Zahrān, Ḥusayn asked: "Don't you remember this boy?"

"No, not at all."

"Ḥāmid Zahrān. One of those who failed the baccalaureate. He's the director of a company. He earns five hundred Egyptian pounds a month!"

Al-Ūrfalī stared at the picture as though he had seen a flying saucer.

"I thought the news wouldn't upset a Ṣūfī," Ḥusayn remarked. They both burst out laughing.

He asked al-Ūrfalī whether he recognized any other classmates in the picture. Al-Ūrfalī looked at it and pointed to a face in the second row, saying: "Muḥammad ʿAbd al-Salām. A clerk in the public prosecutor's office. He worked with me early in my career in Abū Tīg. I don't know anything about him today."

Ḥusayn had to travel to al-Minyā to meet ʿAbd al-Salām at his latest place of work. He seemed older than his age by at least ten years. His shabby appearance, disheveled hair, and wrinkled clothing evoked the image of ruins in Ḥusayn's mind. The man did not remember him, nor did he believe any of his claims until Ḥusayn showed him the old picture. They sat together in a sparsely furnished sitting room in an old apartment crowded with children.

"I don't recognize anyone in this picture. In the civil service I've moved from one place to another."

A pang of pain pierced Ḥusayn's heart. He felt deep sympathy and respect for the man. He inquired about his administrative grade.

"The fifth grade, for a year now. Write this down, sir. It would be wonderful if you published a picture of me and my children! Six girls and four boys. What do you think? Isn't it possible that you were sent to me by God as a consolation in difficult times?"

Ḥusayn wished him well and gradually encouraged him to talk about his experiences at work. Then Ḥusayn requested a detailed account of his family's annual budget and, pointing to Ḥāmid Zahrān in the picture, remarked: "This old schoolmate currently earns five hundred Egyptian pounds a month."

The man was stunned, and his pallor seemed to increase.

"What does he do?"

"He's the director of a company."

"But not even a cabinet minister earns half as much!"

"This is one thing, and that is another."

"How does he spend this money—on what?"

Ḥusayn smiled but did not reply. So the other asked: "What are his qualifications?"

"A secondary school diploma!"

"Good heavens! You must be joking!"

"No, I'm not. The diploma isn't the critical factor."

"Then what is the critical factor? Explain to me. How does a person become so prosperous? Here he is, standing next to me in the same row in the picture. Tell me, how did he reach these heights?"

Gently, Ḥusayn replied: "There is something called luck."

The other man shook his head sadly and confidently. "No job in this country deserves that much money. Otherwise, why haven't we reached the moon?"

Ḥusayn laughed and said: "In any case, you are better off than millions of others."

Protesting, the man responded: "Millions of others—I know that. But Ḥāmid Zahrān is the problem."

He had no difficulty arranging a meeting with his old neighbor, Ḥāmid Zahrān. Because the office was an inappropriate place for an informal interview, Zahrān invited him to come to his house in Dokki. Ḥusayn looked admiringly at the villa situated amid willow trees. It reminded him of ʿAbbās al-Māwardī's country mansion in Qalyūb: the splendid architecture, the spacious garden, and the fragrance of affluence. He wondered how his old neighbor would look today. All he remembered was a thin body with a pale face and a mocking laugh, appearing somewhat hungry. This image no longer befitted a man living in such an impressive villa.

May God have mercy on the old days, Ḥāmid, when you tricked people into loaning you a shilling and would return it only with the greatest reluctance. Had time not separated us, I would have been able to observe firsthand how such great changes come about!

"Welcome, Ḥusayn. Where have you been, old chap?"

He was fully dressed in a suit, as the wealthy are inclined to be in their homes. The living room dazzled the eye with its lights and mirrors and ornaments. As for Ḥāmid, his body had filled out and seemed full of vitality.

"I protest this working visit. You should have made my house your home! You didn't even congratulate me at the time!"

Ḥusayn was nonplussed, but he answered carefully: "I have no excuse! Please forgive me. . . ."

Ḥāmid laughed, satisfied. They forgot the present for quite a while as they reminisced about the past. Then the journalist prepared for work. He avoided questions that could be construed as insulting or mocking and restricted his inquiries to his friend's success and what had made it possible, his policy at the company, his views of his generation, and so forth.

"I had business relations with the former director of the company before he took charge. So he chose me as his secretary, and later as his office manager. He preferred me to others because of my previous experience."

Previous experience! The truth is that you had turned your old house into a gambling club for your bosses—a gambling club and a hashish den to boot! You're one shrewd opportunist!

"During the time that I was employed at his office, I learned every detail, big and small, about the work. I became acquainted with all the important people who did business with the company."

"This is what distinguishes the clever secretary from the ordinary one!"

"And it was my director who appointed me to this job, when he was transferred abroad."

"Yes, the job! But what are your plans for the future?"

He spoke at length on this subject, confident and self-assured, while Ḥusayn summarized his statements faithfully, observing Ḥāmid at close range and mentally registering each movement and pause. When the interview ended, Ḥāmid stood up and headed toward the inner part of the house, saying: "Wait. I'll introduce you to my wife."

Oh, Fāyiqa! Another old neighbor. Ḥusayn wondered how she would look today. Ḥāmid had married her while still at school. Her father, ʿAmm Salāma the tram driver, had been his neighbor. How would she look against the background of this villa?

Ḥāmid Zahrān returned with a girl in her twenties. She was beautiful, radiant, with a face whose features had a touch of the West as well as of the East. O God, it was a new wife!

They were introduced. The conversation was conducted mostly in English. Ḥāmid's laughing face was beaming with pride. But where was Fāyiqa? Dead or divorced?

The report on the picture would be incomplete until he answered this question. He went at once to al-Karmānī Alley in Bāb al-Shaʿriyya, where ʿAmm Salāma's old house had been located. As soon as he entered the alley, a local clothes-presser told him that ʿAmm Salāma had been dead for years. His daughter Fāyiqa had opened a candy and cigarette shop in the lower part of the house. Ḥusayn approached the house nervously, afraid that she might spot him. Then he caught a glimpse of her. She was sitting behind the table smoking a cigarette. All he could see was her face and neck. She looked at least ten years older than she was—just like Muḥammad ʿAbd al-Salām, the clerk at the public prosecutor's office in al-Minyā. She seemed to be at a loss, gloomy, resigned to the fates. He recalled that she had been a model of patience, vitality, and hope, and his heartfelt sympathy and respect went out to her.

Ḥusayn left al-Karmānī Alley feeling suffocated by the turbid air. He began to ponder the material he had gathered for his article and to make a preliminary analysis. He asked himself:

"What message, I wonder, will this old picture convey?"

Comments

This story provides a realistic portrayal of the vicissitudes of life. Ḥusayn, an investigative reporter, is both appalled and intrigued to learn what has happened to his old classmates since their graduation thirty years before. For the most part, those who were successful early on have not prospered, while an academic failure has become rich through shady dealings. One character, Fāyiqa, began modestly, prospered, and has fallen down again. Another, a wealthy aristocrat, has survived the rigors of the Egyptian revolution and agrarian reforms with considerable power and affluence. At the same time, several hardworking civil servants live on the edge of poverty. In an effort to make sense of these baffling contradictions, Ḥusayn sets out to analyze the life stories of these individuals. His intention is not so much to unveil their personalities as to ascertain their social significance—namely, the changes in Egyptian society.

The object that triggers Ḥusayn's investigation is an old picture—a recurrent artistic device in Maḥfūẓ's work.[61] The confrontation with faces from the past evokes old memories as well as curiosity and confusion. In the picture, all the faces look confident and radiant with life; they are unaware of what lies hidden in the unknown. Yet each one of them is a plaything in the hands of time, set on a collision course with the unpredictable and irrational elements of reality.

The story conveys a pessimistic view of human life. There is no relation between people's moral conduct and their fate. It appears that opportunism is more likely to yield success than hard work. The unscrupulous Ḥāmid Zahrān becomes a wealthy businessman, and the virtuous Fāyiqa is deserted by her husband for a younger and prettier wife. In this story, reward and punishment figure only in the context of the afterlife.

Time unravels people's true nature: qualities that are partially hidden during youth become manifest in adulthood. Ultimately, time exposes all men and women to the very core of their being. Time may take a heavier toll on honest characters, such as Fāyiqa and ʿAbd al-Salām, who look much older than their age. But in the end, time is bound to bring everyone to the same final state—aging and death.

Despite the distinctly secular tone of the story, there is an allusion to the spiritual dimension of life. The judge al-Ūrfalī, who sentences people to death, derives strength from Ṣūfism.[62] Nevertheless, the main focus of the story remains on the worldly circumstances of people's lives. Ḥusayn is cast as a journalist to emphasize his concern with the present, the here and now. His investigation raises a cardinal question: why do some individuals prosper and others suffer? His modest inquiry seems to point in the direction of time as the tyrannical force that arbitrarily governs human destiny and the course of history. This theme is depicted in great detail throughout Maḥfūẓ's *Trilogy*.

While in "An Old Picture" Maḥfūẓ presents the relation between human beings and time as tragic on the individual level, he paints it in a more optimistic light on the collective level. In several places, he alludes to a major event in the history of Egypt—the 1952 revolution, which abolished the monarchy in favor of a republic. Hence Ḥusayn's emphasis is on the social significance of his classmates, who represent a generation, and not just their factual accounts. Ḥusayn's findings are mixed: the passage of time has brought about the Egyptian revolution, but the revolution has not lived up to its promise and failed to solve the basic injustice and inequities in society. The lower classes, the peasants and the urban workers, still struggle to make a living while the upper class, the landed aristocracy, still enjoys power and privilege. The only conspicuous difference between the prerevolutionary and postrevolutionary periods is the rise of opportunists like Ḥāmid Zahrān, self-seeking individuals who take advantage of any situation to promote themselves, with total disregard for moral issues and for their fellow human beings.

In the final analysis, perceiving the effects of time is one thing and its *purpose* another. We can look at what time brings about, but what does it all mean? Ḥusayn gives his readers the raw material—the interviews—for his study, but the story ends just at the point where he is ready to sit down and draw some conclusions. Thus he leaves his readers to do their own thinking.[63]

Ghassān Kanafānī
The Viper Is Thirsty

Ghassān Kanafānī (1936–72) was born in Acre, Palestine. His family fled to southern Lebanon in 1948 and later settled in Damascus. He graduated in literature from the University of Damascus and began his career as a teacher. In 1956 he went to Kuwait, where he was engaged in teaching and creative writing. He moved to Beirut in 1960 and worked as a journalist and editor for various newspapers. In addition, he became active in politics, serving as spokesman for the Popular Front for the Liberation of Palestine and as editor of its journal, *al-Hadaf*, which he founded in 1969.

Kanafānī is regarded as one of the leading Palestinian prose writers. His literary output is varied and includes novels, short stories, plays, and studies of Palestinian literature. He was a politically committed writer, and most of his fictional works deal with the loss of Palestine and the tragedy of refugees living in exile. His style combines realism with multiple symbolism and subtle imagery.

"The Viper Is Thirsty" ("ʿAṭshā al-afʿa") appears in the collection *A World Not Our Own* (*ʿĀlam laysa lanā*, 1965). The story portrays time as the harbinger of technological changes that destroy ancestral customs and displace a traditional way of life.

It was the car that dashed toward him. He had been standing still. The whole thing happened so quickly. When he heard the screech of tires, he turned around suddenly and saw the front of a black car and a big wheel. All he knew was that it was *that* car, the selfsame one. He saw a purple cloud approaching him and felt a leaden, quivering numbness filling his limbs. People began to gather around him in silent, slow motion, like fish swimming in a glass tank. He was thrown prostrate on a sharp stone that pierced his waist, so he rolled onto his side. Drops of black oil inched along the asphalt, advancing toward a shiny red stain that stretched up to his cheek.

The sharp stone was still stuck in his waist. He was in pain, but the sensation of numbness spreading through his body felt extremely pleasant. He wished that those mute ghosts would go away and leave him alone to lie in this warm place, watching the black tongue as it crept like a small viper toward the red pool.

"He was trying to cross the street and the car hit him!"

He was unaware of the first time he heard these words, but they began to ring constantly in his ears. The familiar voice might have been his father's, but he was not sure, for he had almost forgotten his father's voice. He could not distinguish anything, except that the voice continued to repeat the same words. What if his father knew he was hit by *that* car? What would he do? No, the voice could not be his father's. If his father knew, he would not just stand there saying, "A car hit him. . . ."

He was still enjoying the numbness circulating throughout his body. He felt many hands carrying him, palpating him, and pressing against parts of his body. But that meant nothing compared to the bliss of the numbness.

"Can you count my fingers?"

The voice that reached him was faint, as if distant. His ears trembled slightly as they caught the sound, swung it around, then hurled it to the back of his head. It was not his father's voice, that was certain. It was a soft, gentle voice. His father had a metallic voice, a loud voice that shook the ceiling of their old house. His mother would always say to his father:

"If your desire to earn a living were as strong as your voice, we'd be a whole lot better off!"

His father's voice! How could he think he had almost forgotten it? Was it possible to forget it? Had he not heard it year after year as he walked beside him along those alleys, paved with smooth cobblestones? What had his father said in those days? He could not remember now. Perhaps he would remember later, but now there was the delightful numbness that flowed pleasantly, though heavily, inside his small veins.

"If you can see my fingers, tell me how many there are. If you can't see them, let me know. Do you hear me?"

Yes. He could hear him. He could always hear his father's voice from the next room telling his mother:

"They're going to marry off Laylā to ʿAbd al-Hādī. You know ʿAbd al-Hādī. He's the son of Ḥasan who used to live above the grocer's before he died."

His mother would be sitting before a bowl full of rice, sifting out the small pebbles.

"When's the wedding?" she would ask.

And the metallic voice would reach him: "Tonight!"

He used to wait for that word. "Tonight!" It was such a beautiful word. As soon as he heard it, he would go off to climb the ladder to the attic. He would quickly find the long stick, which was in plain sight, but he could never find the little drum. Then he would call down the stairs:

"Where did you put the drum? It's not here!"

And his father's angry voice would rise up in reply: "Come down, you little devil! Come down! When will you learn that the drum belongs in the courtyard, not the attic? We've taught you that a thousand times, but you don't get it, do you?"

Coming down the stairs, he would remember that his father had once told him that it was necessary to keep the drum in a dry place where the sunlight could reach it. This would guarantee that the skin on the drum remained taut.

"My dear boy, just tell me. Can you see my hand?"

His father's hand was rough and wide. Its blue veins bulged and pulsated constantly. He would hold the drum and rotate it between the palms of his hands, then tap on it with his index finger. As for him, he would squat in front of his father and watch him eagerly, careful not to miss a thing. He would watch him don the baggy pants with the embroidery on the sides directly below the pockets, fasten the shiny striped vest with the row of small black buttons, then wrap the long black sash around his waist and tie its ends skillfully to conceal the knot. Only then would he walk up to his father and ask:

"May I come with you tonight, Father?"

Without looking at him, his father would reply: "Yes. You may come—but to learn, not just to watch!"

Then, kneeling down before him so that he could hold him by his little arms, he would say: "Tell me . . . If I were to die tomorrow, who would teach you my trade? What work would you do? Keep your eyes open tonight and watch carefully everything I do. You've got to learn! You've got to learn!"

But he had not learned. He must have seen his father more than a thousand times walking at the head of the wedding procession. In fact, he walked right beside him, watching his hands and feet. But he couldn't learn anything. The art was extremely complicated, and he could not imagine how he would ever master it. Would he be able to deliver those rapid, precise strokes on the little drum with such skill? His eyes could not follow his father's hand as it turned the drum behind his back, then between his legs, then behind his neck, simultaneously delivering those astonishing strokes with the stick on the drum and continuing to sing with a voice that never faltered throughout the rapid, wonderful dance.

"We want to help you, son. Why don't you answer my questions? I'm not going to hurt you. Can you see my hand? Nod your head, that's all. Don't speak. Just nod your head. Can you see my hand?"

He had not learned anything! He had tried so often to perform those movements for his father, but he failed repeatedly and came close to tears. He had tried once to rotate the drum behind his back, but it had dropped to the floor. Without picking it up, he ran to the next room and began to cry. Then he had heard his father's voice:

"This boy must be stupid! This is his father's trade, and his grandfather's and great-grandfather's before that. How can he be so stupid? I'm getting old. I may die soon. And this son of yours hasn't yet learned how *not* to let the drum drop from his hands!"

Despite these failures, he was quite happy. He used to look at his father's hands at work at every wedding and imagine this was all an act of magic, some kind of miracle. He held his head up in his neighborhood and was proud that his father was needed at every wedding. It was his father whom the young men gathered around as they led the bridegroom to the bride's house, clapping their hands and joining in the singing. They praised his father's skill in beating the drum with the stick from behind his back, and behind his neck, and between his legs, marveling that the stick never missed the drum and that the timing of the strokes was always perfect!

"Lady, maybe you want to give it a try. I have scores of other patients to see. He's not the only one with an injury!"

He felt a gentle hand wiping his forehead and heard a woman's voice. It had the same soft sound as before.

"Why don't you want to tell us what you see? Can you see my face?"

He did not know when it had happened, but he had heard his father tell his mother in the next room:

"They say that cars are better. Can you imagine that? Since ʿAbd al-Muḥsin got married five months ago, they keep saying every day at the café that cars are better than wedding processions. Have you heard how cars croak like frogs when people are crammed into them like sardines? It's a shame! A great shame! Can you imagine that? They get married without a wedding procession, as if they were ashamed of the marriage! Today the café owner told me that I have to look for another job."

That day he had felt that something terrible had happened. He had gotten out of bed and walked to the door. He had seen his father sitting cross-legged on the mat while his mother oiled the skin of the drum. His father had continued:

"I thought that the other quarters of town had stopped inviting me to weddings because of some competitor. Cars! Good heavens! Imagine the bridegroom sitting in a car—it's as if he were hiding from people. Shame! The wedding day is the happiest day of your life! Cars! All you hear is beep, beep, beep—then the ceremony is over!"

He had returned quietly to bed, and throughout the night he had dreamt about cars that carry bridegrooms and brides without the sound of drum and stick.

"Listen! We'll throw you out on the street if you don't say something. This is an accursed child, believe me! He opens his eyes like a cat, then looks at us and doesn't say a word. Who's your father?"

His father? He had gone out one day and never returned. Our neighbor, Muḥammad ʿAlī the carpenter, was marrying off his son. In the morning, his father had prepared the drum. In the afternoon, he told his mother that Muḥammad ʿAlī the carpenter had not invited him to the wedding. In the evening, the car arrived. When his father heard the horn honking and saw how big the car was and how shiny, as if polished with oil, he went out into the street. He tried to go after him, but his mother stopped him. The two of them heard an uproar in the street, followed by shouting.

His mother peered through a crack in the window and prevented him from seeing what was happening. He sneaked to the door and opened it quietly without her noticing. Sticking his head out, he saw the shiny front of a black car and a big wheel. It was parked directly in front of the door. When he stuck out his head further, he saw a big stone smashing the car window. The shouting grew louder. He closed the door and went back inside.

In the morning he heard his mother saying to a woman visitor:

"He began to throw stones at the wedding car. Then he hit it with his stick and damaged it. And after he had almost killed the driver with his stick, Muḥammad ʿAlī the carpenter had to send for the police."

"He has a serious injury to his waist, but the important thing is to know the condition of his eyes. He has another injury to his head. Is this wretch going to speak or not?"

Again he felt the gentle hand on his forehead and heard a woman's voice saying: "Did you see the car that hit you, my dear?"

It was *that* car! A big black car, shining as if polished with oil, and a huge wheel made of rubber with zigzag furrows. Yes, it was the same car. He knew it without a shred of doubt. That same car had continually followed him since his father had hit it with stones, and when he was walking in the street it had caught up with him and hit him. But why did the car do that? He had not harmed it, he had not harmed it at all. He was walking on the pavement. Why did the car do that?

"Tell us, my dear, tell us. Did you see the car that hit you? Nod your head if you saw it."

If his father were around, if his father knew it was the wedding car itself, he would smash it. But what's the use now? They would never know that the car had hit him deliberately. He was walking on the pavement. He didn't wander off into the street at all. The car drove over the pavement and hit him. If his father were there, would he be standing with those people asking him to count his fingers? Would he be wasting his time on something so stupid?

"What's your name? What's your father's name? Where do you live? Talk to me!"

No use. He could not learn a thing. Once, when he dropped the little drum, it almost broke. Now the drum was stored in the attic. His mother never put it in the courtyard again. And his father never returned after that day.

"Don't you want us to help you, little boy? Why don't you talk to us?"

He wished he could help them, but he did not want to relinquish the pleasant numbness that circulated like hot, heavy mud through his veins. What a dreadful sight it was! He had been lying there, the sharp stone piercing his waist. When he had rolled over, he had seen drops of black oil trickling from the forefront of the car and creeping ever so slowly toward a little pool of blood that stretched up to his nose. He closed his eyes and felt that the black viper was still creeping over to drink from the red pool. . . .

"Leave him alone. Maybe he wants to rest a little. We'll come back later."

The black viper advanced, slow, relentless, repulsive. Then it plunged into the little pool of blood and began to lick the red liquid with its long, thin tongue.

Comments

The story's theme is the impact of modernity—the irresistible product of time—on people and society. Every domain of life is affected: the family, the workplace, the environment, social relations, customs, and traditions. For better or worse, all areas of human activity undergo transformation with the passage of time.

Modernity, as a rule, requires the old to make way for the new. The transition is not always smooth—sometimes it brings about tragic results. In this story, the customary wedding procession, which constitutes the livelihood of the protagonist's family, comes to an abrupt end with the advent of the motor car. From the perspective of a child growing up in the household of a drummer, the car is a fearsome monster which devours his family ruthlessly. The child lies dying in the street after being hit by a car. The car that hit him—the same one that replaced the wedding procession—is the symbol of modernity. It is responsible for robbing the father of his job, undermining his standing in the community, bringing him into a clash with the police, and removing him from his home and neighborhood. As a result, the entire family is fragmented and left without support or protection. Thus modernity is shown here from a decidedly negative perspective. It wreaks havoc and destruction. It terminates not only a mode of life but also a family's life and, ultimately, a child's life.

Despite the simplicity of the story, it is rich in symbolism. The wedding procession signifies the chief function of society, which is to produce future generations. The car, the very hallmark of modernity, attacks the core of society—the family unit. It leaves behind a tongue-shaped oil leak equated with a snake advancing slowly toward the injured child's pool of blood. The snake represents the connection between human beings and knowledge (here, technology). It alludes to the story of Adam and Eve and the warning not to eat the fruit of the forbidden tree. The snake's thirst denotes the fierce and voracious nature of modernity, and the car accident reveals human vulnerability to the effects of science and technology. In fact, the accident is not random. Both the car and the oil leak actively and inescapably seek out and pursue the boy—and humankind.

It is very likely that the author chose the wedding procession to show that the most attractive features of Arab traditional life are threatened by modernity. His sympathy lies with the simple folk who want to preserve the unique customs and authentic character of their culture.[64]

The loss of Arab traditional life to the onslaught of modernity is also depicted by Najīb Maḥfūẓ in his novel *Midaq Alley (Zuqāq al-Midaqq*, 1947). Here, the ancestral custom of reciting stories in public places becomes redundant with the introduction of the radio. The old public reciter, expelled from all the coffeehouses where he used to work because the owners have installed radios to entertain their customers, finds himself facing the same dilemma as the drummer in Ghassān Kanafānī's story: "Old as he was, and now with his living cut off, what was he to do with his life? What was the point of teaching his poor son this profession when it had died like this? What could the future hold for him and how could he provide for his son? A feeling of despair seized him."[65] A similar struggle between old and new is portrayed by Suhayl Idrīs in the story "The Yellow Cotton Bird" (see chapter 6).

3

CHARACTER

The Prison of Life

Among us some are great and some are small,
Albeit in wickedness, we're masters all;
    Or, if my fellow men are like myself,
The human race shall always rise and fall.
—Abū al-ʿAlāʾ al-Maʿarrī[1]

Modern Theories

The ultimate arbiter of people's ability to cope with the many challenges and hardships of life resides in their characters. People with positive mental and ethical traits, attitudes, and habits frequently succeed in achieving their goals and aspirations, whereas those who lack such attributes fail. Moreover, character tends to shape people's lives through a propensity to make decisions that reinforce their basic dispositions, and vice versa. This closed circle ultimately defines the individual's identity in society. The history of a person, reflected in the milestones of a journey to success or failure, becomes largely an account of the unfolding of a particular character. As the dynamics of one's character set the boundaries of one's existence, it is generally recognized that what a person is depends on character—"no man can climb out beyond the limitations of his own character"[2]—and each individual is distinguished from all others on the basis of character.

Is character acquired or inherited? The accepted scientific view is that the distinctive composition of a person's character is the outcome of the interaction of genetic inheritance with the nurture provided by family, education, life experiences, and culture. The question of which is more important to the formation of character—"nature or nurture"—has long been the subject of intense scholarly and public debate. Genes determine one's gender, physical appearance, health, qualities, and basic capabilities or deficiencies. Hence what the offspring inherits from the parents is of paramount importance. The social environment, however, plays a critical role in enhancing or suppressing inherited characteristics. Education in particular provides a powerful tool for both cultivating innate talents and acquiring nonhereditary skills. Material comfort and emotional support are also essential for the steady growth and proper balancing of character. In the main, whenever intrinsic ability is nurtured, human potential is likely to be fulfilled. Thus both heredity and environment—the interplay between nature and nurture—contribute to the development of character and determine what we are and what becomes of us.

"Character as applied to persons is the unified sum of all the elements of personality, intellectual, emotional, instinctive," says Edgar Pierce. Although knowledge is an indispensable attribute of character, it does not fully explain behavior: "Character, then, is not mere knowledge; it is a compelling belief in certain knowledge which forces action, and thus, taken with environment, determines the conduct of individuals."[3] Correspondingly, I. F. Stone points out that in classical times the dominant Greek view before and after Socrates was that lack of virtue stems not from ignorance but from flaws in character. The earliest surviving expression of this view belongs to the pre-Socratic philosopher Heraclitus: "A man's character is his fate" (*ethos anthropou daimon*).[4] Stone adds that this insight forms the basis of Greek tragedy. Citing famous disciples of Socrates who were doomed by flaws in their characters, he elaborates: "The very term, and the idea of 'ethics' originated in the Greek word *ethos*, which meant character. Aristotle's two great treatises on morality were called *ethica*, whence the term ethics derives. It had a hidden corollary. If virtue came from character and not knowledge, it was something the humble could have and the great could lack."[5] It is interesting to note that the prominent Egyptian playwright Tawfīq al-Hakīm, in his play *King Oedipus (Al-Malik Ūdīb*, 1949), portrays the downfall of this mythical figure along the same line of thought. Thus, in al-Ḥakīm's version, the cause of the tragedy is not the "malice of the gods" but Oedipus's character itself, with its obsessive search for the truth and insatiable desire for looking into the origin of things.[6]

As character exhibits itself in conduct, people's deeds or actions are the mirror of their true natures. Until the turn of the twentieth century, the science of psychology concerned itself mostly with the realm of consciousness, investigating behavior and overt mental processes. With the advance of psychoanalytic theory by Sigmund Freud (1856–1939), modern psychology began to explore new frontiers related to the realm of the unconscious. Freud's work, with its explicit criticism of conventional norms and morals, emphasized the role of unconscious motivation in human behavior. According to Freud, phenomena such as slips of the tongue, misreading, forgetting, slips of the pen, bungled actions, and so-called chance actions can be accounted for by unconscious motivation:

"Certain shortcomings in our psychical functioning . . . and certain seemingly unintentional performances prove, if psychoanalytic methods of investigation are applied to them, to have valid motives and to be determined by motives unknown to consciousness."[7]

Psychical determinism, as Freud proceeded to theorize, extends to almost all spheres of life. In fact, people's conscious decisions are frequently determined by unconscious factors over which they have no control; what appears as conscious will is often only an agent in the hands of a deep unconscious motivation.[8] People think they are free, but this impression is due to a lapse in their mental awareness: "Many people, as is well known, contest the assumption of complete psychical determinism by appealing to a special feeling of conviction that there is a free will. . . . If the distinction between conscious and unconscious motivation is taken into account, our feeling of conviction informs us that conscious motivation does not extend to all our motor decisions. . . . But what is thus left free by the one side receives its motivation from the other side, from the unconscious; and in this way determination in the psychical sphere is still carried out without any gap."[9]

Freud further argued that character is shaped mainly by events and experiences undergone in childhood. As such, it can be fully understood only with reference to certain mechanisms—repression, fixation, projection, transference, compensation, sublimation, and so forth—which are essential for the individual's development to maturity. Similarly, aberrations in a person's conduct, from the most severe offenses to mere peculiarities, can be linked with mental disorders stemming from arrested childhood development and unresolved conflicts. Interpretations and diagnoses must always consider the dynamic interplay between the conscious and unconscious elements in one's personality.[10]

Psychoanalysis eventually branched into several schools with different theoretical approaches, yet all shared the basic hypothesis that character and conduct are subject to unconscious influences and controlled largely by unknown motives and drives. As part of this hypothesis, it was generally accepted that because people have limited insight into their actions, frequently they cannot choose otherwise than they do.[11]

Arab-Muslim Perspectives

During the Middle Ages, Arab writers, with a few exceptions, did not take an active interest in the psychological facets of character. Much of classical Arabic biographical and autobiographical literature, for example, is limited to recounting factual information—birth, education, public appointments, outstanding deeds and works—which outlines the intellectual development of the individual under discussion but leaves the personality behind the events obscure.[12] Only rarely is a psychological portrait or a glimpse into the inner world of the personage provided, the most famous example being that of the great theologian al-Ghazzālī, *Deliverance from Error (Al-Munqidh min al-dalāl)*, which describes his spiritual progress.[13] Although the Arabs of the Middle Ages were keen observers, there was lacking a sense of developmental sequence and the need to round out characters in recording life histories.[14] According to one explanation, "dealing too much and too intensely with the psychological experience of one's own self in all its nuances and sentimental finesses was felt to be a kind of almost impious arrogancy."[15] From a strictly religious point of view, a mere mortal was considered unworthy of such introspective emphasis. Moreover, to try to unravel God's secrets—to penetrate the depths of the human mind and soul—was tantamount to a transgression and rebellion against God's will.

It is remarkable that this sentiment has endured to this day and is occasionally expressed in modern Arabic literature. For example, in the postscript to his play *King Oedipus*, Tawfīq al-Ḥakīm writes: "[Oedipus] has left Corinth in search of the truth, plunging into something he lacks knowledge of. His desire to know the truth brought down on him what modern science has brought down on modern man. Take Freud for example. When he started to dig in man's depths, he found that man secretly is his mother's lover. . . . For me the conflict in 'Oedipus' is not with arrogant gods who deal brutally with an innocent person they have selected to pursue. It is a conflict between the will of God and that of man."[16] Al-Ḥakīm cautions that there are "divine traps" for those who rebel against God's will and venture into forbidden zones. They are like the traps that the owner of a field puts out to catch foxes plundering the grapes. Hence human beings should not exceed the limits set for them by God and should not interfere in affairs that are running their own course.[17]

Despite this attitude, when modern psychoanalytic theory percolated into the Arab world from the West during the cultural revival of the second half of the nineteenth and the first half of the twentieth centuries, it did not fall on infertile ground. There already existed a pioneering work on the subject, *A Philosophy of Character and Conduct (Kitāb al-akhlāq wa-al-siyar)*, written by the Andalusian scholar Ibn Ḥazm (994–1064) toward the end of his life. Its discussion of anxiety as the underlying motive for all human actions is considered original within Islamic thought and sounds rather modern now that the concept has been introduced through psychology.[18]

Ibn Ḥazm reports that throughout his investigations to find a goal in human actions which all people unanimously hold as good, and which they all seek, he found only one—the aim of escaping anxiety. Life is full of tensions and pressures, and, knowingly or unknowingly, people spend the greater part of their time looking for relief from their anxieties:

> Those who crave riches seek them only in order to drive the fear of poverty out of their spirits; others seek glory to free themselves from the fear of being scorned; some seek sensual delights to escape the pain of privations; some seek knowledge to cast out the uncertainty of ignorance; others delight in hearing news and conversation because they seek by these means to dispel the sorrow of solitude and isolation. In brief, man eats, drinks, marries, watches, plays, lives under a roof, rides, walks, or remains still with the sole aim of driving out their contraries and, in general, all other anxieties.[19]

According to Ibn Ḥazm, all these forms of escape only promote "a hotbed of new anxieties." In psychoanalytic terms, this situation corresponds to neurotic patterns of behavior that are meant to provide temporary relief from existential stresses. Such responses are usually unsuccessful because they do not address the root of the problem in the individual. Ibn Ḥazm recommends permanent release from anxiety through good and virtuous works: "The good work, one profitable for an immortal life, stands innocent of all defect, free of all imperfection, and is, moreover, a sure way to put aside every anxiety effectively."[20] Again, in psychoanalytic terms, this idea is compatible with "sublimation." It is noteworthy that throughout his discussion, Ibn Ḥazm takes care to point out the importance of developing a mature, well-balanced personality that is able to nurture the well-being of others. These insights, for all the familiar note they strike, antedate modern psychoanalytic theory by almost nine centuries.

There are several expressions in Arabic for character. The term used in Islamic theological literature is *khulq* or *khuluq*, whose plural form *akhlāq* indicates "ethics." The term *fiṭra* is Qur'ānic, meaning "primordial nature" or "a kind or way of creating or of being created." It occurs in Sūra 30:30, where it is stated that the primordial nature upon which God created human beings cannot be altered, although it may be temporarily disturbed.[21] The standard and most common words for character are *ṭab*ʿ and the cognate *ṭabīʿa*, which also translate as "nature" (e.g., *al-ṭabīʿa al-insāniyya*: human nature); *mizāj*, which signifies "temperament" (e.g., *mizāj sawdāwī*: melancholic temperament); and *shakhṣiyya*, which denotes "personality."[22]

The significance of character as the essential foundation for moral conduct and its relation to one's ultimate salvation or damnation are dealt with in the Ḥadīth. For the most part, the traditions support the doctrine of predestination.[23] Just as God determines the course of every person's life from the very beginning, in a similar manner—and with similar finality—God determines the character of each individual. This belief is expressed in the following tradition:

> The seed lies in the womb for forty nights, after which the Angel gives it form . . . and inquires: O my Lord, a male or a female? whereupon

> God prescribes either a male or a female; afterwards he inquires: O my Lord, straight or crooked? whereupon God prescribes a being either straight or crooked; he also inquires: O my Lord, what is its allotment of good? what is its term of life? what is its character? after which God fixes that it shall be either one of the miserable or one of the blessed.[24]

Nothing can change people's God-given characters, which remain with them throughout their lives and compel them to follow a certain way of life. The immutable aspect of God's decree is emphasized in this tradition:

> O Messenger of God, explain to us our religious condition—was it unchangeably written, and predetermined, that we should be so disposed as we are, at this time, touching present conduct, or, on the other hand, is our character a casual incident? to which the Prophet replied: Not so, but rather was it unchangeably written thus, and predetermined.[25]

As to the fundamental question, "What, then, avails conduct?" Muḥammad is reported to have said: "Work ye, for every one is divinely furthered in accordance with his character."[26] The principle upon which this ruling is based comes from the Qur'ān: "For him that gives in charity and guards himself against evil and believes in goodness, We shall smooth the path of salvation; but for him that neither gives nor takes and disbelieves in goodness, We shall smooth the path of affliction" (92:5–10).

Another tradition revolving around an imagined dispute between Adam and Moses seems to imply that divine predestination precludes blameworthiness:

> Said Moses: O Adam, it is thou, our father, who didst frustrate our destiny, and eject us from Paradise; to whom Adam replied: O Moses, thou art he whom God did specially favor with converse with himself, and for whom he traced lines of writing with his own hand—dost thou blame me for doing what God predestined for me forty years before he created me? Therefore Adam got the better of Moses in the dispute.[27]

This account represents a powerful affirmation of the concept of fate. According to an alternative interpretation, the allegorical conflict between Adam and Moses is meant to expose the false sense of freedom that the idea of fate may impart to human beings. In this case, the words put into the mouth of Adam are an *argumentum ad hominem*, designed to silence anyone who fails to recognize the moral liberty of humankind.[28]

The predestinarian view of character finds succinct expression in a popular quatrain by Omar Khayyam:

The characters of all creatures are on the Tablet,[29]
The Pen always worn with writing "Good," "Bad":
Our grieving and striving are in vain,
Before time began all that was necessary was given.[30]

With a note of irony, the medieval poet Abū al-ʿAtāhiya speaks of the human predicament:

Blame me or no, 'tis my predestined state:
If I have erred, infallible is Fate.[31]

As he monotonously reiterates, everything in the universe is carefully foreordained:

Every summary has a trend
Every question has an answer
Every event has an hour
Every action has its account
Every scent has its limit
Every man has his book of fate.

Every guarantee is a symbol of death
Every building is a promise of destruction
Every king and his domain the original of dust.[32]

These verses convey a spirit of gloom and doom with respect to the rigidly set terms of human existence on earth.

The Issue of National Character

The controversial question of "Arab personality" or "Arab character" (*al-shakhsiyya al-ʿarabiyya*) has been the focus of various studies by both Arab and Western scholars attempting to delineate common Arab value orientations and attitudes. They have invariably drawn fierce criticism for stereotyping, overgeneralization, and oversimplification, derived from relying on selected readings, anecdotes, and quotations rather than on field research and empirical data.[33] The topic is so explosive that when L. Carl Brown and Norman Itzkowitz came up with their book *Psychological Dimensions of Near Eastern Studies*, they were advised against its publication by several of their colleagues.[34] Admittedly, the concept of national character is dangerous because it frequently serves as a platform for prejudice and hatred. Despite obvious reservations about the validity of such a concept, it merits some consideration here in view of the fact that leading Arab authors—novelists, short-story writers, dramatists, and poets alike—have dealt with it in their writings.

Among scholars, the Palestinian historian Hisham Sharabi provides some critical comments on the subject. In his article "Impact of Class and Culture on Social Behavior: The Feudal-Bourgeois Family in Arab Society" and his book *Introductions to the Study of Arab Society (Muqaddimāt li-dirāsat al-mujtmaʿ al-ʿarabī)*, Sharabi seeks to uncover the causes of the weakness of Arab society and of the lack of social change. In the first work, he discusses the connection between the feudal-bourgeois family and Arab society in general, and the effect that child-rearing practices and typical childhood experiences have on later social behavior in particular. He identifies authority, hierarchy, dependency, and repression as the values that govern this family, whose structure is carried into, and reflected in, the structure of society. According to his observations, the principal technique of child-rearing in the feudal-bourgeois Arab family is that of shaming, which, unlike playing on guilt feelings, hampers the capacity for self-criticism. Sociability is based on the skills of pleasing and of avoiding direct confrontation, which, in turn, promote hypocrisy and backbiting. Schooling emphasizes physical punishment and rote learning, thus stifling inquiry and experimentation while encouraging passivity and obedience to authority. Sharabi's basic premise is that personality is molded in the family, and the family reinforces and transmits the values and behavioral patterns of society. Hence to change society it will be necessary to change the family, and to change the family it will be necessary to change society, which is where the contradiction lies.[35]

In the second work, Sharabi discusses three prominent traits of feudal-bourgeois social behavior: dependency (*itkāliyya*), powerlessness (*al-ʿajz*), and escape from responsibility (*al-taharrub min al-masʾūliyya*). He finds the expression of powerlessness in fatalism (*al-īmān bi-al-qaḍāʾ wa-al-qadar*), which he sees as a lack of foresight and a failure to prepare for the future. Religion plays a major role in nurturing this attitude: "The individual is taught daily that he was created weak ('Man was created weak'). He lives in a world which he knows he cannot control and in which his fate is preordained ('Whoever lived died, whoever died is gone, and whatever will be will be')."[36] Such an ideology sustains the continuation of the existing sociopolitical order and precludes struggling for change.

While Sharabi's discussion may be open to criticism for its methodology, it seems to be borne out by corresponding depictions in works of literature. For example, the autobiography *For Bread Alone* (1973; *Al-Khubz al-ḥāfī*, 1982) of the Moroccan writer Muḥammad Shukrī, much like Najīb Maḥfūẓ's fictional *Trilogy*, contains a somber account of the father's tyrannical domination over his family. The father's absolute rule invites comparison with that of God: "Each afternoon my father comes home disappointed. Not a movement, not a word, save at his command, just as nothing can happen unless it is decreed by Allah." The son hates his father intensely but submits to his authority and obeys him out of fear. Frequently beaten, abused, and left to starve, he is forced to admit that his father's volition overrides that of everyone else in the family: "His will was necessarily our choice." On comparing the status of his mother and siblings with that of his father, the son ironically remarks: "My father is closer to Allah than we are, and nearer to the prophets and saints."[37] An extreme illustration of the father's oppression is the incident where, in a moment of rage, he wrings the neck of his youngest son and causes his instant death. He is never reported to the police nor made to atone for the crime. Not surprisingly, Skukrī's autobiography appeared first in two European languages (English 1973, French 1980) before it was finally printed in Arabic (1982) by a London-based publishing house.

Another writer known for his fondness for depicting the uses and abuses of authority is the Syrian Zakariyyā Tāmir. In a series of biting social fables and allegories, he illustrates how dictatorial control is extended from the father to the teacher, from the teacher to the employer, and from the employer to the ruler, thus forming an unbroken chain of oppression.[38]

The traditional mode of education comes under attack in *The Days (Al-Ayyām)*, the autobiography of Ṭāhā Ḥusayn (1889–1973). In the second volume, devoted to the years (1902–10) that this blind author spent as a student at the famed mosque-university of al-Azhar in Cairo, he expresses his frustration with, and disdain for, the learning process there. His criticism centers on three points: the method of instruction, the curriculum, and the teachers. The method was based on sterile repetition of scholastic dogma, combined with discipline and indoctrination, all aimed at instilling conformity and respect for authority rather than knowledge and creativity. In class, Ḥusayn's critical comments were invariably met with crushing rebukes and insults. On one occasion, he recalls an argument with a teacher about some remark he had made: "The discussion was lengthy and in the end the sheikh lost his temper and retorted sarcastically: 'Silence, lad. What can a blind boy know about such things?' "[39] The curriculum included the traditional religious subjects and lacked any of the modern sciences. As for the teachers, they were mostly incompetent, intolerant, and vain. In addition, they were constantly quarreling, backbiting, and slandering each other. Expelled from many lectures on account of his dissident views, Ḥusayn concedes that he eventually gave up hope of learning anything at al-Azhar. He continued to attend merely to comply with the regulations, to pass the time, and to look for entertainment. On the eve of his doctorate examination, he was informed by a friend that the chairman of the examining committee had passed the decision to fail him. Advised to withdraw from the examination rather than suffer humiliation, Ḥusayn refused. As predicted, he failed the examination. He then joined the newly founded National University (Cairo University)—Egypt's first secular institution of higher learning. He flourished in the academic freedom he found there, earned his doctorate, and went on to earn another one at the Sorbonne.

Ṭāhā Ḥusayn's illustrious career as a scholar, writer, and reformer is a testimony to the victory of willpower and character over a major physical handicap such as blindness. His accomplishments evoke those of the acclaimed eleventh-century poet Abū al-ʿAlāʾ al-Maʿarrī, who was also blind, and with whom Ḥusayn felt a special bond.

Ṭāhā Ḥusayn's critical account of his years at al-Azhar is supported by his contemporary Aḥmad Amīn (1886–1954), who studied there at about the same time. As he relates in his autobiography *My Life*, his learning experience at the Sharīʿa Judicial School in Cairo was not any different: "They [the teachers] always reminded us of al-Azhar and its method, and of the Middle Ages and their methods. They filled our heads with possibilities and interpretations, and indirectly instilled in our minds the hallowing of authors and books: an author rarely made a mistake, and if he did, there were a thousand ways to interpret his words in a manner that was conceivably correct."[40]

Much has improved in education in the postcolonial Arab world. The nationalist movements, which liberated Arab countries from decades of foreign domination and inner strife, stressed the importance of education as the key to solving the ills of their societies, in particular poverty and underdevelopment. Free compulsory public education for both boys and girls has become widely available throughout the Arab world. New schools have been built, more teachers trained, and standard textbooks published. The curriculum has been revised to include relevant topics and modern subjects, especially the sciences. As a result, illiteracy has declined sharply, and local universities and technical institutes produce large numbers of graduates who take an active part in their country's development.[41]

Despite these advances, education in the Arab world is uneven in quality and not readily accessible to all. In addition, it retains certain aspects from the past: veneration for authority, emphasis on obedience and conformity, reliance on rote learning, and avoidance of sensitive and controversial issues.[42] Thus some of the traditional features criticized by Ṭāhā Ḥusayn and Aḥmad Amīn at the beginning of the twentieth century are still applicable to the contemporary scene. These features, however, are somewhat moderated by the growing trend of Arab scholars who study abroad and then return to their homeland to teach and work. The influence they exert on their students in the sphere of independent thinking and creative discourse is again likely to facilitate future progress.

The relation of education to social psychology is often portrayed in literary works. One of the most distinguished writers to have focused attention on the issue of national character is the Egyptian Yūsuf Idrīs (1927–91). A physician by training, he drew on his medical knowledge to depict the mental makeup and patterns of behavior of the people of his country. Idrīs was especially keen on the medical-diagnostic approach to the problems of his society and the ills which he perceived as afflicting it. His dramatization of Egyptian character traits on both the individual and the national levels is most compelling in stories such as "The Sunken Mattress," "The Chair Carrier," "The Journey," "The Aorta," and "House of Flesh," in which the attitudes of apathy, resignation, escape from responsibility, self-deception, repression, powerlessness, and fatalism are exposed as the shortcomings arresting the nation's development.[43] In these stories, Idrīs reveals the vicious circle between the individual's inability to function and that of his society.

Character in Literary Introspection

On the individual level, the domain of autobiography in modern Arabic literature is a rich and suitable source of examples of the pivotal role of character in shaping a person's life. In *The Prison of Life* (*Sijn al-ʿumr*, 1964) (which inspired the title of this chapter), the playwright Tawfīq al-Ḥakīm tries to understand himself largely in terms of his genetic inheritance and the events and experiences of his childhood. His account begins with a tribute to the driving force of character:

> These pages are not merely the history of a life. They attempt to account for, to interpret, a life. I am taking the lid off my human apparatus in order to investigate this "motor" [*al-muḥarrik*] which we call "nature" [*al-ṭabīʿa*] or "character" [*al-ṭabʿ*]—this motor which determines my ability and controls my destiny [*maṣīrī*].[44]

Al-Ḥakīm portrays himself as the product of an intellectual but rigid father and an emotional but strong-willed mother. His education conformed with traditional conservative upbringing, and his formative years were exposed to influences from both the countryside and the city. While attributing great significance to heredity in the unfolding of his personality, al-Ḥakīm does not fail to recognize the impact of psychological forces at work. In particular, he mentions anxiety—the motivating factor discussed by Ibn Ḥazm in his *Philosophy of Character and Conduct*. As a child, he would get sick at the sight of funeral processions, but even though this passed away with age, "another disease began to grow in me with the growth of my intellect. It is anxiety. I have never been able to find release from it. Even when I find no justification for any anxiety, it suddenly springs up of its own accord. I am its prisoner for all eternity, and know of no explanation for it."[45]

Al-Ḥakīm offers several explanations for his bent toward the drama. The first relates to an unhappy incident with his father: when asked to recite some Arabic verses to him, he failed to elaborate on the meaning of a certain word. His father's reaction was to slap his face, causing a nosebleed. This is imprinted on al-Ḥakīm's memory along with another traumatic event: his father, attempting to teach him to swim, threw him without warning or preparation into the terrifying waters. In retrospect, al-Ḥakīm muses: "I might have loved both poetry and the sea from an early age if my father had taken me gently to the shores of either, instead of casting me to the depths." An alternative explanation is that the dramatic art simply suits his nature. As he readily acknowledges: "Why did I start my writing career with a play? Perhaps it is the essence of drama—i.e., the creation of a character through dialogue, not description, through his own words and not those of another—that suits my temperament."[46]

As to what produced his literary inclination in the first place, al-Ḥakīm falls back on psychical determinism to account for it. His father had harbored a lifelong desire to write, a desire that was repressed by his family, his financial circumstances, and the demands of his job:

> A father's frustrated wish is perhaps what he does pass on to his children. Had my father been able to find an outlet for his literary tendencies and wishes, he would have spared me and freed me from this pull of literature, and I could have turned unfettered to something else. . . . My father therefore cast upon my shoulders what his circumstances did not allow him to carry. I am the prisoner of the wish he did not fulfill, and indeed the prisoner of many things I have inherited from him, some good, some bad.[47]

On the whole, al-Ḥakīm perceives himself as the prisoner of his character. Soberly, he asks: "This prison I live in, made of wall-like inherited traits—could I have escaped from it? I have often tried, as every prisoner does, but it was as if I were moving in permanent fetters."[48] Chained as he is, al-Ḥakīm asserts that he has found freedom in one thing—his thought:

> I am a prisoner in what I have inherited, free in what I have acquired. The intellectual and cultural edifice I have erected for myself is my own. It is in this that I differ from my parents entirely. Here is the source of my real strength, with which I resist. Yes, my thinking, my intellectual formation, this is where all my freedom resides. Man is free in thought and prisoner in his nature.[49]

The theme of character as a prison figures prominently in the autobiographical novella *The Piper Dies (Yamūt al-zammār,* 1982) by Yūsuf Idrīs.[50] In a sad and moving account of his profound disillusionment over the usefulness of his writing, Idrīs describes his decision to give up his work as a writer and look for another occupation. His various attempts to do so fail, and he becomes critically ill. Ultimately recognizing the futility of his action, he yields to his innate bent—"that part of me which dictated that I write"—and comes to terms with himself:

> I did not create my specificity or my selected place, and I cannot change myself, species-wise or organically. All I can do is follow my bent with all my waves, and widen the circle of existence around me. Just the circle of existence—I do not have to catch a wolf by its tail or build a fourth pyramid. Perhaps the mystery of my life lies in that one day I will say a word that will reach someone somewhere, and my wave in the form of a word will conjoin with his wave to activate thousands and millions and billions of waves, and something will erupt which has not yet even occurred to the hearts of men.[51]

The author's hard-won equilibrium is based on the realization that he cannot run away from the mode of life that his character prescribes:

> The piper dies with his fingers on the pipe, for playing is the form of the waves of his existence, and so he will surely keep playing even to the last breath in his body. This is not a matter of frivolity. There is a law to it. And thus, instead of death by abstinence, by refusing your role, is it not more wonderful to play on, however dissonant or dull your playing seems? For surely the day will come when it will rise up and force people by its truthfulness to listen. Or even if that day does not come. . . . What can you do? It is your existence. There is no escape from it.[52]

This realization, however, does not relieve Idrīs of his pressing dilemma:

> The problem still remains. I am still the prisoner of my fate and my waves, however much I scream or invigorate myself or torture myself or die. Can the prisoner be happy? Even if his life's meaning is derived from his imprisonment! Can the prisoner be happy?[53]

The paramount importance of ancestral origins in the composition of one's identity and the formation of one's character is highlighted in *My Life* (*Ḥayātī*, 1950), the autobiography of the Egyptian intellectual Aḥmad Amīn. In the opening lines, he candidly declares:

> I am but the inevitable result of all that happened to me and my ancestors. . . . Since his birth, even since the moment he was an embryonic clot, nay, since the days he was in the blood of his ancestors, all that man encounters in his life abides in the depth of his self and dwells at the bottom of his sensation whether conscious or unconscious, whether remembered or forgotten, whether pleasant or painful. . . . All these ac-

> cumulate and collect, mix and react. This mixture and this reaction are the basis for all actions that issue from him both noble and mean.[54]

This personal account relates how the author rose from humble beginnings to become a distinguished scholar, writer, and reformer. Amīn portrays his journey through life with a keen awareness of the multiple factors that have shaped it and exercised control over it:

> To a great extent, every man is the outcome of all that he inherits from his ancestors and acquires from the environment around him. . . . My formation has been influenced to a great extent by what I inherited from my forefathers, the economic life that prevailed at our home, the religion that dominated us, the language that we spoke, the folk literature that was related to us, and the kind of upbringing that was in my parents' mind though they could not express it or draw its outlines, and so on. I did not make myself: God made me by way of the laws He prescribed for heredity and environment.[55]

It is interesting to note that Amīn traces modern notions such as heredity and environment to the first cause or prime mover—God. This leading thought runs through his autobiography and is emphatically stated at the end:

> These are the most important events that happened to me from boyhood to old age, and that affected me constantly and continuously till they made me what I am today. They could have been different, then I would have been different. It was God's will that they occur to me as they did and make of me what they did.[56]

Amīn's unique interpretation of his life, combining piety with science, derives from his primarily religious education, which he extended through independent reading in Western literature and philosophy.

Jurjī Zaydān (1861-1914), the Syro-Lebanese Greek Orthodox émigré who founded in Cairo the publishing house Dār al-Hilāl, as well as the acclaimed literary magazine *al-Hilāl* (1892), and whose popular historical novels revolve around the glories and heroes of the medieval Arab world, takes the point of view that the environment can do little to change one's basic character. In his memoirs (*Mudhakkirāt Jurjī Zaydān*, 1966), he writes:

> It was my good fortune that during the phase of imitation I did not succeed in emulating my first friends in their vices. I spent a long time amongst them, saddened by my incapability to emulate them. When I met Shawul and his friends, I found myself able to follow them, and I imitated them successfully in their virtuous ways. Perhaps this is the

> root of the saying, "Send your son to the market, and see with whom he associates." This contradicts the other saying, "Wicked company corrupts good character." In my opinion, man is born with certain tendencies and he will only be at ease in the company of those who are agreeable to his tendencies. A youth who is corrupted in the company of educated people has an innate inclination to corruption. He will associate with virtuous men and not benefit from them, but when he meets evil people he will turn to them and keep their company. Though I do not deny the impact education has upon the rectification and improvement of character, I do not believe that it changes the essence.[57]

Zaydān's reflections on human character are intriguing in view of his Christian background and the complicated circumstances of his life. The son of illiterate parents, he was taken out of school at the age of eleven and made to work at his father's restaurant until the age of nineteen, when, determined to resume his education, he hired private tutors and passed the qualifying examinations for medical school at the Syrian Protestant College (American University) in Beirut. While Aḥmad Amīn is the symbol of a self-made man among Muslim Arabs, Jurjī Zaydān is the symbol of such a man among Christian Arabs.

Character in Proverbial Lore

Arabic proverbial lore abounds in references to character, especially the aspects of its fixity and immutability. For example: "Can the shadow be straight when the stick is crooked?" (*hal yastaqīm al-ẓill wa-al-ʿūd aʿwaj?*); "A man's true nature will always prevail" (*al-ṭabʿ aghlab*); "Nature is stronger than nurture" (*al-ṭabʿ ghalab al-taṭabbuʿ*); "Character leaves the body only after the soul" (*al-ṭabʿ yakhruj min al-jism baʿda al-rūḥ*); "A dog's tail always remains curly" (*ʿumru deel il-kalb ma-yinʿidil*, colloquial Egyptian; compare the Bible: "Can the Ethiopian change his skin, or the leopard his spots?" [Jer. 13:23]). At the same time, there are proverbs that emphasize willpower as the key to success: "God helps those who help themselves" (*qum yā ʿabdī ḥattā aqūm maʿak*); "Men are the molders of their fortunes" (*al-rijāl qawālib al-aḥwāl*); "A man stands where he puts himself" (*al-marʾu ḥaythu yaḍaʿ nafsahu*). These sayings demonstrate that folk wisdom recognizes both the potential and the limitations of human beings.

Typically, proverbs express the practical lessons of life learned from experience. Rich in nuances and multifaceted, they can state a fundamental principle in one instance and its total opposite in another. They are not bound by dogma, religious or otherwise, though they may be influenced by it. Middle Eastern proverbs are known for their use of hyperbole and colorful, pictorial, and rhymed forms of expression. Frequently illustrated with the circumstances and events of everyday life, they constitute an important source of folk culture and commonly held ideas and beliefs.[58]

It is interesting to note, therefore, that folk wisdom, which is based on generations of observation, also recognizes the significance of heredity in the ultimate formation of a person's character. For example: "Every man reflects his clan" (*al-marʿu mirʿāt akhīhi*); "Like father, like son" (*hādhā al-shibl min dhāka al-asad*); "Every plant has its sap" (*li-kull ʿūd ʿuṣāra*); "A thorny bush yields no grapes" (*lā yuthmir al-shawk al-ʿinab*); "This cake is made from that dough" (*hādhā al-kaʿk min dhāka al-ʿajīn*).

In view of the factor of heredity, the advice given for choosing a bride emphasizes the value of seeking good "roots" and descent: "Pedigree is an asset" (*al-aṣl ʿawn*); "Marry a well-born woman no matter how poor she may be" (*khud il-aṣīla wi-law kānit ʿal-ḥaṣīra*, colloquial Egyptian). The guiding thought is that both the virtues and the vices of the parents and their family lines are inherited characteristics that are transmitted to their offspring. Outstanding physical features in particular are invariably attributed to genetic inheritance; if they are not directly inherited from the parents, they may be traceable to a grandparent or great-grandparent. Likewise, character traits—whether of meanness, hospitality, piety, wickedness, aggression, or docility—run in families.[59] Considering that agriculture and the raising of livestock have traditionally been the main means of livelihood among the Arabs, it is only natural that they should display a shrewd understanding of the role of heredity, as evidenced by their ability to raise thoroughbred Arabian horses and camels.

In conclusion, character is the aggregate of diverse attributes—partly inherited, partly acquired—which are tenacious and rarely susceptible to change. As such, character limits the choices people can make and the actions they can undertake. According to this view, in the final analysis people are their own prisoners. They can be conditioned by their personal weaknesses, tendencies, and preferences to such an extent that fate seems to assume the shape of psychological determinism.

Maḥmūd Taymūr
The Would-Be Traveler

Maḥmūd Taymūr (1894–1973) was born in Cairo into an aristocratic family of literary talent: his aunt ʿĀ'isha was a distinguished poet, and his older brother Muḥammad (1892–1921) a playwright and prose writer. He received his elementary and secondary education in local schools and then enrolled in the College of Agriculture, but he was unable to complete his studies owing to illness. Subsequently, his main intellectual interest and activity followed the path of his older brother.

Maḥmūd Taymūr is considered the founder and first successful practitioner of the modern Arabic short story. His literary career spanned more than four decades, during which he published numerous collections of short stories, plays, novels, and books of criticism. He received a literary prize from the Arabic Language Academy in Cairo in 1947 and later became a member of this prestigious organization. He is known for his sympathetic depiction of the simple folk of contemporary Egypt and for his realistic description of town and village life.

"The Would-Be Traveler" ("Al-Sā'iḥ") appears in the collection *Shaykh Jumʿa and Other Stories (Al-Shaykh Jumʿa wa-aqāṣīṣ ukhrā*, 1925). The story portrays the character of a man who is a slave to his habits and daily routine.

Muḥammad Bey Nājiʿ has a house in the al-Azhar district, where he lives with his mother, his old nanny, and some servants who are devoted to his family. His income is estimated at one hundred guineas a month, on which he lives comfortably, with no complaints. At forty-eight, his black beard is streaked with gray, foreshadowing the coming of old age. He always wears a frock coat—either black or colored—and a wide, short fez. He was educated in elementary school and by private tutors, though he did not obtain a diploma. He later attended some classes at al-Azhar, but benefited little from them. When he realized that he was nearly forty and had not had much of an education, he became a student of Mabrūk al-Khazāmī, a retired scholar who, for a small fee, taught jurisprudence, Islamic theology and ideology, and other religious subjects at his home. Because of his great thick-headedness, however, Nājiʿ Bey failed to learn anything new from the teaching of his master. Nevertheless, he has recently acquired the title of scholar, granted to him by his friends and dependents, and has been utterly content with it. His most distinguishing characteristic is his passion for reading travel stories and books about old voyages. He owns quite a collection of these books; some of them are valuable, others worthless. He often goes to al-Azhar to visit his friends the scholars—as he refers to them. Each afternoon, he frequents a poor bookshop near al-Azhar, whose owner is also a failed Azhar student, and there he passes his most enjoyable hours.

The bookshop is a dilapidated, damp place, with no chairs to sit on, just a long wooden bench covered with a faded, shapeless piece of rug. As for the books displayed for sale, they include both printed and handwritten material, the most important of which are basic textbooks used by Azhar students. These are all piled haphazardly on wooden shelves and covered with old dust.

Nājiʿ Bey enters the bookshop feigning gravity and dignity, and the owner, Shaykh Sallām, rises to greet him. He approaches Nājiʿ Bey, kisses his hands, and, cleaning the faded, shapeless piece of rug with his big red handkerchief, he mutters in great submission and respect:

"Have a seat, my very learned sir!"

Nājiʿ Bey sits down and asks: "How are you, Shaykh Sallām? God willing, all is well?"

Smiling contentedly, Shaykh Sallām replies: "Praise be to God in any case!"

Nājiʿ Bey shifts in his seat a little. "Could you order me a cup of black coffee and a glass of cold water?"

Shaykh Sallām hastens to fulfill the bey's request. Although the weather changes and turns from cold to hot and from hot to cold, Nājiʿ Bey's request never changes—it has remained the same for the past five years. He always insists on black coffee and cold water, but when they arrive, he does not care if the coffee is sweet or the water is lukewarm. What matters is that he repeats this request each day and then follows it with another one, inseparable from the first, which he utters after clearing his throat:

"Your books, Shaykh Sallām!"

From a nearby shelf Shaykh Sallām brings him three books that are invariably the same: *The Arabian Nights, The Travels of Ibn Baṭṭūṭa,* and *The Wonders of India.* Nājiʿ Bey takes off his shoes and sits cross-legged on the bench. He then stacks the books at his side. Sipping now the coffee and now the water, he occasionally mutters: "Amazing! Beautiful!"

Some Azhar students pass by the bookshop and call out greetings to Shaykh Sallām. Nājiʿ Bey answers them from inside, as if their greetings were meant for him.

Sometimes Shaykh al-Basṭāwīṣī the scribe walks into the bookshop. He wears a robe, a caftan, and a fez. His eyes are always red, and his eyelids have no lashes. His hands tremble constantly, even though he is not yet forty-five. An unpleasant man with dirty clothes, he pretends to be kind, amicable, and well spoken. He also pretends to be knowledgeable, but he speaks in shameful ignorance on every subject. From time to time, Nājiʿ Bey commissions him to copy travel books from the public library or some private collection.

The man comes in, bows before the bey, and kisses his hand. After seating himself on the edge of the bench, with all due modesty and reverence, he begins to discuss the weather, politics, and morality. No sooner has he finished with these subjects than he informs the bey that he has found a hand-written book on the wonders of the islands of the Indian Ocean. The book is illustrated with large color pictures, and costs five hundred piasters, no less. Staring at the scribe, the bey protests:

"Five hundred piasters is a lot of money!"

Wiping his eyes with a torn, dirty handkerchief, al-Basṭāwīṣī replies: "That is what the owner is asking, but we can bring the price down to half."

"I need to see the book."

"I'll bring it to Your Excellency tomorrow, God willing."

The bey returns to the story of Sindbad the Sailor, which he has read more than fifty times, so that he has almost memorized it. Occasionally he exclaims: "Amazing! Beautiful!"

And al-Basṭāwīṣī the scribe repeats after him: "Of course! Amazing! Beautiful!"

Nājiʿ Bey looks up at him and says: "Oh, if only I could travel to the Indian Ocean and visit India and Persia and the sea islands—those islands that no man has set foot upon since the famous Muslim voyagers!"

"Do you intend to travel, honorable sir?"

"There's only one thing that prevents me. It's my mother, Shaykh al-Basṭāwīṣī. My mother is old. I cannot leave her."

"But if somehow you could travel, would you go to the Indian Ocean?"

"Of course. I would go where the Arab Muslim voyagers went in olden times. There are islands there full of treasures that no foreigner has discovered since then. I want to explore these unknown places, and also stop along the way to see the hidden wonders of India and Persia."

"Amazing! Such a glorious enterprise would immortalize your name in history!"

"But I cannot leave my mother, Shaykh al-Basṭāwīṣī. She's old and it's difficult for me to get away."

Nājiʿ Bey returns to his reading and completes the third voyage of Sindbad the Sailor.

The days go by and then the months, and Nājiʿ Bey never changes the pattern of his life. Each afternoon he goes to Shaykh Sallām's bookshop for his usual conversation, after which he asks him to order his cup of black coffee and glass of cold water. Then he delves into the familiar old books.

But fate, from which there is no escape, struck his old mother. God took her unto Him when she was eighty-eight years of age. For a few days the pattern of Nājiʿ Bey's life changed. He divided those days between his home and the cemetery. After the funeral, the daily newspapers published numerous reports about the dearly departed woman, the story of her life—which was filled with splendid, charitable works—and the description of the majestic funeral, attended by local notables and distinguished scholars. Nājiʿ Bey wore black mourning clothes, and his dull face registered sadness and pain. Six months after his mother's death, he returned to the bookshop. Entering with the familiar air of gravity, he greeted Shaykh Sallām with the same old formula:

"How are you, Shaykh Sallām? God willing, all is well?"

Having made his usual request, he assumed his seat on the bench with the old rug. Following the custom that had been established more than five years earlier, Shaykh Sallām brought him the three familiar reference books, and Nājiʿ Bey began to read the story of Sindbad the Sailor. As he was avidly reading, Shaykh al-Basṭāwīṣī walked in. He kissed the bey's hands and proceeded to discuss the weather, politics, and some rare travel books. When he had finished, Nājiʿ Bey cleared his throat with an "ahem" that lasted for five full minutes. Then he shifted peculiarly in his seat, after which he rose in a show of determination and willpower.

"I'm sorry to tell you, my friends, that I'm going away," he said.

Taken by surprise, the two men shouted together: "Your Excellency is going away?"

Their surprise boosted Nājiʿ Bey's pride, determination, and willpower. He replied: "I have decided to undertake an important journey to Persia, India, and the sea islands."

Shaykh al-Basṭāwīṣī drew closer to him, rubbing his red, bald eyes with his ink-stained hand.

"Is this a firm decision, Your Excellency, or just a preliminary contemplation?" he asked.

The bey's jugular vein bulged in anger. Removing an official document from his wallet, he retorted: "Look! Isn't this a visa?"

He fell silent for a moment, while he calmed down, and then proceeded: "Tomorrow I will go to bid farewell to my very learned master, Shaykh Mabrūk al-Khazāmī, and the next day I will be in Suez."

"Will you stay in Suez a few days?" asked Shaykh Sallām, a look of affected sadness visible on his face.

"Certainly. I will spend a week there attending to travel matters. I've heard that the famous, very learned Shaykh Kāmil, who resides in Suez, has a splendid book that contains a complete description of the land roads and sea routes in Persia, India, and the sea islands. I've decided to borrow it from him, so I can study it and learn from it."

Shaykh al-Basṭāwīṣī drew yet closer to him. He was still rubbing his eyes with his ink-stained hand.

"We are saddened by your departure, sir. I swear that my heart is filled with anguish and distress. May your return be speedy, God willing," he said humbly.

Puffed up with pride, Nājiʿ Bey declared: "My journey will last eighteen months!"

The next day, Nājiʿ Bey bade farewell to his very learned master, Shaykh Mabrūk al-Khazāmī. It was a solemn meeting between the master and his student, during which the latter received his last lesson in wisdom, spiritual guidance, and piety.

Four days later, Shaykh al-Basṭāwīṣī walked into Shaykh Sallām's bookshop. To his utter surprise, he found Nājiʿ Bey sitting cross-legged in his usual corner with the three familiar reference books at his side, drinking now from the coffee cup, now from the water glass.

"I thought Your Excellency would be in Suez now," he said to Nājiʿ Bey, hardly able to conceal his bewilderment.

Nājiʿ Bey glanced at him angrily and blurted out: "I delayed my journey for two weeks because of family matters. But, in two weeks, I will be aboard the steamer *Asia*, which belongs to the English-Mideastern Steamship Company."

Ten days later, one of the daily newspapers published the following in the "Local Events" page:

> Good Luck! The Best of Travelers!
>
> His Excellency, the accomplished scholar and great traveler, Muḥammad Bey Nājiʿ ʿAbdallāh, head of the ʿAbdallāh family, which is renowned for its knowledge, refinement, and passion for travel, will be departing for India, Persia, and the sea islands to explore and study these regions. We wish the noble traveler a speedy return and congratulate him in advance on the many benefits that he will reap from this journey, a journey we consider the first of its kind. We call upon the Egyptians to follow the example of the bey in his useful and splendid work.

On May 14, 1920, the steamer *Asia* sailed from Suez, bound for India.

Three months later, Nājiʿ Bey was sitting cross-legged in his usual corner in Shaykh Sallām's bookshop, reading the story of Sindbad the Sailor and muttering now and then: "Amazing! Beautiful!"

At his side, Shaykh al-Basṭāwīṣī was rubbing his eyes and repeating everything after the bey, word for word. Before long, Nājiʿ Bey raised his head from the book and exclaimed: "Oh, if only I could travel to the Indian Ocean and visit India and Persia and the sea islands."

"But Your Excellency was ready to set out three months ago, and then you canceled," Shaykh al-Basṭāwīṣī remarked.

Sighing, Nājiʿ Bey said: "Alas, one thing always prevented me. That was my mother, Shaykh al-Basṭāwīṣī, my old mother who couldn't bear parting from me. But now . . ."

He fell silent, unable to express himself. After a lot of trouble he completed his reply in a stutter:

"Now there is a lot of work . . . collecting the rent . . . loads and loads of work. . . . The farm is in a state of confusion, and sowing is behind schedule. . . . The soil needs fertilizer, and so on . . ."

He fell silent again. After a while, he continued: "But I must travel. I must travel to the sea islands and the lands of Persia and India. I must explore these unknown regions, which are full of treasures. May this be soon, God willing . . ."

Comments

This story offers a character study of a man who has a propensity to substitute words for deeds. For years, Nājiʿ Bey dreams about a trip to foreign lands but always finds an excuse to postpone it. He frequently states his intention without actually following it up with action. Instead, he contents himself with a few travel books, which he reads repetitively. Time after time, Nājiʿ Bey announces his planned departure, then blames the cancellation of his trip on compelling circumstances. In so doing, he continues to adhere to the fixed habits of his dull life.

Nājiʿ Bey's behavior is explained by his shallow character. Although he bears the title of scholar, he is quite ignorant, having failed in his studies with private tutors and at al-Azhar. His impressive title is therefore a mere facade, empty of genuine content. In addition, despite the fact that he is middle-aged, he is not married and lives with his mother and old nanny. This indicates arrested psychological development. To compensate for the monotony of his life, Nājiʿ Bey fantasizes about adventurous journeys and gratifies himself by making travel preparations. However, he never translates his intention into action. He is trapped: his dull life produces a longing for change, but his shallow personality generates a neurotic fear of any change. Consequently, he remains in the same old groove and finds escape in dreams.

Nājiʿ Bey's behavior is also explained by his socioeconomic background. He comes from a middle-class, landowning family. The people who serve him, Shaykh Sallām and Shaykh al-Basṭāwīṣī, come from a lower class. To win his favor, they nurture his ego with flattery and with undue respect and courtesy. Hence Nājiʿ Bey, financially secure and socially comfortable, has no incentive to take any risks. However exciting his plans are, he ultimately recoils into his shell, preferring to persist in the way of life to which he has become accustomed.

Finally, Nājiʿ Bey's behavior is in conformity with the traditional values of his community. There are several facts in the story indicating that the conservative attitudes of the social milieu in Cairo, where the story takes place, contribute to Nājiʿ Bey's passivity. First, Nājiʿ Bey's education is primarily religious, with no exposure to modern science or philosophy. Second, the prevailing cultural orientation reflects devotion to the models of the past rather than those of the future. This preference is evident from the type of books which the bookshop in the shadow of al-Azhar carries and which Nājiʿ Bey favors (e.g., *The Arabian Nights* and *The*

Travels of Ibn Baṭṭūṭa), old books recounting Arab history and the glories of the past. In fact, Nājiʿ Bey literally lives on a legacy from the past—the estate which he has inherited. His ideal is to imitate the past, not to tread new ground. He is attracted to the ancient civilization of the Far East (*The Wonders of India*), not to the technological advances of the West. Class distinctions make his companions submissive to him, and their servile attitude, marked by hypocrisy and affectation, is dictated by custom and convention.

Altogether, Nājiʿ Bey is the product of both nature and nurture. He has a poor character, and his environment further reinforces his negative traits. Full of vain talk, delusions, wishful thinking, and self-deceit, he enjoys social standing and prestige without any real merit. Hence, despite his splendid dreams, he goes nowhere, and despite the easy circumstances of his life, he achieves nothing. Significantly, the story ends with Nājiʿ Bey using the standard formula "God Willing" to shift the responsibility for his inactivity onto God or fate, rather than his own character.[60]

Yūsuf Idrīs
The Sunken Mattress

Yūsuf Idrīs (1927–91) was born in the village of al-Bayrūm in the Nile Delta and grew up in the countryside. In 1945 he went to Cairo to study medicine, graduating in 1952. Subsequently he worked as a physician in various public posts, including that of health inspector in the poor districts of Cairo, where he collected firsthand material for many of his stories. He began to publish during the early 1950s and achieved immediate success. In 1967, after a long period of a dual career as a physician and a writer, he stopped practicing medicine and devoted all his time to writing.

Idrīs was one of the most innovative and influential writers in Egypt and throughout the contemporary Arab world. His literary output is varied and includes novels, novellas, plays, articles, and especially short stories—the medium in which he made his name. He is credited with perfecting the modern Arabic short story by introducing new themes and modes of narration.

Idrīs's medical background is reflected in his creative writing. His stories offer a unique insight into the psychological forces that shape the mentality of the people of his country and motivate their actions and reactions. His style is remarkable for its spontaneity and novelty of expression, as well as for its blend of the colloquial and standard registers. Whereas the first decade of his literary activity (1954–64) is marked by realism, the later decades (1965–85) reveal a transition to symbolism and surrealism. Idrīs's subject matter is diverse and includes the rural and the urban scene, simple folk and intellectuals. He excels at cameo portraits that effectively depict the nature of a particular situation, event, place, or person.

"The Sunken Mattress" ("Al-Martaba al-muqaʿʿara") appears in the collection *The Siren (Al-Naddāha,* 1969).[61] One of the author's ultrashort stories, it dramatizes the notion of character as fate.

On the wedding night, the mattress was new and thick and puffy. He laid his tall, heavy body on it and relaxed into its luxurious softness. He said to his wife, who just then was standing by the window:

"Have a look. Has the world changed?"

The wife looked out of the window.

"No," she said, "it has not changed."

"Then I'll sleep for a day."

He slept for a week. When he woke up, his body had sunk a little into the mattress. He glanced at his wife and said:

"Have a look. Has the world changed?"

The wife looked out of the window, then said:

"No, it has not changed."

"Then I'll sleep for a week."

He slept for a year. When he woke up, the hollow his body made in the mattress had become deeper. And he said to his wife:

"Have a look. Has the world changed?"

And the wife looked out of the window and said:

"No, it has not changed."

"Then I'll sleep for a month."

He slept for five years. When he woke up, his body had sunk still deeper into the mattress. As usual, he said to his wife:

"Have a look. Has the world changed?"

And the wife looked out of the window and said:

"No, it has not changed."

"Then I'll sleep for a year."

He slept for ten years. By that time, the mattress had made a deep groove for his body, and he had died. They pulled the sheet over him and its surface was smooth, without a bulge. They picked him up in the mattress which had become his tomb and threw him out of the window onto the hard ground of the street.

Then, after she had witnessed the mattress–tomb fall to its final resting place, the wife looked out of the window, lifted her eyes to the open sky, and said:

"O God, the world *has* changed."

Comments

This story offers a cameo portrait, in a surrealistic setting, of Egyptian society, represented by its basic unit: the family. To explore this unit, Idrīs takes a man and a woman on their wedding night, pictured with the bare essentials of their environment—a room and a mattress—and makes of this a single enduring scene: the man sleeps, while the woman looks on.

There is no action in the story, which is a flat, matter-of-fact account of stasis. The sinking man on the mattress and the woman by the window project apathy and passivity. Their common anticipation of change is marked by total inertia: there is no initiative on their part to bring about change. Their whole existence is made up of waiting—it has become a way of life. As the man is slowly buried alive, the wife quietly stands by and watches. They hardly communicate, and the few terse words they exchange betray alienation and a failure to relate. As a couple united in marriage to create future life, they are not functioning. But why?

The husband's bizarre behavior—namely, his heavy bouts of sleep—provides a clue to this puzzling situation. Here Idrīs draws on his medical knowledge to portray a mental condition known as narcolepsy. Psychoanalytic theory ascribes this condition to a severe form of depression in which the affected individuals unconsciously seek escape from a reality they are unable to bear. Sleep, like drugs, provides the mechanism of escape. The prognosis for such a condition is bleak because these individuals are caught in a vicious circle of unbearable reality–depression–sleep. Only a drastic change in their circumstances can bring a cure. In this case, the wife could be the agent of change, but she is too passive and submissive. Her behavior is culturally bound and traditionally ordained in Arab society, leaving her devoid of any power to act.[62] Thus, while her husband surrenders to sleep, she surrenders to her fate. The overall effect of the husband's illness and the wife's weakness is to produce a dysfunctional family unit. As the family is a microcosm of society, the implication is that society as a whole is dysfunctional.

A fatalistic outlook and an attitude of surrender are frequent features of Idrīs's portrayal of Egyptian men and women. In exploring the ailments of his society, he often focuses on the shortcomings in the psychological makeup of the people of his country, which he sees as the underlying causes of the harsh and unchanging social reality.

At a deeper level, the motif of sleep in this literary work alludes to the Qur'ān. Sūra 18: 9–12 tells of the People of the Cave, a story which is generally identified with the legend of the Seven Sleepers of Ephesus. The story revolves around a group of Christian youths who took refuge in a cave to avoid persecution by their pagan and hostile society. In the cave, they fell asleep for several generations or centuries. When they woke up, they discovered that the world had changed and that Christianity had become the state religion. The story's spiritual lessons are those of the ultimate victory of belief and of the potency of faith. The miracle of the prolonged sleep and the salvation of the youths is explained as a wonderful manifestation of God's bounty.[63]

Idrīs's point of view in this story is somber and critical. The escape into sleep in anticipation of a miracle that will change the world results in the husband's demise, not in salvation. It is the way not to a new beginning but to the very end. In this portrayal, Idrīs conveys his exasperation with the character of his compatriots and a grave concern for their future.[64]

4

CUSTOM

The Yoke of Tradition

> Custom causes human nature to incline toward the things to which it becomes used. Man is the child of customs, not the child of his ancestors.
>
> —Ibn Khaldūn[1]

Custom, Habit, and Usage

Every person is exposed to the influence of the social environment. Human beings are essentially social creatures, many of whose basic needs are met through their integration into society. They therefore attempt to interpret the dynamics of their society and form adaptive responses to it. Through centuries of evolution, each society has developed its own particular codes, values, and institutions, the aggregate of which constitutes culture. Broadly defined, culture is "that complex whole which includes knowledge, belief, art, morals, law, custom, and any other capabilities and habits acquired by man as a member of society."[2] In essence a man-made environment, culture consists of behavioral patterns transmitted by social rather than hereditary means.[3] Of all these behavioral patterns, the most rigid, formal, and ritualistic is custom. Chiefly serving as a mechanism of social regulation and control, custom determines the parameters within which a person can act freely. It also establishes a range of expectations for the individual and lays down mandatory guidelines for actions that have the force or validity of law.

In the *Prolegomena (Muqaddima)* of his *World History (Kitāb al-ʿibar)*, considered to be the earliest attempt by any scholar to discover a pattern in the changes that occur in human political and social organization,[4] the Arab historian Ibn Khaldūn (1332–1406) offers numerous insightful observations about human behavior. Describing the marked differences in character traits between Bedouins and sedentary people, he says:

> Man is a child of the customs and the things he has become used to. He is not the product of his natural disposition and temperament [*al-insān ibn ʿawāʾidihi wa-maʾlūfihi, lā ibn ṭabīʿatihi wa-mizājihi*]. The conditions to which he has become accustomed, until they have become for him a quality of character and matters of habit and custom, have replaced his natural disposition.[5]

In discussing the factors leading to the decline and splintering of a ruling dynasty, Ibn Khaldūn again highlights the role of custom in this irreversible process. The politically conscious ruler, he remarks, often assumes that he can save the dynasty by rectifying his predecessors' negligence in areas such as injustice and limited access to the authorities, but in reality this is not so:

> Customs that have developed prevent him from repairing it. Customs are like a second nature. A person who, for instance, has seen his father and the older members of his family wear silk and brocade and use gold ornaments for weapons and mounts and be inaccessible to the people in their salons and at prayer, will not be able to diverge from the customs of his forebears in this respect. He will not be able to use coarse dress and apparel and mingle with the people. Custom would prevent him and expose him if he were to do this. Were he to do it, he would be accused of madness for his brusque disregard of custom.[6]

Custom is closely connected with both habit and usage, all being socially based and mutually interactive. The distinction of one from the other lies in the scope of practice, range of influence, and degree of enforcement. According to Wilhelm Max Wundt, habit is a voluntary action that serves as an individual rule of conduct. If the acts of the individual agree with the habitual action of the community, habit becomes usage. Custom forms a smaller circle within the general field of usage, but, unlike usage, it has a normative character. Conformity to custom is not a matter of individual choice, for custom has the sanction of a moral constraint, which the individual cannot ignore without risking retribution. Hence, whereas individual habit is left entirely to choice as long as it does not conflict with the general rules of social conduct, usage exercises a practical compulsion through the example that it sets, and custom brings this compulsion to the level of a restraining norm.[7]

Edward Westermarck sums up the general characteristics of custom, once it has gained sway: "Custom regulates external conduct only. It tolerates all kinds of volitions and opinions if not openly expressed. It does not condemn the heretical mind, but the heretical act. It demands that under certain circumstances certain actions shall either be performed or omitted, and, provided that this demand is fulfilled, it takes no notice of the motive of the agent or omitter."[8] He stresses that when the course of conduct dictated by custom is not followed, the motives for the transgression are likely to be dealt with harshly and in a manner that does not allow any measure of individualism. Thus custom tends to override the exercise of personal judgment and to become dissociated from true ethical or religious considerations.

Conformity is an inevitable corollary of custom. It ensures the orderly conduct of social life by making prediction possible. Child-rearing practices and education are designed to instill behavioral norms at the deepest possible level of the individual's awareness. When conventions are organized according to class, gender, age, and so forth, the process of socialization is set in motion and guarantees the hierarchical structure of the community. Those members who have been trained in childhood along traditional lines will be inclined to show the same action pattern and motivational system, because of pressure to conform to group standards. In this manner, the individual's personality is molded as it matures under the formative influence of this potent cultural force.[9]

Custom dominates every area of human life, from the sacred to the profane. Louis H. Gray notes that in the domain of religion, it is custom that has influenced ritual and led to the rise of myth. Custom is also the chief factor in the evolution of law, which, to primitive man in the early stages of civilization, was inseparable from religion. Custom conditions the pattern of existence of almost every individual, even in highly civilized societies, from the cradle to the grave.[10] As for the origin of custom, it is presumed to have one course of development, which is from preceding customs of related substance. The origin of custom is of little consequence to a simple tribesperson: "For him it is enough that such and such a custom exists; and his sole explanation, if one be sought from him, is that . . . 'it was so done by my fathers.' "[11] A custom may persist even after its original cause has become obscure, in which case it may acquire an entirely different motive or purpose.[12]

The Arabic word for custom is *ʿāda* (plural: *ʿādāt* or *ʿawāʾid*). Another term is *ʿurf*, which means "what is commonly known and accepted" and indicates collectively the unwritten laws of local custom and practice, as opposed to established law—the *sharʿ* or *sharīʿa*.[13] Scholars have observed that the realities of Muslim social life have never entirely reflected the *sharīʿa*—the ideal Muslim law corresponding to God's will. The canonical law, in its ritual provisions as well as in its juridical aspects, has been overridden by pre-Islamic traditional usages on many occasions.[14] Both *ʿāda* and *ʿurf* have been the product of "longstanding convention, either deliberately adopted or the result of unconscious adaptation to circumstances, and they have therefore been followed where practical considerations have been uppermost."[15] This compromise is still at work in numerous communities in the Arab world, where there are native codes of unwritten laws and traditions by which life is regulated. Reuben Levy writes that in southern Palestine there existed as late as the middle of the nineteenth century a peasant code called *sharīʿat khalīl* (i.e., "the law of Abraham"), besides the *sharīʿa*. Among the Bedouins of Arabia there have always been, apart from the *qāḍīs*, special judges knowledgeable in the customary lore of their tribe, to whom people could resort in all matters involving tribal interests.[16]

Levy points out that in many situations tribal law diverges sharply from the *sharīʿa*. The important instance of the blood feud shows how Muslim law failed to abolish established custom, for the Qur'ān teaches that no Muslim may slay another who is innocent of offense, yet to this day blood revenge remains an important part of tribal life. Where family life is concerned—in marriage, divorce, and the allocation of inheritance—the regulations of the *sharīʿa* appear to be widely neglected. For example, it is the exception rather than the rule for daughters to inherit, and this exclusion is as prevalent in North Africa as it is among the Muslims of India. Temporary marriage (*mutʿa*),[17] though banned by the Caliph Omar and regarded as forbidden to Sunnites, has in various Muslim communities at different times been permitted by local custom, and to this day it is practiced among the Shiites of Iran and Iraq, who consider it lawful.[18] Numerous traces of pagan beliefs, customs, folklore, practices, and rituals surviving in the popular religion of Islamic peoples have been collected and described by Edward Westermarck.[19] It is noteworthy that Muslim puritanical movements, such as the Wahhābīs of late–eighteenth-century Arabia, have struggled to cleanse Islam from such impurities.

The Role of Tradition

Tradition lies at the heart of the cultural identity of every nation, comprising an intricate web of shared beliefs and bequeathed customs that serve to form community bonds and models of social conduct. In discussing aspects of formality and rigidity among the Arabs, Sania Hamady remarks: "Arab society is permeated with tradition and impregnated with strictly defined and fixed ways of behavior set by past usage. Tradition occupies a strong position as a regulator of individual and group actions. The qualities of Good and Bad are defined by following the traditional way of behavior or deviating from it. If an act is in accord with custom, it is good, and if not, it is bad. Tradition is always there to uphold or condemn people's actions; and even where some form of behavior has no precedent and therefore no traditional norm to guide it, it is expected to be conducted in the spirit of tradition in general."[20] A similar observation about the power of tradition in Islamic society is made by John L. Esposito, who states that "while tradition plays an important role in most cultures, in Islam it has been elevated to an almost sacrosanct status."[21]

The Arabic word for tradition is *taqālīd*, the plural form of *taqlīd*. A key term in Islamic theological literature, *taqlīd* is derived from the verb *qallada*, "to imitate, follow, obey someone," meaning acceptance of or submission to authority."[22] The term has a predominantly negative connotation, implying uncritical faith and thoughtless imitation: "*Taqlīd* lastly means 'clothing with authority' in matters of religion; the adoption of the utterances or actions of another as authoritative with faith in their correctness, without investigating reasons. . . . In this sense, *taqlīd* is the opposite of *ijtihād*. The historical beginnings of the *taqlīd* coincide with the formation of the juristic *madhāhib*."[23] Hava Lazarus-Yafeh notes that in al-Ghazzālī's writings, *taqlīd* usually indicates "blind adherence to, or following, ancestral tradition and pronouncements by teachers, without independent examination, meditation and reflection. It has a distinctly negative, derogatory connotation, and appears as the contrary to the faith which is founded on examination and study or on personal religious experience."[24] For the most part, al-Ghazzālī opposed the *taqlīd*, emphasizing the principle that "knowledge lies in inquiry and verification, not in blind acceptance of another's authority" (*al-ma'rifa bi-al-ḥaqīqa, lā bi-al-taqlīd 'an al-ghayr*).[25] Nevertheless, the doctrine of *taqlīd* exerted such a strong influence on Muslim religious sciences, especially Islamic law and jurisprudence, that it arrested intellectual exploration and creative activity.

In Arab society, respect for tradition is part of the enormous respect and admiration for the past, which contains the Arabs' glorious history and highly developed civilization. While tradition derives its power from being rooted in the distant past, it is not merely the fact of its antiquity that makes traditional usage absolute. Generally, it is sufficient for a custom to be once established, even if recently, to enjoy the same prescriptive character. Its potency lies in being associated with ideas steeped in religion—not that each and every custom carries a primarily religious or quasi-religious sanction but rather that veneration for tradition is the doctrine most characteristic of and most strongly stressed in Islamic teaching.[26]

The close relation between tradition and religion is reflected in the essentially ritualistic nature of numerous customs. According to Raphael Patai, "the entire field of custom—wide and infinitely ramified in its permeation of everyday life—cannot be divorced from religion either in theory or in practice. Whatever man does, he must always conform to custom, tradition, and religion." Altogether, religion, tradition, and custom form an inseparable "three-in-one constellation" which determines the pattern of Middle Eastern life.[27]

The Syrian poet Adonis, in his essay "Language, Culture, and Reality," explores the connection between the state of Arabic language and Arab culture and social reality. He begins by discussing the Arabs' attachment to the traditions of the past: "The dominant cultural trend in Arab society is a devotion to the culture of the past. It is presumed that if traditions are preserved, so is the existence of society itself." Adonis points out that this devotion is manifested in educational programs, cultural institutions, and intellectual currents: "It reflects a specific idea of culture, namely, that it is knowledge of the texts of the past, or knowledge of that which does not contradict such texts." The representatives of this trend—the educated, the intellectuals, and the writers—treat this knowledge in a manner that resembles religious reverence. They believe that the strength of Arab society depends on the power and persistence of traditional culture. As a result, Arab culture continues to be based on transmission and imitation: "The relation between the Arabs and their traditional culture remains analogous to the relation of the fallible with the infallible, the pupil with the teacher. Questioning, rejecting, and transcending are viewed not only as transgressions of culture, but also as attacks on society itself." In addition, the Arab masses live in closed circles: since their culture is a part of their forefathers' (*salaf*) culture, their concern is not to innovate but to emulate. Adonis stresses that language is not only a means of expression but also a way of thinking. Every social situation has its own language: when the prevailing circumstances are backward on all levels, so is the language. As for Arabic, it has lost the vitality of innovation and has become the language of rhetoric, artifice, and ornament. Adonis argues that without a revolutionary language, it is impossible to create a revolutionary Arab culture. Then again, it is impossible to generate consciousness by studying the cultural legacy (*al-turāth*), which constitutes a dead weight on the shoulders of the Arab world. For these concrete reasons, Arab social reality undergoes no development and shows no radical change.[28]

Adonis's conclusions echo those of the nineteenth-century English philosopher John Stuart Mill. In his provocative essay "On Liberty," Mill writes: "The despotism of custom is everywhere the standing hindrance to human advancement, being in unceasing antagonism to that disposition to aim at something better than customary, which is called, according to circumstances, the spirit of liberty, or that of progress or improvement."[29] Mill maintains that the contest between the spirit of progress and the sway of custom constitutes the chief interest of the history of humankind. As he sees it, the greater part of the world has no history because the despotism of custom is complete. As an example, he mentions the East: "This is the case over the whole East. Custom is there, in all things, the final appeal; justice and right mean conformity to custom; the argument of custom no one, unless some tyrant intoxicated with power, thinks of resisting. And we see the result." The nations of the East once had originality and rose to be the greatest and most powerful in the world. When they became ruled by custom, they ceased to possess individuality and creativity—the leading essentials of well-being and development—and suffered inevitable stagnation and decline.[30] Mill is unequivocal in his attitude to custom: "The human faculties of perception, judgment, discriminative feeling, mental activity, and even moral preference, are exercised only in making a choice. He who does anything because it is the custom, makes no choice."[31]

From a sociological point of view, the Arabs' loyal adherence to custom and tradition appears to be connected with the family structure and the emphasis placed on group cohesion. Halim Barakat describes the traditional Arab family as a socioeconomic unit in the sense that all its members cooperate to secure its livelihood and improve its standing in the community. The success or failure of an individual is perceived as that of the family as a whole. Every member of the family is held responsible for the acts of every other member. The sexual misbehavior of a girl, for example, reflects not just upon herself but upon her father, her brother, and the entire family. In such a close-knit unit—typically patriarchal, pyramidally hierarchical (in respect to sex and age), and extended—the pressures on the individual to obey the rules of conduct are considerable.[32] This situation is not peculiar to the urban setting. In a small tribal society or village community, where many people are related by birth or by marriage and all know each other well, group cohesion and kinship solidarity come first and foremost. The individual is expected to live by the norms of the group and uphold its code. The fact of the matter is that without the effective support and protection of the group, the individual would be unable to survive and advance. The mutual obligation underlying this interdependent relationship requires the individual to conform to the group's manners and mores and internalize them to the point of identifying personal interests with those of the group. Such a commitment may involve a large measure of self-sacrifice and self-abnegation.[33]

On the whole, in tradition-oriented Arab society, customs represent values that are long-lived and hard to change. They pass from generation to generation through various channels, including the family, schools, religious institutions, political organizations, and the social environment. Child-rearing practices, methods of education, male–female relations, sexual morals, and patterns of work, marriage, divorce, and childbearing are all codified by custom. The pivotal role of public opinion in influencing one's conduct is manifested especially in situations of internal crisis and conflict, when one's actions may well be contrary to one's own judgment but consistent with the group's established custom, because that is regarded as the proper thing to do. The process of socialization begins early on: "By the time the child reaches adolescence, the do's and don'ts hammered into him by his elders will have become internalized, so that he will continue to obey them in adult life even without external compulsion; and, what is more important for sociocultural continuity, he will insist on imparting them to his children."[34] This is largely how the cultural heritage of human societies is handed down from the past to the present.

Custom as a Literary Theme

Arabic proverbial lore recognizes the potent force of custom. To the four classes into which Arab physiologists used to divide human nature (the choleric, bilious, melancholy, and phlegmatic), a popular saying adds another: "Custom is a fifth nature" (*al-ʿāda ṭabʿ khāmis*). Another proverb states: "Custom is the twin of the innate character" (*al-ʿāda tawʾam al-ṭabīʿa*). And yet another declares: "Everything is habit, even piety" (*kull shayʾ ʿāda ḥattā al-ʿibāda*).

In the story "Caught Red-Handed" ("Ḥālat talabbus") by Yūsuf Idrīs,[35] the traditional attitude to custom comes under attack. The story centers on a faculty dean who catches sight of a female student smoking under his window. As smoking is traditionally prohibited for girls, his immediate, conditioned response is to expel her:

> When it caught his eye, it was not the Dean in him who was angry and in whose veins the blood boiled, but the child born and bred in Sohag. Since he was first conscious of anything, he had understood that it was permitted for men, shameful for youths, strictly forbidden for children, but a crime for women. More than a crime, it was tantamount to a violation of honor.[36]

However, the girl's sensuous style of smoking captivates the dean and generates erotic feelings that reawaken his doubts about the merit of custom in general and of this prohibition in particular:

> Why do we forbid it to a body vibrant with youth and allow it for a married lady or an old woman who hacks and coughs and spits with every puff she takes? Did he not hold the same principles in his twenties and thirties when his mind was awakening, when he thought that the basic problem of his society was that the individuals in it live in one age according to the customs of other dark, long-past centuries; that it was impossible for his country to make any progress, scientific or technological or cultural, unless there was complete freedom, and people lived in it according to the customs of their own age, the values and forms of freedom of their own age? Did he not hold that progress would be made by giving people freedom even to make mistakes, by not preventing them with advice and rebukes from gaining experience, or bequeathing them our right deeds and our mistakes; rather, by leaving them alone so that they can derive, from their own experience, what they see to be right and what they see to be wrong.[37]

In this story, a sexual revolt—symbolized by the girl's act of smoking—is presented as a liberating force, capable of releasing people from servitude to oppressive conventions, and enabling them to channel their energies toward positive goals. Despite this realization, the dean eventually succumbs to the yoke of custom and tradition, and takes steps to punish the girl:

> His passage back to being a Dean was slower, mixed with a greater shame, a more terrible blame. He moved, eyes lowered, tall, thin, old, shoulders bent, carrying once more all the troubles of the world. There was nothing clear in his mind save duty, and what he must inevitably do. The small smooth white knob on the desk, and the punishment. With a finger once more as irritable as before, reaching out as if from a world-weary heart, he pressed the bell.[38]

The degree to which custom controls behavior in Arab society is further exemplified by the concept of honor (*sharaf*), one of the most sensitive issues in the Arab code of ethics. The myriad facets and subtle nuances of this value are manifested in various social situations. Hospitality, generosity, and a strong sense of family loyalty are matters of honor, and the same applies to actions such as fulfilling a pledge and protecting a guest. Under all circumstances, a man must be cautious lest his "face" should be "blackened"; he must always strive to "whiten his face" and the face of his kin group. Any affront to a man's honor must be avenged, or else he becomes permanently dishonored. Further, there is the sexual honor of the woman, through which her entire paternal family can suffer the loss of their honor, and which is, therefore, the most important factor for the preservation of their honor.[39]

The extreme vulnerability of this value makes it imperative to guard it at all costs. If honor is damaged, great efforts are needed to restore it. If lost, it is almost impossible to regain. Honor is perceived as the collective property of the family: "If any single member of the family incurs dishonor, the whole family is disgraced. It is like a life-raft designed to carry the family over the dangerous waves of the inimical sea which is the social environment."[40]

In the story "The Free-for-All Dance" ("Al-Raqṣa al-mubāḥa") by Yaḥyā al-Ṭāhir ʿAbdallāh,[41] two village boys are caught in a homosexual act. The parents' reaction is swift and harsh: the boy who is the passive partner is forced to meet his death by jumping into a water well, while the boy who is the active partner is doomed to a life of exile and vagrancy by being banished from the village forever. Mourning for his dead son, the grief-stricken father says: "I'm poor, Ḥājj, I'm poor . . . I possess nothing but my honor. . . . Would you have respected me, Ḥājj? Would anyone have respected me? Who could have carried this shame but I? Now I possess my honor."[42] As for the other boy, his banishment implies that he "will live as a stranger, will die as a stranger, just like the wandering gypsies, people without honor, poachers of chickens."[43] Denys Johnson-

Davies comments: "For the peasant, the worst thing that can happen to a man—worse than death itself, for death is inevitable—is dishonor, and one form of dishonor is banishment from the land in which he was born. . . . For people who possess little of this world's goods, honor is central to their existence. . . . It is interesting to note, in this same story, that in a society where woman's honor is so highly prized, where woman is the bearer of the family's honor, it is the passive partner in the homosexual act who must pay the heavier penalty."[44]

An ancient, pre-Islamic custom, closely bound up with the concept of honor, is the inexorable *lex talionis*, or law of retaliation, which not only required the individual and his immediate relatives to take revenge for any injury sustained, but made it their duty under the threat of losing their honor.[45] Here, too, a direct connection is perceived to exist between the survival of this custom and certain features of traditional Arab society: "A society in which great emphasis is placed on the kin group, in which individual interests are subordinated to the interests of family and lineage, and in which, in addition, honor is given the highest priority, it is inevitable that every homicide, premeditated or accidental, should give rise to blood revenge and trigger a chain reaction that soon involves an increasing number of men and groups."[46] While the consequences are invariably tragic, the fighting spirit of the feuding parties finds consolation in the belief that the fate of every individual is "written" (*maktūb*), that is, preordained.

The story "Blood Feud" ("Al-Tha'r"), by Yūsuf al-Shārūnī,[47] offers a forceful account of this relentless custom. In the opening paragraph, the narrator introduces his village in general and the chronic malady that afflicts it in particular:

> My village, like the rest of the villages of Upper Egypt, is still ailing. Water pipes, electric lights and a Collective Unit that includes a hospital and school, together with agricultural and social supervisors, have recently been introduced into it and yet it remains ailing. Its ailment has many symptoms, perhaps the most important of which is that of the blood feud. Hatreds, like the seed sown by the people of my village, are buried only so that they may reappear, may grow. Over their seed they wait patiently for months; over their hatreds they wait years, till the fruit ripens, the tragedies hatch out. No sooner have the stalks of maize or sugar cane become strong and taller than a man than everything has ripened, both fruit and hatreds, and the harvest season is on the way. Life and death walk side by side, in fact the one seeks protection in the other; thus everyone who must take revenge or who sees that the time has come for him to cleanse himself of dishonor, goes and hides himself among the towering green stalks of maize to lie in wait for his enemy. From time to time one hears the sounds of gunshots followed by the noise of the crashing of stalks under the rush of quickly

> fleeing feet. Then, for some moments, silence reigns, until some passers-by find their way to the body of the victim, to be followed by the man's relatives, for the news of the tragedy will all too quickly have reached them. So they will take up the body of their murdered relative and will neither inform the police nor receive condolences on his death. With the murder of the man there will sprout in their hearts a new black seed of hatred, which the mothers will tend in the breasts of their children for years and years until they become young men capable of handling a weapon; this hatred will be tended, too, by paternal and maternal uncles, by custom and environment.[48]

As the story unfolds, a gang member from the village of Ṭanāsh is shot dead during an attempted robbery. His relatives, seeking vengeance, demand that his killer, Maḥmūd, who denies any wrongdoing, be subjected to the trial by ordeal—*al-bashʿa*. This is a Bedouin ritual which requires the accused to lick a piece of red-hot metal; if his tongue is burned he is found guilty. In parentheses, the narrator ironically remarks: "The educated among us try to explain the phenomenon of the *bashʿa* by saying that anyone who has committed a wrong would be so frightened that his spittle would dry up so that when he brought his tongue close to the white-hot metal object he would at once be burned. As for someone innocent, his spittle would suffice to lessen the effect of heat on his tongue."[49] It is worth mentioning that the branding associated with this ritual and the serious nature of the cases for which it is reserved provide the title and the subject matter for a story written by the Jordanian author Ghālib Halasā.[50]

When Maḥmūd is killed, despite his acquittal in the trial, his brother Mahrān undertakes to avenge his blood by assassinating the leader of the gang of Ṭanāsh. Having succeeded in his purpose, he proceeds to dance by the body of the victim and sing:

> Justice is my destiny
> Revenge was for the taking
> Shame is wholly washed away
> Cooled my fire of aching.[51]

The next casualty in this saga of killing is Mahrān's village mayor, who announces his intention to go to the notorious gang "bearing with him his shroud"—a symbolic act that is automatically accepted in place of further bloodshed and thus can end a blood feud.[52] It is unclear whether he is killed by his own people who oppose his intention or by the vengeful gang of Ṭanāsh. The story ends with the government establishing, for the first time, police posts in these villages in an attempt to preserve the peace and prevent further bloodshed.

The religious nature of several customs, in particular the worship of saints and the idolatry of shrines, is brought to the forefront in the novella *The Saint's Lamp (Qindīl Umm Hāshim*, 1944) by Yaḥyā Ḥaqqī. In this work, the protagonist, Ismāʿīl, grows up in the Cairene district of the mosque of al-Sayyida Zaynab—the granddaughter of the prophet Muḥammad. As a child with a traditional upbringing, his life is centered around the mosque and its holy shrine. He becomes attached to all the practices and beliefs connected with this shrine, such as the miracle cure in the oil of the saint's lamp and the saint's power of blessing and protection. As a young man, however, he comes under the influence of Western civilization when he goes to England to study medicine and falls in love with Mary, a fellow student. As a result, his values and way of thinking change:

> In the past he always looked for something outside himself to lean against, something like religion or tradition, a peg on which to hang his precious coat. But she used to tell him that whoever resorted to a peg, would remain all his life a slave to that peg, sitting next to it to keep an eye on his coat. She insisted that one's peg should be inside oneself. . . . One day he woke up to find his soul completely in ruins. Religion appeared to him to be only a superstition invented to rule the masses, and the human soul to be unable to find its strength and hence its happiness except by detaching itself from the crowd and facing it as a separate being. . . . Luckily for him he managed to pass through that crisis which many of his young countrymen experience in Europe, and emerged from it with a new self, confident and secure. His lost religious faith was replaced by a stronger faith in science. Instead of thinking of the beauty and bliss of Heaven he now thought of the beauty of nature and its secrets.[53]

After an absence of seven years, he returns to Egypt as an eye specialist, infused with the logic of science and determined to free his people from the shackles of ignorance, superstition, and tradition. But he fails miserably. He finds that his cousin Fāṭima suffers from trachoma, which his mother is treating with drops of oil from the saint's lamp. Outraged by this harmful practice, he storms the mosque and destroys the lamp, whereupon he is attacked by the attending crowd and barely escapes with his life. He then begins to treat Fāṭima's eyes with the prescribed medical cure, but her eyes do not get better; on the contrary, they become worse. Unable to understand the failure of his therapy, he suffers a severe existential crisis, after which he comes to terms with himself and his environment. He now treats Fāṭima both with the prescribed medication and with drops of oil from the saint's lamp. Curiously enough, Fāṭima's eyes begin to heal, until they are completely cured. This ending suggests that

Ismāʿīl has discovered that science without faith is blind and incapable of answering all human needs. But the fact remains: he cannot change reality, and in the end he gives up the struggle and conforms to the "three-in-one constellation": custom, tradition, and religion.

In the novel *The Seven Days of Man (Ayyām al-insān al-sabʿa,* 1969) by ʿAbd al-Ḥakīm Qāsim, the custom of annual pilgrimage to the shrine of the saint al-Sayyid al-Badawī in Ṭanṭā, a town in the center of the Delta, forms the theme around which the work revolves. Ḥājj Karīm, the leader of a village group of Ṣūfī brothers who worship this saint, spends most of his resources on meeting the expenses of conducting the pilgrimage. His young son, ʿAbd al-ʿAzīz, is alarmed at the rate at which his father's plot of land shrinks while that of his neighbor, al-Mitwallī Sārūkh, expands:

> The thin slice of land Sārūkh owned next to Ḥājj Karīm's property kept getting wider and wider every year. The anxiety that was building up in ʿAbd al-ʿAzīz's heart could only be eased by his father's deep voice and trusting words.
>
> "We own nothing ourselves. We are merely guardians of what we have."[54]

As Ḥājj Karīm refuses to concern himself with the future and in utter improvidence continues to sell his land and other assets in order to observe this traditional festival, he undermines the economic basis of his family's existence. In the end, the family is totally impoverished, having lost practically everything they owned. In this instance, the tendency of custom to become an addictive emotional and physical need is reflected in zealous adherence to religious ritual. Here custom turns into an instinctual drive that dominates every aspect of Ḥājj Karīm's life to the point of self-destructive behavior. This situation is analogous with certain trends of migration in nature, where the migratory instinct of birds and fish becomes counterproductive and overrides the instinct of self-survival. Thus, while custom may achieve a state of coexistence with progress, as in Yaḥyā Ḥaqqī's *The Saint's Lamp,* it may also fail to strike such a balance, in which case it is likely to have negative consequences for the individual and society.

The foregoing illustrations from modern Arabic literature present another perspective on human fate: the idea that people's cultural background exerts a decisive influence on their mentality and conduct. According to this view, people are bound by their cultural inheritance and the system of values into which they are born. They can be trapped in a maze of custom and tradition to such an extent that fate seems to assume the shape of sociocultural determinism.

Ḥabīb Jāmātī
Blood Feud

Ḥabīb Jāmātī (1887–1968) was born in a village near Jūniyya in northern Lebanon. He attended the Lazarist college in ʿAynṭūra, after which he went to Egypt and worked as a journalist. Later he traveled to France, where he founded an Arabic printing house and published his journal *al-Shuhra* for one year before taking up a job as a translator at the French Ministry of Foreign Affairs. Between 1916 and 1918, he joined the independence movement in Saudi Arabia and became close to King Faisal. After World War I, he returned to Egypt and resumed his journalistic and literary career. His output is substantial and includes fiction as well as nonfiction. Jāmātī was concerned with the traditional values of Arab society, indicating aspects of needed reform. His favored technique was to investigate true events and report them in a semifictional form, which he published in a series entitled *What History Has Forgotten (Taʾrīkh mā ahmalahu al-taʾrīkh)*. His style is conservative and reflects old literary usage.

"Blood Feud" ("Qātil wa-qatīl") appeared in the Saudi cultural magazine *Qāfilat al-zayt* in 1960. The story depicts the tyrannical hold of the custom of blood revenge on Bedouin society by recounting the events leading to the extinction of an entire family.

The silence of that moonlit night was disturbed only by our faint voices. We rested in front of the tent we had erected behind a sand hill. We had spent the entire day hunting game, which was available in abundance. After dark, we sat drinking coffee as we reminisced about the past.

Throughout the week, we had continually moved from place to place—sliding between the rocks looking for partridges or rushing along the plains on the trail of wandering gazelles—oblivious to the scorching rays of the sun. The refreshing desert night replenished the energy and strength that had been depleted by our exhausting day.

There were eight of us in the group. That night we decided that the next day we would depart from this area, each of us going his own way, to return to face life's hardships and the city's din. We had forgotten—or had pretended to forget—all of that in this wide desert with the open sky and the beautiful natural scenery.

It was the year 1928 of the Christian era, which corresponded to the year 1347 of the Muslim era, just after the glorious uprising that shook Syria for over two years in an attempt to free it from foreign rule.

I said to my friend, Shaykh Fulayḥān the Bedouin, who had invited me on the hunting trip:

"Tomorrow we will be parting, as we did once before, more than ten years ago. Before we do, would you tell me the latest developments in that affair of blood revenge, whose violent stages you described to me during our previous journey in Hejaz and the Syrian Desert?"

Fulayḥān replied: "Your wish is my command, but only if you keep your promise not to include any of this account in your published stories and memoirs. At least, not until there is an end to this tragedy, and the chain of retaliation among our family comes to a stop—either through the extinction of those who seek vengeance or through a reconciliation that will erase the hatred from people's hearts and replace animosity and feuding with peace and harmony."

I repeated my promise to the Bedouin shaykh and renewed my oath.

The tragedy, whose details I was acquainted with and whose stages I followed, was neither the first nor the only one in the Syrian Desert between families, clans, and tribes. This tragedy comprises a part of history and a certain aspect of life. It undoubtedly includes many manifestations of pride and demonstrations of heroism. At the same time, it contains roots of destruction and elements of disintegration. Therefore, the matter needs to be handled according to modern thinking and in a way that will preserve the family within the sphere of Arab nationalism.

Decades ago, a dispute arose among members of a single Arab family over a weapon, an old-fashioned rifle that was once common in Syria.

A girl named Farḥa wanted to appropriate it, but her cousin Faraj scolded her, saying that such weapons were meant for men, not women. He told her that women were supposed to stay in their quarters and let the men rush into the danger of battle with rifles in hand. The girl became angry and answered that women are frequently more courageous than men. She recited a verse of poetry, which was the spark that ignited the fire:

> The feminine gender does not disgrace the sun,
> Nor the masculine exalt the crescent moon.[55]

The young man's reaction was to slap Farḥa on the cheek. The girl reached for the rifle—the subject of the dispute—and fired a bullet that struck her cousin dead. And so began the chain of retaliation, blood for blood, among the sons of one and the same family.

When I met Shaykh Fulayḥān the Bedouin during World War I, thirteen people had been killed over the rifle incident. At that time Fulayḥān remarked:

"We observe a custom that we have inherited from our fathers and forefathers from olden times: all the names we choose for our sons and daughters begin with the letter *F*. We still follow this custom, without knowing the reason or justification for it, except that it is in imitation of those who preceded us on this earth. Likewise, we have inherited the hatred and the need to seek vengeance from each other since that ill-fated incident in which the young man Faraj met his death at the hands of his uncle's daughter, Farḥa.

"We belong to the tribe Ḥuwayṭāṭ. We have relatives in the Syrian Desert, Hejaz, Najd, the Eastern Desert in Egypt, the Sinai Peninsula, and even in the oases of Barqa.[56] But the events that are connected with the blood feud and are stamped by it—on account of the incident involving the rifle and the verse of poetry—remained limited to our family alone and did not extend to other families. Today, each of us is either a killer seeking vengeance or a victim who met his death because of this vengeance, and 'the rope is on the tug.' "[57]

This was the story Shaykh Fulayḥān the Bedouin had told me ten years earlier. Now, the hunting trip of 1928 had reunited us. For this reason, I was eager to hear all about what had happened during the past ten years, which had been filled with great events. While one state had emerged, another had vanished; the Ottoman sultanate had shrunk, and the Arab countries had separated from it. A bright star had shone in the sky, that of Abdel Aziz Ibn Saud, who established the Kingdom of Saudi Arabia. In 1928 there was still unrest in the Arab East, and tremors of nationalism erupted here and there among the Arab lands. All this time, the hatred remained deeply embedded in the hearts of the vengeance seekers of this divided family, the family of Shaykh Fulayḥān the Bedouin.

After I had repeated my promise and renewed my oath, the shaykh said:

"Since we last parted, there have been other killers and victims among us. The latest occurrence was the death of my younger brother Fāḍil at the hands of his cousin Fātik, who was also our brother-in-law. He had married our sister Faḍīla, and we believed that this marriage would end the bloodshed. The marriage was my idea and at my suggestion. Then it suddenly fanned the fire, and my sister caused her brother's death at the hands of her husband. That was the most terrible thing that has happened in our family. The killer attacked the victim while he was in my home. In doing so, he not only violated the sanctity of my home but also disgraced me, by killing my own brother and guest. It therefore became incumbent on me to take revenge for the death on the offender, who was my brother-in-law.

"But the killer fled—no killer had fled from us before—and what's more, he offered himself to the service of the French army. I pursued him for some time, but he eluded me. Fate decreed that he should die during a military operation on the Taurus Mountains and that I myself should not be his killer.

"He left behind a wife—my sister Faḍīla—and a boy named Fāris, of the same age as my son Fāyiz. Fāris's mother turned him over to a Frenchman who adopted him. This Frenchman was married to an Algerian woman with whom he was not blessed with children, so the couple found consolation by adopting the boy. I don't know whether Faḍīla told them about the dreadful bloody secret that had caused her to flee with her husband the killer. She agreed to part from her only son, believing that she was safeguarding him from the imminent danger of retaliation.

"I think that she succeeded in doing what she wanted, but she was killed during the Syrian uprising, on the day the French bombed Damascus in 1925. She was among the victims of this barbarous act. I later heard that the man who adopted her son either returned to his own country or went to another country. Perhaps the death of my brother Fāḍil will end this tragedy, since both the killer and his wife have died, and his son has vanished."

Fulayḥān fell silent. Two tears welled up in his eyes and rolled down his cheeks into his small beard, which was streaked with gray. He wiped his eyes with the edge of his sleeve and remained silent for a few moments. Then, turning to me, he continued:

"However, please do not tell our story yet. Perhaps the next stage is still to come, for my brother-in-law has left one son behind, and I also have a son. If revenge escaped me, it may not escape my only son."

Fulayḥān called his son, who was accompanying us on the hunting trip. The youngster came up.

"Fāyiz, what's your uncle's name?" he asked.

"Fāḍil," the boy replied.

"And the name of my cousin who killed him?"

"Fātik, the husband of my aunt Faḍīla."

"And his son's name? And his age?"

"His name is Fāris, but he may have changed it to something else. He is ten years old, just like me."

"What's the first verse of poetry that you memorized?"

The youth recited:

> The feminine gender does not disgrace the sun,
> Nor the masculine exalt the crescent moon.

Again, Fulayḥān asked: "And the second?"

Fāyiz recited:

> We will contend with our foe in enmity as long as we live,
> And, dying, bequeath this enmity to our sons.

Fulayḥān said: "This has been going on for the last ten years. Whenever we tried to end the animosity, something would happen in our family to add further fuel to the fire. If I die, however, and this boy dies after a long life, with neither of us having taken revenge for the last person killed, then the tragedy will end."

Fulayḥān fell silent again. He stretched out his hand and uncovered his forearm. Then he took his son's hand and uncovered his forearm as well. To my surprise, each had a tattoo—both father and son.

The tattoo showed a clear picture of a dagger dripping blood. . . .

The last thing Fulayḥān said to me was:

"This mark is like a written oath and a printed pledge. It is unnecessary to explain its meaning."

Indeed, the tattoo required no explanation.

Twenty years had passed since I last met Shaykh Fulayḥān the Bedouin in a tent in the desert. All I heard about him afterward was that he had died on a business trip, returning from Najd to Kuwait. In 1948, I was surprised by a visit from his son, Fāyiz, in Cairo.

He was in the prime of life, just over thirty years of age, with a true manly demeanor. A well-spoken man, widely read, and fluent in English and French, he had a passion for Arabic literature and could recite dozens of odes.

The first thing he said to me was: "My father told me, before he went on the trip on which he died, that you should be the first person I visited in Egypt if I should ever happen to be here. He told me that you knew the story of the blood feud in our family, and that you would no doubt want to know more. So I've come to tell you the end of this tragedy."

In the desert of Hejaz, I heard from Fulayḥān the first part of this moving story; in the Syrian Desert, he told me the second part; and on the banks of the Nile, his son told me the third and last part.

Fāyiz said: "My father died telling me over and over what I've learned from early childhood, and reciting continually the two verses of poetry that triggered the chain of killing in our family and infused us with the spirit of vengeance. My mother died soon after, repeating, in her turn, what my father had constantly said. I grew up and attended school in Beirut, but I never forgot anything of what I learned and what was implanted in my soul, whether in a desert tent or in a house in the city. I began to believe that the revenge I sought was unattainable. Where was the man I was seeking in order to quench my thirst with his blood and fulfill the quest for revenge?

"But fate had made preparations for revenge on my behalf. In 1941, I went with some companions to Iraq to take part in the revolt that had broken out there. On our way, near Palmyra, we met a platoon of French soldiers. They, together with their young officer, had become lost in the desert and had run out of food and water. We helped them by escorting them to a city nestling between the sand hills. To my surprise, their officer began to thank us in good Arabic, saying that we had rescued him and his soldiers from certain death. Then we parted, and wished each other safe travel, which is customary in the desert in such circumstances.

"Afterward, I returned to Syria and then went on to Palestine. In 1945, World War II was about to end, and a new revolt erupted in Syria against the French. I hastened to join it, as is traditional in our family and clan.

"One day I found myself among freedom fighters on our way from Ḥawrān[58] to Damascus. We clashed with a small French force and exchanged fire with them. Then we fought hand to hand with cold steel and revolvers. I found myself facing an officer—a captain—who fired a bullet at me, but missed. Then I shot him, hitting a vital part of his body. He fell to the ground, the blood gushing from his chest. When his companions saw that the villagers were rushing to help us, they fled in their armored cars.

"The French left five men dead on the battlefield, among them the captain. I cast a quick glance at his torn clothes. A mark that appeared through them made me curious and uneasy. I uncovered his forearm and saw the dreadful tattoo! The bullet had touched it on its way to his chest. Yes, there it was—the dagger dripping blood that my father had drawn on my forearm, just as Fātik, my uncle's killer, had drawn it on the forearm of his son, Fāris. I realized that I had killed the man whose father had killed my uncle Fāḍil. That French officer I killed was the same one I had rescued, along with his companions, near Palmyra. I met him once and saved his life without knowing who he was. Then I met him again and killed him, also without knowing who he was. But the tattoo revealed the dreadful truth to me. Fāris—my cousin, and my father's nephew, and my aunt's killer[59]—had become an officer in the French army, and fate led him to the place where his father had committed his crime, so that he should meet his death at my hands, according to the requisite revenge."

And now, the reader may wish to know Fāyiz's fate, after he had killed his adversary.

Fāyiz, the last living member of the family whose legacy of hatred and vengeance was bequeathed by fathers to sons generation after generation, also died—but for the cause of Palestine.

He hurried to join the Arab freedom fighters in 1948 and was killed, weapon in hand, in a battle among the citrus orchards of Jaffa.

His death ended the tragedy that I have recounted for you. By that time, the entire family had perished, which released me from the pledge that had bound me to Shaykh Fulayḥān the Bedouin.

I hope that this tragedy will be the last of its kind among the members of a single family and the sons of a single clan, and that the verse of poetry sung by the Bedouins in their desert will be:

> We will contend with our foe in "love" as long as we live,
> And, dying, bequeath this love to our sons.

Comments

The events of this story extend over a period of more than three decades and a geographical area comprising several Arab lands: Saudi Arabia, Syria, Iraq, Egypt, and Palestine. By using such an elaborate frame of reference, the author accentuates the fact that the custom of blood revenge transcends the boundaries of time and place. He succeeds in showing the ruthless nature of this custom by setting it within the framework of a single family. The lack of a rational basis for this custom is illustrated by analogy with another custom: the members of this family invariably choose names for their children that begin with the letter *F*. They know of no reason, except that they inherited the custom from their forefathers. By judiciously exposing the untenable background of the blood feud, the author places the reader in a defensive position and expresses his moral indignation at, and condemnation of, this Bedouin custom.

Although the Bedouins today constitute a small percentage of the population of the Arab world, many people in villages and cities are of Bedouin origin. Regarded as figures from the glorious and heroic past, the Bedouins are looked up to as the "ideal" Arabs, and their ethical code is considered a model to emulate. Hence Bedouin values such as honor, courage, hospitality, and generosity extend to rural and urban areas alike, and Bedouin manners and mores can be found throughout the Arab world.[60]

Jāmātī's intent is to persuade the reader to abolish vengeance killing. For this purpose, he introduces several carefully tailored arguments, which are designed to create acceptability for the reader. For example, the different stages of the blood feud are connected with specific political events in Arab history: one episode happens during the uprising of the Syrians against the French, another during Iraq's revolt against foreign rule, and the last during the Palestinian war of 1948. By setting the incidents of the blood feud in the shadow of these historic events, Jāmātī impresses on his reader the idea that the Arabs have far more important matters to attend to: national struggle and independence. Their energies, therefore, should be directed outward, against the real enemy, and not inward, against themselves. Moreover, the success of most of these campaigns demonstrates that if the Arabs are capable of shaking off oppressive colonial rulers, they are also capable of shaking off oppressive customs. Jāmātī is primarily concerned that ancient customs such as blood revenge will impede the development of Arab nations. As he recounts several milestones in modern Arab history, especially the rise to power of Abdel Aziz Ibn Saud, who established the Kingdom of Saudi Arabia, he deliberately contrasts them with the pointless and relentless pursuit of blood revenge.

It is interesting to note that the story traces the cause of the blood feud to a girl, Farḥa, who claimed equality for women. It is not clear whether Jāmātī is trying to argue for or against women. The issue he raises involves the role of women in the persistent custom of blood revenge. The author's position is ambiguous and can be interpreted as either critical or supportive.

Ironically, the author uses the traditional concept of fate as an argument for relinquishing the custom of blood revenge. Fāḍil's killer ran away, but fate caught up with him and he was killed while in the service of the French. His wife gave her only son for adoption to a Frenchman. Yet just as Oedipus could not prevent what the Fates had decreed and killed his father unknowingly, so here, the son cannot escape his fate: he is killed by his blood-seeker Fāyiz in tragic circumstances and without the killer knowing his true identity. Is the author suggesting that the Arabs should leave vengeance to fate? Clearly, Jāmātī avoids a direct confrontation with his audience, whom he is reluctant to alienate. Instead, he seeks to convince his readers to abolish one tradition by drawing on a still more powerful one. As a result, not only is the concept of fate present in this story but it actually plays an active part in the saga of this family.

As for Fāyiz, Fulayḥān's only surviving son, he perishes too—for the sake of Palestine. Symbolically, the blood feud ends when the last son is sacrificed as a freedom fighter. The author concludes the rather complicated story with a pietistic paragraph wishing the Arabs to learn to settle their disputes amicably and to recite poetry that commemorates love rather than hatred. This aspiration, echoing the ideal of seeking a rational and practical resolution to conflicts, is still relevant to the contemporary scene.[61]

Zakariyyā Tāmir
The Beards

Zakariyyā Tāmir was born in Damascus in 1931. He did not pursue formal education after elementary school and is largely self-taught. Early in his career, he worked at several manual crafts and was an apprentice to a blacksmith. He began to publish during the early 1960s and achieved immediate success. An established writer and journalist, he has served as editor for various literary magazines, including the prominent Syrian journal *al-Maʿrifa*. He moved to London in 1980 and currently resides in Oxford, where he continues to contribute articles to the Arabic press and to write fiction.

Tāmir is regarded as one of the leading practitioners of the short story and the foremost Syrian author of children's literature. He has published several collections of short stories and books of stories for children. His stories often contain political and social fables and allegories. A master fantasist, he combines dream with reality, innocence with madness, and satire with tragedy. Most of his stories deal with political oppression, sexual frustration, and personal alienation. His style is remarkable for its vivid images and metaphors, frequently referring to animals, nature, or the countryside.

"The Beards" ("Al-Liḥā") appears in the collection *Thunder (Al-Raʿd,* 1970). The story depicts the prominent role of custom and tradition in a fierce conflict between men of religion and a new ruler.

The birds fled our skies, the children stopped playing in the alleys, and the singing of the caged sparrows turned into soft, trembling sighs. Sterilized cotton began to disappear from the pharmacies. There they were, gentlemen. The armies of Tamerlane[62] were besieging our city. Only the sun was not struck by fear; it continued to rise every morning.

We, the men of the city, were not afraid. We smiled bravely and thanked God for creating us bearded men rather than smooth-faced women. We held a meeting to discuss what to do to preserve our safety. The first speaker was a reckless youth who worked as a salesman of women's apparel. He shouted enthusiastically: "Let's fight!"

Contemptuous looks instantly assailed him. He fell silent and blushed in shame. Then the man with the fullest beard in the city stood up and declared: "Only a person who doesn't exist needs war. We, praise be to God, have beards. Therefore we exist."

At once there were shouts of approval and support, and, after a brief debate, we decided to send a delegation to negotiate with Tamerlane. It would be led by an old man whose beard was so long that it reached his knees when he walked.

The city had seven gates. The delegation departed from one of them, preceded by a person holding a white flag. They walked through a mass of troops whose number exceeded that of the stars and the locusts. The troops, however, were exhausted from searching for lice in their underclothes, and their swords had been left in the sun for the stains of blood and mud to dry.

The delegation entered Tamerlane's tent with deliberate, dignified steps. Surprisingly, Tamerlane was but a youth with a child's eyes and an old man's smile!

The head of the delegation spoke: "We seek peace. Our city is yours without war. But our city is small and poor. It has neither gold nor petroleum. And our women look like goats. We would be glad to be rid of them."

Tamerlane replied: "I hate shedding blood, and I seek neither gold nor beautiful women. But I have learned that in your city the barbers are starving because of your custom of growing beards. I condemn this injustice, especially as my life is dedicated to vindicating ill-treated souls and spreading justice throughout the world. Human beings should not go hungry!"

The delegates were taken by surprise. They exchanged puzzled looks.

Tamerlane went on: "My army will leave your city once you have shaved your beards and the barbers' business has begun to prosper."

The head of the delegation replied: "Your demand is a serious matter. We must return to the city to deliberate before giving you a final answer."

But Tamerlane declared: "Either shave your beards or die. The choice is yours."

Silence and horror seized the delegates. At that moment, life seemed very precious to them. The skies appeared deep blue, and the red roses more beautiful than popular songs sung by a tormented lover. The babies' first cries were producing green grass in the drops of blood, and a woman's trembling mouth was a moon slaughtering the nights with a silver knife. But when the delegates imagined themselves staring into the mirror at clean-shaven faces, they were overcome by repugnance and offense. At that moment, death became a red fish shining under a golden sun.

Aware that all the men of our city were listening submissively, the head of the delegation replied coldly: "Tomorrow our city will decide its future."

The delegation returned to our city and related Tamerlane's demand. Anger erupted, and someone shouted: "What's the point of saving our lives if we lose our beards?"

The next day, the armies of Tamerlane attacked our city. They smashed the walls, demolished the gates, and slaughtered all the men.

Thus Tamerlane was given the opportunity to stare at a mountain of heads. The faces were sallow and covered with blood, but all were smiling, proud of their beards. It is said that they neither frowned nor lost their joy and pride, until Tamerlane ordered the barbers to shave their beards.

And thus, gentlemen, we were defeated without being avenged, and covered with shame that no blood can ever cleanse.

Comments

This story is a satirical account of the conquest of Damascus in 1400 by the ruthless Turkish-Mongolian leader Tamerlane. Instead of a bloody tyrant and clashing armies, there is only a youth "with a child's eyes and an old man's smile." The mocking recital of history is further accentuated by glaring anachronisms: the pharmacies are said to have run out of sterilized cotton, and the besieged men protest that their city has no petroleum.

Beneath the sarcasm lies the dilemma of the men of Damascus faced with Tamerlane's imminent attack: What must they do to save their lives? The bearded men have no qualms about surrendering the city without a fight, or giving up their freedom, or handing over their women. However, when their beards are threatened, they are willing to die rather than lose them. Ironically, they end up losing both their lives and their beards.

The beards take center stage in the unfolding drama of the new conqueror and the men of Damascus. The significance of the beards is evident from the statement of the spokesman of these men: "Only a person who doesn't exist needs war. We, praise be to God, have beards. Therefore we exist." This assertion, which is a distortion of Descartes's famous saying "I think, therefore I am," equates the beard with the mind and serves to inform the reader that the men of Damascus are thoughtless.

The predicament of the men of Damascus derives from the high value attached to their beards by custom and tradition. First, the beards represent their gender identity: they are strong, superior males, not weak, inferior females. Second, the beards denote their pious nature, for traditionally only an atheist or a nonbeliever lets his face be clean-shaven. Socially, a man's prestige is enhanced by the size and color of his beard: the longer and grayer it is, the more respect it evokes. Orthodox Muslims swear by their beards and believe that a man disgraces his beard by an evil action. Consequently, forcing an orthodox Muslim to shave off his beard is tantamount to striking at the core of his masculinity, piety, and prestige. The shaving of one half of a person's beard as a form of punishment is known to have been practiced in modern times. It is an ancient means of inflicting personal and public humiliation, which is also recorded in the Bible (2 Sam. 10:4).[63]

The ensuing confrontation between the besieged men and the invading dictator reveals the underlying motivation and ideology of these men. Based on custom and tradition, their beards symbolize the essence of their existence: sexual, religious, and social. They cling to their beards and would rather die than sacrifice them. Even after death, their faces can still react to an insult directed at their most prized attribute—their beards.

Inevitably, negotiations with a tyrant like Tamerlane are doomed to fail. Tamerlane is a shrewd and unpredictable adversary. His unique skill lies in being able to identify his enemy's most sensitive spot; his goal is to attack where the pain is mortal. The author indicates that once people give in to a tyrant, their fate is sealed, because a tyrant is never satisfied until he achieves his opponent's total destruction.

The story is safely set at the turn of the fifteenth century for the author to be able to attack the present regime in Damascus and still avoid censorship and persecution. Damascus itself is equated with hell. This allegorical portrayal is implied by a vital detail: the city which the bearded men inhabit has seven gates. In the Qur'ān, hell is described as having seven gates: "And verily Hell is the promised abode for them all! To it are seven Gates: for each of those Gates is a special class of sinners assigned" (15:43–44).

It is most likely that Tamerlane represents the Baʿth regime in Syria, while the bearded men represent the religious leadership (*ʿulamā'*) or Muslim fundamentalists. Since the accession to power of the Baʿth regime in Syria in 1963, a fierce conflict developed between the traditional conservative men of religion and the new rulers. The Baʿth regime carried out a secular policy aimed at reducing the role of Islam in public life and practically separating Islam from the state. This policy clashed with orthodox Muslims and with all those whose livelihood—and social standing—depended on knowledge in the customary religious disciplines. Further, the Baʿth regime implemented extensive social reforms that damaged the economic interests of the urban notables. The predominantly Sunnite population was also largely antagonized since 1966, when the new regime became dominated by the ʿAlawite sect—a small minority in Syria regarded as socially inferior and religiously heretical.[64] Hence, throughout its rule, the Baʿth regime has had to contend with opposition to its leaders and to its secular socialist party both from the *ʿulamā'* and from the fundamentalists. The challenge of the Islamic opposition was met with acts of repression and bloodshed. The conflict reached its climax in 1982, when government troops killed twenty thousand residents (mostly fundamentalists) of the city of Hama to crush a religious uprising, and membership in the outlawed Muslim Brotherhood was declared a capital crime by the judicial court.[65] In a curious analogy, when Tamerlane entered Syria, he is reported to have extorted from the *ʿulamā'* a *fatwā* (formal religious ruling) approving his conduct, before sacking their cities.[66] To a certain extent, then, this story is prophetic in that it depicts events that later actually happened.

Obviously, the author does not sympathize with either the dictator or the bearded men: his portrayal shows them both to be blind and inhumane. While this satire exposes the brutal reality of the Syrian political scene, it nevertheless offers a ray of hope: in the end, even the mightiest dictators succumb to human fate. In the chronicle of history, however, these rulers do not fade into oblivion. Rather, they tend to evolve into fearsome legends, which in time become archetypes of oppression deeply embedded in the collective memory of generations of people. In his portrayal of his society and its leaders, Zakariyyā Tāmir often draws on such mythical figures, particularly that of Genghis Khan.[67]

5

GENDER

The Female Experience

> Our people prefer boys, because a girl's life is difficult. It's difficult in every sort of family and among all nationalities. A girl's life is not like a man's life. She has no assurance of being happy in her marriage. And her main purpose in life is to marry and to have children. A girl's and a woman's lives are a trial whatever happens.
>
> —Umm Gad[1]

Differential Evaluation

That the fair sex does not fare well in the Arab world is borne out by such widespread practices as segregation, veiling, seclusion, arranged marriage, and crimes of honor. In this instance, fate assumes the form of gender: to be born a girl is to be destined for a harsh life; to be born a boy is to be destined for a more privileged life. As the heroine of "A Woman for Sale" by the Saudi writer Maḥmūd ʿĪsā al-Mashhādī confirms: "We all begin and end the same, or so we are told. But the difference in between! Some are born male, to find all doors opening for them, while others are born female, to find all doors slamming in their faces."[2]

The distinction between the sexes begins early on, even prior to the child's arrival in the family. For example, it is customary to wish a newlywed couple many sons, but not daughters; during pregnancy, the wife hopes and prays that she will be blessed with a son. When a boy is born, there is celebration in the house, but when a girl is born, the mother is likely to be disappointed and the father displeased, because he must shoulder the burdensome responsibility of guarding the girl's—and the family's—honor and must find her a husband in due course. The overwhelming preference for boys results in a situation where a woman who has only daughters is not much better off than a childless wife.[3]

In the short story "Bahiyya's Eyes" by the Egyptian woman writer Alīfa Rifʿat (1930–96), the heroine wishes to see her daughter one last time before she becomes completely blind. Her affliction, she explains to her daughter in a letter, did not come from the flies and the dirt, as the doctor claims, but from "the tears I shed since my mother first bore me and they held me up by the leg and found I was a girl." Her sad experiences are not in themselves unusual: "The fact is there's no joy for a girl in growing up, it's just one disaster after another till you end up an old woman who's good for nothing and who's really lucky if she finds someone to feel sorry for her." What befell her, she attempts to rationalize, is all "a question of fate and destiny"; it's all "written on the forehead" and determined by God's will. Looking back on her unhappy life, she soberly concludes: "All my life I'd been ruled by a man, first my father and then my husband." And again: "Daughter, I'm not crying now because I'm fed up or regret that the Lord created me a woman. No, it's not that. It's just that I'm sad about my life and my youth that have come and gone without my knowing how to live them really and truly as a woman."[4] In another story by Alīfa Rifʿat, "The Long Night of Winter" ("Fī layl al-shitāʾ al-ṭawīl"), the motif of harsh fate recurs. A wife, who is waiting for her habitually unfaithful husband to come to bed at long last, wonders to herself: "Had her mother suffered the same sort of nightmare of a life as she did? Was this the fate of all women?"[5]

In the novel *Memoirs of a Woman Doctor (Mudhakkirāt ṭabība*, 1965) by Nawāl al-Saʿdāwī, the heroine describes her experiences growing up female in Egypt:

> All I did know at that time was that I was a girl. I used to hear it from my mother all day long. "Girl!" she would call, and all it meant to me was that I wasn't a boy and I wasn't like my brother. . . . My brother went out into the street to play without asking my parents' permission and came back whenever he liked, while I could only go out if and when they let me. My brother took a bigger piece of meat than me, gobbled it up and drank his soup noisily and my mother never said a word. But I was different: I was a girl. I had to watch every movement I made, hide my longing for the food, eat slowly and drink my soup without a sound. My brother played, jumped around and turned somersaults, whereas if I ever sat down and allowed my skirt to ride as much as a centimeter up my thighs, my mother would pierce me with a glance like an animal immobilizing its prey and I would cover up those shameful parts of my body. Shameful! Everything in me was shameful and I was a child of just nine years old. I felt sorry for myself and locked myself in my room and cried. The first real tears I shed in my life weren't because I'd done badly at school or broken something valuable but because I was a girl. I wept over my femininity even before I knew

what it was. The moment I opened my eyes on life, a state of enmity already existed between me and my nature.[6]

The differential treatment of women is manifested in many areas: in marriage laws, men are allowed four wives and an unlimited number of concubines whereas women must be monogamous; in divorce, men have the prerogative of repudiation, but women's right to divorce is severely restricted; in inheritance, a woman is entitled to half the share of a man; in a court of law, a male witness is worth two female witnesses. In addition, education and work opportunities—despite progressive efforts in recent decades—are still limited for women, who are largely relegated to a dependent social and economic position. Women's domain is the home, and their traditional roles are those of wife and mother. The strict allocation of space prevents most women from active participation in public life.[7]

The subordination of women is not devoid of ideology. The prevailing religious view considers women to be a source of evil, temptation (*fitna*), and trickery or deception (*kayd*). Those who uphold the traditional view contend that women are subordinate to men by God's will and design. They base their claim for male domination on a Qur'ānic verse: "Men have authority over women because God has made the one superior to the other, and because they spend their wealth to maintain them" (4:34). They also cite another verse: "Women shall with justice have rights similar to those exercised against them, although men have a status above women" (2:228). Such verses have provided conservative forces with divine sanction for their control over women. The traditional view has dominated the Islamic establishment, the moral code, and the personal status code. Contemporary Muslim apologists attribute the subordination of women to misinterpretation of Islam rather than to Islam itself.[8]

The Realm of Sexuality

Sexual matters constitute the area in which the differential treatment of women is most pronounced. Female sexuality is surrounded by strict taboos that are designed either to discourage girls from attempting to engage in premarital sex or to make it altogether impossible for them. One of the most powerful deterrents is the value attached to virginity. In traditional Arab society, virginity is a highly guarded property. It represents not only the honor of the girl but also that of her family. While honor in its nonsexual connotation is termed *sharaf*, a woman's sexual honor is called *ʿirḍ*. The *sharaf* of the man depends on the *ʿirḍ* of the women in his family.[9] Under all circumstances, a girl must preserve her virginity intact until her first marriage. To lose her virginity to anyone but her husband is the gravest sin she can commit. In parallel, the greatest dishonor that can befall a man results from the sexual misconduct of his daughter, sister, or female cousin (*bint al-ʿamm*). The roots of this perception of male honor are grounded in the structure and dynamics of the Arab kin group: the ties of patrilineal descent cannot be severed, and they do not weaken throughout a person's life. Even when a woman marries into a different kin group, she remains a member of her own paternal family, which, in turn, continues to be responsible for her.[10]

In a situation where a girl brings dishonor on her family by losing her virginity, it is incumbent on her paternal relatives—her father, brother, or uncle—to avenge the family's honor by severely punishing her. In conservative circles, punishing her means putting her to death. Public opinion permits crimes of honor, and the courts treat them with leniency.[11] Condemning this culturally bound, age-old state of affairs, the renowned Moroccan sociologist Fatima Mernissi spares no words:

> Like honor, virginity is the manifestation of a purely male preoccupation in societies where inequality, scarcity, and the degrading subjection of some people to others deprive the community as a whole of the only true human strength: self-confidence. The concepts of honor and virginity locate the prestige of a man between the legs of a woman. It is not by subjugating nature or by conquering mountains and rivers that a man secures his status, but by controlling the movements of women related to him by blood or by marriage, and by forbidding them any contact with male strangers.[12]

Sexual aggression against female children and the controversial customs surrounding female sexuality are openly discussed by the Egyptian author Nawāl al-Saʿdāwī, a physician by training and a staunch advocate of Arab women's rights. In her courageous social studies *Women and Sexuality (Al-Marʾa wa-al-jins*, 1971) and *The Hidden Face of Eve (Al-Wajh al-ʿārī lil-marʾa al-ʿarabiyya*, 1977), as well as in her imaginative works *Two Women in One (Imraʾatān fī imraʾa*, 1975), *God Dies by the Nile (Mawt al-rajul al-waḥīd ʿalā al-arḍ*, 1976) and *Woman at Point Zero (Imaʾra ʿinda nuqṭat al-ṣifr*, 1977), she exposes the systematic brutalization and exploitation of Arab women and depicts their desperate struggle for freedom and justice. Al-Saʿdāwī often highlights the class dimension of the oppression of women, as well as its religious and patriarchal basis. Not surprisingly, her dauntless criticism has brought her into conflict with the authorities: in 1972 she was dismissed from her post as Egypt's director-general of health education for writing *Women and Sexuality* and had to take refuge in Lebanon, and in 1981 she was arrested for alleged "crimes against the state" and spent several months in jail.

Another woman writer, Laylā Baʿlabakkī of Lebanon, attacks the tyrannical imperative of virginity in her novel *The Disfigured Gods (Al-Āliha al-mamsūkha*, 1960), where she sarcastically calls the hymen "the sacred membrane" (*al-jidār al-muqaddas*). In this work, the heroine is married to a university professor who, for all his education and progressive views, refuses to have sexual relations with her because she was not a virgin on her wedding night. Although all the characters in this work suffer from the "disfigured gods" of custom and tradition, it is the women who are affected the most. Baʿlabakkī's first novel, *I Am Alive (Anā aḥyā*, 1958), proclaims the need to overthrow all oppressive social norms. The heroine's passionate outcry "I am alive," as a declaration of self-awareness, rebellion, and independence, constitutes a revolutionary testimony in modern Arabic literature.

Several Arab male writers, such as Ṭāhā Ḥusayn in *The Tree of Misery (Shajarat al-bu's*, 1944), Yūsuf Idrīs in *The Sinners (Al-Ḥarām*, 1959), and Najīb Maḥfūẓ in *Love in the Rain (Al-Ḥubb taḥta al-maṭar*, 1973), express sympathy for women's plight and criticize the conventions that hold them in bondage. For Maḥfūẓ and Idrīs in particular, the "sins" of women—the loss of their honor and their inevitable downfall—are attributable to economic circumstances of poverty and deprivation. On the symbolic level, these authors frequently link the liberation of the nation to the liberation of women and, conversely, present the aggression committed against women as aggression against the nation. The first theme is portrayed, for example, in the novel *Love Story (Qiṣṣat Ḥubb*, 1956) by Idrīs, and the second in the novel *Miramar (Mīrāmār*, 1967) by Maḥfūẓ.

An explicit and unequivocal male acknowledgment of women's intrinsic value and indispensable contribution to society can be found in *My Life*, the autobiography of Aḥmad Amīn. Upon visiting several European countries—England, France, the Netherlands, and Italy—Amīn is struck by the differences he discovers between East and West, especially with regard to women:

> I returned to Egypt after having seen the sights of modern civilization and understood some of the secrets of the progress of these nations. In most of what I saw, my mind was occupied with comparing the East and the West. I would think of that when I saw machines, factories, and their progress or when I saw streets, houses, and their cleanliness, and people and their discipline, or when I saw the important place of woman in social life to the extent that most of the credit for modern civilization should go to her. For it is the woman who brings up the nation and it is she who accustoms her sons to discipline and good manners. It is the rain that puts order in nature and gives it a beautiful look, clothing the rocky mountains with trees and plants and fashioning gorgeous scenes. On the whole, the woman and rain are behind every aspect of civilization. If I say that the measure of the progress of the nations I saw is commensurate with the degree of the woman's progress and the amount of rainfall in various times, I would not be far from the truth.[13]

Amīn's tribute to women echoes the sentiments of his compatriots Rifāʿa Rāfiʿ al-Ṭahṭāwī (1801–73) in *The Refinement of Gold in the Summary of Paris (Takhlīṣ al-Ibrīz fī talkhīṣ Bārīs*, 1848) and Qāsim Amīn (1865–1908) *The Liberation of Women (Taḥrīr al-marʾa*, 1899) and *The New Woman (Al-Marʾa al-jadīda*, 1901). These pioneering works were landmarks on the road to the emancipation of Arab women.

The Closed Circle

In traditional Arab society, the excessive emphasis on female virginity has several ramifications. For one thing, girls are placed under severe constraints to safeguard their proper sexual conduct. For another, the mutual interest of parents and prospective husbands to ensure that the bride will be a virgin leads men to take very young wives and compels parents to marry off their daughters at an early age. Consequently, there is a predominance of young marriages.[14] Theoretically, marriage should answer the needs of all parties concerned, but in reality, being arranged and forced, it holds little promise for the girl: "In a culture which provides few other means of fulfillment for a woman, marriage is of paramount importance. But marriage is unlikely to be a joyous affair for the bride, first because she will have no part in choosing her future husband, and second because marriage becomes, for most women, a state of oppression and imprisonment as severe as that which they experienced as adolescents in their own homes."[15] It should be noted that in an extended family living together, the husband's female relatives, especially his mother, help to enforce the rules when the males are absent—a situation that underlines the impossibility of escape from captivity.[16]

The denial of ordinary human aspirations—freedom, self-expression, and recognition—to Arab women is at the core of their existential crisis. The French anthropologist Germaine Tillion declares: "The female veil became a symbol: a symbol of the enslavement of half the human race. . . . Widely plundered despite legislation, sometimes sold, often beaten, coerced into forced labor, murdered almost with impunity, the Mediterranean woman is among today's serfs."[17] A similar observation is made by the Lebanese feminist writer Evelyne Accad, who states that the majority of Arab women are "deprived of personal and social freedom, subjected successively to the will of their fathers, husbands and sons, economically dependent and intellectually circumscribed."[18]

Under such circumstances, it is exceedingly difficult for Arab women to realize their potential. A much-discussed topic in many critical writings is that they are defined not in terms of themselves and what they are, but in terms of their relationships to others and who they are: daughter of, sister of, wife of, mother of, mother-in-law of, and so forth.[19] The point at issue is the essence of self-image and personal identity. The Iraqi woman poet Nāzik al-Malā'ika (b. 1923) addresses this question in the poem "I Am" ("Anā"):

The night asks me who I am
  Its impenetrable black, its unquiet secret I am
  Its lull rebellious.
  I veil myself with silence
  Wrapping my heart with doubt
  Solemnly, I gaze
  While ages ask me
        who I am.

The wind asks me who I am
  Its bedeviled spirit I am
  Denied by Time, going nowhere
  I journey on and on
  Passing without a pause
  And when reaching an edge
  I think it may be the end
  Of suffering, but then:
        the void.

Time asks me who I am
  A giant enfolding centuries I am
  Later to give new births
  I have created the dim past
  From the bliss of unbound hope
  I push it back into its grave
  To make a new yesterday, its tomorrow
        is ice.

The self asks me who I am
  Battled, I stare into the dark
  Nothing brings me peace
  I ask, but the answer
  Remains hooded in mirage
  I keep thinking it is near
  Upon reaching it, it dissolves.[20]

This poem betrays the tormented spirit of a woman who cannot define her true identity. Her melancholy, stemming from a vision of centuries-long suffering and denial, brings to mind the tragedy of the pioneer woman writer Mayy Ziyāda (1886–1941), who fell into a severe depression that cut short her brilliant career.

In "Ice and Fire" ("Thalj wa-nār"), al-Malā'ika reflects on the strained relations between the sexes:

You may reproachfully provoke
   my guilt.
Would I retreat?
Would the sharp icicle of your plaque
   cut through my flames?
Would I yield,
   and not go mad?

No.
I should revolt.
I scream inside.

But
were I to trespass
darken the air
with some bitter phrase
   perhaps misplaced word
You would be offended
turn dry like sand
Rise
and quietly
disappear.

Don't ask me why
I am gagged.
Here, I remain
a bed of roses bent
   under your snow;
a puzzle of unanswerable questions
in some corner of your heart.
It is destiny's prescription:
Adam is the ice
Eve the fire.[21]

This poem reveals the consequences of the tragic polarity between men and women: estrangement, loneliness, bitterness, and frustration. The conflict in the male-female relationship is here insoluble and determined by fate.

In "Washing Off Disgrace" ("Ghaslan lil-ʿār"), al-Malā'ika takes up the issue of crimes of honor. With a deep sense of anguish and indignation, she exposes the injustice, savagery, and hypocrisy which characterize this custom. Here the perpetrator, having just murdered his sister to avenge the family's honor, goes to a tavern to celebrate the event with a prostitute and plenty of wine:

> "Mother!"
> A last gasp through her teeth and tears.
> The vociferous moan of the night.
> Blood gushed.
> Her body stabbed staggered.
>   swayed with crimson mud.
> "Mother!"
> Only heard by her man of blood.
> At dawn
> If her twenty years of forlorn hope should call
> the meadows and the roseate buds shall echo:
> She's gone
> washing off disgrace!
>
> Neighborhood women would gossip her story.
> The date palms would pass it on to the breeze.
> It would be heard in the squeaking of every
>   weather-beaten door,
> and the cobbled stones would whisper:
> She's gone
> washing off disgrace!
>
> Tomorrow
> wiping his dagger before his pals
> the butcher bellows,
> "Disgrace?
> A mere stain on the forehead,
> now washed."
> At the tavern,
> turning to the barman, he yells,
> "More wine
> and send me that lazy beauty of a nymphet
>   you got, the one with the mouth of myrrh."
> One woman would pour wine
>   to a jubilant man
> another paid
> washing off disgrace!
>
> Women of the neighborhood
> women of the village
> we knead dough with our tears
>   that they may be well-fed

we loosen our braids
  that they may be pleased
We peel the skin of our hands washing their clothes
  that they may be spotless white.
No smile
No joy
No rest
for the glitter of a dagger
                    of a father
          of a brother
     is all eyes.
Tomorrow who knows
what deserts may banish
you
washing off disgrace![22]

This compelling poem reveals the precarious existence of Arab women, whose bodies and minds are at all times controlled by the men to whom they are related.

In *Woman at Point Zero*, a fact-based novel by Nawal al-Saʿdāwī, the heroine, Firdaws, is an orphan married off by her uncle to a miserly old man who habitually abuses her. She runs away from him, only to fall into the hands of a café owner who uses her as a servant by day and as a sexual commodity by night. She again runs away and, with no one to turn to, ends up a prostitute—but her own master:

> How many were the years of my life that went by before my body and my self became really mine, to do with them as I wished? How many were the years of my life that were lost before I tore my body and my self away from the people who held me in their grasp since the very first day? Now I could decide on the food I wanted to eat, the house I preferred to live in, refuse the man for whom I felt an aversion no matter what the reason, and choose the man I wished to have, even if it was only because he was clean and well manicured.[23]

For Firdaws, then, independence is worth the risk of living on the street and being exposed to crime as well as to shame. She prefers to exist on the fringes of society as a free person rather than remain in society as a helpless and abused slave. Her freedom, however, is short-lived; before long, she is forced to kill a pimp in self-defense and is condemned to death. Stubbornly, she welcomes death—the price society exacts for her rebellion—as the only freedom available to her.[24]

In the novel *The Story of Zahra* (*Ḥikāyat Zahra*, 1980) by the Lebanese fiction writer Ḥanān al-Shaykh, Zahra is a troubled woman haunted by memories of abuse in her early childhood and rape and seduction in her adult years. After a failed marriage and several bouts of mental illness, she seeks her redemption in a relationship with a sniper in the Lebanese civil war. In the midst of chaos reigning around her, she seems to find sexual fulfillment. However, when she tells the sniper that she is pregnant, he kills her. The novel demonstrates that even in a state of anarchy marked by the collapse of accepted norms, values, and symbols, the rules of conduct, insofar as they relate to women, still apply. While the freedom fighters use the war to revolt against authority and tradition, displaying an attitude of indifference and permissiveness, the patriarchal system that oppresses women is still at work. The heroine is tempted to believe that the liberation sought by the freedom fighters will be extended to her, too. In fact, instead of destroying the old sexual code, these men reinforce it and bring women to the brink of self-annihilation.[25]

Finally, the Palestinian poet Fadwā Ṭūqān (b. 1917), in her poem "Siege" ("Ḥiṣār"), depicts the painful experience of physical and psychological entrapment:

> When all sorrows are released at night,
> and when our true face is uncovered,
> our face sinks into the bottom of the sorrows,
> and sleep from our eyes is stolen.
> The cracked world in us appears
> like a gloomy desert on our forehead
> where fate's hand has drawn our misery.
> Fate played his hand, and there was no defence.
>
> Oh heart, you suffer hell and fate.
> You are a broken boat with a torn sail
> struggling with the wind; you miss the port.
> Every evening's battle in our depths
> removes the mask from our eyes,
> and frees our sorrows from captivity.
> When will a hand be stretched out
> to save the chained and drowned face
> from the net of fate and captivity?[26]

The poem expresses the direct connection which Fadwā Ṭūqān perceives between her personal tribulations and preordained fate.

Breaking through Barriers

Since the 1950s, when almost every Arab country in the Middle East and North Africa gained its independence from foreign or colonial rule, one of the proclaimed goals in every national charter was the improvement of women's status. To achieve this, certain laws were passed to adjust the inequality between men's rights and women's rights, and certain steps were taken to ensure that both men and women would benefit equally from government reforms in education, health care, and welfare.[27]

Although few of the social, economic, and political imbalances between Arab men and women were rectified, and although many of the promises were not fulfilled, some progress is clearly evident. The traditional pattern of women at home and men in the workplace is slowly eroding, mainly because of necessity. Women recognize the advantage in the necessity of obtaining more income for the family and insist on their right to work outside the home. The spread of free compulsory public education has benefited women greatly. Not only has it liberated them from the fetters of ignorance and illiteracy, but it has also opened the door to new employment opportunities. In many Arab countries today, women have access to male-dominated occupations, serving as journalists and editors for newspapers and magazines, as physicians and lawyers, and as high civil servants. Modernization has also had a dramatic effect on women's liberation by changing the structure of their everyday lives with respect to veiling, segregation, and seclusion. Educated women can venture into public places on their own and meet their male counterparts in different settings: in school, on the street, and on the job. Thus members of both sexes get a chance to communicate with each other and foster new relations.

Women in the Arab world, particularly the social elite and those who live in major urban centers, are breaking through barriers of custom and convention. While this trend has not yet engulfed the rural areas and the lower classes, it has definitely laid the foundations on which more is expected to come. Allowed to vote, study, choose professions, and assume public roles, this hard-won freedom has brought a growing number of women to a closer realization of their potential. Nevertheless, the influence of age-old values and traditions and of patriarchal and religious institutions is still pervasive in contemporary Arab society. Yet despite the various obstacles they face, women continue to emerge from the isolated world in which they have been kept, seeking self-expression, recognition, and fulfillment. The process of emancipation, though slow, is irreversible, and the many leading men supporting it emphasize its significance in the wider context of the quest for social change and national rebirth.

"The strongest principle of growth lies in human choice" runs a dictum by the English woman writer George Eliot. The majority of women in the Arab world are still limited in their choices solely because of their gender. Thus for these women fate is equated with gender: this biological factor plays a decisive role in shaping their life experiences and in determining the pattern of their existence.

Nawāl al-Saʿdāwī
She Is Not a Virgin

Nawāl al-Saʿdāwī was born in 1931 in the village of Kafr Ṭaḥla on the bank of the Nile. She studied medicine at Cairo University, graduating in 1955. Throughout the next decade, she worked as a physician in both the countryside and the city. In 1966, she received a degree in public health from Columbia University in New York. In 1967, she became Egypt's director-general of health education, a post from which she was dismissed in 1972 for writing *Women and Sexuality (Al-Mar'a wa-al-jins*, 1971). Her activities on behalf of Arab women's liberation landed her in jail in 1981, when Anwar Sadat was president of Egypt. She founded the Arab Women's Solidarity Association in Cairo in 1982 and served as its president until 1991, when the organization was shut down by the authorities because of its publicized opposition to the Gulf War.

Al-Saʿdāwī is a leading feminist writer. She uses the firsthand material she gathered as a physician to expose the oppression of women in Arab society. Her style is direct and realistic. A prolific author, she has published a large number of books, both fiction (novels, short stories, and plays) and nonfiction (social studies and memoirs). Many of her works have been translated into various European languages.

"She Is Not a Virgin" ("Laysat ʿadhrāʾ") appears in the collection *A Little Tenderness (Ḥanān qalīl*, 1962). The story revolves around an impending crime of honor—the common fate of a girl who loses her virginity before marriage. The harsh lot of women is shown in the double victimization of the girl: first through rape, then almost through ritual murder—both at the hands of her uncle.

Hājj Badawī locked the door of his shop and brushed the dust off his hand. He then reached into his pocket for a clove, which he placed under the molar that had been hurting for the past three days. Unlike his habit, he did not bring out snuff to smell and sneeze, for he was worried and despondent. He had no desire for the snuff, or for anything else.

Along the way he passed Bayyūmī's café. Usually he sat there at night with Ḥājj Muḥammad, smoking the water pipe, chatting, and watching Sitt Ḥamdiyya, who sat behind slightly open shutters, wearing a red silk scarf perched somewhat askew on her head, so that it clung to her right brow and exposed the left brow as it framed her sad, honey-colored eyes. But today Ḥājj Badawī could not stop at the café, nor even turn his face toward it. He passed it at a distance, pressing hard on his turban to hide his forehead. He wanted neither to see anyone nor to be seen himself. He had heard enough from people, who had had nothing to do but gossip for the past three days about him and his honor. His conduct had been the subject of general discussion since the night of the scandal. Had it not been for the financial necessity to conduct his business, which was selling spices such as cloves and ginger—had it not been for that, he would have remained at home and never ventured forth.

Ḥājj Badawī arrived at his house gasping for air—he was unaccustomed to such rapid walking. He took out the key, opened the door, and went into the bedroom. There he removed his clothing listlessly and got into bed. As soon as his head touched the pillow, he heard his wife's soft snoring rise with her breathing. He turned toward her, but she seemed unconscious, like a dead person, fast asleep. He began to contemplate her wrinkled skin and dry lips. Fuming and smacking his lips in contempt, he turned his back toward her and covered his head with the blanket in order to sleep. But an image flashed through his mind. It was Saʿdiyya in wedding clothes and a white crown, sitting in the middle of a platform decorated with plants and flowers. The bridegroom, dressed in a dark blue suit, moved among the guests, who were gazing at each other and gulping large quantities of sherbet. The grand reception pavilion had been erected, and the microphone transmitted the songs, the shrieks of joy, and the rhythm of the dance and the cymbals. The people of al-Sayyida Zaynab district, who usually remained awake after the evening prayer, looked out from their windows at this unusual wedding and recounted the story of the bride and bridegroom a hundred times.

Ḥājj Badawī suddenly turned his face toward his wife. His narrow eyes glittered like the eyes of a hawk when he observed the sharp, protruding bones of her jaw. As far back as he could remember, her face had never looked any different. How often—in fact, every night since his wedding—had he invoked evil on Umm Yūsuf the matchmaker, and cursed her and her forefathers, and spat on her and on them. Ten years had passed, and every night he rained down curses on the matchmaker's head whenever he saw his wife's face.

Saʿdiyya was a ten-year-old girl, running and playing. Sometimes she would jump and he would see her plump legs and thighs. He did not know why he used to stare at her. Whenever he drew her to the balcony and seated her by his side and ran his fingers over her legs, feeling her soft skin, a voice inside him seemed to cry out: "Shame, Ḥājj Badawī! You're her uncle! You've been raising her since her father died. . . . Shame, man! You, who made the pilgrimage to the House of God!"

But he could not resist this persistent desire whenever he saw her jump. There was such a difference between her soft legs and his wife's thin, dry ones.

Sometimes, when he lost control over his desire, he would press her to his chest and stroke her soft, fresh skin with his thick mustache. He would not release her until the odor of tobacco on his breath choked her and she screamed or bit his finger.

On one occasion, there was no one in the house except Saʿdiyya. He was stretched out on the bed smoking noisily from the water pipe and watching her play as usual, when he was seized by an overwhelming desire, as though the blood were boiling in his veins, which he could not resist. He got up and carried her off, and placed her on the bed. . . . The recollection made Ḥājj Badawī sweat all over, and he pushed the blanket away. He remembered his messy appearance when he had put on his clothes, replaced the turban, and left the house in a hurry to go to the market. When he returned, he found that she had stopped crying. And when he gave her a bag of candy, she smiled sweetly and forgot everything—and he felt relieved. She did not understand anything, so she would not tell her mother.

Ḥājj Badawī's sweat dried, and he felt cold. He pulled the blanket to cover himself, baring, as he did so, his wife's thin legs. He glanced at her angrily. He had hated his wife from the first night, but even more so after the incident with Saʿdiyya. He felt remorse. He began to run away from the house to the café to smoke the water pipe and chat with Ḥājj Muḥammad. At the same time, he stared at the legs of the women who crossed the street in front of him.

Sitt Ḥamdiyya—that fat widow who lived opposite the café—rescued him from his perdition. When he sat at the café, he could see her watching with one eye through the aperture of the window. He could also see her fat white hands holding the slats of the shutters. Sitt Ḥamdiyya helped him to become acquainted with her, and to visit her. He replaced his "worthless" wife with her, and forgot Saʿdiyya with her.

No longer did the sight of Saʿdiyya's legs and thighs arouse him when she jumped. Even after she had grown up and filled out and developed a conspicuous bosom, he felt nothing toward her—were it not for that painful incident for which he was responsible, and which came to mind each time he thought of marrying her off. He had chosen Ḥusayn Effendi to be her bridegroom because he thought he was a good man. His late father had been a stupid man, and Ḥusayn Effendi could not have inherited his mother's intelligence because he had failed in the taʿmiyya business.[28] His eyesight was weak and he was unfit for any work except the menial job that one of his relatives had mediated for him.

Ḥājj Badawī trembled in his bed when he remembered the voice of Ḥusayn Effendi—that stupid good man, as he had thought. How loudly and harshly he had screamed, and insulted his dignity, and spat on his honor, and insisted on divorce by repudiation before sunrise. He also insisted on getting back his bride payment and all his presents, and demanded that Ḥājj Badawī should waive the balance and the expenses, and put an end to the matter in private—or else he would make him a laughingstock throughout the neighborhood.

Ḥājj Badawī felt a fire erupting in his body. He kicked the blanket away from him and threw it on his wife's inert body, then got up and started pacing up and down the room.

He had been humiliated and could not show his face in the neighborhood, nor could he sit at the café or even see Sitt Ḥamdiyya. He was now, in the eyes of all the people, a man without honor—until he cleansed his honor. And among these people, a man could cleanse his honor only with blood.

The blood rushed to his face. Saʿdiyya was sleeping now in her room and only an unlocked door separated him from her.

He imagined he was again the Ḥājj Badawī who walked with his chin up, the Ḥājj Badawī who sat at the café with Ḥājj Muḥammad, smoking from the water pipe and chatting, the Ḥājj Badawī whom everyone greeted. And Sitt Ḥamdiyya . . . oh, he would be able to go to her again, and she would embrace him warmly. He had been deprived of all this for three whole days!

He placed the kaffiyyah on his head and put his folding knife in his pocket. Then he tiptoed away and slowly pushed Saʿdiyya's door.

The room was pitch dark, and he had to grope his way to her bed. His whole body was trembling and his breaths followed rapidly one on the other. He would have fled from the room, had Sitt Ḥamdiyya not appeared to him lying on the bed with her arms outstretched to embrace him. Infused with fervor, he took the knife from his pocket and reached for the bed, searching for Saʿdiyya's neck, but he could find nothing. He used both his hands to search, but the darkness hindered his efforts. He turned on the light and hurried to the bed, only to discover it was empty. He looked under the bed and in the wardrobe and behind the clothes rack, but Saʿdiyya was nowhere to be found.

He returned to his room, his body drenched with perspiration, and crept into bed beside his wife. Saʿdiyya had fled before he could kill her, before he could prove to the neighborhood that he was a man who cleansed his honor with blood. He should have killed her right away, the first night. Now they would all say he was a coward. He would never again be able to sit at the café. He would never again be able to hold up his head among the people. He would never again enjoy the embrace of the passionate Sitt Ḥamdiyya. His eyes bulged in anger and confusion. The knife was still in his hand, behind his wife, who lay unconscious, as though she were dead.

He did not know why he began to stare at her familiar thin neck as it rose and fell with her snoring. The knife trembled in his hand, and he imagined that he raised his hand and thrust the knife into her neck and her blood exploded in his face and mingled with his sweat. But he did no such thing. With the knife still in his hand, he turned over, his back toward his wife. When he closed his eyes and dozed off, the image of

Saʿdiyya appeared before him. A little girl, ten years of age, carrying the bundle of her clothes and walking in the streets without a place of refuge. . . . He opened his eyes and felt something as hot as blood flowing down his face. Then he heard the sound of his sobbing rising above the sound of his breathing.

Comments

This story portrays the sad reality of sex relations in Arab society. It highlights the heavy chains of custom and tradition, which put both men and women in impossible situations of crisis and conflict. Ḥājj Badawī is a sexually frustrated man. He has been tricked into marrying a woman whom he intensely hates, for she is dull and lifeless and sleeps by his side like a corpse. He can find neither physical nor emotional satisfaction in her. Trapped in a situation brought upon him by the custom of arranged marriage, he is bound to seek solace outside his marriage.

Ḥājj Badawī's sexual frustration drives him to commit a terrible crime. Saʿdiyya is a ten-year-old girl who is entrusted to him as her uncle and adoptive father. In the absence of any other relief, he does not control his urges and rapes her on one occasion. After the rape, he repents; however, he is now caught in the iron grip of yet another custom governing the sexual code in traditional Arab society: protecting the family's honor. The high value attached to virginity requires that he continue with his criminal conduct and wash the shame—which *he* has brought on himself—with blood, by killing Saʿdiyya.

Ḥājj Badawī is a religious man, and his shameful transgression bothers him. He therefore puts off his problem for as long as he can. He works hard in his little shop, then spends his time with friends in the local café. He seems to have a good social standing, enhanced by having made the pilgrimage to Mecca. His life improves dramatically when he meets a passionate widow, Sitt Ḥamdiyya, who welcomes him into her arms. By now, he is oblivious to the time bomb ticking in the body of his niece Saʿdiyya, who has blossomed into a beautiful woman. In an attempt to cover up the wrong that he has committed, he decides to marry her off to Ḥusayn Effendi, a man who is mentally retarded and almost blind. Ḥājj Badawī hopes that because of these deficiencies, the groom will not notice that his bride is not a virgin, and thus his old crime will be laid to rest.

With mockery and derision, Nawāl al-Saʿdawi exposes the male obsession with female virginity in traditional Arab society. The absurdity of the situation is demonstrated by the fact that even a half-witted, half-blind man like Ḥusayn Effendi can tell the difference between a virgin and a nonvirgin on the wedding night. He can make demands for restitution, even though he is marrying well above his station and getting a pretty girl like Saʿdiyya for a wife. The hypocrisy of the community is accentuated by the fact that Ḥājj Badawī is ostracized by his neighbors not for his potential role in the scandal or for his sinful relationship with Sitt Ḥamdiyya, but rather for the perceived loss of his honor, which he has inflicted on himself in the first place by raping Saʿdiyya. Regardless of the truth, public opinion now demands that Ḥājj Badawī should cleanse his honor with Saʿdiyya's blood. Thus the sexual code of traditional Arab society lays the blame on the innocent victim—the woman—and makes the victim pay for the crime.

Al-Saʿdawī portrays a closed circle of female brutalization. Although Ḥājj Badawī is not a violent man—there is no evidence in the story that he physically abuses his wife—he must satisfy the tyrannical demand imposed on him by a society in bondage to ancient customs, or else he will have no life. Indirectly, Ḥājj Badawī is also a victim of the oppressive value system of his community. He inevitably follows the prescribed course of action. Ironically, while Saʿdiyya's flight saves him from committing a second crime—murder—at the same time it seals his fate of living in shame for the rest of his life.[29]

Samīra ʿAzzām
Fate

Samīra ʿAzzām (1927–67) was born in Acre, Palestine. Early in her career, she worked as a schoolteacher and published poems and articles in the newspaper *Filasṭīn*. In 1948 she fled to Beirut and then moved to Baghdad, where she worked in broadcasting and journalism. Several years later, she returned to Beirut and became editor-in-chief at Franklin House, a company for translation and publishing. A highly regarded literary figure, she was deeply involved in community affairs and took an active part in Lebanese and Palestinian cultural life.

ʿAzzām was a short-story writer. Her stories deal mainly with the Palestinian experience in exile and the oppression of the weak and defenseless in Arab society: women, children, and the poor. She wrote in a realistic mode, and her stories are carefully crafted and meticulously styled. Her literary output includes five volumes of short stories: *Little Things (Ashyāʾ ṣaghīra*, 1954), *The Big Shadow (Al-Ẓill al-kabīr*, 1956), *And Other Stories (Wa-Qiṣaṣ ukhrā*, 1960), *Time and Humanity (Al-Sāʿa wa-al-insān*, 1963), and *The Festival from the Western Window (Al-ʿĪd min al-nāfidha al-gharbiyya*, published posthumously in 1971).

"Fate" ("Naṣīb")[30] appears in the collection *The Big Shadow*. The story focuses on the custom of arranged marriage, which is perceived by traditional Arab women as the ultimate expression of their inability to decide their own fate.

"Take her! My authority over her ends here and now!"

Her father had not actually said anything of the sort when handing her over to her bridegroom at the church door, yet that was the feeling she had as she was taking the hand stretched out toward her, and as she started to make her way through the assembled congregation who strewed basketfuls of lilies at their feet.

She did not look up. Yet she felt the intensity of the atmosphere around her; she felt that a mass of humanity had come to watch her, to supply themselves with material for conversation which would last for a good few days.

So it was all real. . . . And there she was coming, of her own accord, to witness before God, before the assembled congregation, and before the man standing on her left that she would be a faithful wife, as Sarah was to Abraham.

Did she really want all that?

Oh, how confused she was, wavering between saying "yes" or "no," and how feeble she felt in the face of that strange power which her mother's female friends agreed to call "Fate." Earlier, as a schoolgirl, she had consistently refused to recognize the existence of this reactionary word in her vocabulary, a word which had filled her mother's and her grandmother's minds before her time. But she did not subscribe to this school of believers in "Fate," for "Fate" is the drug of those whose will is broken, and she was *not* one of them.

But was it really within her power to rebel against "Fate" which had led her to where she was now without any significant resistance from her, and without the least attempt on her part to prove herself or to assert her right to choose? Still, what was stranger, in a way, was that she had not said "no."

For that matter, why had she not said "no"?

To her mind, saying "yes" was a positive act of will suffused with a spirit of acceptance, carrying with it the savor of satisfaction and bearing the aroma of desire, but her "yes" did not hold any of this positive feeling. It was just a "yes" and no more.

And the story did not begin long ago.

About four months ago, this man's mother—or let's say "Fate"—had come knocking at her door. She had not met this woman before, but she instinctively understood the significance of a strange woman calling on a household with a young girl in it. Her mother had understood as much, so she had called her to beg her to put on her new gray dress.

She had felt contemptuous of her mother for asking her to do this, and still more contemptuous of this woman for wanting to make out the color of her flesh under the simple linen dress she was wearing.

The very same night the woman had returned, bringing her son with her. The girl had rebelled and had refused to come out to welcome them; though she later gave in after her parents had insisted. She had sat down without speaking, and had spoken reluctantly only when she felt obliged to answer the questions that the man—trying to be friendly—addressed to her. She was sure she would not win his approval; she must have seemed rather pathetic in his eyes. This infuriated her all the more, for she had always liked people with whom she could give full rein to her personality; yet with this man she did not feel that she could be herself, even though he tried to sweet-talk her. As the visitors stood up to leave, she had rushed to her room and so avoided her mother's reproaches.

A few days later, the same woman returned to visit them.

The woman's visit infuriated the girl all over again. For one thing, she was not in a hurry to get married; and, for another, she saw herself as a modern woman who would never be given in marriage in the same way that her mother and her father's sisters had been. What's more, she did not feel at ease with people like this; people who behaved in an affected way, and from whom she shrank so that either her personality dwindled to nothing or she no longer cared to assert it.

She had not come into the room to greet the woman, but through the door, which was ajar, she had heard the woman's voice as she questioned her mother about her.

The feeling of tension returned to her; and she had run off to see her nearest girlfriend. On her return, she had found her mother in a state of great eagerness, with her mouth agape and her arms outstretched: "A bridegroom, my daughter! A bridegroom! What a wonderful chance to make you the envy of other girls!"

But who had told her mother that she wanted a bridegroom who would make her the envy of other girls? Who had told her that she would accept an engagement in this fashion? Who had told her . . . ?

"Do you refuse?"

"Yes!"

So saying, she walked out, leaving her mother in a fit of rage.

In the evening the man had come to call.

Why did she keep calling him a "man"? Was it because he deserved this term? Sure, he was a man in years, a man in his demeanor, a man in his way of thinking, and he was all too proud of all this for her liking.

And he asked for her hand.

She had lived in turmoil for a month, and at first she had stuck to her "no," but later she started to have second thoughts.

Her father had not tried to cajole her; all he had done was to expound the man's merits and commend him to her as a husband. Although her mother had tried to play a neutral role, her woman's instincts had got the better of her. She was a woman and so she could not stop herself from having a quiet word with her daughter at every opportunity she could find.

But what about herself?

In the face of insistence from her mother, her female relatives, and the neighbors, she found herself abandoning her determination and entertaining thoughts which deviated from her previous firmly held ideas.

She might as well take this man lock, stock, and barrel. He had an acceptable appearance—that was obvious; he was successful in his business—his shop in the town center testified to that, and so did the way he looked and the evidence supplied by anyone who volunteered to talk about him. He had a strong personality—yes, otherwise he would not have been a successful businessman. He was not uneducated, or rather life had educated him more than his formal schooling had—and experience is more effective in life than formal education, as men successful in the affairs of the world testify. There were certain things in his character she had not liked: vanity, though not to the extent of corruption; a taste for showiness that was alien to her own character—she was, for example, scornful of the fact that his watch had a gold bracelet, and she intensely disliked the way he had stuck a tiepin in his tie. Apart from this, she had known nothing about him.

He had told her that he was fond of reading and listening to music, but she was not inclined to believe him, for when she asked him who his favorite singer was he had hesitated a little before memory came to the rescue and provided him with an answer. There was no reason why he should not have a collection of books and records, but does everybody who has books and records necessarily read and listen to music?

Also, she had not been able to understand why whenever she thought of him, her thoughts immediately turned to her cousin. He was her own age, or slightly younger. It was not that she longed to get married to him, as he still had a few years at school and his future was hazy and uncertain.

But she was constantly impressed by the simplicity of his character and its openness, and by his childlike enthusiasms, for if he came across a new record, he would come running with it to her house and immediately put it on the turntable and start dancing, bounding with energy and life.

In contrast, this man could never be simple or natural, for he epitomized the character of a businessman in a manner not devoid of affectation. He would certainly have laughed if she had shown him her attempts at painting in watercolors, or he might have played the role of the "well-informed" person and tried to criticize her painting, puffing away at his cigarette all the while.

But these were trivial things that she might be able to get him to give up, or she might get used to them once she knew him better. Besides, what good would it have done her to insist on refusing him? Did she have any choice?

She was not in love with any man. If she were—and oh, how she wished she were—it would have been easy for her to decide the direction of her life; but she did not have this luxury. Her life was devoid of excitement. It had in it those moments of happiness and excitement that young women experience: compliments from young men, or an affection such as the one she shared with her cousin.

But none of these people would have qualified as a husband; even if any of them wanted her, she had no means of knowing that they did.

Opportunities for love might still have been within her grasp, if only she had known how to change her pattern of life just a little. And yet—had the creation of opportunities really been within her grasp? Probably not!

Her relationship with other people had been limited and superficial. Her father continued to have an old-fashioned outlook on life, and did not believe that his daughter could have a better life than the one he gave her. It was sufficient for her to eat, dress up, and visit and entertain the few family friends and relatives, or to die of boredom—if she wanted to—watching her father play backgammon with one of his ancient friends.

Her mother had always had the same outlook on life and the same standards. Now in her fifties, all that concerned her was the chance to be the one to choose a husband for her daughter—a husband to whom she could entrust her. Her first aim was that he should be well-off, for to her money meant a comfortable life and a social status which must be secured.

But she herself would have liked a somewhat different husband: one who was just a little older than she, who knew a lot of romantic poetry by heart, who liked her paintings, and was willing to wear an apron round his waist and help her make an orange cake or a potato omelette, and to kiss her once every ten minutes. This was how she pictured "her man," and she had not yet come across someone who could be all these things, apart from her cousin.

If only she had an older brother, opportunities for meeting young men would have been within her reach; but her brother was a lot younger than she. So, as things were, she had no choice. Like every Oriental woman, she could not exercise her will, for her whole being was paralyzed.

She had remained in turmoil. What should her answer be? Should she refuse? But would not her refusal be considered rash? The man had merits; nor could she deny that the reason for the psychological gap between them was a simple one: she did not know him well enough. Was it not possible that he might cast off these outward trappings once they became better acquainted with each other? Could she not turn him into a simple person like herself?

Why had he chosen her of all girls?

Often the question came into her mind and impressed itself upon her; she had longed with all her heart to find the answer to it, but the opportunity never came. When she asked her father: "Haven't you asked him?" he looked at her and replied: "How absurd! How could I ever ask him a question like that? He took a fancy to you, so he asked for your hand. What more do you want? Daughter, don't behave like the heroine of a romantic novel."

Indeed, why had he chosen her? Was it because of her beauty? Her share of beauty was modest: average figure and looks; there was nothing stunning about her; many girls were more beautiful than she.

When she had asked him this question after their engagement, he smiled in a knowing way and said: "Do you want the truth? I got tired of women, so I said to myself: I'll choose my wife in a traditional way. I'm chary of goods that are laid out for sale."

Selfish! Selfish! He wanted to bind what for her was a beginning to what for him was the beginning of the end, for in his view the two beginnings were one. He had got tired of women! But she had not had the chance to get tired of anything yet. What had she done to deserve all this? She had accepted him out of weariness with her own indecision, and after her mother had succeeded in making her feel that she would regret it if she refused him. Her father left her to think things over, but she had not found within herself anything that could be effective in pronouncing the final word in such a situation.

Yes, she had accepted him as a bird in the hand. The other ten in the bush were nothing but a gamble. So said her mother and many of her friends who were still without husbands. And so she, too, had believed, or thought she had believed, when she said: "Yes, I accept."

She was engaged to him for four months, during which time she tried, in the light of her "yes," to love him, understand him, bring him closer to her, to her way of thinking, but she could not claim to have succeeded. He remained in her eyes the man who had sent his mother to select a wife for him, and it was sheer coincidence that she had been selected. What if, when his mother had called, she had been out, or his mother had taken it into her head to visit the neighbors first? In her eyes, he remained the man who viewed life from a different perspective, a man with a mentality that mocked her dreams.

One time she had gone to purchase kitchen utensils for her home; she had shown them to him, saying jokingly: "This will be my little world in your home!" He said: "Do you think that your husband is just a grade-nine civil servant who'll let you spend your life among the pots and pans? No, my little one! I wouldn't like my wife to have hands that smell like a maid's." And she had once asked him: "Will you help me dry the dishes when I've washed them?" He said, laughingly: "That is if I let you wash the dishes."

He had annoyed her with his many presents of perfume and silk, so she said to him: "Could you not love me without flooding me with all this?" He replied: "Do you want me to recite reams of love poetry for you?"

These trivia, along with other things he had done which surprised her, had accumulated and deepened the gulf which she felt existed between them. Surely they should not be of any great consequence to her, yet they aggravated her—but then she tried to reassure herself and laugh at such small details, which could not possibly stand in the way of a happy marriage.

And now, there she was!

Why should these ideas rage in her mind now? At this very moment when she was actually getting married? Why didn't they leave her alone to be wed to this man in peace? She had not been apprehensive or afraid; on the contrary, when saying "Yes, I accept this man," she had acted as a firm believer in the realities of life. She had wondered whether success in adapting to each other might not be counted as a victory for the mind of the modern young woman.

Who could claim at that very moment that she had failed? If she had lost the first round . . . then she still had the second and third rounds, and her entire life ahead of her. But how could she be sure of success? Could it not go the opposite way and end up with him indoctrinating her with his ideas?

There he was, smiling, not at all embarrassed by the people he had invited to come and watch him; her father was smiling too; even her mother's tears were smiling; and everyone was so happy for her.

She felt tension and anger play havoc with her nerves. She had grown tired of standing and wished that the four priests who were conducting her wedding ceremony, and raising their voices in competition with one another, would finish the whole affair quickly. What if she were to say just one word to spoil their enthusiasm?

"Do you take So-and-so to be your wedded husband?"

"No!"

What a dramatic ending she could put to this story by uttering a single word!

"No!"

She would triumph; and so would her old ideas. She would live for some time drugged by her dreams of what might happen, thus annoying this man who had sent his mother to select a wife for him; and she would watch the utter astonishment on the faces of the congregation.

"No, I don't!"

Stupid! stupid! Who was forcing her to do this, making her feel angry enough to say "I don't want him" in the middle of her wedding? Was the whole affair imposed upon her by force? No!

But would not her "No! I don't want to" express all that used to go through her mind before she became dull-witted, preferring easy and secure ends?

If only she could let go of her senses for a moment and say it. Everything, yes, everything would come to an end.

"I don't want to! I don't want to!"

Overwhelmed by her confusion, tiredness, and nervousness, she began repeating it, saying it aloud, shouting it. But the cry was blotted out. No one heard her, not the priests, not the congregation, not even this man standing next to her. It was lost in the reverberations of a sound that engulfed the church, the voices of all those present sealing her marriage with the wedding hymn: "With glory and dignity he wed her!"

Comments

Given the happy topic of marriage, this is a sad story. It is fairly clear from the first encounter between the girl and the man that the girl is being maneuvered into giving up everything she has hoped for in a husband. She will not experience romance with him; he will not be a soulmate for her; he will not allow her to develop or express her personality. Instead, he will shower her with material comforts and insist that she delegate the household chores to a maid—not for her own sake but for the sake of his prestige and social standing. With her deep-seated feminine intuition, she recognizes that he will be the exclusive owner of her future and that she will dangle miserably, attached to him like his tie, pinned to adorn his world.

In a traditional society that offers few legitimate means of self-fulfillment for a woman outside marriage, the choice of a suitable husband becomes all-important. However, the custom of arranged marriage excludes the bride from taking any real part in this critical process. The story illustrates the psychological pressure that accompanies the custom. Although in this case the girl is not physically coerced into giving her consent, as, for example, in "The Assassination of Light at the River's Flow" by the Saudi woman writer Khayriyya al-Saqqāf,[31] she is subjected to constant persuasion: her father sings the man's praises, and her mother and the other females of her circle nag her with their concern that she will rue the day she refused the proposal. Above all, they allude to the presence of that inescapable and relentless power—fate.

It is interesting to note that the story is set in a Christian family. This fact indicates that, with regard to certain customs, there is practically no difference between Muslim Arabs and Christian Arabs, and that similar norms apply to women in both groups. In particular, male domination and the polarization of the sexes pervade all sectors of traditional Arab society.

The girl in the story comes from a middle-class family. She is well educated, likes poetry and music, and is idealistic and romantic. She has a mind of her own and is capable of analyzing her situation soberly. Her heart tells her that this suitor is not suitable for her. But her mind tells her that she has no alternative. For one thing, opportunities for meeting other men are not within her reach. For another, she cannot exercise her will, even though she has some freedom of self-expression, because the norms and mores of her society deny her the power to act. She therefore tries to look for a silver lining in her situation, reassuring herself that, despite the overwhelming differences between her and her prospective husband, he may change or they may adapt to each other eventually.

As for the groom, he seems to be ill-matched for the girl. His answer as to why he has chosen her is very revealing. He has tired of women who are available to him as "goods laid out for sale" and has decided to choose his wife in the traditional way. In his view, women are either cheap sexual objects or pure, virtuous wives. The sexual commodity is for him to find by himself, and the virtuous wife is for his mother to find for him. This attitude suggests that he sees liberated women as fallen and degraded, unworthy of being taken seriously, and he, as an experienced man, can choose those easily enough. But when it comes to a woman of importance—his wife and the future bearer of his children—he is not mature enough to choose and must turn to his mother.[32]

The girl understands the gravity of his answer. She intuitively dwells on whether he deserves the title of "man." As she stands at the wedding ceremony, all the negative impressions that she has gathered of him whirl around in her head. When the priest asks her whether she takes this man to be her husband, she finally speaks her mind and shouts "No!" But her answer is drowned in the cheering and singing of the guests, who can conceive of only one response. Her spontaneous attempt to reassert herself is defeated. She is forced by her congregation to accept her lot quietly and consider herself lucky. Belatedly, she recognizes what she previously tried to deny: a woman's fate is sealed with her marriage, because her husband holds the reins of her happiness.

It is worth mentioning that in a significant number of imaginative works by women writers, the male protagonist is presented in a distinctly negative light. This is illustrated in the present story as well as in those by Nawāl al-Saʿdāwī, Ghāda al-Sammān, Ulfat al-Idilbī, and Laylā Bin Māmī included in this book. In these stories, the main male characters are, at least from the viewpoint of the female characters, depicted as hostile, selfish, hypocritical, and vain. The heroines make severe accusations against the men who rule their lives and rob them of their self-esteem. The male protagonist appears not as kind or affectionate but rather as a slave to his lust, pride, and greed. He is capable of exploiting, raping, and even murdering a woman for the sake of his ego and honor. Above all, he has no understanding whatsoever of a woman's soul, and his thoughts revolve primarily around ensuring his comfort and gratifying his desires.[33]

Arab women writers display a variety of styles in their creative work. Their writings express keen sensitivity, profound emotion, and intense awareness of a woman's vulnerable existence. The courage to speak out, however, does not go unpunished. Many are condemned for their liberal views: they are prosecuted by the courts (Laylā Baʿlabakkī), driven out of their country (Nawāl al-Saʿdāwī), and boycotted by readers and critics alike because they dare to expose what is considered sacred and taboo in traditional Arab society.[34]

6

CLASS AND CAPITAL

The Trap of Poverty and Tyranny

Man is only man by his money.
—Nuʿmān Ibn Mundhir[1]

Social Justice in Islam

The material aspect of people's day-to-day existence has a great influence on the course of their lives. Possessing adequate resources enables people to realize their potential by concentrating their energies on the pursuit of education, career, creative leisure, and other forms of social, cultural, and spiritual attainment. Exceptionally endowed individuals can rise above circumstances, but the life stories of most people are closely tied to their economic condition. The availability of the basic necessities, the benefits of schooling and health care, the range of exposure and social interaction, the experience of travel, and the presence of opportunities are all dependent on one's means.

Islam recognizes the importance of material assets in life. The Qur'ān explicitly states: "Wealth and sons are the ornament of this life" (*al-mālu wa-al-banūna zīnatu al-ḥayāti al-dunyā*, 18:46). Throughout the Qur'ānic text, the righteous are promised that they will be rewarded with wealth and sons, whereas wrongdoers are threatened with the loss of their fortunes and children. While the Qur'ān admonishes those who glory in their riches and warns that such things will be of no avail on the Day of Judgment, it urges believers to live well and enjoy the wordly goods bestowed upon them: "O children of Adam, wear your beautiful apparel at every time and place of prayer; eat and drink, but waste not by excess, for God loveth not the wasters" (7:31). The emphasis is on spending in moderation, so that one's fortune will not be squandered away, and on abiding by moral rules of conduct.[2]

The important role of wealth in the lives of believers is also reflected in the Ḥadīth literature, which depicts in detail the luxurious attire, perfume, and meticulous beard-styling of the pious. The saying "When God blesses a man with prosperity He likes to see the signs thereof visible upon him," attributed by tradition to Muḥammad upon seeing well-circumstanced people appear before him in shabby clothes, is diametrically opposed to any puritanical principles.[3] In this connection, it should be noted that asceticism, as a philosophy, is not part of Islam proper. Though fasting and penitence are respected, they are not prescribed as a way of life.[4] Muḥammad's statement that "There is no monasticism in Islam" (*lā rahbāniyya fī al-Islām*) and the injunction "Complete your religious duties by marriage" (*akmil dīnaka bi-al-zawāj*) indicate that the concept of abstinence is alien to Islam. Asceticism was incorporated into popular Islam through the school of Ṣūfism and its teachings, which arose in reaction to the accumulation of unlimited fortune and power by Muslim rulers. As a spiritual revolt against materialism and despotism, Ṣūfism advocated the abdication of two kinds of things: worldly possessions and worldly desires, the former an external obstacle, the latter an internal one, on the path to obtaining the knowledge of God.[5] The early promoters of this view were a group of highly pious men, among them the famed ascetic Ḥasan al-Baṣrī (d. 728), who preached that poverty facilitates the attainment of salvation. The rich are more strongly connected to this world than the poor, and a share in this world is likely to entail a threat to one's share in the next. Moreover, poverty perfects human confidence in God: people should not worry about their sustenance, because the almighty God who created them will also provide for them. Hence complete trust (*tawakkul*) in God will result from complete renunciation of the world.[6]

Islam further recognizes that while people are all equal before God, they are not equal among themselves. God has created them different, so that they may learn from one another: "Men, We have created you from a male and a female, and made you into nations and tribes, that you might get to know one another" (49:13). God has also conferred different degrees of prosperity on people: "See how We have bestowed more on some than on others" (17:21). Similarly, God has established gradations of power among people: "It is He Who hath made you (His) agents, inheritors of the earth: He hath raised you in ranks, some above others: that He may try you in the gifts He hath given you" (6:165). The allocation of the means of subsistence is not necessarily the same for all: "It is We Who portion out between them their livelihood in the life of this world: and We raise some of them above others in rank, so that some may command work from others" (43:32). Given that there is no uniformity in God's gifts to people and that creation includes different individuals, who, by God's design, possess varying levels of physical and mental ability, there are bound to be class distinctions among them. Hence, to provide a measure of social justice, the Qur'ān enjoins believers to give charity to the poor and needy.

Almsgiving, *zakāt*, is one of the five pillars of Islam. The great value attached to this duty is reflected in the prominence given to the matter in the Qur'ān. In almost every chapter, this duty is urged upon Muslims: "You shall never be truly righteous until you give in alms what you dearly cherish. The alms you give are known to God" (3:92); "Have faith in God and His Apostle and give in alms of that which He has made your inheritance; for whoever of you believes and gives in alms shall be richly rewarded" (57:7). The recipients of alms are carefully defined: "The alms are only for the poor and the needy, and those who collect them, and those whose hearts are to be reconciled [to Islam], and to free the captives and the debtors, and for the cause of Allah, and for the wayfarers" (9:60). Alms are said to be of two kinds: obligatory, denoted by the word *zakāt*, which entails an annual tax at a fixed rate imposed on one's total wealth; and voluntary, denoted by the word *ṣadaqa*, which entails gifts and donations.[7]

Other channels for the redistribution of wealth instituted by the Qur'ān are inheritance and endowment (*waqf*). The laws governing inheritance limit the extent of what one can give away in one's will to a third of one's estate. The remaining two-thirds is then divided among all the members of the family—sons, daughters, father, mother, wives, brothers, and sisters—according to a fixed ratio. Thus, in a couple of generations, a rich estate will be broken down and redistributed among hundreds of heirs. The *waqf* is the dedication, made in perpetuity, of up to a third of one's property to charitable uses or to the service of God.

Islam's concern with social justice extends also to the spoils of war. Military booty played an important role in the regulations, promises, and expectations of the early adherents of Islam. The Qur'ān stipulates: "Know that one-fifth of your spoils shall belong to God, the Apostle, the Apostle's kinsfolk, the orphans, the destitute, and those who travel the road" (8:41). Thus four-fifths of what was taken in war was divided among the warriors, and the remaining fifth was retained for special purposes, including charity to the poor and needy.[8]

The Arabic word for wealth is *māl*. It includes concrete things such as money, property, land, livestock, goods, and the like. The word is presumably formed from *mā* and *li* and properly means "anything that belongs to anyone."[9] The attitude of Islam toward property and its acquisition is often characterized as a middle way between capitalism and communism. On the one hand, capitalism recognizes the right of the individual to private property, granting everyone unlimited freedom to amass huge capital and monopolize the means of production. Communism, on the other hand, does not recognize the right of the individual to private property, and all the means of production are owned by the state. Islam offers a compromise between these opposing systems: the right of the individual to ownership is fully acknowledged, but it is subjected to such limitations as to render it harmless to the greater good of the community.[10] This approach is reflected, for example, in the strict prohibition on hoarding, speculation, and usury, as well as in the insistence on moderation in consumption, the continuous utilization of property (e.g., land), and justice in the manner of distribution (i.e., *zakāt*). It has been argued that whereas in the capitalist system redistribution of wealth plays a peripheral role, amounting to a safety net designed to catch those who fall through the cracks, and whereas in the communist system redistribution of wealth is the primary goal, amounting to a net that is indiscriminately thrown over all the people, in Islam the issue of redistribution of wealth is given due consideration without jeopardizing either the individual or the collective interest.

It is generally recognized that Islam is both a religion and a social, economic, and cultural system. As a total way of life, Islam embraces all the domains of activity of the individual and the community. This unique aspect sheds light on the movement of Muslim fundamentalists and their demand for the return of the canonical law of Islam (*sharīʿa*). Frustrated with the failure of existing governments and imported ideologies to solve the socioeconomic problems in their societies, the fundamentalists fall back on the one alternative—Islam—which is both familiar to them and emotionally satisfying in its consistency, providing answers to all human needs, physical as well as spiritual.[11] The compelling force of this argument helps to explain the popularity of the Islamic views of the late Egyptian radical Sayyid Quṭb, considered to be the ideologue of the Muslim Brotherhood organization, and of the Sudanese radical Ḥasan al-Turābī.

Central to the doctrine of social justice in Islam is the notion of God's will. The circumstances of people's earthly existence are regarded as dependent on God's will and subject to His sublime judgment. The Qur'ān emphatically states: "To Him belong the keys of the heavens and the earth: He enlarges and restricts the sustenance to whom He will: for He knows full well all things" (42:12). A. Yusuf Ali comments: "The source of all gifts is God; His bounty is inexhaustible, and He gives to all; but He does not give to all in the same measure, because, out of the fullness of His knowledge and wisdom, He can judge best what is best for any of His creatures."[12] Thus God dispenses His grace according to His will and His plan. No one has exclusive possession of God's generosity or can influence its granting or withholding: "Grace is in His hands alone, and He vouchsafes it to whom He will" (57:29); "Such is the Bounty of God, which He bestows on whom He will: and God is the Lord of the highest bounty" (62:4).

While God distributes material blessings unequally to His creatures in this life, He is expected to compensate the unfortunate but worthy of His benevolence in the afterlife: "But verily the Hereafter is more in rank and gradation and more in excellence" (17:21). The description of paradise includes not only spiritual bliss but also physical comforts and pleasures and the enjoyment of abundance: "In it are rivers of water incorruptible; rivers of milk of which the taste never changes; rivers of wine, a joy to those who drink; and rivers of honey pure and clear. In it there are for them all kinds of fruits; and Grace from their Lord" (47:15). Hence, for the multitudes of the poor, many of whom suffer privation until the end of their lives, religion, with its solemn promise of future reward, is a great source of consolation and reconciliation.

Vested interests in the class system in Arab society have conveniently downplayed the value of this world and stressed that of the next: "The typical situation in the Middle East was for centuries the concentration of great riches in the hands of a very few, with great poverty the share of the many. This was, and in many places still is, a factual reality. The ideological counterpart of this situation was that the division of worldly goods is willed by God, that the possession of wealth is not one of those really important things for which man should strive, that there is a certain religious virtue in poverty, and that it is a religious duty of the rich to dole out alms to the poor. In this manner extreme economic inequality was organically incorporated into the culture, not only by being accepted realistically, but also by being underpinned ideologically."[13] The coherence, balance, and inner consistency of this traditional situation were disturbed with the intrusion of foreign ideological influences.

Marxist Ideology and Arab Response

The orthodox Islamic view of human welfare came under scrutiny following the cultural encounter with the West, the groundwork of which was laid with Napoleon's invasion of Egypt in 1798, and the effect of which was the spread and adoption of Western ideas. During the nineteenth century, Karl Marx (1818–83) introduced his revolutionary theory, which delineated the economic factor as the determining force in the evolution of human history. The particular appeal and dramatic influence that Marxist ideology enjoyed in the Arab world require a brief examination of its basic tenets.

Marx's theory of history suggests that people's social and cultural life, their political ideas and aims, reflect their material conditions of existence. Human beings are products of their environments in general and of their economic environment in particular.[14] The materialist assumption is expressed as follows:

> In the social production of their existence, men inevitably enter into definite relations, which are independent of their will, namely relations

> of production appropriate to a given stage in the development of their material forces of production. The totality of these relations of production constitutes the economic structure of society, the real foundation, on which arises a legal and political superstructure and to which correspond definite forms of social consciousness. The mode of production of material life conditions the general process of social, political and intellectual life. It is not the consciousness of men that determines their existence, but their social existence that determines their consciousness.[15]

Raised to the level of historical law, this hypothesis was applied to capitalist society. According to Marx, the capitalist system creates two basic social classes that oppose each other: the owners of the means of production, or bourgeoisie, and the workers, or proletariat. The relations between these classes are inevitably antagonistic because the allocation of what is produced is based on exploitation rather than justice. Moreover, the class that has control over material production has at the same time control over mental production. It establishes a distinct cultural style and a dominant ideological orientation, which are supported by a corresponding political system.[16] As Marx states: "The ideas of the ruling class are in every epoch the ruling ideas: i.e., the class, which is the ruling material force of society, is at the same time its ruling intellectual force. The class, which has the means of material production at its disposal, has control at the same time over the means of mental production, so that thereby, generally speaking, the ideas of those who lack the means of mental production are subject to it."[17]

The concept of class struggle is central to Marx's thought. The history of society is essentially the history of class struggles, and conflicts are the driving force of change. The dialectical approach assumes a pattern of thesis–antithesis–synthesis as the process of social evolution. History progresses from one stage to its opposite and then to a higher level of development that preserves something of both earlier, negated states.[18] Eventually, the tensions arising from the stratification of society into classes based on their material assets rather than on their value and contribution to society are bound to lead to the workers' revolt and the overthrow of the capitalists in favor of a proletarian dictatorship. The final synthesis—a new order consisting of a classless society—will be conducive to personal development, economic prosperity, and political stability.[19]

Marx's concept of class struggle was extended to the relationship between colonizing and colonized nations, which was regarded as revealing class subordination and exploitation at their worst. The liberation of the oppressed from their oppressors, whether capitalists or imperialists, was to be achieved through a revolution that would ultimately unite all the workers in the world under the banner of socialism and eliminate geographical and national divisions.

Marx's ideology of class struggle, social equality, and freedom has inspired revolutionary movements worldwide and stimulated many people in occupied countries to rise up against their rulers. The political interpretation of Marxism, in its most popular form, served as the basis of socialism and as the doctrine of communism.

In the Arab world, the intellectuals' response to Soviet Marxism—that is, communism—was one of newfound ideals, aspiration, and expectation.[20] Communism provided a concrete program for the Arabs: first, to liberate themselves from colonialism and imperialism; second, to free themselves from feudalism and capitalist exploitation. Radical Arab intellectuals were also fascinated by the possibility of replacing religion with secularism. Communism offered a strategy and a course of action: it reduced all social ills to one cause—the economic—and promised a complete cure. In Marxist ideology, Arab intellectuals found a plausible explanation for the lack of development and sorry state of affairs in their societies. They also hoped that through social solidarity the Arab nations would attain unity, rising above traditional divisions and rivalries. Thus both Marxist and communist doctrines gave the intellectuals a practical framework for revolutionary action to gain national independence, achieve social change, restore Arab unity, and secure an equal place among the nations.

In "The Appeal of Communism in the Middle East," Walter Z. Laqueur points out that World War II brought a great upsurge in Middle Eastern communism. The main reason was the emergence of the Soviet Union as one of the two great superpowers. The effectiveness of communism as a method for modernizing the Middle East and overcoming its backwardness in the shortest possible time was of paramount importance. Capitalism was identified with imperialist rule, while democracy was not a militant creed and did not provide the answers to many questions relevant to Arab reality. It failed to inspire the masses and did not give firm spiritual support to the elite. Communism, by contrast, had all the force of a secular religion. Laqueur notes that in the 1940s and 1950s it was almost universally believed in the West that economic and technical assistance was the most efficient way to curb the influence of communism in underdeveloped countries. Ironically, many people who rejected Marx's teachings became, in fact, strong believers in historical materialism, perceiving in economic progress the key to the whole situation.[21]

Bernard Lewis, in an early article discussing communism and Islam, suggests: "We of the West can do much to promote the material well-being and raise the material standards of the lands of Islam."[22] Attempting to explain the power of attraction of communism in the Muslim world, he enumerates the elements that make communism and Islam compatible. As an accidental factor, he mentions the anti-Western motif: the communists were against the Western powers, their institutions, practices, and ideas; therefore, they had a strong appeal in the Arab world, which was undergoing a reaction against colonialism and the impact of the West. As an essential factor, he mentions the authoritarianism of the Islamic political tradition, which might provide an easy transition to communist dictatorship. The traditional Islamic autocracy is based on three pillars: the bureaucracy, the army, and the religious hierarchy. In this pattern, only the religious hierarchy need be changed to pave the way for a communist state.[23]

Lewis finds additional similarities: both Islam and communism profess a totalitarian doctrine, with complete and final answers to all questions on heaven and earth. The traditional Islamic division of the world into the House of Islam (*dār al-Islām*) and the House of War (*dār al-ḥarb*), including the collective obligation to struggle against the latter, has a parallel in the communist view of the world. In the final analysis, however, communism is not and cannot be a religion, while Islam is, and this is the core of the popular resistance to communist ideas. The Islamic peoples are still profoundly religious and cannot tolerate an atheistic creed.[24] Communism sparked the imagination of the elite but failed to enlist the support of the masses; therefore, it never became a grassroots movement.

Following World War II, many Arab leaders sought solutions to the socioeconomic ills of their countries in Arab socialism, which combines nationalist and Islamic principles with Marxist ideology. In Egypt, the socialist-oriented regime established by Gamal Abdel Nasser after the 1952 revolution carried out the nationalization of the Suez Canal and radical agrarian reforms. In Syria, the Baʿth Socialist Party ascended to power in 1958 and formed a political union with Egypt. The union collapsed in 1961, bringing down the party, but the Baʿth regained control in 1963, and, headed by Hafez Assad for three decades (1970–2000), it has brought political stability to Syria. In Iraq, the local branch of the Baʿth Socialist Party seized power in 1963, and, led by Saddam Hussein since the coup of 1968, it continues to rule the country. In South Yemen, revolutionary Yemenis ousted the government in 1969 and the South became a communist state, renamed the People's Democratic Republic of Yemen, until 1990, when it was reunited with the North and declared an Islamic state. In Sudan, Colonel Gaafar Nimeiri launched a successful coup in 1969 and declared Sudan "democratic, socialist, and nonaligned." However, the renewal of the civil war in 1983 brought this secular leftist leader back to the Islamic path, resulting in the imposition of the *sharīʿa* as state law and the enforcement of Islamic economics. Although Nimeiri was deposed in 1985, the Islamization of Sudan has continued. Other Arab countries, such as Algeria, Tunisia, and Libya, have adopted socialist policies in education, health care, and welfare.

The economic reforms pursued by Arab socialist regimes indicate that Islam, for all its concern with the poor and needy, is conditional, as is the case with other religions, upon the goodwill of the people to give charity. Hence it cannot provide a reliable mechanism of social justice and equity. Nevertheless, the initial appeal of communism in the Arab world derived in part from a certain "religious" quality that it possesses, a kind of affinity with "a doctrine of the future" (i.e., eschatology), in that it looks forward to an earthly paradise, or heaven on earth.[25]

The Revolt against God's Justice

Even before World War I, Arab writers, such as Gibran Khalil Gibran in his romantic novel *The Broken Wings (Al-Ajniḥa al-mutakassira,* 1912) and Muḥammad Ḥusayn Haykal in the first Egyptian novel *Zaynab* (1913), under Western influences of humanistic values, were criticizing the tyranny of feudalism, patriarchy, and the religious authorities in Arab society. Their imaginative works reflected new attitudes toward traditional Arab beliefs, customs, and norms.

The spread of socialist realism and Marxist ideas in the Arab world during the 1940s and 1950s focused attention on the economic factor in challenging the traditional concept of fate. At every level, Arab reality grew increasingly harsh during and after World War II. Struggles for independence from Western colonialism and numerous regional conflicts, oppressive and corrupt governments, limited resources, and natural disasters like drought and famine combined to aggravate the already acute living conditions of the masses. In urban areas, the working classes had to endure overcrowding, unemployment, and a cumbersome bureaucracy. In rural areas, the peasants were exploited by feudal landlords and impoverished by antiquated methods of irrigation and cultivation. Overpopulation compounded the problems of poverty, disease, and illiteracy, robbing the majority of Arab society of any future prospects. The plight of the common people, and the glaring social injustice that emerged, led the intellectuals to reexamine their religious beliefs and seek other, more satisfying explanations for existing social ills.

Under communist ideological influences from translated literature and visits to the Soviet Union, many Arab writers began to express the idea that human fate is controlled not by God's will but by the established system of social organization. They laid bare the appalling conditions of the weakest strata of Arab society—the poor, women, and children—and questioned the notion of divine justice. For example, in the novel *Egyptian Earth (Al-Arḍ,* 1954) by ʿAbd al-Raḥmān al-Sharqāwī, the life of a simple village community is disrupted when a corrupt government official orders their quota of irrigation water cut in half. The local religious leader, Shaykh Shināwī, attributes the shortage of water to an act of God, interpreting it as a divine retribution for evil behavior. But ʿAbd al-Hādī, a stubborn peasant with a mind of his own, doubts that the unfair distribution of water is caused by impiety and that it is related to the principle of reward and punishment:

> So the lack of water was a divine punishment, because the village was irreligious? The village's punishment was the Pasha's reward. Yet did the Pasha pray? The Sheikh said that he gave alms, and the village did not. But what alms did the village have to give? At least the village said its prayers. And ʿAbd al-Hādī thought of other villages, far off, of which he had heard, where the landlords owned everything, where the farmers were hired serfs, owning nothing at all. Yet those landlords did not pray nor give a farthing in alms, and the wrath of God had not struck them. Their canals continued to flow merrily with water, their trees were bowed down with fruit. Such landlords would drink alcohol in the holy month of Ramaḍān, they would seduce any girl that took their fancy. Yet they were not struck down by the wrath of God, nor was their water cut off by the Government.[26]

A schoolteacher from Cairo, Shaykh Ḥassūna, with relatives in the village, urges the peasants to rebel. However, as the traditional attitude of the peasants is one of servility, it takes several attempts before they join forces against their oppressors. In this instance, the tenet of the inevitability of class struggle provides the theme around which the novel revolves.

In "The Scorpion Hunter" ("Al-ʿAqrab"), also by ʿAbd al-Raḥmān al-Sharqāwī,[27] the need for subsistence drives Ḥasan to try his hand at catching scorpions, whose poison is in demand by the government. In pondering his desperate situation, Ḥasan's thoughts center on getting plain bread to survive:

> Ever since the day His Reverence the Sheikh kicked you out of the mosque, you've been shifting aimlessly from one job to the other. . . . You try to get yourself drafted into the army, but you're turned down. And the only way left for you to get a bite to eat is by catching scorpions. Catching scorpions? Just one sting from a scorpion is enough to get rid of you once and for all. You're in a fix, Ḥasan. But a scorpion sells for a piaster—ten for the price of a measure of corn. Ten scorpions, man, will buy you enough bread to fill a sack.[28]

Ḥasan cannot help thinking about the exploitative behavior of the shaykh, the religious leader who showed no mercy toward him when he fired him, thus sealing his doom:

> In Ḥasan's mind, memories whirled around in rapid succession. From the day that the sheikh refused to raise his pay to ten piasters a month,

> and hired someone else for the job, everything had gone against him. He could not get work in the fields anywhere. There was none there for him, nor for twenty others like him in the village.[29]

In the end, Ḥasan goes to hunt scorpions, but sure enough as soon as he finds one it stings him and he dies. While the story condemns the unscrupulous religious leadership, it also illustrates the tragic fate of a helpless man caught in a vicious circle of poverty and tyranny.

In the story "Uncle, Help Me Across" ("ʿAmmī, ʿabbirnī") by the Iraqi writer Ghā'ib Ṭuʿma Firmān,[30] a blind girl who is abandoned in the street without a companion begs for someone's help to cross to the opposite side. Drenched by the pouring rain, cold and barefoot, she is finally led to safety by a male passerby. The warm touch of the man's hand arouses sexual desires in her and throws her soul into turmoil. Contemplating her wretched existence, she wonders: "What is this life of hers? Mud, rain, and blindness! Desolation, hunger, and orphanhood!" Agitated, she sarcastically remarks: "Of course, You Lord. You have a hand in this. A blind girl and this muddy, slippery world!" At the same time, Umm Khumayyis, a destitute woman who makes a living selling beans on the street, is vexed by the constant rain, which frustrates her efforts to light a fire. Exasperated, she grumbles: "Even God resents the poor. . . . How many times have I started the fire today, only to have it go out again! That's the way it is. God can rule only over poor people!"[31] These ironic remarks by the needy women betray a spirit of revolt against the notion of God's justice.

Similar sentiments of indignation and resentment are expressed in *For Bread Alone* (1973; *Al-Khubz al-ḥāfī*, 1982), the autobiography of Muḥammad Shukrī. The author describes how the great famine in the Rif forced his family to leave for Tangier, where he grew up in extreme poverty. He recalls the difficult time when his father was put in prison and he and his mother were left without any means of support. To a hungry child, the idea of divine justice does not make sense:

> She goes to the city in search of work. She comes back disappointed, just as my father used to do when we first arrived in Tangier. She sits biting her nails distractedly. She sobs. Sorcerers make her talismans to wear around her neck; perhaps my father will get out of prison and she will find work. She says her prayers and lights candles at the tombs of the saints. She looks for luck at the fortuneteller's. There is no way out of prison, there is no work, no luck, save by order of Allah and Mohammed his prophet; this is what she says. I began to think: Why doesn't Allah give us our good luck the way he gives it to other people? I passed the question to my mother. That's something we can't ask, she

> said. He knows much better than we do, and when he wants us to know, he'll tell us.[32]

When the young Shukrī goes to visit his brother's grave, he is shocked to find that there are class distinctions at the cemetery as well:

> I went to the graveyard in Bou Araqia. Large bunches of myrtle had been left on some of the richer tombs. I gathered them up and carried them to my brother's grave. There were many graves without tiles marking them, and without myrtle on them, like my brother's. A mound of earth and two stones of different shapes, one for the head and one for the feet. The sight of the neglected graves hurt me. I thought: Even here in the cemetery there are rich people and poor people.[33]

A classic example of the closed circle between social and economic prospects can be found in the novel *The Beginning and the End (Bidāya wa-nihāya*, 1949) by Najīb Maḥfūẓ. Set in Cairo among the lower middle class, the work depicts the crisis of several members of a fatherless family confronted with poverty. The eldest son turns to criminal activities, the middle son is forced to stop his education to support the family, and the only daughter drifts into prostitution. Hard as he tries, the youngest son, an army officer, cannot escape his humble past, which keeps haunting him and frustrating his efforts to achieve respectability and a career. In the end, when his sister is arrested in a brothel and jumps into the Nile to save his reputation, he realizes the consequences of his selfish conduct, and, seeing no way out of his predicament, he commits suicide. As can be noted, the title itself suggests the idea of inevitability, which the novel develops in great detail.

The same theme figures prominently in the novel *War in the Land of Egypt (Al-Ḥarb fī barr Miṣr*, 1978) by Yūsuf al-Qaʿīd. In this work, set in a village in rural Egypt, the powerful mayor—*ʿumda*—whose son has been drafted into the army, persuades the night watchman to send his own son instead. In return, the mayor promises to allow the watchman to farm the small plot of land which was given to him under Nasser's agrarian reforms but which was decreed to be restored to the mayor following a new law by the Sadat regime. The watchman's son, who bears the symbolic name Maṣrī ("Egyptian"), agrees to the bargain, which involves an impersonation plan, because of lack of choice. Utterly destitute and powerless, he has no say in his own fate, which is manipulated by those around him with means and influence. This point is emphasized by the fact that the novel, which consists of six chapters, each narrated by a different character, has no chapter for Maṣrī, although he is the central figure around which the work revolves and the only one with a name.[34]

Maṣrī is sent to the front and is killed in action, but his sacrifice is in vain: his father neither gets the plot of land promised to him by the tyrannical mayor nor the monthly compensation offered by the government to a fallen soldier's family. Maṣrī's army friend, in whom Maṣrī has confided, is unable to accept such a great tragedy as simply a matter of fate:

> The chapters of his [Maṣrī's] life were filled with unending agony. Even so, I won't say that what happened was completely due to such things as "predestined fate" or an "inevitable destiny," because there was more to it than that. The answer lies in the gulf between the ʿumda's huge white mansion, which gleams even at night, and the house, or rather shack, where Maṣrī's family lived, and in the contrast between the ʿumda himself, with his huge elephant's carcass, and Maṣrī's father, with his skin stretched so tight over his bones they look as if they might pop out at any moment.[35]

Pondering the sad events in Maṣrī's doomed life, his friend is left to struggle with unresolved feelings of anger, frustration, and disillusionment:

> Where was divine justice in Maṣrī's story? If there were any justice, God would grant the poor the rights they're trying to uphold. They've got right on their side, but since when has right mattered against power? Right on its own is helpless—it's a rifle that fires back into the breast of the person holding it, it's a broken wooden sword. Maṣrī's family own nothing but their bare hands, while the ʿumda is powerful and never tires of repeating that his power comes from God—which is apparently true! The simple truth is that if God has chosen to be the Lord of the rich alone, then the poor's only recourse is to look for a Lord of their own. . . . Every bullet fired toward occupied Sinai should have been matched by another one fired back toward enslaved Egypt, which has occupiers of a different sort—poverty, backwardness, injustice, and oppression.[36]

Al-Qaʿīd's novel exposes the harsh reality which forces a decent and talented peasant to forsake his identity and lose his life.

In contrast to the angry social protest expressed in the preceding examples, in the novella *Faraḥāt's Republic (Jumhūriyyat Faraḥāt*, 1956) by Yūsuf Idrīs,[37] a Marxist frame of reference is used to paint a vivid picture of a social utopia, in which a wise leader undertakes to build an equitable society for his people:

> He didn't make any profit at all from workers' sweat. The man who did work worth five piasters got five piasters, the one who did work for ten

> got ten. Forgive my saying so, but a worker will put his heart and soul into his job when he's properly paid. . . . That's how it was—give and take, give me my right and take yours.[38]

Equality and justice produce healthy, happy, and motivated people:

> Also the worker himself was completely changed, with tip-top clean clothes, his overalls nicely ironed to go to work in, then returning in the afternoon to change into his best suit. . . . And what cafés there were! What gardens! What casinos![39] What splendor! And the people all looking nice and gay and happy. . . . Every row of houses had its own canteen in which they all ate and then they'd all go home for a siesta and later they'd file off to school so as to learn to read and write and get to know their rights and duties.[40]

Thus a change for the better in people's material conditions has a dramatic effect on the pattern of their lives and their future prospects.

The Cause of the Masses

The writers who espoused Marxist ideas belonged to the secular-rational group among Arab intellectuals. Distinguished for their emphasis on nationalism, secularism, and socialism, the members of this group aspired to establish a modern society by replacing traditional Arab-Muslim values with Western scientific models and democratic ideals. In Egypt, the secular-rational trend was led by Syrian Christian émigrés such as Shiblī Shumayyil (1850–1917), Faraḥ Anṭūn (1874–1922), Fāris Nimr (1857–1951) and Yaʿqūb Ṣarrūf (1852–1927), as well as the Copt Salāma Mūsā (1887–1958). The secular-rational trend embraced a multiplicity of views, ranging from laissez-faire liberalism to Marxism. In some instances, there were even attempts to formulate a historical-materialist interpretation.[41]

Two works of literature merit mention in this connection. Faraḥ Anṭūn's didactic novel *Religion, Science, and Money (Al-Dīn wa-al-ʿilm wa-al-māl,* 1903) revolves around class conflict and social inequities, which are depicted in lengthy discussions by representatives of different groups, including workers, capitalists, religious leaders, and intellectuals. At one point, the workers argue that the founders of the great religions all taught that God created all people equal, but greedy employers abandoned the egalitarian principles of Moses, Christ, and Muḥammad. They quote Marx to the effect that they serve capitalists as slaves serve their masters and demand that the factories and land should belong jointly to the whole nation. The intellectuals defend the workers and accuse the religious leaders of abetting the capitalists by teaching the workers to submit to their lot. When attempts to reach a compromise fail, the workers revolt, troops fire on them, and the cities perish in a holocaust.[42]

In ʿAbd al-Raḥmān al-Sharqāwī's imaginative biography of the Prophet, entitled *Muḥammad, Apostle of Freedom (Muḥammad rasūl al-ḥurriyya,* 1962), Muḥammad is portrayed as an exemplary Marxist revolutionary. As M. M. Badawi observes, the accepted epithet of Muḥammad, which is found in the profession of faith (*shahāda*), is *rasūl Allāh,* that is, God's Apostle. True to the work's title, the portrait of Muḥammad is that of a radical reformer—the apostle of freedom, but not necessarily of God. Further, the author describes the struggle of Islam as a class struggle between the haves and the have-nots. In this framework, the opposition to Islam came from the capitalists of Mecca, the merchants and moneylenders, and their supporters, the priests who served the gods. The poor were left unprotected and deprived of any rights, the males among them forced into slavery and the females into prostitution. Muḥammad himself was an orphan who belonged to the poor and identified with their tribulations. His mission was to bring liberation, fraternity, equality, and justice. In this dramatic account, the author shows Muḥammad "glorifying manual labor, attacking monkery because it involves having to support a privileged class of people who do not earn their living by their own efforts, standing for the freedom of slaves, for free scientific inquiry, and even for Arab nationalism." Badawi remarks that to all appearances, the secularization of Muḥammad is here virtually complete, for he is presented as a committed Marxist idealist and activist.[43]

It should be noted that in the context of the Arab struggle for national independence and social change, the cause of the masses became an essential component of the literary concept of commitment (*iltizām*) and was not limited to a few Marxist writers or poets.[44] World War II brought a recoil from romanticism, which came to be regarded as a form of escapism, a preoccupation with ideals remote from reality and irrelevant to the pressing needs of the common people. Realism, with a marked socialist tendency, became so widespread that most Arab writers and poets fell under its influence.[45] Some of the leading practitioners of this trend were, for example, the poets ʿAbd al-Wahhāb al-Bayātī, Ṣalāḥ ʿAbd al-Ṣabūr, Badr Shākir al-Sayyāb, and Muḥammad Miftāḥ al-Faytūrī, as well as the fiction writers Yaḥyā Ḥaqqī, ʿAbd al-Raḥmān al-Sharqāwī, Najīb Maḥfūẓ, Yūsuf Idrīs, Suhayl Idrīs, Ghā'ib Ṭuʿma Firmān, and Jabrā Ibrāhīm Jabrā. As Arab writers shifted their interest to the suffering and dehumanizing poverty of the masses, their visions of reality were depicted in concrete images. The famous poem "The People of My Country" ("Al-Nās fī bilādī"), by Ṣalāḥ ʿAbd al-Ṣabūr, reads:

The people of my country wound like falcons
Their songs are like the chill of winter in the rain's locks
Their laughter hisses like flame through firewood
Their footsteps dent the firm earth
They kill, steal, drink, belch,
But they have their human worth and are good
When they have a handful of money
They hold fast to their belief in fate.

As one entered my village there sat my Uncle Muṣṭafā
Who loved the Prophet
Who spent the hour
Between dusk and nightfall surrounded
By musing men
To whom he told a tale
Rooted in experience
A tale that stirred
Within their souls
The pain of man's mortality.
And it made them weep and bow their heads
Staring into silence
Into the gulf of deep terror and silence.
"What is the purpose of man's striving, what is the purpose of life?
Oh God!
The sun declares Thy glory, the crescent moon is Thy brow
And these unshakable mountains are Thy steadfast throne
Thou art He whose will is accomplished, oh God!
A certain man rose to eminence, erected castles
with forty rooms filled with glittering gold
And on one faint twilight evening
Azrael came to him
his fingers grasping a small book
And Azrael stretched out his staff
with the secret of life and death
and that man's soul was pitched into Hell!
(Oh God! . . .
How cruel and full of menace thou art,
Oh God!)"

Yesterday I visited my village
Uncle Muṣṭafā had died
They laid him to rest in the earth
He built no castles (his hut was of mud)
And behind his ancient coffin
Walked those who, like him, owned only an old cotton gown

They said no word of God or Azrael
For it was a year of famine
And at the door of the tomb stood my friend Khaleel
Uncle Muṣṭafā's grandson
And when he stretched up his brawny arms toward the sky
A look of contempt flickered across his eyes
For it was a year of famine.[46]

In this poem, the rejection of the belief in fate is expressed by the look of scorn which surges in the grandson's eyes when he lifts his arms to the sky. Uncle Muṣṭafā died not from lack of faith but from lack of food—hunger—and it is hunger that leads the younger generation to rebel against the traditional value orientations of their elders.[47]

The foregoing illustrations from modern Arabic literature reveal another perspective on human fate: the recognition that faith is a fantasy and freedom a fallacy because people are prisoners of their historical and material circumstances. Born into a class system which defines their reality and shapes their consciousness, people are compelled to follow a mode of life not of their own choice. According to this view, people are creatures of circumstances: they can be trapped in their social and economic background to such an extent that fate seems to assume the shape of socioeconomic determinism.

ʿAbd al-Raḥmān al-Sharqāwī
Little Dreams

ʿAbd al-Raḥmān al-Sharqāwī (1920–87) was born in the Egyptian province of Munūfiyya. He studied law at Cairo University and graduated in 1943. Subsequently he worked as a lawyer, civil servant, and journalist. He became chairman of the popular weekly magazine *Rūz al-Yūsuf* and secretary-general of the Supreme Council for the Arts, Literature, and Social Sciences in Cairo.

A poet, playwright, and fiction writer, al-Sharqāwī gained much acclaim with his novel *Egyptian Earth (Al-Arḍ,* 1954), which offers a sympathetic depiction of the Egyptian countryside and the peasants. It was made into a popular film and translated into several European languages. He also published poetry, verse dramas, and collections of short stories. He is known for his sensitive portrayal of Egyptian rural life and for his realism and social commitment.

"Little Dreams" ("Aḥlām ṣaghīra") is the title story of a collection published in Cairo in 1956. The story depicts the social and economic obstacles facing a little village boy who aspires to go to school in the city.

Everything was asleep in his little world—his mother, his father, the goat, and the chickens—but Muṣṭafā could not fall asleep. He was watching the pale rays of light that emanated from a rustic old lamp and filtered into the corners of the room. The lamp gave off more smoke than light. He watched the light and waited for his mother to wake up—for dawn to break. Tomorrow, he would wear a suit and a pair of shoes for the first time. He would wear these new things and let the wind play with the tassel of his fez. He was going to a city that he had never seen before to take the entrance examinations for elementary school!

On this trip he would ride the donkey. He would finally climb up on the donkey that he so hated to walk behind on the way from the house to the field. How often had he wished to ride it! In fact, he had ridden it once. If Muṣṭafā were to forget everything that had ever happened in the village, he would never forget that incident. His uncle had surprised him with a slap so hard that he fell from the donkey. His uncle cared dearly for the donkey, as he considered it far more useful to the family than twenty worthless children like Muṣṭafā. He thought that carrying loads of earth was a sufficient burden for the old donkey. Muṣṭafā could not understand, however, how his uncle could allow the donkey to carry loads of earth and would not allow it to carry him. He was, after all, the only child in the family!

The small household included Muṣṭafā, his mother, his father, and an uncle. They owned the old donkey, a goat, and some chickens. Formerly, his father had studied at al-Azhar and had hoped to obtain a teaching post there and don a turban.[48] One evening, he came to the village with a wide turban wound down his forehead and walked about arrogantly. His brother had been the first person to meet him. Grinning, he said:

"Why are you wearing the turban like that? Do you think this spectacle will earn you money? Come off it! You won't make a penny!"

The village had laughed at his wit and continued to laugh to this day, incorporating these comments into its treasury of sayings and anecdotes.

The uncle had been correct. The young Azhar student did not go back to Cairo. Instead, he got married and settled in the village, but he continued to wear a wide turban, wound down his forehead. Although he never obtained a teaching post at al-Azhar, he eventually achieved some influence over the peasants by rendering legal opinion on issues related to paradise and hell, and marriage and divorce. He also presented written complaints for them whenever they were oppressed by the mayor. He sent Muṣṭafā to the village school, and then decided to send him to a city school, to enable his son to accomplish what he himself had been unable to do.

The uncle had disagreed with this plan. He thought that Muṣṭafā should remain in the village to give him a hand in farming the land and, in due course, to learn how to handle the stick. With this skill, he could help his uncle protect the family interests from intruders who stole the family's share of irrigation water and let their sheep and goats graze on their small field.

The uncle was a small, thin man whose bronzed face was etched with stern and bitter lines. Sometimes he made wisecracks, delivered with great composure, which the peasants laughed at and remembered for many years. Whenever the mayor seized the peasants' chickens or took their money unlawfully, they turned to the uncle, and his ironic comments and deadpan delivery made them laugh and forget their troubles.

This small man had continually opposed his brother from the moment the latter declared his intention to send Muṣṭafā to a city school. That very night, as the family sat down to supper, the uncle took a big bite from an onion and, munching on dry bread with old red cheese, said:

"Leave him here, man, I tell you. We need him. If he goes away, who will fight the thieves? It's not like he will bring independence to the country. Will he? Bring independence? Ha!"

Muṣṭafā heard the words "independence" and "country" without understanding. Finally he blurted out angrily:

"Yes! I *will* bring independence to the country!"

The uncle burst out laughing in a strange way, and his father laughed, too, saying: "God willing."

Still grinning, the uncle muttered dreamily: "Who knows? Perhaps . . ."

His uncle was now asleep on the bench in front of the adjacent courtyard so that he would awaken at the crack of dawn. But the day never dawned for the group to accompany the boy to the city. The room in which Muṣṭafā's heart blazed with emotion was completely enclosed, leaving no crack through which the warm sunlight or the dreamy moonlight could enter. The sound of snoring mingled with the panting of the goat and the noises of the night. The rustic old lamp quivered with a pale and feeble light, just like the quiver of a ray of hope inside some hearts. It did not clearly illuminate the surroundings, but neither did it go out.

The moments passed like eons. Muṣṭafā wished that a miracle would suddenly find him dressed in his new clothes—just like the son of the chief of police, who wandered about the village protected by his father's authority and in the care of the chief guard. The boy was exactly Muṣṭafā's age, but his hair was well combed, his face was rosy, and his knees were white! He would dash around the village, behaving arrogantly toward the other children, who regarded him with admiration. He would run around bothering the people and the animals, kicking whatever crossed his path, as the chief guard followed behind, smiling indulgently and waving at the children.

Muṣṭafā remembered the time that he might have killed the boy, if the chief guard had not grabbed his hands and allowed the son of the chief of police to slap him repeatedly. Then he had flung Muṣṭafā down, cursing his father, his forefathers, and the entire village population! When Muṣṭafā told his family about this incident, his mother scolded him and his father shook him by the shoulder, but his uncle pinched him on the back of the neck, shouting:

"What a black day! Do you fancy yourself the equal of the rulers? You're a chip off the old block! Your father, too, had to leave Cairo because of a similar incident!"

Muṣṭafā recalled this incident and wished morning would come so that his mother would awaken him to leave for the city. He would enter elementary school and be just like the son of the chief of police, or perhaps even like the son of the magistrate. He would wear a suit, and when he spoke everyone would pay attention. He would become sophisticated and knowledgeable—just like that fat, grand inspector who had visited the village school early last autumn. He had driven a car that made furrows in the dusty alleyways. The old women stood by their doors discussing the old days and God's saints and their miracles, while the older girls covered their mouths and chins with black veils and sized up the "gentleman" with their glances, eager to hear a few words from the man who came "from beyond the fields."

Finally, the inspector had reached the school, followed by a throng of youngsters. He entered Muṣṭafā's classroom, and the teacher rushed to greet him. The children noticed that the teacher, always ready to inflict pain with his stick, lowered his voice and stopped cursing; he even attempted to hide the stick. Their hearts filled with affection for this wonderful visitor. Silence mixed with awe prevailed. They extended their hands beneath the desks, and when the inspector spoke, they all joined hands and everyone stared at the man's mouth and clothes. He spoke with rare, unfamiliar eloquence, as though he had been sent from heaven on the Night of the Divine Decree!

The inspector had asked the children to draw something called . . . an apple. Muṣṭafā would never forget this word. The entire village still laughingly recalled the tale of the inspector and the apple. This tale, too, had become a part of the village's treasury of anecdotes.

In fact, the children had not understood what the inspector wanted them to do. So he turned toward the teacher and asked him to draw an apple for them on the blackboard. The embarrassed teacher was taken by surprise. He hesitated in bewilderment, as though trying to recall something, and the children's laughter trilled like the chirping of birds.

Now Muṣṭafā would go to the city and learn what an apple is. He would undoubtedly discover many such secrets scattered among the city streets like clear facts of life!

Why wouldn't his father wake up and get everything ready for him? His snoring still mingled with the panting of the goat.

Muṣṭafā felt a strange pride as he cast a long, gloating glance at the goat. How often had it made him cry when he had dragged it in the morning or in the evening! It would always jump along the side of the road and then escape, leaving him to be cursed and beaten by his uncle. At long last, he would be delivered forever from this creature's miserable company!

The goat answered him with a frozen look from its big eyes.

But when would morning ever come so that he could put on his suit and shoes and fez?

He rose cautiously and glanced at his father and mother, sleeping nearby on a mattress on the floor. The lamp was almost extinguished. He slipped away from his place, his heart pounding with excitement. He reached out carefully and unlocked the chest in which his mother placed baked goods and fine clothes and other valuables. The goat moved and made a noise like a cough. Muṣṭafā noticed it shifting uncomfortably. Realizing that the goat was tied down, he hurried to free it. His body trembled with joy as he opened the chest easily and removed the new suit. He carried the suit to his bed, spread it out, and hugged it warmly in hope and ecstasy. The fragrance of the new fabric permeated his nostrils and penetrated him through and through. He felt it invigorating him like a splendid, powerful perfume. His hand began to stroke the rough clothing as he thought of the city and its dwellers who ate apples, and bread made of wheat, and meat, and rice.

He could no longer contain his happiness and shut his eyes with delight. He felt a pleasant intoxication slowly coursing through his limbs. He began to plunge into a strange abyss filled with all kinds of cheerful, vibrant colors. The sounds faded away . . . far away . . . until the dreams . . .

Suddenly Muṣṭafā felt a sharp pain all over his body. Confused screams reached his ears—his mother, his uncle, his father! He jumped up, rubbing his eyes, still yawning. A slap struck his face and he reeled a little with pain and fright. He called for his mother's help, but she was clinging to his father and uncle in a strange way, asking whether they were going to kill her only child over a piece of fabric! She was sobbing and talking about the demons that would possess him because they had beaten him while he was asleep!

He opened his eyes fully and began to search for the suit—the suit that would take him to the city and deliver him from all this. All he found was a piece of chewed-up rag!

He did not know what to do. He looked around him, choking with tears, and saw the goat standing behind his uncle, still chewing the remains of the fabric. He tried, like his mother, to pounce on the goat, but his father pushed both of them away. How could he bear his losses if the goat, too, were wasted? Muṣṭafā felt that his uncle and father were protecting the goat in the same way that deaf, tyrannical fate protected the son of the chief of police!

He was still crying when his uncle pulled him by the hand and told him to lead the goat and the donkey into the field, for he was unfit to do anything else. He was a complete good-for-nothing!

Never before had the goat jumped so stubbornly along the road as on that day. Grimacing with grief, Muṣṭafā threw numerous stones at it, all of which failed to reach their target.

His father could not afford another suit for him this year.

When Muṣṭafā arrived at the field, he was no longer crying. He began to dream about going to school in the city the following year. He swore that next time he would shut the chest containing the suit that his father would buy him, and keep it under lock and key. He would guard it all night. He would even sleep on top of the chest, after removing the goat from the room altogether!

Comments

Muṣṭafā is a child who carries a heavy burden: he has to fulfill two people's dreams—his own and his father's. The father tried in his youth to escape the harsh peasant life in rural Egypt, but failed. He is therefore determined to improve his son's lot through education and saves money for a whole year to buy him a suit and a pair of shoes for school. Muṣṭafā yearns to escape the confining environment of his village, where his life is terrorized by a tyrannical uncle and a capricious goat. However, when the goat chews up his suit, both he and his father have to put off their dreams for another year.

The story portrays the grinding poverty of the peasants and the great difficulty of breaking away from the prison of their economic reality. Without the money to buy proper clothing, Muṣṭafā cannot attend school in the city, and hence he cannot escape the narrow path of his family's precarious existence.

Muṣṭafā's material circumstances include only the bare essentials. His living quarters consist of one small room, shared by all the members of his family, as well as the farm animals. As an image of his life, the room in which Muṣṭafā sleeps is shut and dark, leaving no crack through which sunlight or moonlight can penetrate. Muṣṭafā is an inquisitive, intelligent, and ambitious child. Like his father, he is rebellious. He clashes with the son of the chief of police, oblivious of the dire consequences which this incident might have for his family. As for his father, he studied at al-Azhar in his youth and aspired to become a teacher, but his hopes were dashed when he got expelled for a similar act of lèse majesté.

The story highlights the tyranny endured by the peasants. Despite their poverty, they have to contend with an oppressive mayor who unlawfully seizes their chickens and money, fight the thieves who covet their few possessions, and watch out for selfish intruders who steal their share of irrigation water and allow their goats to graze on their small fields. The peasants are ignorant and illiterate. They depend on Muṣṭafā's father to provide them with legal and religious advice and to act as scribe for their formal complaints against their oppressors. In their endless trials and tribulations, they find solace in telling witty anecdotes and making jokes, even when the joke is on them.

One of the dramatic points in the story is the visit of the school inspector, who arrives from a distant city. The inspector asks the village children to draw an apple. To his utter surprise, they have never seen this fruit and cannot visualize what it is. This lack of awareness is due to the fact that apples are a luxury rarely enjoyed in the poor villages of Egypt. The inspector's request reveals that his urban world is far removed from that of the peasants and that he has no understanding of the reality of their lives. At a deeper level, the apple evokes the forbidden fruit of the tree of knowledge in the Garden of Eden. The village children, who are raised in ignorance, have no access to this fruit—knowledge. Hence Muṣṭafā dreams of eating an apple when he goes to school in the city, and he hopes to discover the meaning of many other secrets that ought to be perfectly clear to everyone.

The story further demonstrates that poverty breeds aggression against children and disregard for human life. For the destitute peasants, a beast of burden is more valuable than a child, even when that child is male, and even when he is an only child. Thus Muṣṭafā's uncle forbids him to ride the donkey and treats the donkey more kindly than the boy.

Although the story presents a classic example of socioeconomic determinism, it nevertheless alludes to the power of fate. Muṣṭafā has suffered a heartbreaking disappointment. How does he deal with his calamity and face his responsibility? On the one hand, he resolves to sleep on the chest next time, which indicates that he recognizes his fault. On the other, when his father and uncle prevent him from retaliating against the goat, he sadly concludes that the same deaf, tyrannical fate which protects the son of the chief of police also protects the goat that has shattered his hopes.

Despite this major setback, however, neither father nor son relinquishes their plan. Stubbornly, they intend to wait another year. With this ending, the author expresses the peasants' unshaken resolve to obtain an education and better their lives.[49]

Suhayl Idrīs
The Yellow Cotton Bird

Suhayl Idrīs was born into a conservative Muslim family in Beirut in 1923. His early education was primarily religious, and he attended Islamic schools. He took his baccalaureate in philosophy at the Islamic Maqāṣid College in Beirut, after which he worked in journalism. In 1949, he went to Paris and enrolled in the Sorbonne, from which he obtained his doctorate in literature in 1952. After returning to Lebanon, he founded the influential literary journal *al-Ādāb* (1953), of which he is still editor-in-chief, and the prestigious publishing house Dār al-Ādāb, which he continues to run.

Suhayl Idrīs has written short stories, novels, and literary criticism. His first three collections of short stories, published in the late 1940s, were later reprinted in one volume entitled *The Early Stories (Aqāṣīṣ ūlā,* 1977); they comprise what the author describes as his "romantic phase."[50] The next three short-story collections, published between the late 1950s and the early 1970s, were also reprinted in one volume entitled *The Later Stories* (*Aqāṣīṣ thāniya,* 1977); they are marked by realism. Idrīs's works of fiction include the acclaimed novel *The Latin Quarter (Al-Ḥayy al-lātīnī,* 1954), which contains autobiographical material related to his stay in Paris.

"The Yellow Cotton Bird" ("Al-ʿUṣfūr al-quṭnī al-aṣfar") is from *The Later Stories.* The story portrays the closed circle between one's aims and one's means: a simple porter wishes to improve his son's life through education, but his dream clashes with the stark reality of his dire poverty.

I'll surely have half a pound left over. Now I've got three and a half pounds. God has blessed my work today. True, I've worked harder than usual, but it was worth it. Praise be to God, He rewards us with what we deserve. After the evening prayer, I'll do two additional prostrations in gratitude. Three and a half pounds—that's not bad. One pound for meat, half a pound for eggplant, forty piasters for bread, sixty for rice, and half a pound for oil. Have I made a mistake? One pound, plus a half, plus another half, add forty piasters, and another sixty piasters. . . . No, no mistake. Half a pound, then, will be left. Ziyād will be happy today, may God preserve him. I'll make his dream come true after putting it off for the last six days. This evening, Ziyād. Tomorrow, darling. In the afternoon, my precious boy. I promise, son, tomorrow morning. I was almost ashamed to face him and wished that I would find him asleep when I came home, despite my great love for him. This evening, at long last, I won't be a liar any more. He'll touch the yellow bird's soft back with the palm of his little hand and hold it against his heart. May God protect him from harm. Forgive me, sweetheart. I kept promising every day that I would buy it for you. Can I forget how you stood in front of that shop window, looking disappointed at the yellow cotton bird, and how you reached out to touch it? I picked you up and kissed you, and promised to buy it the next day. Many days have passed since then. But what could I do, Ziyād? There was very little work this week. You know, or you may not know, how little money I make at my job. This week I've carried few loads, so few that I've even rested my back and the pain in my thigh has eased up. People are getting stingier all the time, Ziyād. Some of them carry their bags and suitcases by themselves instead of calling a porter, and some prefer to call a taxi to carry them and their luggage. The car competes with us for our livelihood, Ziyād. Imagine what will happen if this continues. I'm not fit to do any other work. I won't allow you to do such menial work. You'll become something better than I am. A son should outdo his father. The porter's son become a porter? I'll never agree to that. You'll do better than I, Ziyād. You'll go to school next year. I wanted you to begin school this year, but they told me you were too young. To be honest, Ziyād, I was a little relieved to hear that because I didn't know where to get the money for tuition. But from now on, I'll work much harder to save money for your next year's tuition. Perhaps in a year or two tuition will be reduced, or even abolished. Who knows? The other porters who are my friends always complain when they talk about school and their children. They all have children like you, Ziyād, and it's strange, but not only do they all want their children to go to school, it's got to be a good school at that. But, as they say, the cost is high. Yesterday, the head of our group said that tuition in our country is the highest in the world. He said that education here is a matter of business and profit, and he wonders why the government doesn't make education compulsory and free of charge. If only that would happen! But if it doesn't, then I'll work day and night, Ziyād, to save money for your tuition, and pray to God to change this corrupt government.

Strange. Is this the grocery store? It seems to have suddenly popped up before me, as if it wasn't here before. I must have wandered off. Well then, Ḥājj Maḥmūd, give me a kilogram of rice, a pound's worth of oil, and bread. I still need eggplants. I'll get those at Mūsā's. As for the meat, I'll buy it at the butcher's. We haven't had meat for three days. Now, God has sent us some relief. Not bad. We won't die of hunger. Salīma's a good woman. She doesn't ask for anything and never complains. May God give her health. Her only concerns are Ziyād and the single room in which we live. Our room looks so clean every evening! It's always so nice and relaxing at home. I feel as if I've returned from a distant trip. But I don't spend much time there. True, the room is clean, but it's also very small. It won't be suitable for Ziyād when he grows up. Hopefully, the future will be better and I'll earn more money. Who knows? Maybe I'll give up being a porter and find a better-paying job. Honestly, I don't understand why they don't set up big factories here, as they do everywhere else. I'm very strong. I could work in a big factory behind a powerful machine, and I'd run it with pride and honor. People wonder how I can lift any bag no matter how full it is. Believe me, Ziyād, I almost feel that I deserve something better than this job. Not that I'm ashamed of it, God forbid, but I want a better job. What's wrong with wanting to improve my condition? Anyway, let's leave that for the future.

And now, ʿAmm Saʿīd, give me an ounce and a quarter of meat. Yes, the beef. Give me some bones, too. Clean them a little bit, ʿAmm Saʿīd. May God bless you and keep you well.

I feel very hungry today. Praise be to God, I'm satisfied quickly once I begin to eat. Only a few bites fill me up. Then I wonder how I could have been so hungry. The eggplant tastes very good, and luckily it also cooks quickly. I'll suggest to Umm Ziyād that we fry one or two, and save the rest with the meat for tomorrow's dinner. After I finish off my meal with a few olives, I'll take Ziyād on my lap and watch him play with the yellow cotton bird. He'll have fun with it for a while, and then he'll tuck it beside him in bed and fall asleep with a smile. Wait for me, Ziyād. In another ten minutes you'll have the bird. You'll hold it in your sweet little hand, and I'll carry you in my arms and kiss you and smell you and hug you. Wait for me, Ziyād. Wait.

What's this? Why is that damned kid beating that boy? Hey, you! Why are you beating him? He's your brother? Then your crime is twice as bad! Don't you hear him crying in pain? Don't you see that the pieces of gum are falling from his little cardboard box and that he's picking them up one by one? Why don't you help him, you wretch? Where did you learn to be so cruel? What? The boy's crying because he hasn't sold all the gum in his box? Is that why you're beating him? He'll sell the remaining pieces tomorrow. Your father will beat up both of you because of this? He might throw the boy out and make him sleep on the doorstep? But what kind of a father is he? Is he sick? Woe to the tyrant who has such a disease! Is being sick sufficient reason to inflict such suffering on a child? You've sold all your pieces of gum, but your brother hasn't? Then help him sell what he has left. No, I don't know your father, that's true. But I'm a father, too. He's very cruel? How can that be? You swear by God that he'll give your little brother a severe beating? Then why are you beating him, too? Because he wants to sell you the rest of his gum, so that you'll get the beating instead? Enough. Enough. He's crying because he hasn't sold all his gum. That's clear. Leave him alone. Come here, little boy. Wipe your tears and stop crying. How old are you, son? Four? Just like my little boy, Ziyād. May God keep both of you safe and sound. How many pieces of gum have you got left? Nine? And how much is each one? Nine francs? That comes to forty-five piasters. Yes, forty-five piasters altogether. But . . . what about the yellow cotton bird? The yellow bird? The bird? The five piasters I'd have left aren't enough to buy it. What should I do? O God, help me solve this problem. Are you crying again, little boy? Look at me. Strange. Why didn't I notice this before? You look like Ziyād. I swear by God that you look like him. And you're the same age. But I—I don't beat him. I'm not sick, thank God. And even if I were sick, I would never lay a finger on him. Enough. Enough. Don't cry any more. Wait a second. Come here. I don't want your father to beat you. It would be like me beating Ziyād. Imagine me beating Ziyād! May my hand be cut off before I do that! Come here. Take this. It's half a pound. I'm buying the remaining pieces of gum from you. Hand them over. Don't be shocked, son. The other five piasters? No, keep them for yourself. Take them, too. They're a gift. A gift from Ziyād to you. Yes. Smile like this. Hold your brother's hand. And you, don't you beat him again! Don't you ever beat him. He is little, and beautiful, and he looks just like my son Ziyād. Do you hear? Don't you ever beat him again. And now, give my regards to your father. No, I don't know him, but tell him that Abū Ziyād sends his regards. Goodbye. Goodbye.

Strange. Why does this basket feel so heavy when it contains so little? What happened? It's as if an invisible hand has placed the misery of the entire world inside it, and that's why it feels heavier and heavier. I can no longer bear it. It's not only the world's misery, but its injustice too. Misery as well as injustice. I'm going to rest on this doorstep for a few minutes so that I can continue. It's all right, now. I've rested a bit. I should be on my way so I can see Ziyād before he goes to sleep.

May God give you health, Umm Ziyād. Take this. It's some food. God has protected us today. Listen to this story, Umm Ziyād. But where's Ziyād? I don't hear his voice. He's asleep? Why did he go to sleep so early? Oh, he waited for me for a long time and he kept asking about the yellow bird and then got tired and fell asleep.

Never mind, Umm Ziyād. Tomorrow. Tomorrow, I'll buy him the yellow bird. Absolutely. With what they pay me for the first load I carry, I'll buy it. Without fail.

The room looks so nice, Umm Ziyād! May your hands be blessed. I have no money, Umm Ziyād, but you are my wealth and my fortune. You and Ziyād.

O God, what do I see? Thank God, it was only a dream. I dreamt that Ziyād had turned into a bird, a little yellow bird. He began hovering in the room, then he flew out of the window far, far away. . . .

May God preserve you, Ziyād. May you continue to smile when you're awake and when you're asleep, as if an angel's wing were protecting you. Come, let me kiss your forehead. Come, Ziyād, before I fall asleep again.

But I cannot fall asleep. My eyes are wide open, staring into the night, into this long, thick night. I feel weighed down, just as I did a while ago when I was carrying the basket. I want the night to pass quickly and lift my burden. When will the morning dawn?

Comments

This story consists of a single monologue narrated through the stream-of-consciousness technique. The man whose chain of thoughts unfolds before the reader belongs to the lower strata of society and has a wife and child to support. His occupation as a porter serves as a symbol for the multiple burdens that he bears on the personal, emotional, and social levels. As a porter, he meets all kinds of people and is in a unique position to observe the inequities and distinctions in society. Barely able to provide his family with the basic necessities, he is still better off than the unemployed and homeless people whom he encounters. Thus the porter occupies the borderline between two groups, the poor and the utterly destitute, and dangles between bare existence and lack of subsistence. In this situation, he is inclined to feel sadness for the selfishness which predominates in human behavior.

The image of the bird dominates the story. The bird signifies the gift of freedom which the porter wants to bestow on his son. However, the intended bird is made of cotton; it is not alive or real, but a mere toy. The artificial bird reveals a faint hope of success. The porter has a dream in which his son flies like a bird out of his confining environment. The only way to achieve this dream is through education, which the porter ardently seeks for his son. However, his meager income and failing health suggest that he is unlikely to succeed in accomplishing this goal on his own.

The somber atmosphere of the story is brightened by the porter's act of compassion. His love for his boy enables him to recognize the anguish of another boy, who is abused by his brother for not selling his assigned quantity of gum. Using the few piasters with which he intended to buy the bird for his son, the porter instead buys the gum. His humane gesture shows the basic goodness in human nature and puts the whole story in an optimistic light. As a porter, he relies on people to give him tips, based on their goodwill. His decision to buy the gum from the child is his way of contributing to the chain of generosity on which he, too, is dependent.

The porter's economic condition is harsh, yet he is able to endure it through his complete trust in God (*tawakkul*). This trust lends him emotional strength and comfort: "God rewards us with what we deserve." Highly moral and righteous, his piety sustains him in times of need and reassures him that better days will come. While he humbly expresses gratitude to God for whatever he receives, he is critical of the existing social order and painfully conscious of the misery and injustice that pervade God's world. Hard as he tries not to complain, he wishes for a better lot, especially for his son.

The porter's precarious existence is further compounded by the invasion of modernity. The advent of the motor car has made porters' service superfluous. The porter is all too aware that the car competes with his trade and threatens his livelihood (compare "The Viper Is Thirsty" by Ghassān Kanafānī, in chapter 2). Unskilled to do any other work, his only asset is his physical strength, but it, too, is failing. In his despair, the porter dreams of working in a big factory behind a powerful machine as the solution to all his problems. He yearns for social reforms that will make education compulsory and free for all, while industrialization will provide jobs for all. In addition, government corruption will be eliminated and the rights of the individual will be fully protected. This dream, which contains elements of a social utopia, reflects the mood of many writers at that point in Arab history.

Finally, in this story the author shows that for the destitute, who live in constant material want, faith in God constitutes an indispensable coping mechanism. Religion is the only possession of the poor. They therefore cling to it, nurture it, and arm themselves with it against life's misfortunes. At the same time, the story illustrates the ambition of the working classes to obtain an education and better their lives. The porter's wish to send his son to school is shared by all his colleagues, who want their children not only to go to school but also to a good school. It is noteworthy that in both stories in this chapter, the fathers—the older generation—have given up making anything of themselves and see the hope for the future in their educated sons.[51]

7

CHANCE

The Random Arbiter

Chance rules the world.
—Ghāda al-Sammān[1]

The Idea of Chance

Chance chooses a single sperm cell, out of millions, to meet the ovum and form human life. The blending of two sex chromosomes, an X with an X, or an X with a Y, determines the individual's specificity and identity as, respectively, a female or a male. Mere chance, free but blind, is at the root of this momentous biological event, which has lifelong repercussions: a female's assigned role in many societies is fundamentally different from that of a male.

"Chance, in the most general sense of the word, is the negation of necessity and the opposite of determinism," suggests one definition.[2] Stated differently, chance is the way that things happen with no obvious cause or plan and with total lack of predictability. The word, however, contains a wide range of meanings: "To some, chance denotes human freedom, but to others, fate. Chance can be haphazard; it can be fortunate or unfortunate. It is a highly equivocal, bifacial term, in that one meaning can easily turn into its opposite. This ambivalence may be traced back to the essential unpredictability and unknowability of any occurrence."[3] Given the ambiguous nature of chance, "plain bad luck" may be the explanation when an unfavorable outcome results from obscure factors or when the causal connection is missing, while "plain good luck" may be the conclusion when the outcome is unexpectedly and inexplicably positive.[4]

The relationship between chance and fate can be seen as one of complementary polarity: "Chance and fate—these initially contradictory notions are but two counterinterpretations of the experience of unexpected coincidence or happenings that seem arbitrary but nevertheless have a decisive impact on one's life and in some cases totally change it."[5] From a strictly fatalistic perspective, mere chance does not exist, because all events are determined prior to their occurrence and every single detail is already fixed.

An outlook based on the notion of chance may be experienced positively or negatively and is generally reflected in the attitudes and expectations of people. Common statements such as "Luck is everything in life" and "Being in the right place at the right time" (or conversely, "Being in the wrong place at the wrong time") indicate the importance which people attach to chance in the unfolding of their lives. Frequently, the workings of chance are likened to a lottery—the result is equally uncertain and depends entirely on luck. Hence there are expressions such as "Life is a crap shoot" and "It's better to be lucky than smart." Arabic proverbial lore abounds in sayings to this effect: "A handful of good luck is better than six assloads of learning" (*kaff bakht khayr min kurr ʿilm*); "An ounce of good luck is better than a pound of cleverness" (*qīrāṭ bakht wa-lā faddān shaṭāra*).

There are people who view life as a chain of chance occurrences and others who view it as an interplay of chance with character. Chance may place a person in a certain position or present a certain opportunity, but ultimately the individual's character will determine whether this opportunity is seized and nurtured or ignored and wasted. "A wise man turns chance into good fortune," counsels one folk saying. "Opportunity never knocks twice," warns another. While the interaction of chance with character is readily discernible, the intermingling of chance with other orderly factors in life and nature is barely perceptible. This leads David F. Bell to suggest that "the claim that there is an essential chance should probably be tempered in favor of a formulation . . . that the universe is composed of a combination of orderly and disorderly phenomena and that the place where such phenomena meet is something like the moment of contingency which is the present."[6]

Leonard W. Doob argues that from a cognitive standpoint there is no difference between ascribing a past or future event to chance or to fate-destiny when both terms are used as "verbal clichés without any reference to retrodiction or prediction." Chance entails "the absence of both Necessity and Impossibility"; people do not know "where or whether the figurative or literal lightning will strike." He concludes that chance doctrines serve as substitutes for inevitability doctrines either as a result of uncertainty or as an explanation of it.[7]

The interest in chance is not a phenomenon of modern times, though it has been influenced by certain discoveries and advances in science. Ancient cultures had a mythological notion of chance as a kind of antideity, Tyche (Greek) or Fortuna (Roman). At the end of the Renaissance, the development of scientific and mathematical reasoning brought the question of probability and how to deal with chance within the framework of the scientist's goal, which is to find regularities and formulate general laws. The fascination with chance increased, along with the preoccupation with games of chance, in early–seventeenth-century England and France. Thus, while interest in chance promoted new scientific theories, these, in turn, were achieved through the gradual elimination of chance phenomena.[8]

Chance in the Arab-Muslim Context

In the Arab world, the prevailing religious view excludes chance as a force in human life. The traditional beliefs of orthodox Islam attribute every event that transpires in the universe to God's omnipotence and the divine design. A theistic position that negates chance is predicated on the theory of a dynamically stable world comprising codes of order that give direction and meaning to life. In most cultures, the interpretation of chance is part of a worldview, be it deterministic or indeterministic. According to one explanation, the fundamental mystery of events can inspire awe. The religious mind has seen in chance something sacred or an expression of the divine will. Some have placed chance under the control of divine providence. Others reject it out of reverence for the divine providence, asserting that whatever happens is in conformity with the transcendent scheme. Consequently, an apparent chance event, either fortunate or unfortunate, assumes the meaning of fate. In contrast, chance seen as indicating the total uncertainty of things would imply the presence of free will. In the main, the perception of chance is anchored in people's outlook on life, be it secular or spiritual.[9]

The Qur'ān teaches that there is no room for chance in God's creation. Everything in the universe has been created by God with a definite purpose and in precise measure: "Verily, all things have We created in proportion and measure" (54:49). A. Yusuf Ali comments: "God's Creation is not haphazard. Everything goes by law, proportion, and measure. Everything has its appointed time, place, and occasion, as also its definite limitation. Nothing happens but according to His Plan, and every deed, word, and thought of man has its fullest consequences, except insofar as the Grace or Mercy of God intervenes, and that is according to law and plan."[10]

The idea of chance is null and void in the Qur'ān especially as God, the almighty creator, has foreknowledge of the most inscrutable events on earth: "God knows what every female bears: He knows of every change within her womb. For everything He has a finite measure" (13:8). A. Yusuf Ali interprets: "The female womb is just an example, a type, of extreme secrecy. Not even the female herself knows what is in the womb—whether it is a male young or a female young, whether it is one or more, whether it is to be born short of the standard time or to exceed the standard time. But the most hidden and apparently unknowable things are clear to God's knowledge: there is no mere chance: all things are regulated by God in just measure and proportion."[11] This assertion is repeated in numerous verses: "And there is not a thing but with Us are the stores thereof. And We send it not down save in appointed measure" (15:21); "It is He who created all things, and ordered them in due proportions" (25:2). Such verses are widely quoted in support of the predestinarian views of the Qur'ān, which, as previously noted, preclude the presence of chance.

Fazlur Rahman writes that the Qur'ān refutes not only the argument that the universe is a phenomenon of chance but also the claim that God created the world as a sport, for among the Ṣūfīs there are those who adhere literally to a famous Ḥadīth report in which God said: "I was a hidden treasure, but I wished to be known, therefore I created the creation."[12] His commentary sheds light on the Qur'ānic verse "It was not in sport that We created the heaven and the earth and all that lies between them. Had it been Our will to find a pastime, We could have found one near at hand" (21:16–17). As stated by Rahman, the point at issue is that if the world is a sport, all talk of guidance and error and the Last Judgment becomes irrelevant. The Qur'ān must therefore reject the notion that the universe, organized and functioning the way it is, could be a casual product and establish conclusively that creation points to a purposeful creator. For the same reason, belief in a cyclic universe must also be dismissed, for however attractive it may be, cyclic motion is incompatible with any purposefulness.[13] Hence the Qur'ān constantly asserts: "Not without purpose did We create heaven and earth and all between!" (38:27). Insofar as chance is linked to risk taking and probability (gambling, betting, dice), the Qur'ān prohibits such activities, as they imply dealing with the unknown—the future—which is in God's hands.[14] Invariably, these activities are castigated as vices: "Believers, wine and games of chance, idols and divining arrows are abominations devised by Satan. Avoid them, so that you may prosper" (5:90).

There are various words in Arabic for the cluster of meanings surrounding the term "chance." *Ṣudfa* and *muṣādafa* convey the sense of "coincidence" or "happenstance." *Ḥaẓẓ* and *bakht* denote "fortune" or "luck" and can be modified by adjectives to indicate good or bad luck. In folklore, *ḥaẓẓ* can be foretold by a fortune-teller through diverse methods of divination, such as reading the palm of the hand or the residue in a cup of coffee, as well as by means of geomancy and astrology.[15] *Qadar* (fate), however, is inscrutable; it cannot be foreseen; it becomes evident only after the conclusion of events. *Ḥaẓẓ* is perceived as an episode that happens occasionally and lasts temporarily, whereas *qadar* represents a set course of events that dominates a person's entire life. The sense of "opportunity" is expressed by *furṣa*, and "random" is rendered by *'ashwā'ī*. Lastly, there is the word *naṣīb*, which is richer in meaning. It signifies "portion," "luck," "chance," "fate," and "lot." A colloquial saying runs: "God brings one's lot" (*Allāh bijīb illi fi n-naṣīb*, Levantine).[16]

The role of luck is acknowledged in the Qur'ān. Good fortune originates from God and is contingent on good conduct: "And no one will be granted such goodness except those who exercise patience and self-restraint, none but persons of the greatest good fortune" (41:35). The bestowal of good fortune (*ḥaẓẓ ʿaẓīm*) is inevitably a cause of envy and admiration: "Lo! he is lord of rare good fortune" (28:79). Arabic proverbial lore recognizes the crucial factor of luck. A couple of popular sayings state: "One's fortune depends on God" (*al-bakht ʿinda Allāh*) and "Life is a matter of luck" (*al-dunyā ḥuẓūẓ*).

Chance in the Literary Context

In classical Arabic literature, which, as noted earlier, was essentially an Islamic literature, authors did not take an active interest in the issue of chance in conveying a meaningful message about human life. Inspired by religious and ethical motivations to produce texts that are beneficial for study and instruction, they tended to regard the topic of chance as unsuitable for serious literary treatment. In the popular narrative tradition, however, including epics, romances, and sagas, the motif of chance found creative expression. Nevertheless, even in *The Arabian Nights*, where chance and prominent—along with fantasy, improbability, and extravagance—play a prominent role, the general thrust of the narrative is to show that ultimately people are propelled by fate and controlled by God's will. The idea of chance emerges as a major theme in modern Arabic literature, where, under the influence of surrealism and existentialism, it is often employed to point out the profound uncertainty at the heart of reality.

Whereas other views of human destiny, such as those previously discussed, emphasize the rational and orderly nature of life, the concept of chance stresses the opposite. If all events are occasioned and experienced by mere accident, if there is neither plan nor purpose, neither observable pattern nor causal connection, then reality becomes increasingly ambiguous and erratic. People are perceived as dangling in a terrifying world in which extraordinary things happen with no explanation or power of intervention. A chaotic, irrational world produces alienated individuals who live from one moment to the next, from one opportunity to another, vulnerable to the most mundane daily affairs. They are involuntarily entangled in bizarre relationships and absurd circumstances from which they cannot extricate themselves. In this reality, people are alone, with nothing to guide them but their basic instincts. Social structures are inherently flawed, and justice is seldom seen in the endless and mostly tragic procession of life.

Within such a frame of reference, it is entirely conceivable for an underdog to become a hero without the slightest effort or intention. This is what happens to the protagonist in Najīb Maḥfūẓ's story "The Drug Addict and the Bomb" ("Al-Masṭūl wa-al-qunbula").[17] Ayyūb goes to visit his friend Muḥsin, a clothes presser. Stoned from taking drugs, he sits on the sidewalk in front of his friend's shop when a political demonstration happens to pass by. A violent attack on the captain, followed by a bomb explosion in the vicinity, sends the police looking for the culprit and the people fleeing to safety. The only person remaining on the street is the semiconscious Ayyūb. Seized as a scapegoat, he is arrested and charged with both crimes. After spending years in prison, he emerges as a national hero and a symbol of courage and self-sacrifice. Taken with his new image, Ayyūb is smart enough to avail himself of the favorable circumstances: he announces his intention to run as a district representative in the upcoming elections.

Extreme elements of chaos, irrationality, inopportune timing, and happenstance are featured in Yūsuf Idrīs's story "The Aorta" ("Al-Awurṭā").[18] The story opens with a scene of utter turmoil on a square through which swarms of people are running frantically in every direction in search of a starting point or a goal. The compulsive running is accompanied by shoves, blows, and collisions, which throw people to the ground, screaming and groaning. But this physical friction has no effect on the overall flow, which continues uninterrupted. Before long, a violent conflict unfolds: the first-person narrator bumps into ʿAbduh, a petty thief whom he suspects of having stolen his money. The narrator's outspoken accusation is sufficient to attract a crowd and transform the aimless, divided individuals into a cohesive mob, viciously intent on its newfound target, ʿAbduh. Here, however, the handy scapegoat is not provided with an opportunity to redeem his life but is deprived of his life: he is led to a butcher's shop and hung on a meat hook in an outburst of hatred, brutality, and madness.[19]

In Fatḥī Ghānim's novel *The Man Who Lost His Shadow (Al-Rajul alladhī faqad ẓillahu,* 1962), the protagonist, Yūsuf Ḥāmid, tries in vain to discern the logic in his life. He is particularly at a loss to understand how his life has become so intertwined with that of Mabrūka, the servant girl whom his father has unexpectedly married. That their paths should cross defies reason:

> What happened was so ordinary. She was Mabrūka. . . . I was Yūsuf. She was a maid working in someone else's house. I was the son of a schoolmaster. She was a peasant from the country, I was from Cairo. We had nothing in common. Nothing but the link of coincidence. She was growing up. . . . I was growing up. Thoughts ran through her mind, thoughts ran through mine. Her flesh had urges, so had mine. She swept, cleaned, answered a servant's bell while I studied geography, geometry, English, French and law. Yet, like fate she forced her way into my life and I forced my way into hers.[20]

After Mabrūka's husband dies, leaving her with no means of support, she becomes a prostitute, while Yūsuf becomes a famous journalist. Yet he, too, has to prostitute himself to his corrupt master to obtain his means of subsistence. The correlation is astonishing:

> Nothing covers her body. Nothing covers me. Thinking about life drives a man mad. Life is irrational. I, who write about socialism, who urge the people to believe in planning and in a hopeful future, I who tell them that life is logical, with a reasonable purpose—what logic has my life had, to equip me to teach the logic of theirs? . . . No surety, no logic. We control nothing—except our own suicides.[21]

In "The Picture" ("Al-Ṣūra") by Nawāl al-Saʿdāwī, a mere accident triggers a new awareness that changes the life of a little girl forever: "Everything could have gone on as before in Narjis's life, had her hand not collided accidentally with Nabawiyya's backside, and had her fingers not hit a soft sphere of flesh, and had her amazed eyes not seen a pair of small protrusions wobbling along under Nabawiyya's dress in time with the jerking of her arms as she stood washing at the sink."[22] Suddenly awakened to her femininity and sexuality, the little girl then inadvertently stumbles upon her much-admired father raping the maid in the kitchen. As the godlike image of her father is shattered to pieces in her mind, the girl instantly matures and loses her childhood innocence.

The story "An Encounter" ("Liqāʾ mā"), by the Tunisian author Ḥasan Naṣr (b. 1937), contains a tragicomic portrayal of the role of chance in everyday life. As the story consists of a very short text, it is presented here in full:

> When she saw me, a spark of happiness flashed across her wide eyes. Her almond-shaped face overwhelmed me, and I was entirely captivated by its charm.
>
> Her dainty mouth parted in a childish smile as she extended her hand to shake mine. As I launched forth into profuse greetings, she cried out:
>
> "Is it really you? When did you return?"
>
> The warmth of the voice I had yearned so much to hear enveloped me.
>
> "Only a short time ago."
>
> Looking me straight in the eyes, she repeated after me: "Only a short time ago! My heart told me you were back."
>
> I wondered whether she really had thought of me during my absence.
>
> I muttered, unable to take my eyes off her: "I saw you that evening after my return."
>
> Surprised and bewildered, she asked: "Did you really see me? Where?"

> "You were walking slowly toward the café on Liberty Street."
>
> "Why didn't you speak to me?"
>
> "That was exactly what I wanted to do when I saw you. But then I realized that you were not alone, that you were in the company of a man."
>
> Her wide, intelligent eyes sparkled, and she smiled enticingly. "Was that a reason not to speak to me?" Still smiling, she added: "And who was this man? What did he look like?"
>
> "He had a dignified look about him. He seemed a little old, but despite his age he was quite handsome."
>
> Grinning from ear to ear, she immediately responded: "You say he was old—that was my father! I was out with him last Thursday. I've told him a lot about you. He knows about the letters you wrote to me."
>
> I couldn't help but laugh with her. So the two of us laughed . . . and laughed. . . .
>
> The clever girl forgot that she had introduced me to her father before I went on my journey, and that he was *not* the old man who had been escorting her and flirting with her![23]

While this story illustrates the coincidence of events in time and place, it also highlights the absurdity of such occurrences and their decisive impact. In this case, the chance encounter clearly determines the future relationship between the narrator and the woman.

Finally, in Yaḥyā al-Ṭāhir ʿAbdallāh's story "A Tale Told by a Dog" ("Ḥikāya ʿalā lisān kalb"), chance accounts for the survival of a newborn puppy:

> I am the child of blind chance [*anā ibn al-ṣudfa al-ʿamyāʾ*]. My name is Maḥẓūẓ [i.e., "lucky"], and there's a story to my name which my mother tells:
>
> "I gave birth to two puppies, then to two more, then to two more. You were one of them. The man of the house said to his children's mother: 'Choose, O mother of my children, from amongst these puppies one that will live with our children.' His wife pointed to you and said: 'The one that's half white and half black.' So the man of the house got up and took up your brothers and sisters and threw them onto the faraway waste land, to hunger and the cold and the winds and the rain and wild animals. Your father went up to you and smelled you and licked you lovingly, saying: 'You're lucky.' So I said: 'What about our calling him Maḥẓūẓ?' Your father answered: 'Agreed, Mother of Maḥẓūẓ.' "[24]

The story develops into an allegory about human life.

The fuzzy line of demarcation between fate and chance is depicted by Tawfīq al-Ḥakīm in his autobiography *The Prison of Life (Sijn al-ʿumr*, 1964). The author recounts how his parents' marriage came to be arranged: "[My mother] told me the story of that marriage. Because the prospective groom's mother had died, it was his paternal aunt and his sister—both provincial—who came to Alexandria in search of a bride. Fate [*al-qadar*], or chance [*al-muṣādafāt*], or that mysterious Wisdom [*ḥikma*] which remains unknown to mankind to this day and which always manifests itself in such circumstances and brings together two out of millions with unimaginable consequences—Fate, then, led them to my mother."[25] It is interesting to note that for al-Ḥakīm, mathematical reasoning (two out of millions) points in the direction of fate.

Chance and Existentialism

Arab writers who draw on the notion of chance to interpret life represent the existentialist trend in Arab thought. As a philosophical theory, existentialism occupies an important place in modern Arabic literature, and its expression is found in almost every domain of creative art, whether verbal or visual. While the basic issues of social justice, political struggle, and the human condition figured to varying degrees in Arabic writing of the first half of the twentieth century, they became the dominant themes after World War II, concurrent with the shift from romanticism to realism and the appearance of the French existentialists on the Arabic literary scene.[26] Jabrā Ibrāhīm Jabrā (1920–94), a critic, poet, and fiction writer, describes the response of Arab intellectuals to existentialism:

> When Sartre and Camus . . . were translated and studied all through the fifties, they took Arab intellectual life by storm. Sartre was the special favorite of Beirut's literary workshop, and the reaction in Baghdad and Cairo was tremendous. One did not have to agree with everything Sartre said, but his ideas became pivotal to the new generation of writers who sought involvement in the political and social issues of their times. Whether novelists, essayists or poets, their preoccupation was with radical change and the concepts concomitant to it.[27]

Jabrā notes that the Arabic word *iltizām*—"commitment"—became a key word in the vocabulary of writers and critics alike. It covered a wide range of meanings, from Marxism to nationalism to existentialism, but its primary sense was the need for the writer to convey a message rather than to produce art for art's sake. Theory was put into practice, and a new journal, *al-Ādāb*, appeared in Beirut in 1953. It was guided mostly by Sartre's philosophical and dramatic writings, and its message centered on commitment.

As Jabrā explains, the 1950s witnessed intense conflicts with the West (e.g., Palestine, the Suez Canal, Algeria), which generated a demand for a literature wholly committed to Arab causes. There was a heightened realization that "to meet the challenge of the West, society had to change through action, and action was to be attended by a great deal of philosophical speculation."[28] Existentialism, with its strong affinity to socialism and nationalism, was perceived as conducive to regeneration on several different levels: the moral and individual as well as the political and national. The new writers' main motifs were freedom, anxiety, protest, struggle, social progress, individual salvation, rebellion, and heroism. The prevailing mood was one of commitment to humanity: "A 'Third World' was being born and writers were its prophets."[29]

Owing to the interactive nature of the arts, when poetry changed, fiction and drama changed, and so did painting and architecture. All these creative domains have shared the same influences and motivations: "Man's alienation, his exile, his hope, whether 'man is a useless passion' (Sartre), whether tragic confrontation is the determining factor in human existence, whether, as Camus advocates, man accepts the absurd in life in order to transcend it in praise of the glory of life itself, these are some of the questions put to us in all our arts."[30] In the literary realm, modern Arabic drama merits special mention because of the theater of the absurd, which, as "an offshoot, however unexpected, of existentialist philosophy, is itself a paradoxical comment on the meaningful in life."[31] This type of response characterizes primarily the work of Egyptian playwrights, foremost among whom is Tawfīq al-Ḥakīm.

The point of connection between existentialist thought and the concept of chance lies in the denial of the existence of God and the assertion that chaos and absurdity are at the basis of human reality. Jean-Paul Sartre defines the existentialist position on the human condition: "When we speak of 'abandonment' . . . we only mean to say that God does not exist, and that it is necessary to draw the consequences of his absence right to the end."[32] One of these consequences is that human beings are peripheral to the universe: "Mankind, instead of being the central figure on the stage of reality, the rational creature for whom the nonrational world exists, is actually an accident, a late and adventitious newcomer whose life is governed by contingency; and the proof, paradoxically, comes from rationalism itself from the Darwinian idea of evolution."[33] Another consequence is that human beings are responsible for their own fate: "All man's alibis are unacceptable: no gods are responsible for his condition; no original sin; no heredity and no environment; no race, no caste, no father, and no mother; no wrong-headed education, no governess, no teacher; not even an impulse or a disposition, a complex or a childhood trauma. Man is free."[34] Freedom, however, is a mixed blessing, both a great gift and a great burden: "Man stands alone in the universe, responsible for his condition, likely to remain in a lowly state, but free to reach above the stars."[35] Hence existentialism, while potentially life-enhancing, accentuates the tragic element in the human predicament.

A classic example of the existentialist outlook can be found in Najīb Maḥfūẓ's story "Under the Bus Shelter" ("Taḥta al-miẓalla," 1969).[36] Passengers waiting for a bus are witnesses to bizarre events that unfold before their eyes: cars crash into each other, people assault people, they kill, make love in the street, dance in the nude, and dig graves to bury the living with the dead. Chance is the driving force of these senseless happenings. The story focuses on the negative side of what happens when affairs are left alone to take their own course. The result is a nightmarish world in which anarchy reigns supreme, the most primitive human instincts take over, and crime and immorality are the norms of society. In this series of scenes seemingly from a motion picture, there is no "movie director"—that is, there is no God, no leader, no system. In addition, the internal turmoil parallels the external rainstorm: in the absence of sensible guidance and control, both human beings and nature regress into a state of self-destruction. The story expresses the profound loneliness of human beings and the pressing need to put their minds to work in order to create a meaningful structure to life. Without self-consciousness and social responsibility, people fall prey to disaster, oppression, and exploitation. Significantly, the story was written in the aftermath of the Six-Day War with Israel.

In an early article entitled "Arab Inquietude in Modern Times,"[37] Jacques Berque, one of France's distinguished Islamic scholars, discusses the perturbing effect the West has had on Arab society. In examining the intellectuals' attitudes through their literary works, he identifies three major characteristics: confusion between nature and the political world (nature, for the Arabs, is the "other"), preference for the symbolic over the real (words are not only informative but also creative), and resentment. Berque notes that in this psychological climate, existentialism emerges as a key idea, which can lead to political and social commitment, despair and nihilism, or revolt.[38] Contemporary Arabic writing manifests all these forms of response. This is not to say that one author may be committed to one response to the exclusion of others. On the contrary, Arab authors tend to be dynamic in their approach to the problems of modern life, and their vision of reality is subject to change. Najīb Maḥfūẓ, most notably, wrote the allegorical novel *Children of Gebelawi (Awlād ḥāratinā)*, an expression of despair and nihilism, in 1959. His later works, however, show a tendency toward the mystical experience, and Ṣūfī or semi-Ṣūfī characters often appear in them. Some examples are the Ṣūfī shaykh in "Zaʿbalwī" (1963) and in *The Thief and the Dogs (Al-Liṣṣ wa-al-kilāb*, 1961), Samīr ʿAbd al-Bāqī in *Autumn Quail (Al-Summān wa-al-kharīf*, 1962), and ʿUmar al-Ḥamzāwī in *The Beggar (Al Shaḥḥādh*, 1965).[39] The mystical tendency is still evident in Maḥfūẓ's most recent work, *Echoes of an Autobiography (Aṣdā' al-sīra al-dhātiyya*, 1995), in which a Ṣūfī sage bearing the symbolic and intriguing name "ʿAbd Rabbihi al-Tā'ih," that is, "the lost slave of his Lord," plays a prominent role.

Despite the enthusiasm with which existentialist philosophy was received in the Arab world, on the whole this secular outlook has remained the preoccupation of the intellectual minority and has failed to filter down to the common people. The existentialists' hope of revolutionizing Arab attitudes to life by eliminating the influence of religion, replacing fatalism with activism, and focusing on the present rather than the past has not materialized. Existentialism did lead to a surge of creativity in Arabic literature but not to the desired radical change in Arab society.

In conclusion, the concept of chance, as a perspective on human fate, represents the antithesis of the concept of God's will. If Arab thought may be perceived as a continuum, at one extreme of this continuum stands the religious belief in God's will as determining the fate of each and every individual. At the other extreme stands the secular belief in chance. In between lie the various rational approaches to human fate, such as the philosophical (time), the psychological (character), the cultural (custom), the biological (gender), and the economic (class and capital).

Ghāda al-Sammān
Another Scarecrow

Ghāda al-Sammān was born in Damascus in 1942. She comes from an intellectual family: her mother was herself a writer, and her father was rector of the University of Damascus and Syria's minister of education. In 1961, she received her B.A. in English literature from the University of Damascus. In 1964, she moved to Beirut, where she earned her M.A. from the American University of Beirut. In 1967, she went to London to pursue postgraduate studies. She returned to Beirut in 1969 and worked as a translator, university lecturer, and journalist. Her first collection of short stories appeared in 1962 and was followed by novels, volumes of poetry, and books of essays. The outspoken nature of her social and political criticism put obstacles in the path of her career, so in 1977 she founded her own publishing house to enable her to disseminate her works. In 1984, the Lebanese civil war forced her to leave Beirut for Paris, where she currently resides.

A leading fiction writer, al-Sammān is known for her liberal views. The major themes in her work include the Arab national struggle against colonialism and imperialism, the tension between tradition and modernity, the oppression of women, and the importance of self-realization. In her novels and stories, she makes frequent use of symbols and poetic language, and her chosen images, while vivid and original, tend to be provocative. She is one of the most prolific women writers in the Arab world, and many of her works have been translated into various European languages.

"Another Scarecrow" ("Fazzāʿ ṭuyūr ākhar") is from the collection *The Night of Strangers (Layl al-ghurabā',* 1966).[40] The story depicts the role of chance in the life of a barren woman whose culture regards procreation as the main purpose of marriage and as the most important task of women in society.

It's raining. It's raining.

It's raining ash-gray hail, and boredom. It's been raining since morning, on and on, on and on.

I feel I'm in a slow train crossing vast, dead deserts. The passengers don't know each other; everyone speaks a different language; and no one knows where he's going, or where he's come from.

It's raining, dull, ceaseless rain.

In the garden, the cat wails continuously, a low, sorrowful wailing. It's like a sharp knife blade sinking slowly and ceaselessly into my belly. I don't know why I dare not get rid of the cat, just as I don't know why I killed her kittens a few weeks ago.

During the night I had heard an appalling mewing. It was the first time I had heard my pampered cat wail like that. I followed the sound. I found her in my studio, near the window, and on the pillow were five little creatures moving and squeaking. Five kittens, just like that, and all at once! I don't know why I snatched them away, ignoring the claws clinging to my hands, or why I opened the window and threw all five of them out, one by one. The cat was still wailing, and in her eyes there was a dreadful accusing look. A human look, like that in the eyes of a woman whose children have been flayed in front of her. On the studio walls were dozens of paintings of dozens of children. Their faces were all alike, as if they were all the face of a particular child, a child who wasn't born yet, but whose features I knew very well. Even the men in my paintings had that child's face. Even the flowers. Even the things had the face of my still-to-be-born child. As I closed the door on the cat's wailing, I heard the hundreds of children in my paintings crying tears of bitterness and hatred.

It's raining. It's raining.

It's raining a new melancholy evening. If only the sky would explode with thunder, and lightning would burst open the clouds. If only the wind would howl and whistle in the cracks of the window. That would silence the cat and stop the terrible boredom. Anything, anything, but the meaningless existence that dominates my days in this dreadful villa.

Despite the cold, he has been fixed, rigid and motionless, on the balcony for more than an hour, just as the scarecrow is fixed, rigid and motionless, at the bottom of the garden.

He's always silent. Since our marriage, we've exchanged words only rarely. I wonder if he talks to the scarecrows and the ghosts of the garden.

He takes out another cigarette. Why doesn't he offer the scarecrow a cigarette? In the early days of our marriage, this cold silence made me miserable. It would throw me into a winding yellow garden in which even the echo of my voice would vanish. In the early days of our marriage, he was already capable of making me miserable. I would often search for an excuse for him, as I painted pictures of children, one after another, wishing that one day one of the pictures would scream and a living child would jump out of it. I could think of dozens of excuses: he is a judge, and in everything that goes on he judges me wrong. But he is also an important businessman. Perhaps that part of his personality has crept into our relationship. His feelings obey the law of supply and demand. If I frown, he smiles at me. If I am silent, he drowns me in unexpected eloquence. If I express desire for him, he rejects me; and if I turn away from him, his passion is aroused.

Then I learned how to burn the superfluous words of love on my lips, just as they burn coffee in Brazil so that its price will not go down.

I've become tired of the taste of ashes.

It's raining between my skin and my flesh. It's raining inside my bones, in my throat. I can't answer his question; it slaps against my face with the current of hail pouring in from the opened door.

"Did the doctor call with the result?"

"No . . . he didn't . . ."

"Who was it then? Who called?"

"It was them! They're waiting for you!"

I hear my voice, harsh and wounding.

"They're waiting for you!" I say it as if I were firing bullets at him. But he doesn't stagger, he doesn't drop dead. Instead, he closes the balcony door behind him and goes out to his scarecrow. I hear myself repeating, "Them!""Them!" "They're waiting for you!"

I see them there, waiting for him.

I see them there, ready. I see him come into the room, a combination of happy contradictions: the eyes of an old man and the smile of a child, the calm movement of a judge and the athletic appearance of a handsome businessman.

I see them scrutinize him. Then they will say many things. They will make grave accusations against him. They will talk voraciously, like crows tearing at the wounds of a man chained down and still alive.

He will not answer. I know he will not defend himself. He will confront them with the same coldness that has often burned me.

Then they will challenge him: they have a witness for the prosecution. He will laugh contemptuously. One of them will scream in his face: "We are sure of the accusation. You never studied a single defendant's file. You neglected everything—the legal proceedings, the prosecution, everything. You used to come to the courthouse with a bundle of folded papers in your pocket. On each paper you had written a single word: 'guilty' or 'innocent.' Your blind fingers would choose one paper from the darkness of your pocket. Then you would open it and read what was on it, 'guilty' or 'innocent,' at random. Just like that, without logic or justification. This is no justice!"

And you will look at them attentively, smiling and silent.

Then the final blow will come: "The witness for the prosecution is your wife!" Perhaps only then will the gag fall from your mouth, and perhaps you will scream in their faces, just as you screamed in my face that fearful night a year ago.

It was also raining, but ferociously. I still loved you. I couldn't sleep unless I buried my face in your chest. I still believed there were rare treasures at the bottom of the seas of your silence.

Light was shining from under the closed door of your study. I crept up on you, barefoot. I had decided to persuade you to come to bed by planting a kiss on the back of your neck. I moved up behind you slowly and silently. Then I stopped. As I was about to bend over and kiss you, I caught sight of something that stunned me. On the desk were dozens of scraps of paper with nothing written on them except the words "guilty" or "innocent." And the black book you had brought with you and said you were going to study was lying on the floor, under your feet!

I groaned. When you turned to me, and I saw the dreadful expression on your face, I understood everything. In an instant, like a flash of lightning, I understood everything. Your face remained contracted, dripping sweat. So that was what your silence was hiding! Despite your great success in business, you had hung on to your position as a judge in order to kill, and to do so from behind a veil! Your face advanced toward me. I remembered the faces described in Dante's hell. I was afraid. I wanted to run away. You held my hands tightly, pinning me down. I tried to escape but couldn't. I felt I had somehow been sentenced to death. But you would never dare carry out the sentence yourself.

"You wouldn't dare!"

"You fool!"

"You wouldn't dare! . . . This time it would be a crime that leaves blood and a corpse behind."

"You fool!"

"And you couldn't do it in the name of justice."

"You fool!"

"And you won't get paid for committing it!"

"You fool! That's terrible . . . terrible. . . ."

"You're supposed to represent the justice of the gods."

"I apply it in their way. . . . Try to understand."

"That's heresy. What can the gods be to blame for in this?"

"I honestly try to do as they would do."

"And leave people's fate to mere chance?"

"Chance rules the world."

"You're crazy!"

"And you're a fool. You're still deceived by the game."

I convinced myself that I was no longer deceived by the game, that I had to do something to save my ideals and the thousands of accused people whose fate was being decided by chance. But when he ordered that something be done to scare off the birds in the garden, I came to the painful conclusion that perhaps I was doing all this because my husband would not talk to me, because the dead silence had made my life an empty desert. Even wailing over a dead person is better than waiting for a joy that will never come!

The telephone rings. Perhaps it's the doctor. Perhaps he has good news for me. I stay stock-still. I don't want to move. I'm afraid it might be "them," those who are "waiting for him." The maid, Tuffāḥa, rolls along the hall, carrying her swollen belly in front of her. She lifts the receiver. She mumbles. She comes toward me, holding the receiver in one hand. How ugly she is! Ugly! With her dead, expressionless face, her step like that of a farm bull, and that belly. I watch that belly swelling, growing bigger day by day. Why aren't its muscles ripped apart? Why doesn't it drop to the floor and smash to bits? How could any man in the world make love to such a beast? How disgusting to think of them. I hate her. It tears me apart to imagine there is a little child inside the shabby clothes that envelop her huge form. And it belongs to her! Whereas I, with all that I possess, and with all the men who eye me hungrily—I cannot have anything like this!

A few minutes pass. I let the receiver fall from my hand.

So, I shall never have a child! Never, never, never. . . .

The doctor has now told me. The decision is final, not open to appeal or reversal.

Why? He doesn't know. Nobody knows.

Why?

Above a cloud stretching to a dark horizon, I see the hundreds of papers I saw before on my husband's desk: "guilty," "innocent," "barren," "fertile," "guilty," "innocent," "barren," "fertile." Then devilish, jesting fingers pick up one paper. Then the doctor says: "Sorry, you're barren." And on the pillow the cat had borne them all at once, five kittens.

Barren. Perhaps the scarecrow had children like itself, but they hated the silence and so flew off with the songs of the birds of the fields.

It's raining. It's raining.

It's raining a low moaning that rises slowly, so slowly, merging with the wailing of the cat in the garden. We are three scarecrows, each of us fixed far away from the others, never conversing, never meeting. Who's moaning?

He comes in from the balcony. He doesn't seem to hear any strange voice. He says he's going out but won't be back late.

As usual, he doesn't hear any moaning. He goes off, and I see torn papers flying under his feet, "guilty," "innocent," "guilty," "innocent". . . .

I'm alone in the house.

The moaning rises. Where does it come from? It's all in my imagination. There's no one in the secluded house except me, and the maid. Tonight Beirut hasn't turned its lights on, one after the other, in the corners of the windows. The fog, like a whale, has swallowed it up. Perhaps the scarecrow is weeping. I wonder if it gets sad or angry. Does it ever feel hatred or revolt? Does it talk to my husband, Najm? Does it sneak into the study every night on its cane legs and sit with him? Do the two of them tear up the papers together and write "guilty," "innocent"? Why don't silent men marry scarecrows? Why am I unjustly condemned to silence? Why is there no child to fill the place, screaming in protest, tearing off the veil from Najm's face?

It's raining. It's raining.

The moaning turns to punctuated screams. Perhaps the children in my paintings are hungry. To this day, I haven't found a way to feed them. Perhaps they need to go for a walk, and play. My children are prisoners in the paintings. Why don't the gods free them, let them burst into the world from my insides, from my belly?

It's raining screams. . . .

Who's screaming like that? Perhaps the faceless figure in the picture which I haven't yet finished is protesting.

I run to my studio. I turn on the light. There's nothing. There's no one except my twenty children, nailed to the walls, and the picture, still incomplete, awaiting a face. The window is open. The pillow on which the cat gave birth to her kittens lies in its place. I dare not approach the window. I have the impression that behind it, outside in the darkness, there are five little cats lurking, their fangs pointed. If I look out, they will sink their claws into my face and tear it apart.

I run away.

It's still raining screams. I know where the voice is coming from. It's calling my name. It's not my imagination. I hate Sunday night, when all the servants are away. Tuffāḥa is the only one who hasn't been given time off since I noticed her belly growing. I hate her, and I hate the patient way she endures my torture. I want her to stay *here*. I don't know why I like to oppress her. I see her gasping with fatigue, wiping away her smelly sweat, moving like a stupid animal, and I try in vain to convince myself that there's a goat in her belly, or a cub, or mice. . . .

I look in the kitchen. She isn't there.

I make my way to her miserable room. She's stretched out on her back on the bed. Her hands are on her big belly. She's silent. The muscles of her face are still contracted with a pain I've never seen before on her features. Her face is pathetic and horrifying!

At her side are the needles I've often seen her working with, knitting garment after garment. I've seen the delicate hands of little children come out of the openings of the unfinished garments as they grow day by day with the continuous knitting. I feel an infuriating urge to thrust the needles into her belly. I shall thrust them in until they tear her insides apart and destroy what lies there. Why is she screaming? The needles are still in their place. She opens her eyes for a second, and a terrible look of feminine triumph flashes across them. Her eyes challenge me. Then they drown in a dark sea of mingled pain and pleasure that draws over her face—the pain of a nun who is being raped and is tormented by the pleasure it gives her.

She mumbles, pleading. She wants a doctor.

Why? Why should the doctor come for her sake and not for mine? And for the child that is hers and not mine?

Something black wells up from the depths of me and merges with her crying. Black bubbles form. They rise up, gush out from my throat, my eyes, my pores. Black bubbles of burning acid submerge everything. Everything is torn, burning. I want everything to be torn, to burn. I want to protest, to revolt, to engulf everything around me in senseless destruction. Why? Why? Who? Who? How? When? Who? Who passed this sentence on me? Why shall I never stretch out on the bed and get up with a child in my arms? Why shall I not feel the kicking of little feet in my belly, and the body of a child turning over inside me, then wake up from my sleep to cuddle him when his screaming fills the house?

I gaze at her with a dead face, expecting the black bubbles to gush out from my eyes and drown her. Why? Who? Who? Who plays with the papers marked "barren" or "fertile," scattering them in the wind, to be carried away by the blind chance? Is Najm to blame for being so quick to grasp the fact? Is he to blame for believing in his heresy and being devoted to his calamity?

It's raining. The rain falls outside the window. I wonder if it's raining in Beirut too. Why doesn't it rain everywhere at the same time?

Who decides where the rain falls and where the children come? Who has made chance into justice?

It's raining. It's raining.

The maid screams, pleading. For weeks she's been begging for time off. She must have known.

I stay stock-still, exploding with black hatred. I'll bury her with black bubbles. I'll pile earth on her like a grave and choke the screams of the child inside her. Her pain provokes something like jealousy in me, but much more bitter, more stinging, more miserable.

She becomes silent, semiconscious. I have the urge to draw a child! Let her give birth to her child by herself. I have nothing to do with it. I shall go to my studio and give birth to a new child as well. I shall finish that picture. I shall ignore what the doctor said on the phone. Her screaming starts up again, then turns to crying.

Let her scream. No one will ever hear her in our secluded house in al-Yarze.[41] Let her die. If she manages to give birth, as the cat did, I won't dare throw the child out of the window. I won't dare because since that night I no longer see the looks of love and friendship with which the faces of the children in my paintings used to envelop me. They've begun to frown at me; they've stopped their nighttime singing. They've started to hate me, and fear me. I shall bear a new child now. I shall lay it down on the paper and get rid of all the others.

The maid's moaning stirs a similar wailing in the depths of me, a wailing of black bubbles, a raging current of tense, impetuous, acid screams. I feel the urge to draw. My hand races ahead of me, pulling me to the studio. I'm a prisoner of my hand. The black current moves my hand. The maid's screaming provokes it. I'm incapable of controlling a single muscle in my body. My hand is drawing on its own, madly, frantically. Outside, it's raining ferociously. The maid's screams are like the cries of a sailor cast up on the shore, being eaten by crabs. My hand is drawing on its own, madly, frantically. . . .

It's raining ferociously. The thunder sounds like a minefield high above, being set off by devilish feet. Lightning flashes. I'm afraid. The maid screams. I'm afraid. Afraid. I feel something on the back of my neck. The claws of vicious cats. I feel them tearing at my flesh. I'm afraid. Out in the field, millions of scarecrows are marching. They're carrying torches in a terrifying ceremonial procession. The thunder sounds like one vast minefield. The lightning flashes periodically, setting alight the children on the walls. I draw. I want to draw a child, but I don't know what I'm drawing. The scarecrows advance toward the window. The electricity fails. The children in my paintings suddenly grow huge. The lightning strikes the faces with their gouged-out eyes. The faces freeze, their teeth fall to the floor, their hair turns white, they weep. Then they change into more scarecrows. They jump down from the paintings and out of the open window, joining the throng singing under it. Their weeping-singing screams have a terrible rhythm. Meanwhile, the wind beats against the window. I want to run away. I can't. My hand chains me to the picture. So I draw on and on, and I can't run away. The electricity is back. I can't run away. Then suddenly one scream rings out at the door of my studio.

It's the other woman, leaving a trail of blood behind her.

The screaming of the procession outside quiets down. It seems as if millions of scarecrows are now peering furtively through the windows, staring silently with their gouged-out eyes, timidly submissive. The other woman braces herself, comes in, and drops onto the chair, onto the very same pillow on which the cat gave birth to five kittens. I wonder if she, too, will give birth to five babies.

She seems huge, so huge to me. A great giant. In her eyes there is a commander's challenge, an amazing creative power, and a pain that is beautiful and radiating and bitter.

I begin to be conscious of things again.

A cruel, calamitous calmness fills me.

She wants a doctor or else she will die.

I am the absolute ruler.

I try in vain to remember my ideals. I try in vain to reawaken in myself my sweet old world. I search in vain for the face I once had.

In the picture that I've drawn unconsciously, I find a strange face, a mixture of my face and Najm's face! A mixture of cruelty and calamity, even of indifference. The picture suddenly seems like a mirror to me. I smile, and the face in the picture smiles. I move my lips, and the face moves its lips.

The moaning turns to screaming and rises up to me again. What sentence shall I pass? The frost of calamitous cruelty fills me. It becomes petrified inside me. At the threshold of my world all the voices vanish in utter silence. I go to my husband's study. I sit down where he sat. I take out a blank sheet of paper. I cut it carefully into two equal parts. On one piece I write, "I shall fetch the doctor," and on the other, "I shall not fetch the doctor." I fold each of them, I put them in my pocket, I muddle them up.

Then I take one of them out.

I open it and read: "I shall not fetch the doctor." The decision is final, irrevocable. I can't hear any voices when I go into my room. I dress calmly and carefully. I pick up my car keys. I take care to leave my husband a note: "I'm with Nūrā and Nīllī. We're going to play bridge with the rest of the group."

Comments

This story describes the severe identity crisis of an Arab woman who cannot fulfill her traditional role as mother owing to the fact that she is barren. In a culture where a much-quoted dictum by the prophet Muḥammad runs: "Paradise lies at the feet of mothers" (*al-jannatu taḥta aqdāmi al-ummahāt*), the heroine's existential nightmare becomes apparent. Here, the author attacks the traditional notions of female fulfillment through motherhood and of marriage as existing primarily for the purpose of procreation. The author is critical not of motherhood per se, but rather of the culture that sanctions childbearing as the key to a woman's self-realization and social standing.

The woman in this story belongs to the upper class. She is well educated, intelligent, and passionate. She lives in a villa in an affluent neighborhood, and her household includes servants. Yet despite all the material comforts, her life is joyless: her relationship with her husband is strained to the point where there is a wall of silence, contempt, and hostility separating them. Without children, she has no meaningful outlet for her personality. Further, her prestige is affected, her integrity is threatened, and her life loses its raison d'être. She tries to occupy her time by painting—and all her paintings are of children.

The story depicts the gradual mental transformation of the woman who, unable to cope with the stress of her predicament, becomes ruthless and psychotic. In her loneliness, she equates herself with a scarecrow: she realizes that her whole being is paralyzed, that she has become as mute and lifeless as a scarecrow. Disillusioned and frustrated, she emerges from her isolation a monster ready to strike at the well-being of others who have what she desires—babies. As her condition deteriorates, she proceeds from killing five kittens born to her pet cat to denying medical assistance to her pregnant maid who has gone into labor. In both instances, she is aware of her actions and derives sadistic pleasure from them. Symbolically, the five kittens stand for the five fingers of her hand, which endeavors to draw a child as creative compensation for her inability to give birth to one. However, she ends up drawing a composite picture of herself and her husband. Both of them have turned into horrifying scarecrows—a distorted microcosm of society.

The heroine's inner turmoil is mirrored in a scene of domestic and external chaos: the cat wails, the maid screams, the wind whistles, and the thunderstorm rages. In the heroine's tormented mind, images turn into hallucinations and paranoid delusions. The author relies on the interior-monologue technique and rapidly shifting time frames to convey the heroine's dangling position between the past and the present, fantasy and reality. The story abounds in forceful and shocking images: crows tearing at a man's flesh, a sailor being eaten by crabs, a nun being raped. These macabre images are designed to show the heroine's disintegrating personality and to elicit a response from the reader.

The story also abounds in symbols. The cat represents fertility, for it delivers five kittens all at once. It is contrasted with the scarecrow, which represents barrenness and lifelessness. Knitting, like weaving, in which the maid is engaged, signifies creation and life, whereas painting, with which the heroine busies herself, is an escape from reality. The picture-mirror, into which the heroine stares near the end of the story, stands for truth, for it reveals her subconscious identity, which is a mixture of herself, her husband, and the desired child. The thunderstorm denotes a state of tremendous emotional upheaval and uncontrollable rage. On the whole, the author's stylistic characteristics of dense imagery and multiple symbolism come to the forefront in this story, where form and content combine to leave an indelible impression on the reader's mind.

As the heroine finds it increasingly difficult to cope with her ordeal, she is inclined to ascribe it to the force of chance in life. The realization that chance is responsible for her fate is enhanced by her discovery of the random manner in which her husband, a prominent judge, convicts or acquits the defendants brought before him on trial. She laments the unfair rules of the chance–luck–fate game and turns to punish those over whom she retains some power. In the heroine's metamorphosis from oppressed to oppressor, victim to victimizer, the author expresses her condemnation of the patriarchal values of Arab society, which she sees as the underlying causes of the degradation and dehumanization of women.[42]

The idea that chance rules the world and determines the course of people's lives is central to the story's message. The woman equates the arbitrary way in which her husband passes judgment on the accused with her own allotted fate of barrenness: in either case, there is no relation between deeds and reward or punishment, yet the decision is final and irrevocable. The husband equates his role as a judge with that of a god. She rebels against the two alter egos of her husband and perceives that they both play dice with her life. Chance, in her view, is the most cruel arbiter of justice because it offers no logical explanation or justification for her affliction to make it bearable. Chance is also cruel in its obliviousness to the identity of the recipient—she is completely irrelevant, and her particular personality is immaterial. Moreover, chance trivializes her suffering, which aggravates her frustration and blunts her compassion. In her mind, the killing of the kittens and the abandonment of the maid are considerably less harsh than her own fate because at least they are of her own making, a punishment originating in her jealousy, whereas she is doomed by a totally erratic and irrational force to live like an inanimate scarecrow.

In conclusion, the story presents the existential dilemma of many Arab women trapped in a prison of gender and fertility that is entirely governed by chance. Under pressure to conform to prevailing norms, some women may be driven out of their sanity or lose their humanity.[43]

Fu'ād al-Takarlī
The Boil

Fu'ād al-Takarlī was born into a middle-class family in Baghdad in 1927. He studied law at Baghdad University and graduated in 1949. He became a judge in 1956, serving in that capacity in the Iraqi capital until 1979, when he left for Paris. Since then he continues to live abroad. He began to publish during the early 1950s and played a pivotal role in developing the Iraqi short story.

Al-Takarlī differs from other Iraqi fiction writers in matters of theme and technique. He frequently depicts people in illegitimate sexual relationships, with tragic consequences for themselves and for others in their social environment. His carefully crafted stories focus on the private, interior world of the protagonists, and it is through their consciousness that the narrative unfolds.

Al-Takarlī's literary output is small yet influential. His first collection of short stories, *The Other Face (Al-Wajh al-ākhar,* 1960), was reprinted in 1982 with eight additional stories. He also published a widely acclaimed novel, *The Distant Echo (Al-Rajʿ al-baʿīd,* 1980), and a volume of one-act plays.

"The Boil" ("Al-Dummala") appears in the second edition of *The Other Face*. The story revolves around a man whose immoral sexual conduct leads him to commit an act of suicide in which an unrelated person, who happens to be at the scene by chance, is also killed.

It was just after midnight when they left the Mashriq bar. They walked along the pavement, puffing on cigarettes in the fresh night air, and their gait was slow but not unsteady. One man coughed violently and then spat as he addressed his companion:

"Where's your car, Abū Ḥusayn?"

Abū Ḥusayn wanted to say that he had not brought the car with him. Instead, he replied: "I'm not sure. It's probably nearby."

Abū Ḥusayn did not want the man's company. He glanced around looking for the car and saw it parked a short distance away. Damn! He walked toward it, followed by the black shadow. They got into the car, and he turned the key in the ignition. They shook as the car plunged forward. The cool, soft air brushed his face, and his body relaxed with the monotonous motion of the car. Glancing at his friend from the corner of his eye, he saw that he was crumpled silently like a hedgehog, giving no sign of life except for the swirls of smoke.

The empty street was long. Its lights vanished on the horizon, and the trees on either side passed swiftly. He felt as though an electric current in his soul were flowing together with the car, the lights, the trees, and the night—with the events of his life, the memories, the dreams, and the obscure images. If only he were alone with these feelings!

"Abū ʿAlā', where's your house?" he asked.

The latter sat bolt upright, as though a snake had bitten him.

"What did you say, Abū Ḥusayn?"

"Where do you want me to take you?"

"Wherever you please, Abū Ḥusayn. I'm not busy. To al-Karrāda Street."

"What do you have to do in al-Karrāda Street?"

The man burst out laughing, and then began to cough and gasp.

"Nothing," he replied, and spat forcefully.

"Are you still with that old woman?"

The convulsive laughter along with the gasping and the spitting rang out again. "What can I do, Abū Ḥusayn? We've got to live, haven't we?"

The street was dark, the car lights wavered, and he did not know the way to al-Karrāda Street. If she were riding with him in the car, she would know that he could not find the way. Leaning on her arm against the side of the door and tapping on the edge of the radio with her fingertips, she would sing or listen to music while shaking her head, and he would be elated by her movements. She would speak to him with her eyes and say things without moving her lips. She had long black hair and hazel eyes.

"You know, Abū Ḥusayn, I don't drink every day. Just once or twice a week. After that, I like to spend some time with my friends."

"This time you'll spend the whole night with her!"

The man almost choked with laughter and smoke.

He still did not know why he had kissed her that scented evening in a dark corner of the garden. She was luscious and alluring. As she spoke about things he did not understand, he found himself leaning over and touching her mouth with his lips. He had not told her that he loved her—he had not known that himself. She had been slightly startled. Then they had returned to the house silently. She had said nothing to her mother—his wife—about what had happened. And he, feeling utterly wretched, had wanted to infuse her silence with some meaning.

There was an alley in front of him and he made two wild turns, after which he entered a wide, dark street. Loneliness had affected him greatly during the past few days. He still felt tired for no apparent reason and experienced a fierce rage. When he accidentally ran into this friend, he thought he would manage—by spending the evening together drinking arrack and eating shish kebab—to remove the black shadow that lay across his shoulders. They finished a bottle of arrack during the course of the evening and ate a lot and laughed a great deal. But the sheer stupidity that clouded his friend's eyes clearly indicated that it would be futile to pour his heart out to such an insensitive soul.

The car now moved without shaking. The cold air enveloped his face and tousled his hair. The night was quiet. She had not been startled to discover his face in the darkness of her small room. She had said nothing in particular that he could remember, and her smile concealed a vague secret. He had slipped into her room without premeditation after his son and wife had both gone to bed. The house was quiet, and he had not hesitated. He wanted to be sure that he had truly kissed her, that he had touched her lips, that he had not been dreaming, and that she had not been a phantom. And that night—with her soft lips and the touch of her shoulders—she had given him happiness and joy he had never before experienced. He had spoken to her with meaningless words about things he had scarcely understood, and he had seen her eyes shine in the darkness.

He heard his friend speaking. "What did you say, Abū Ḥusayn? When I drink, my ears get clogged up. Are we almost at al-Karrāda Street?"

Those memories wrenched his heart, and he mumbled: "Perhaps, perhaps."

Had he been alone in his dark car—alone with the sky and the stars—he would have burst into tears and sighed deeply with every hot tear. That was impossible, though. At his age, crying was useless.

"Do you have any matches, Abū Ḥusayn?"

He had not noticed her when he married her mother a few years before. It was only for the past few months that he had begun to feel her pleasant presence in his life and discovered that she was indispensable to him. That happened simultaneously with the budding of her young body—the exciting sight of the lines of her thighs and waist, and her curving hips and breasts. That she should expose her body like that was flagrantly indecent frivolity. She had not appeared to have any designs in mind. Nor had he, in turn, had designs on her.

"Do you have any matches in the car, Abū Ḥusayn? I want to light a cigarette. May God preserve you."

"Here, help yourself."

He had failed to understand what was happening to him. The day he admitted to himself that he desired her and that he would stop at nothing to achieve his ends, he felt as though he were plunging into a dark, infinite abyss. He was deeply depressed. She was not a naive girl who could be led blindly into an affair. She was not merely the subject of his passion and dreams, but life and death as well as light and darkness. He was bound to her, and he felt humiliated at the realization that his very life was jeopardized by such a sleazy desire.

The air in the car was foggy with smoke, despite the cold wind that rushed through the small window. Misery, like a burning rock or a sharp knife, tore at his heart. It surged and clashed like sea waves, rising up from the depths of his soul. He felt a choking in his chest and a lump in his throat. He clenched his teeth and pressed harder on the gas pedal. He was not waiting for tears—tears would not wash away his anguish, and he was unwilling to cry.

"The difference is not worth it—one or two minutes. Why are you driving so fast, Abū Ḥusayn? I'm in no hurry."

He eased up on the gas pedal, and the car slowed down a little.

"I'm in no hurry either," he said, his voice hoarse and unstable. "Why should I hurry? How often can a person die?"

"What? What did you say, Abū Ḥusayn? My ears seem to get clogged after one drink."

"I'm talking about death. Death is what I'm talking about."

"What has happened to you, Abū Ḥusayn? Have you had a quarrel at home?"

"No."

"Then why are you so depressed, my friend?"

When was there a reason for death that the mind could grasp and the soul accept? Yet every moment we come closer to this unknown experience. When he heard about her affair with another man, his heart suddenly sank and he felt that most of his life was lost in a few moments. What was left until death was only for these moments to be relived. In fact, she had not spared his feelings. She turned up, after a few weeks of work at one of the companies, with lips painted red and eyes—oh, those hazel eyes—too dark with kohl. She appeared to have won. The fire within him failed to subside, and everything seemed bleak.

"Abū Ḥusayn, please drop me off. I'll take a taxi home."

She let him know, through her loud laughter, swinging gait, and bare arms and thighs, that she was playing with life—a life she did not understand—as well as with his feeble, trembling heart, and his humiliation.

He was tapping lightly and monotonously on the frame of the small window as he gazed in bewilderment at the spot on the street where the wavering light fell. His friend, like him, was quietly staring ahead, trying to find the way.

"May I have a cigarette, Abū ʿAlāʾ?"

"Of course."

He quickly handed him a cigarette, saying: "I don't have any matches, Abū Ḥusayn. But you have a lighter in the car."

"Yes, yes."

"Maybe if you turn to the right, we'll come to al-Karrāda Street."

He exhaled the smoke, which the night wind swept back in his face.

"Could you please pull up a minute so I can get out and take a taxi?"

"Why, Abū ʿAlāʾ? Do you think I don't know the way? We'll be there soon. Are you in a hurry?"

"No, my friend. Why should I be in a hurry?"

Why not let him go, leave him alone? Why should he condemn this fellow when he had done nothing wrong? Just like him, a man eternally condemned for no wrongdoing except for wanting to satisfy his desires in his own wicked way.

"Don't be angry, Abū ʿAlāʾ. I want to take you home, but the way is a little long."

"Yes, yes. I know."

"I like being with you. You know, Abū ʿAlāʾ, for three days . . . for several days, I've had no idea where I am . . . no idea."

"Yes, yes, I know. Turn to the left, Abū Ḥusayn, and we'll come to Abū Nuwās Street. To the left."

She had not compelled him to end his misery and confusion. She knew with absolute certainty that he had no part in her life. He had tried in vain to ignore those frequent conversations on the telephone, her prolonged absences, and the signs of absentmindedness and exhaustion. She intuitively sensed that he was an ill-fated man, but he was unable to accept that. After her constant flights from him and the banal excuses that she used to rebel against him and her mother, the idea occurred to him to visit her one night. At first it seemed a crazy, futile idea, but then it took root and branched out in his mind and heart like a malignancy. Eventually, as the days passed, it became an obsession that obliterated all rational thought. He could not escape. The idea became the turning point and the fever spreading through his limbs. It never occurred to him that he might die afterward; rather, he believed that he would surely die if he failed in his purpose.

"Abū Ḥusayn, please slow down. The street is narrow and the river is high. Why are you in such a hurry? May God preserve you."

He noticed that the car was shaking violently on the muddy ground of the street, and then he saw the lights of the distant shore reflected in the rising waters of the Tigris River. He eased his foot on the gas pedal and shifted in his seat. His head was buzzing with thoughts and his eyes were weary, but he felt neither tired nor eager for sleep. He wished he could sing a sad song on the deserted shore, a song that would waft away on the wind without an echo. He heard his friend mumble things he neither understood nor wanted to understand. They were driving at the edge of the pier and the river. Do we have to understand life properly and deeply, or sing it, just as we sing any sad song with no particular meaning? Perhaps, through the melody, we would be able to accomplish our goals.

That springlike night, a few days ago, when he had slipped away from their room to the garden. . . .

"A cigarette, Abū Ḥusayn? I'm almost home."

That night he had kept on walking and inhaling the humid air in order to give himself courage. He was waiting for some obscure, unknown sign before proceeding. It seemed to him that the stars glittered more brightly than usual in the sky and that ghosts were hiding behind the silent trees. He did not know how to cope with his loneliness. Images flashed rapidly through his mind, but they were meaningless, meaningless. He felt exhausted, his steps were sluggish, and he was fearful of the wave of crying that racked his chest. Such an outburst would be merciless. The flowing tears would overpower him and turn him into a crushed cricket. Alarmed by this sudden sign, he rushed to her room. She did not awaken when he reached her bed, groping in the dark, and she did not answer him when he twice whispered her name. He waited, full of fear, shame, and humiliation, and then he touched her soft, naked shoulder. He wished, for a moment, that she were dead, that she were incapable of answering him, of completing his tragedy. She was startled when she discovered him and drew back, covering her breasts. He looked through the dark at her beautiful face and glowing arms, and forgot what he had wanted to say. That movement of hers made him realize that he was finished. There was nothing left for him to do but begin at the point where he ended—that is, begin his end. It would have sufficed, had she remained in that position, shrunken and distant, for him to go away quietly and kill himself under the silent trees of the garden. But that she should have screamed for no reason, jumped like the devil, and gone running to her mother—that was only because she was a cheap and corrupt girl.

"Abū Ḥusayn, slow down. May God preserve you."

He had been unable to purge her from his soul during the past few days, and he had experienced an overwhelming loneliness. He could not stop his tears, which surged like the sea, nor could he extract that excruciating boil from the depths of his heart. Now he was crying piteously. . . .

"Abū Ḥusayn, be careful! The river, be careful! For God's sake!"

He was leaning on the steering wheel, trying to turn the car toward the river. His tears obstructed his vision. He felt, through the violent convulsions of his chest, that he was separating from himself, ridding himself of the man he was. There was no room for a humiliating return. Then he felt a clash that shook him, and a heavy blow on his temple. He did not lose consciousness. He heard his friend utter terrible screams, clutching desperately at his arm. The car was lurching erratically on the pier while the shining water level was rising from side to side. It would be pointless for people to judge him because they—their private worlds and their common interests and concerns—are transitory. His head was spinning as the car slammed into the river and the waters slowly parted and swallowed it. The deadly silence and choking darkness engulfing them did not frighten him. He felt the flagging of his body and the chill of the gushing water. They would not be able to find their traces easily. And he was all alone.

Comments

This story describes the existential crisis of a married man who is obsessed with his young stepdaughter. Despite his awareness of the incestuous nature of this forbidden relationship, Abū Ḥusayn's sexual desires steer him unremittingly toward a shameful encounter with her. The story unfolds through the consciousness of the protagonist, who is driving his car at night with a passenger at his side. The journey becomes a process of soul-searching and self-evaluation as Abū Ḥusayn contemplates the turbulent events of the last few days in his life. Symbolically, when he recalls his final fall—his late-night intrusion into the girl's room, which leads her to expose him to her mother—the car sustains its final fall, plunging with its two occupants into the river and into oblivion.

The story depicts the emotional turmoil of a restless man who encounters a girl's blossoming sexuality in his household. The girl symbolizes the mystical fountain of youth with which the man hopes to revitalize his life. In his desperation at his inner emptiness, he is compulsively drawn toward an untenable and distorted sexual relationship. Despite the gravity of the situation and the girl's mere adolescent teasing, he attaches himself to her in a frenzied and neurotic way. His obsession with her is likened to a boil in his heart. The boil signifies a moral malignancy; it connotes decay, depravity, and pollution. Like a time bomb, it is bound to explode, causing ruin and confusion. When one night Abū Ḥusayn tries to force himself on the girl and is flatly rejected, his world collapses. He cannot have her, yet he cannot live without her. By exposing his secret he has inflicted unspeakable disgrace on himself. Thus the boil in his heart leads him to self-defeat and self-destruction. As a reflection of his predicament, when Abū Ḥusayn is driving his car, he takes the wrong turns and gets lost in the city, paralleling the wrong path he chose to follow and the loss of direction in his life.

Through flashback and interior monologue, the role of the passenger in the sequence of events is clarified. Confused and disoriented, Abū Ḥusayn tries to drown his anguish and humiliation in drinking. He goes to a bar, where he accidentally runs into an old friend, Abū ʿAlāʾ. He hopes to find consolation in pouring his heart out to him, but his friend appears to be totally insensitive to his need. After they leave the bar, Abū Ḥusayn does not want his friend's company any more and tries to shake him off; however, Abū ʿAlāʾ follows him and asks for a ride. The car ride turns into a painful process of self-examination, at the end of which Abū Ḥusayn realizes that he has crossed the line and gone beyond the point of no return. He can no longer face life. He drives the car faster and faster toward a violent crash, inevitably killing both himself and his friend.

The story illustrates the role of chance in everyday life. Abū ʿAlāʾ is unaware of his friend's inner turmoil and does not perceive any danger to his safety. He is an unfortunate man who happens to be in the wrong place at the wrong time. As a random victim, he suffers the consequences of someone else's fatal mistakes.

Nevertheless, the story conveys a moral message. Abū Ḥusayn has a questionable character. He has been contemplating an incestuous relationship, in his own home, with the daughter of his wife, who is the mother of his son. Thus the boil in his heart may have its origin in his character. This flaw in his character is most likely the cause of his tragedy (compare Tawfīq al-Ḥakīm's *King Oedipus*, in chapter 3).

In addition, Abū Ḥusayn's attitude to life is neither rational nor serious. He wants to "sing" life like "any sad song with no particular meaning"; he speaks to the girl "with meaningless words about things he had scarcely understood." These sentiments reflect Abū Ḥusayn's superficial mindset. His desire to enjoy the moment without any regard for the consequences clashes with both the Islamic code of ethics and the existentialist principle of personal responsibility.

Likewise, Abū ʿAlāʾ is also somewhat to blame for his own death, since he is willing to ride along aimlessly on life's waves, in no hurry to go anywhere and with no ultimate destination but an illicit sexual encounter. In this respect, he is not innocent either. Once again, character and chance interact. This "along-for-the-ride" flaw in Abū ʿAlāʾ's character is arguably the reason that he is punished too.

Finally, both men drink alcohol, which is strictly forbidden in Islam. This fact highlights their moral decay and plays a role in their downfall.[44]

8

TO WISH OR NOT TO WISH?

The Double-Edged Sword

> I know not, when I journey to a land,
> desiring good fortune, whether will
> betide me the good fortune of which
> I am in pursuit, or the misfortune
> that pursueth me.
>
> —Unknown Arab poet[1]

The Instinct of Dissatisfaction

Human history, according to the Qur'ān, began at a point of unique advantage: after fashioning Adam, God "breathed into him something of His spirit" (32:9), endowing him with creative knowledge that set him above the rest of creation. God then asked all the angels to honor Adam by prostrating themselves before him, which they did, except for one of the jinns, who refused to acknowledge Adam's superiority, disobeyed God's command, and became Satan—Adam's archenemy and the personification of temptation and evil (7:11–18). Thereafter, God placed Adam in a state of unparalleled bliss. God said: "O Adam! dwell thou and thy wife in the Garden, and enjoy (its good things) as ye wish: but approach not this tree, or ye run into harm and transgression" (7:19). No sooner had Adam and Eve settled in the garden than Satan began to "whisper suggestions to them." Cunningly, he said: "Your Lord only forbade you this tree, lest ye should become angels or such beings as live for ever. And he swore to them both that he was their sincere adviser" (7:20–21). And so they ate from the tree, and "their shame became manifest to them, and they began to sew together the leaves of the Garden over their bodies" (7:22). When their sin was exposed, God said to them and to Satan: "Get ye down, with enmity between yourselves. On earth will be your dwelling-place and your means of livelihood, for a time" (7:24). Their expulsion was decreed to encompass their entire life cycle: "Therein shall ye live, and therein shall ye die, but from it shall ye be taken out (at last)" (7:25).[2] Thus Adam and Eve fell from the state of felicity which had been theirs, only to embark on a lifelong quest to try to regain precisely what they had lost.

This story, which has its parallel in Genesis, raises an intriguing question: Why did Adam, in such a state of sublime bliss, care to listen to Satan at all? The answer, according to the Qur'ān, lies in the weakness of human nature in general and in certain innate qualities in particular: greed, ingratitude, and haste. There is a whole series of Qur'ānic verses that speak of the fundamental deficiencies of human beings: "Man was created weak" (4:28); "Men's souls are swayed by greed" (4:128); "Most ungrateful is man!" (17:67); "Man is a creature of haste" (21:37); "Truly man was created very impatient; fretful when evil touches him; and niggardly when good reaches him" (70:19–21). According to Fazlur Rahman, Satan's tentacles are not in themselves so strong; it is only human weakness that lends Satan a powerful image.[3] This weakness (*ḍaʿf*), the origin of which is a petty mind, obscures people's vision and makes them oblivious to the long-term consequences of their actions: "[Man's] self-destructive selfishness and the greed to which he is a constant prey, his hasty, panicky behavior, his lack of self-reliance, and the fears that perpetually haunt him arise ultimately from the smallness of his mind."[4] Erratic behavior and going from one extreme to the other are thus inevitable.

Al-Ghazzālī sees another lesson in the story of Adam and Eve. From a didactic point of view, a strict prohibition may not be a productive measure with human beings, given their nature, for it may only provoke greed and desire for the forbidden. In the *Book of Knowledge (Kitāb al-ʿilm)* of his *Revival of the Religious Sciences (Iḥyāʾ ʿulūm al-dīn)*, al-Ghazzālī elaborates on the various duties of the teacher toward his profession and his students. One point he makes is that the teacher, in dissuading students from their bad habits, should do so by suggestion rather than openly, and with sympathy rather than with rebuke. Al-Ghazzālī explains that open dissuasion destroys awe and encourages disobedience. He quotes the prophet Muḥammad, who is reported to have said: "If men had been forbidden to make porridge of camels' dung, they would have done it, saying that they would not have been forbidden to do it unless there had been some good in it." The same principle, al-Ghazzālī asserts, is brought out in the story of Adam and Eve and the prohibition imposed upon them, the purpose of which is to emphasize the necessity of spiritual guidance and deductive reasoning in directing human behavior, for these alone can prevent people from erring.[5]

The story of Adam and Eve highlights the absurdity of the human condition: the only state in which people can exist seems to be one in which their aspirations and wishes are *not* met. At the core of their being, people reveal a basic inability to be satisfied. A morbid pattern of behavior is thus established at the outset of their careers: as soon as they obtain their desired goals, they are dissatisfied and seek something else or more.

With a note of irony and exasperation, several Arabic verses express the human instinct of dissatisfaction:

> Man wishes for summer when it is winter,
> And when summer comes he rejects it.
> Man is impatient with any situation.
> Cursed be man, ungrateful creature that he is![6]

Evidently, restlessness is a dynamic condition that translates into a motivating force, while contentment is a static condition that translates into a debilitating force. People are damned if they wish and damned if they wish not. In the first case, they set themselves up for trials and tribulations; in the second, they are likely to undergo stagnation and decline. Inevitably, the human spirit is riddled with nagging doubts: What next? Is that all? Should I stop here or go further? Have I got what I really wanted, or have I made a terrible mistake?

"There are two tragedies in life. One is to lose your heart's desire. The other is to gain it."[7] This simple truth is reiterated in subtle variations: "Granting our wish one of Fate's saddest jokes is!"[8]; "When the gods want to punish a man, they answer his prayers." What these sayings encapsulate is the same deep-seated paradox in human nature. While that which is unattainable is highly valued, passionately worshiped, and rigorously pursued, that which has been attained creates a sense of malaise, anxiety, and disillusion. In other words, instead of bringing happiness, it inflicts misery. As the Sage in Gibran Khalil Gibran's poem "The Processions" ("Al-Mawākib") observes:

> Happiness is a myth we seek,
> If manifested surely irks;
> Like river speeding to the plain,
> On its arrival slows and murks.
>
> For man is happy only in
> His aspiration to the heights;
> When he attains his goal, he cools
> And longs for other distant flights.
>
> If you should meet a happy one
> Who is contented with his lot,
> Unlike the rest of all mankind,
> Pray his Nirvana disturb not.[9]

A tragicomic illustration of the discontent embedded in human nature can be found in Yaḥyā Ḥaqqī's story "So Be It!" ("Kun . . . kāna").[10] A middle-aged schoolteacher regrets the way he has lived his life—the profession he has chosen and the woman he has taken for a wife. His life seems to him nothing but a chain of mistakes and misfortunes, and he wishes he were a lawyer instead, and married to his charming neighbor rather than to his dull cousin. "If only I could go back ten years," he says to himself. If he were ten years younger, he would change the whole course of his life: "He would enjoy whatever he had denied himself and avoid all the mistakes he had made." When by a stroke of magic (or in a dream) his wish comes true, he discovers that he is utterly miserable slaving away as a lawyer and terribly unhappy living with an attractive but selfish wife. He then begins to think that he would have been much better off had he married his cousin and become a teacher. By the time he realizes this, however, his life is over. He passes away with a flash of recognition and "a faint smile on his lips."[11]

This story highlights the fact that people have a predilection to question their lot and to feel disappointed with their lives. In many instances, such feelings are not entirely groundless. Life is frequently tragic, and reality seldom conforms to the dreams and aspirations of the individual: "Very few live by choice. Every man is placed in his present condition by causes which acted without his foresight, and with which he did not always willingly cooperate; and therefore you will rarely meet one who does not think the lot of his neighbor better than his own."[12] Typically, in facing their reality, people's reaction can be either to accept, to rebel, or sometimes just to gripe.

"Complaining is a weak man's only weapon" (*silāḥ al-ḍuʿafāʾ al-shikāya*), states an Arabic proverb. But does it help to revile fate? Mikhail Naimy offers the following thoughts:

> What profits it to rail at Fate?
> No ear has she to hear you prate,
> Nor eye to see, in misery's murk,
> The scorpion's bitter sting at work,
> Nor heart to soften, though you cry
> Until your very tear-ducts dry;
> It's all the same to her, my friend,
> A blithe career, or wretched end,
> All one to her, whether it be
> A love-song or a threnody;
> The cradled infant's smiling eyes,
> The helpless failure's sobbing cries,
> The man who's happy with his lot,
> The clamorous rebel who is not—
> Her equity consists therein:
> She favors neither, lose or win.
> What profits it to rail at Fate?
> She simply doesn't hear you, mate!

She is your shadow—strange, I know,
Your shadow should deceive you so![13]

The Arabic word which Mikhail Naimy uses for "fate" is *al-ayyām*, that is, "the days."

Considering that human life rarely proceeds smoothly and that often "What man proposes, God disposes" (*al-ʿabd yuʾammil wa-al-rabb yukammil; al-insān fī al-tafkīr wa-Allāh fī al-tadbīr*), it is questionable whether people should wish at all. Life is full of irony, of flukes, of the unexpected. The journey through life resembles a ride on a roller coaster: there are plenty of ups and downs, twists and turns, and narrow escapes. Whatever good one wishes for oneself may be bestowed on someone else, and the evil one wishes upon someone else may befall one personally. There are no guarantees—the vicissitudes of life strike arbitrarily and indiscriminately. Arabic proverbial lore abounds in sayings to this effect: "Life is a day of honey and a day of onions" (*al-dunyā yawm ʿasal wa-yawm baṣal*); "Life has its ups and downs" (*al-dunyā yawm lanā wa-yawm ʿalaynā*); "Some days you win, and some days you lose" (*id-dunyā yōm tiddi wi-yōm tākhud*, colloquial Egyptian).

The Virtue of Contentment

In Arab culture, the traditional attitude has been to emphasize the virtue of contentment with one's lot and to caution against the danger of ambition, castigated as greed. A popular saying attributed to the prophet Muḥammad runs: "Whoever is contented with fate foreordained by God is never in need" (*man raḍiya bi-qismat Allāhi istaghnā*).[14] According to al-Ghazzālī, the most important of all the qualities that follow from the mystical virtue of love of God is satisfaction with His decree (*qaḍāʾ*).[15] While it is easy for people to be satisfied with those works of God that are agreeable and beneficial to them, the true test of their sincere love for God is being satisfied with those of His works that entail personal suffering or misfortune. For al-Ghazzālī, satisfaction with sufficient material wealth is the virtue of contentment. Moreover, the less one possesses, the greater is one's contentment—a view that agrees with the mystical virtues of poverty and asceticism.[16] Al-Ghazzālī warns against the long-term consequences of greed, which extend into the afterlife, for "the soul which has contracted covetousness as a fixed habit will necessarily in the next world suffer from the pangs of unsatisfied desire."[17]

There are numerous maxims in Arabic that pay tribute to the virtue of contentment (*qunūʿ, qanāʿa*): "Contentment is better than all the riches of the world" (*khayr al-ghinā al-qunūʿ*); "Contentment with one's lot is a limitless treasure" (*al-qanāʿa kanz lā yafnā*); "He who accepts his lot is happy" (*illi yirḍa bi-qismitu yirtāḥ*, colloquial Egyptian). Another related value, patience (*ṣabr*), defined as the ability to bear hardships, is considered an indispensable asset: "Because life is just like this, it has to be endured with patience" (*mā al-dahr illā hākadhā, fa-aṣbir lahu*); "Patience is the best medicine against the changes of fate" (*dawā' al-dahri al-ṣabr ʿalayhi*); "Patience is the key to relief" (*al-ṣabr miftāḥ al-faraj*).

While Arabic proverbial lore exalts contentment, it denounces greed (*ṭamaʿ, ḥirṣ*). For example: "Grasp all, lose all" (*al-ṭamaʿ gharrār ʿuqbāhu khasār*); "Greed leads to privation" (*al-ḥirṣ qāʾid al-ḥirmān*); "A greedy man doesn't get more than his allotted share" (*laysa al-ḥarīṣ bi-zāʾid fī rizqihi*); "Only the grave can put an end to man's greed" (*il-bani ādam ma-yimlā-sh ʿeenu illa t-turāb*, colloquial Egyptian).

The conviction encapsulated in these sayings is also expressed in the Ḥadīth literature. A tradition attributed to the prophet Muḥammad asserts that there are two types of people whose hunger is never satisfied: the seeker of knowledge and the seeker of wealth. While the first is praised, the second is condemned.[18] In a tradition attributed to the Caliph Omar, it is said: "Greed is a cause of poverty, and despair is a cause of freedom from want" (*al-ṭamaʿ faqr wa-al-yaʾs ghinā*). [19] This sentiment can be traced back to pre-Islamic Arabic poetry, as illustrated by the following lines of al-Nābigha al-Dhubyānī (d. *c.* 604):

> And despair of what has become beyond reach occasions, as its result, rest:
> And assuredly many a cause of coveting, is, in its result, like a disease in the fauces, or a poisonous plant.[20]

These lines affirm the benefit of the psychological relief imparted by resignation and contentment as opposed to the emotional stress caused by ambition and greed.

Between Rebellion and Compliance

In modern Arabic literature, with the impetus of new ideas from the West and the challenge of social change, there has been a growing rejection of traditional values and attitudes—the maxim "Contentment with one's lot is a limitless treasure" being a case in point. The adoption of rationalist and existentialist theories has led to a heightened awareness of the need for people to nurture a spirit of activism, confrontation, and involvement in order to gain control of their destinies, fulfill their potential, and reform society. New values, such as self-assertion, self-reliance, self-betterment, self-expression, self-determination, and rebellion against all forms of deprivation, have become not only desirable but essential to defeat poverty, injustice, ignorance, and oppression. Consequently, themes of defiance and heroic revolt by individuals struggling to improve their lot and attain their aspirations against the constraints of family, culture, and society figure prominently in modern Arabic literature. Imbued with local flavor, they reflect a universal quest for a life lived in freedom, dignity, and fruition.

Not always does personal rebellion bring about the desired results. More often than not, it ends in failure, tragedy, escape, or suicide. These motifs are depicted in novels and novellas such as *The Saint's Lamp (Qindīl Umm Hāshim,* 1944) by Yaḥya Ḥaqqī, *I Am Alive (Anā aḥyā,* 1958) by Laylā Baʿlabakkī, and *Season of Migration to the North (Mawsim al-hijra ilā al-shimāl,* 1966) by al-Ṭayyib Ṣāliḥ, as well as in short stories such as "The Barren Woman" ("Al-ʿĀqir") by Mikhail Naimy, "The 'A' of Freedom" ("Alif al-aḥrār") by Yūsuf Idrīs, and "The Crush of Life" ("Al-Ziḥām") by Yūsuf al-Shārūnī.[21] In these works, the spontaneous rebellion is the inevitable outcome of the characters' oppressive conditions, yet the same system that propels the rebellion is also responsible for ultimately crushing it.

Rejection of the traditional roles assigned to a woman in Arab society and of the conventions governing male–female relations is an important theme in the work of women writers such as Ghāda al-Sammān, Nawāl al-Saʿdāwī, Laylā Baʿlabakkī, Ḥanān al-Shaykh, and Alīfa Rifʿat, and women poets such as Fadwā Ṭūqān and Nāzik al-Malāʾika. Their critical writings shatter the myth that women are content to live in their accustomed way and portray desperate attempts of female characters seeking an exit from a state of physical and mental entrapment. Again, more often than not, these attempts fail; nevertheless, they are not devoid of merit. Their value lies in the mere fact of the heroines' actual endeavor, in the measure of catharsis that the experience provides, and in the likelihood that the seed sown will one day bear fruit. As the heroine of Iḥsān Kamāl's story "A Mistake in the Knitting" ("Saṭr maghlūṭ") acknowledges: "We've left our old traditions and plunged into the sea of life, striking out for the opposite bank—liberation. But it seems we haven't reached it yet. Perhaps our daughters will manage to get there. Our generation is the generation of sacrifice."[22]

Sometimes the heroines succeed in their rebellion. These women are exceptional in that they have strong willpower and unusual talent. They manage to rise above circumstances and escape the narrow path of their sisters' existence by demonstrating great resolve, courage, and self-sacrifice. For example, in the novel *Memoirs of a Woman Doctor (Mudhakkirāt ṭabība,* 1965) by Nawāl al-Saʿdāwī, a young woman decides to overcome the age-old restrictions imposed on her gender, search for her own identity, and carve out a career for herself in a domain of her own choice:

> All that was left for me was to reject, to challenge, to resist! I would reject my femininity, challenge my nature, resist all the desires of my body; prove to my mother and grandmother that I wasn't a woman like

> them, that I wouldn't spend my life in the kitchen peeling onions and garlic, wasting all my days so that my husband could eat and eat. . . . I would become a doctor then, study medicine. . . . I'd prove to nature that I could overcome the disadvantages of the frail body she'd clothed me in. . . . I wouldn't give it a single chance to drag me into the ranks of illiterate women.[23]

Once in medical school, she learns through her personal encounters with both male students and male corpses in the anatomy room that men are not gods, as her mother had led her to believe, that science does not provide an answer to every problem, and that she cannot be happy to lead only an intellectual life. She then seeks marriage, finds herself bound to the wrong man, and opts for divorce. Thereafter, she immerses herself in her work and becomes a successful physician. Her professional success, however, does not blind her to the injustice and hypocrisy in her society:

> Why wasn't there a greater understanding of truth and justice? Why didn't mothers recognize that daughters were like sons, or men acknowledge women as equals and partners? Why didn't society recognize a woman's right to lead a normal life using her mind as well as her body?[24]

In times of disillusion and despair, she pulls through by relying primarily on herself and by drawing on her inner resources: "My acts of rebellion had given me a sort of strength and willpower which made it impossible for me to cling to anything outside myself for protection."[25] Eventually she finds both fulfillment and love. The novel, though a work of fiction, derives its authenticity from similar events in al-Saʿdāwī's own remarkable life.

Two personal accounts of men who succeed in their goal to improve their lot and realize their potential are those of Jurjī Zaydān (1861–1914) and Muḥammad Shukrī (b. 1935). Jurjī Zaydān's memoirs (*Mudhakkirāt Jurjī Zaydān*, 1966) tell of his tenacious efforts as a young boy to obtain an education and develop a career in a direction other than that of his father, a restaurant owner who has never learned to read or write. Taken out of school at the age of eleven to serve as a cook, waiter, and accountant for his father, he continued to read and study on his own. Despite all odds, after an eight-year break from school, he managed to pass the entrance examinations to the Syrian Protestant College (American University) in Beirut and get into medical school. Hard work and self-discipline paid off, and Jurjī Zaydān completed the first year successfully. However, he never became a physician. An internal dispute that broke out among the professors of his college and caused a student strike forced him to leave for Cairo, where he hoped to continue his medical training. Instead, he became a famous journalist, publisher, and novelist.

Muḥammad Shukrī's depiction of his colorful life is remarkable for its vivid detail and the outspoken quality of its language and subject matter. Born into extreme poverty in Morocco, he ran away from home in his youth because of an abusive father and lived in the back streets of Tangier and Tetuán with thieves, prostitutes, and smugglers. At the age of twenty, he made the decision to become literate. Within a period of five years, he progressed from learning the Arabic alphabet to writing poems and stories. Today, his works are published both in the Arab world and in the West. His struggle for survival and his journey of discovery are chronicled in *For Bread Alone* (1973; *Al-Khubz al-ḥāfī*, 1982).

Despite such successful accounts, given the pressure to conform and the lack of freedom in traditional Arab society, most people find it easier to resign themselves to their lot and accept the demands, norms, and expectations of the social environment rather than to defy them and rebel. Moreover, the high value attached to contentment promotes compliance as a convenient alternative for individuals who seek to resolve their conflicts with the established system by adapting themselves to its requirements, however repressive. Dissatisfaction with the existing order is then suppressed or redirected, and submission becomes the main course of action.[26]

Arabic literature abounds in novels of compliance, foremost among which are those of Najīb Maḥfūẓ. In many of his works, the characters are caught in the grip of social forces beyond their control. They make futile attempts to change their harsh situation and, for lack of legitimate means, resort to opportunism and illegitimate activities. Such strategies are usually ill-fated and bring about disastrous results.[27] In the long run, however, these characters adjust to their conditions and endure their lot with stoic patience and a semblance of contentment. This theme is portrayed, for example, in Maḥfūẓ's *Trilogy (Al-Thulāthiyya*, 1956–57); *The Thief and the Dogs (Al-Liṣṣ wa-al-kilāb*, 1961); *Autumn Quail (Al-Summān wa-al-kharīf*, 1962); and *Miramar* (1967). In *The Beggar (Al-Shaḥḥādh*, 1965), ʿUthmān Khalīl, a socialist revolutionary who has spent years in jail, says of his prison experience: "If we were thrown into hell, I believe we'd get used to it eventually and to its fiery minions."[28] In *Love in the Rain (Al-Ḥubb taḥta al-maṭar*, 1973), the protagonist, Ḥusnī Ḥijāzī, denounces the poor waiter ʿAbduh Badrān and the entire generation that he represents. His thoughts are: "God damn them! They accept injustice, tyranny, and servitude, but when it comes to love and fun they turn into vicious lions."[29]

In *Midaq Alley (Zuqāq al-Midaqq*, 1947), also by Najīb Maḥfūẓ, one of the characters, Raḍwān Ḥusaynī, has suffered successive disappointments and sorrows. The years he spent studying at al-Azhar ended in failure, for he did not manage to obtain a degree. Then all his children died young. Despite his many hardships, he is content with his lot and speaks in favor of acceptance and against revolt:

> Never say you are bored. Boredom is disbelief in God. Boredom is an illness that destroys faith. Does it mean anything other than dissatisfaction with life? Life is a blessed gift from God Almighty, so how can a believer become bored or dissatisfied with it? You say you are dissatisfied with this or that, and I ask you from where did this or that originate? Doesn't everything originate with the Glorious God who in His kindness rights all wrongs? Never rebel against the work of the Creator! All of life has beauty and taste, although the bitterness of an evil soul will pollute the most appetizing tastes. Believe me, pain brings joy, despair has its pleasure, and death teaches a lesson.[30]

While Raḍwān Ḥusaynī is kind and generous to his neighbors, he is strict and unyielding in his own house, imposing his authority on the only person who would submit to his will—his wife. As for the wife, she accepts her position and does not complain: "Apart from those wounds indelibly engraved on her heart by the deaths of her children, she considered herself a fortunate woman, proud of her husband and of her life."[31]

Between rebellion and compliance, Arab writers find themselves functioning in societies that conceal a considerable degree of inner tension. Pulled in opposing directions, they oscillate between the individual's aspirations and society's gravity. The struggles, contradictions, and conflicting values that permeate their culture frequently translate into a creative force that yields an output of original literary works.

Ulfat al-Idilbī
Hard Luck

Ulfat al-Idilbī was born in Damascus in 1912. Having married early, she did not pursue formal education and is largely self-taught. She began to publish during the early 1950s and received critical acclaim for her sensitive style and sympathetic description of life in the Syrian capital.

Al-Idilbī is regarded as a pioneer woman writer of fiction, especially the short story, which is her preferred medium. She excels at portraying the lives of women in traditional Damascene society. She has published several collections of short stories, the first of which is entitled *Damascene Stories (Qiṣaṣ shāmiyya*, 1954). She has also published books of literary articles, a study of *The Arabian Nights*, and two novels: *Sabriya: Damascus Bitter Sweet (Dimashq yā basmat al-ḥuzn*, 1980), which has been dramatized for Syrian television, and *Grandfather's Tale (Ḥikāyat jaddī*, 1991).

"Hard Luck" ("Al-Ḥaẓẓ al-ʿāthir") appears in the collection *Damascene Stories*. The story depicts the fundamental tendency in human nature to be dissatisfied with any situation.

One bright night, three young girls who were students at a boarding school took advantage of the headmistress's preoccupation to leave their beds and slip away to the roof terrace to chat in the moonlight. It was a peaceful night, and cool, damp breezes carried the fragrance of flowers in the air. The delightfully intoxicating atmosphere infused the girls' souls with joy and tranquility, and enticed them to abandon themselves to sweet, lovely dreams.

The Angel of Luck and the Angel of Mercy happened to be strolling about. They heard the chattering girlish voices.

"Come, my brother," said the Angel of Mercy. "Let's feast our eyes on the sight of those young girls in their flowing white gowns and enjoy listening to their innocent, sweet talk." So the two angels landed on the roof.

A fair-haired, rosy-cheeked girl was speaking. Her words had a magic ring and an enchanting tone.

"Ask me, my friends, what kind of man I would like for a husband, if I were given the opportunity to choose?

"I would like him to be rich, very rich, with an important position and great prestige. I wouldn't care if he were old and ugly or stupid and dull, because I would spend most of my time with other people rather than with him. It would be enough for me that I could live in a lofty palace, buy the finest car, wear the latest fashions, and adorn myself with the rarest and most expensive jewels. Besides, I would give banquets and parties for prominent people. I would be a grand hostess, and my house would be a haven for celebrated artists, literary prodigies, and brilliant leaders."

Hardly had she arrived at this point in her speech when a slender, dark-skinned girl with long eyelashes interrupted her, saying:

"I feel just the opposite, because I would like my husband to be smart, good-looking, elegant, witty, knowledgeable, and well versed in literature. It wouldn't matter if he were poor and destitute or unknown and obscure, for it would be enough for me if we loved each other and belonged to each other."

She had no sooner finished than a small, ivory-skinned girl with pitch-black hair gave a mocking laugh that pealed through the air.

"Oh, what nonsense!" she cried. "Are wealth and prestige only to be found together with old age and unattractiveness? Are youth and beauty only to be found together with poverty and destitution? I would like my husband to be both young and handsome, smart and rich, and have position and prestige."

The three young girls fell silent as they began to delight in their sweet dreams.

The Angel of Mercy said to the Angel of Luck: "My brother, what if you were to fulfill the wishes of those girls?"

"Fulfill their wishes! Oh, my brother! You know nothing of their affairs!"

The Angel of Mercy retorted: "Indeed, we were correct to call you ruthless, stupid, and frivolous. By God, if I were in your shoes, I would fulfill each girl's wish!"

Slapping his palms together in despair, the Angel of Luck exclaimed: "Fulfill each girl's wish? I've spent my entire life exerting efforts on their behalf, and never have I succeeded in pleasing them!"

But the Angel of Mercy remained resolute and refused to budge.

"By God, I won't leave until you smile upon those girls in that special way of yours that makes the most difficult wishes and the rarest dreams come true!"

The Angel of Luck had no desire to frustrate his friend, so he smiled upon the girls in such a way that a bright light shone like a flash of lightning. It momentarily blinded the girls' eyes and their hearts quickened. Regarding it as the Night of the Divine Decree, they muttered supplications and presented their requests, then humbly arose to return to their beds. They slept contentedly, full of dreams.

The year had hardly ended when the Angel of Luck fulfilled his promise. The first girl married a rich old man who showered her with material comforts, exactly as she had wished. The second girl married a handsome sports hero who was much admired for his elegance and wit. The third girl married an heir whose youth and good looks were combined with wealth and noble lineage.

And the wheel of time turned. The Angel of Luck forgot about the three girls. He went about his work, neither tired nor bored, smiling upon those he raised to the heights and sneering at those he reduced to the lowest level.

One day he happened to pass by the boarding school. He became suspicious when he saw unusual activity going on there, so he inquired and learned that the school was giving a party to celebrate its fiftieth anniversary. All of its graduates, as well as their families, were invited to the celebration.

The gathering was hosted by the fair-haired, rosy-cheeked girl whose voice had a magic ring. At her side was an old, rather dull-looking man. The girl was bejeweled and draped in a splendid fur, but the Angel of Luck was alarmed at her clearly melancholy expression. She attempted to conceal it by chatting animatedly and smiling occasionally, but the truth could not be hidden. The Angel of Luck cast a searching glance at her, which penetrated her soul and reached her innermost depths. And there she was, talking to herself and saying:

"*Oh, what hard luck*! I made a terrible mistake when I married this old man who is as ugly in the morning as he is when he chases me in the evening. He has attached himself to me like a second skin. We do not agree about anything—ever. We are merely polite to each other. It is all a sham, and I can no longer bear it."

As she pondered these thoughts, she gazed at a handsome young man who was the center of attention. Many guests were gathered around him, enjoying his anecdotes and admiring his elegance and finesse. At his side was the slender, dark-skinned girl with the long eyelashes, but she seemed silent, somber, and absentminded, as though preoccupied with something that distracted her from her surroundings. Again, the Angel of Luck cast that searching glance of his, which probed the soul's very depths. And there she was, talking to herself and saying:

"*Oh, what hard luck*! I made a terrible mistake when I married this young man who has no interest beyond dispensing wit and charm in company, because he never seems to get enough praise and flattery. I'm fed up with his endless repetition of these tiresome jokes. What good are his looks and manners and elegance and wit to me, if I must remain at his side obscure and forgotten? I wish I had married a rich man!" At that thought, she glanced at her plain clothing, then sized up her fair-haired friend with a sharp look that enabled her to assess the price of the splendid fur. Her eyes settled on the large diamond ring, but its bright sparkle interfered with her attempts to estimate its size and price.

The Angel of Luck said to himself: "Where is the small, ivory-skinned girl with the pitch-black hair? Perhaps I've succeeded with her, although I've certainly failed with her friends."

He began to look for her all around the school, but he was unable to find her. Then he heard her two friends ask the headmistress about her. The headmistress replied that she had received regrets that the lady would be unable to attend. The two friends shook their heads and said to themselves:

"Oh, how happy she must be! Her life is so full of fun and banquets and parties that she cannot find time to squeeze in such a stupid affair as the school party."

The Angel of Luck wanted to see for himself, so he flew swiftly to her home. The spacious garden delighted him, and the lofty palace stunned him. Servants and attendants floated in and out. He was dazzled by the splendid furniture and priceless ornaments. He began to search for the mistress of the palace, until he stumbled upon her just as she had shut her bedchamber door and begun to cry bitterly.

"What ingratitude!" he said. "This one has a problem, too?"

And there she was, sobbing to herself and saying:

"*Oh, what hard luck*! I made a terrible mistake when I married this spendthrift youth who squanders his money indiscriminately. The clubs monopolize him, the associations compete for his presence, evil men try to lure him with their schemes, and loose women try to seduce him with their charms. Then he cannot find the time to accompany me even to a function that means as much to me as the school party. I was ashamed to attend alone when my friends were accompanied by their husbands.

"If only he were an old man! Then he would try hard to please me and would not refuse my wishes!

"I wish he were poor! Then no one would want to share him with me!"

At this, the Angel of Luck slapped his palms together and moaned:

"*Oh, what hard luck*! I made a terrible mistake when I agreed to be the Angel of Luck.

"Where is the Angel of Mercy? He should see and hear firsthand how I've spent my entire life trying to help these people, but I've never succeeded, and neither will I ever succeed, in pleasing them!"

Comments

This story revolves around the question of "to wish or not to wish" and offers a tragicomic illustration of the pitfalls associated with gratifying human desires. The popular point of view is expressed by the Arabic proverb "Man always covets what he does not possess" (*al-mar'u tawwāqun ilā mā lam yanal*).

Three young girls, shortly before their graduation from high school, list the attributes they wish for in a husband. The Angel of Luck is pressured by the Angel of Mercy to oblige them. Actually, the Angel of Luck knows better: satisfying human wishes may be the surest route to achieving the opposite result.

Several years later, the Angel of Luck discovers that what he predicted earlier has come true, and that despite his granting the girls' wishes, they are all dissatisfied. It appears that now the girls need the Angel of Mercy's compassionate touch.

The girls' dilemma is not peculiar to their sex but rather universal. It is difficult to satisfy human wishes. For one thing, people often have great expectations of life, which are at variance with their objective ability to judge their circumstances accurately. Some lack the qualities that would enable them to work toward achieving their desires; for others, the work may be difficult and success slow in coming. In either case, there is bound to be a measure of discontent. In addition, immaturity and inexperience often lead individuals to make poor decisions that they later regret and are unable to correct. Moreover, people are frequently dependent on each other, and inasmuch as they pin their hopes on others, they are likely to be disappointed. In this particular instance, the girls' inability to be satisfied is directly related to their lack of personal means of self-expression and total reliance on their husbands for a sense of fulfillment. One should bear in mind that in traditional Arab society, women's education is not necessarily career oriented, and it does not afford them full freedom. Women are always under some form of male domination, be it the father's or the husband's. Marriage marks a girl's transfer from the authority of her father to that of her husband, on whom she becomes thoroughly dependent. Hence each heroine is preoccupied with the ideal profile of her future husband.[32]

It is significant that the story contains an allusion to the Night of the Divine Decree (Laylat al-Qadr). A common belief holds that on this night a light appears to a chosen few, who thereby acquire fulfillment of a wish (compare "Our Lord Qadr" by Mubārak Rabīʿ, in chapter 1). Besides the message that people may get what they wish for, the author is making the point that wishing itself gets in the way of doing. The girls substitute wishing for the exercise of whatever skills they may possess. They do not try to achieve their own success within the framework of socially sanctioned activities available to them.

Presumably, for the three young women, the key to long-lasting satisfaction is to pursue their own self-development. While this goal appears to conflict with the patriarchal values of Arab society, it is noteworthy that much has changed over the years. Arab women have become more involved in public life, and their presence as highly trained professionals—physicians, lawyers, and teachers, as well as journalists and writers—is growing in number and influence. The tradition that confined them to the home is slowly changing, and women in many Arab countries today participate in almost every domain of public and productive life—with or without wearing the veil. However, as Arab women gain greater freedom and more career opportunities, they—like their sisters in the West—encounter new difficulties, such as the hazards connected with freedom and the strain of maintaining a job and a family. These dilemmas—and sources of dissatisfaction—are inseparably linked to the process of liberation and modernization.[33]

Laylā Bin Māmī
I Want Him to Be Free

Laylā Bin Māmī was born in Djerba, Tunisia, in 1944. She received her elementary and secondary education in local schools and then attended the University of Tunis, from which she graduated in Arabic literature. She has worked as a journalist for the Tunisian newspaper *al-ʿAmal* and has published many poems in various journals and magazines.

The appearance of her collection of short stories, provocatively entitled *A Burning Minaret (Ṣawmaʿa taḥtariq,* 1968), created an uproar similar to that surrounding the Lebanese woman writer Laylā Baʿlabakkī's *Spaceship of Tenderness to the Moon (Safīnat ḥanān ilā al-qamar,* 1963), in that it was perceived as a direct attack on religion and tradition. Regarded as a feminist writer, Bin Māmī is mainly concerned with the problems of women in Arab society: the issues of liberation, self-realization, and male–female relations. Her stories contain a mixture of lyrical poetry and simple prose. A salient feature of her style is the use of short, pithy sentences, ending in elliptical dots. The rapid succession of such sequences results in a vibrant rhythm, at times creating a feeling of excitement and at times a sense of bewilderment.

"I Want Him to Be Free" ("Urīduhu ḥurran") is from the collection *A Burning Minaret.*[34] The story depicts a feminist rebellion.

I'm in a strange state tonight, strange, strange. I used to live in a whirlwind of thoughts, opinions, and principles, which removed me from the reality of life, from its original course, carrying me off suddenly toward what was outside the realms of life, what was far away from it and from its reality!

My hand was a part of me. I'd forgotten all about it until . . . one day I became aware of its existence again. Its tasks multiplied, so I limited myself to a few of them, and refused the hand its freedom. I didn't respond to its rebellion—I, who am a woman, and who want everything to respond to my rebellion. The hand was a part of me. It was demanding, together with my other parts, the ultimate rebellion that I myself was seeking. But it wanted to have a rebellion of its own, alone; it was demanding a rebellion from me—me, an integrated whole, with the exception of my hand!

Why? I don't know! I refused the hand its freedom. I believed in the freedom of the individual, but I forgot the freedom of the part. I neglected it. My mistake was . . . to neglect it.

I neglected my hand, a piece of me, an inseparable part. But I was neglected too. I needed a person confronting me who would make me feel the need for inner rebellion, for external rebellion. But my hand—it too needed to be confronted with another hand, to arouse it to rebel. And it rebelled against *me.* Wasn't I a believer in freedom? I was . . . pieces . . . parts, scattered abroad in the distant past and coming together to form *me.* The hand knew how it worked together with its sisters—the small parts—to ignite a rebellion in my soul. And today it wanted to conduct its own rebellion, alone, without asking its sisters for help, so that its rebellion would be against *me,* and against what was outside both of us.

It was rebelling for itself. By itself. Against me. Because I taught it to rebel. Or rather, it learned to rebel by itself. . . .

What did the hand want? It answered: "Something simple. My ideal is a part of your ideal! You wanted your freedom in order to subdue another person. I want my freedom in order to subdue another hand!"

I asked myself just how much my freedom had helped me in subduing the other person. The answer came to me. I knew now. I had subdued the other person by raising my word when he raised his, by expressing my opinion when he expressed his, by making choices when he made his, by becoming as indispensable to him as he was to me. I had subdued him, and we lived as I wanted, and as he wanted. But today my hand was provoking me. It wanted to rebel against me, to subdue the other hand. I hadn't yet noticed the signs of its rebellion when it began. The hand broke its prison chains and set itself free, looking for the other hand in order to subdue it. Its fingertips spread out toward the fingertips of the other hand, responding—I don't know how—to thousands of calls. Calls of which I was unaware. My hand was becoming free, living, and I had only got as far as asking what the benefits of its liberation would be. It was living, and I had only got as far as asking what the benefits of its rebellion would be. My own rebellion hadn't been destructive. It had enabled me to subdue the other person.

And what of the hand's rebellion? I don't know. What is its purpose? What will it accomplish? I hesitate between waiting and yielding to the urge to forget it. Waiting is something I'm not used to. I live. The minutes pass—they have to. I don't wait for them. I don't wait for what they might bring. I let them pass. They pass because . . . they have to. I don't want to wait because . . . I don't have to. I yield to the urge to forget the hand, but I can't. Even though I no longer feel it, I see it, I notice it. It has disengaged itself from my feeling, but it hasn't disengaged itself from my mind. I have neglected it. My senses have lost track of it, but the fragments of its attributes have remained in my memory, in my mind. I see the hand's movements, and I wait. No, I'm not waiting. I'm paying heed, until the moment the hand achieves a result. Until it becomes what it wants—what that is, I don't know—or until it fails to become what it wants. It is enough that it has rebelled; it has *felt* its existence, and wanted it. It doesn't matter what it achieves; it will definitely achieve something.

The hand said it had adopted my ideal. It, a part of the whole, had adopted a lesser ideal from the great ideal. The ideal that I had formulated, with its help. It is a part of my parts. It is *my* part of the parts, the only one able to formulate an ideal. It formulated it by itself, because it had learned what power is. It knew how to derive benefit from what was around it. Its experiences are bits of my experiences. Its participation in my experiences, its partial participation, taught it the entire experience. And it set itself free, to experiment. . . .

I was amazed. Had the other hand—the thought startled me—had the other hand set itself free from its master or had it merely obeyed him? You have to understand that what my hand does isn't in obedience to my will, my own will. I don't want what it's doing!

I had wanted to become free, and I had gathered the small components of me, my parts, my limbs, and turned them into a great power, with which I demanded my freedom. I led them in the quest to obtain my freedom. Then I obtained it, and subdued you, the other person.

And here was my hand, assuming my character, and rebelling in its turn. It wanted its freedom. It, the little part, the part of my parts, wanted its freedom. Then it demanded it, and took it, without my being able to prevent it.

And now it's practicing its freedom with your hand, which I regard merely as submitting to your giant will, your deadly will.

You are a human being. You didn't obtain your freedom alone; you didn't defend yourself for its sake; you didn't rebel against a condition that deprived you of it. You are a human being born free. Yes, they granted you your freedom. They gave it to you as a gift, because you were incapable of demanding it. They knew you. They had tested your ability before, and your hand came out bearing your stamp. It wanted to be granted everything. It expected to be given something. It submitted to you, to your will, which you were granted at no cost.

As for my hand, it's like me. It doesn't want to be offered cold food, free of charge. It wants to struggle to obtain, in order to feel the pleasure of obtaining.

So he rebelled. A self-defeating pride stirred up in him. It made him lose the dearest thing he had. He pulled his hand from my hand. He set it free in a rebellion, a negative rebellion, which made him lose the hand he loved.

He retreated somewhere or other, urged on by a negative rebellion, pushed into it by a senseless pride. He wanted to be liberated from the love of freedom. He went away because he didn't understand. Why? I wanted to arouse him to rebel. He, who had always lived under the nightmare of submission, regarded me . . . as crazy. I freed my hand from myself. I gave it its independence. I avoided selfish behavior. And so I set my parts free. My hand became free, in order to lead its life in liberty, in order to subdue the other hand.

And his hand became free, in order to lead its life under the nightmare of submission, in order that he should subdue it. He was a person subdued by society, subdued by life, and then he subdued his hand. Whereas I was a person who subdued society, who subdued life, and then my hand subdued me.

He refused life; he refused freedom. I preferred them to him, and left him forever, left him to live in the nightmare of submission. I couldn't tolerate his senseless and self-defeating pride.

Comments

This story presents a woman who is the very antithesis of the girls in the previous story. Whereas in "Hard Luck" the girls, though dissatisfied and unhappy, display the traditional attitude of compliance and resign to their lot, here the heroine demonstrates the new spirit of self-assertion and rebellion against oppressive conditions and norms.

The feminist narrator rebels against her domination by her male companion—possibly her husband—as well as by her society. The breakdown in the relationship of this couple is signified through the separation of their linked hands: the man pulls his hand away in a disapproving gesture, after which the woman chooses to leave him and follow her own path.

The cause of the conflict in this relationship is the woman's demand for freedom and equality, which clashes with the dictates of society and the customs to which the man subscribes. She has fought stubbornly to live as an equal partner with him. However, he has neither responded to her demands nor demonstrated any concern or fighting spirit on her behalf. The intolerable situation compels the woman to free herself from the man, in an effort to preserve her own identity and the ideals that she holds dear.

There are three rebellions in this story. The first is the woman's rebellion: it is depicted as positive, for the sake of freedom. The second is the man's rebellion: it is negative, for the sake of custom and tradition. The third is the hand's rebellion: it is allegorical and constitutes a replica of the woman's own rebellion. The woman's personality is funneled into her rebellious hand, which moves in an autonomous fashion, demanding full freedom. This vivid depiction provides additional insights into the woman's original rebellion.

The choice of the hand as the rebelling agent is symbolic. The hand stands for action—it is the organ that regularly performs the tasks dictated by the individual's will. In body language, a gesture of the hand is often used to convey a thought or an attitude of the mind. The fact that the hand has five fingers is also significant: first, because of its analogy with the human figure, which is composed of four extremities plus the head; second, because of the symbolism of the number 5, which denotes love, health, and humanity.[35] In addition, the number 5 corresponds to the five senses. In Berber tradition, the hand represents protection, authority, and strength. In Islamic cultures, the image of the hand is widely used as an amulet (*khamsa*) to ward off the evil eye or other evil spirits. This practice is based on the belief in the mystic power of the number 5, which is considered a sacred number. There are several reasons for its special status. To begin with, God is one; therefore, the odd numbers are better than the even ones. Then there are five pillars of faith in Islam, five keys of secret knowledge, and five daily prayers.[36] In universal terms, two hands linked together signify union, marriage, fraternity, and solidarity in the face of danger. Altogether, the hand is imbued with positive connotations and is intimately associated with the individual's will and state of mind. Hence the struggling hands indicate a conflict of human wills. The woman, in her inner turmoil, discovers that her hand is in conflict not only with the man's hand but also with her own other hand.

The heroine has chosen rebellion rather than passive resignation to her lot. Her rebellion is directed not only against the man but also against the notion that she has to be content with her lot—a prevailing value in traditional Arab society. In her desire to have a meaningful existence, she is mature enough to understand that her freedom can be achieved only in concert with the man's own liberation from the chains of custom and tradition. She also recognizes the risks involved in rebellion, as allegorically illustrated by the action of her hand: the hand's lack of discipline may be harmful to the integrity and proper functioning of the body (i.e., herself, matrimonial union, or society). While retaining its freedom, the hand must remain connected to the body and fully coordinated with it. Further, the woman is aware that her hand is in danger of demanding too much and thus itself becoming oppressive: in the allegory, the rebelling hand does not accept equality but rather aspires to dominate the woman's other hand. It appears that the hand is getting carried away and seeking to achieve retribution and control rather than justice and parity. In like manner, the woman realizes that she is in danger of replacing the man's tyrannical domination with her own. An excessive demand for freedom can be hazardous and possibly disruptive. In the final analysis, however, this woman is courageous and outspoken in her approach to the dilemma of her existence.

The story's title, "I Want Him to Be Free," conveys an important message: men, as well as women, need to be liberated in Arab society. Joint liberation will benefit both sexes, restore harmony to them, and allow them to develop and prosper. While the heroine seeks a dialogue with her male counterpart, she perceives no possibility for normal relations prior to his disavowal of the social norms that deny her justice. The tragedy of the male–female relationship depicted in this story lies in the inability of the man to ignore his pride and stand up for the woman at his side. Instead, he has forsaken her to espouse the mores of a society that holds her gender in bondage.[37]

9
CONCLUSION

> What we should take hold of and imitate is the flame of questioning which animated our ancestors, so that we can complement their work with a new vision and new approaches to knowledge.
>
> —Adonis (ʿAlī Aḥmad Saʿīd)[1]

Fatalism: The Popular Outlook

This study has focused on the concept of fate in the Arab world as mirrored in modern Arabic literature. Several views of human destiny have been examined: the religious, the philosophical, the psychological, the cultural, the biological, the economic, and the existentialist. All these views, diverse as they are, have the same basic concern: making sense of life. This concern, in itself, is not culture-bound but universal. Throughout the ages of human history, people have been puzzled by the mystery of life and propelled by a need to know and understand the world. In contemplating their existence and the forces of nature, they have invariably sought some kind of explanation, purpose, or meaning. A theory of fate provides a conciliatory answer to the apparent contradictions in the phenomenon of human life. Serving as a shield and a coping mechanism, it helps people to interpret their experiences and adapt themselves to their circumstances. Such a theory restores order and harmony to an otherwise terrifying reality, and affirms the underlying uniformity and rationality of the universe.

While there is remarkable variety among the perspectives on human destiny presented by modern Arab writers, not every one is unique to the Arab world. The role of chance and of economic and psychological factors in shaping a person's life is recognized in most contemporary societies, Western as well as non-Western. The effect of ancient customs and traditions on people's way of life, including the position of women, is manifested in other parts of the world, notably Africa and the Far East.

The only outlook that is genuinely Arabian and that distinctly typifies the Arab world as a culture area is the belief in divine predestination, epitomized in the Qur'ānic verse "And the Sun runs his course for a period determined for him: that is the decree of (Him), the Exalted in Might, the All-Knowing" (*wa-al-shamsu tajrī li-mustaqarrin lahā, dhālika taqdīru al-ʿazīzi al-ʿalīm*, 36:38).[2] According to this outlook, the universe runs its predestined course, determined by the will of God, who not only directs all the affairs of the world but also foreordains the fate of each and every individual. As shown in this work, the notion of fate was adopted from pre-Islamic Arabic poetry and pre-Islamic Arab beliefs. Rooted in the nomads' conception of time (*dahr*) as the cause of whatever happened to people, fate in Islam was attributed to God and assimilated into a doctrine of predestination, which, as an article of faith, was considered to be compatible with freedom of choice and human responsibility.[3]

Some orientalists suggest that for an accurate analysis of fatalism in Islam, it is necessary to distinguish between the popular point of view and the theological or philosophical one: "Eastern people have a psychological tendency to fatalism; but this species of popular fatalism, numerous traces of which are found in their folklore, is a sentiment rather than a doctrine. It is, moreover, limited to the outstanding accidents of human life, and especially to death, which it represents as happening of necessity at such and such a time and in such and such circumstances, no matter what one may do to avoid it; it is, we may say, a physical fatalism. The fatalism of the scholars is rather a moral fatalism; it does not apply specially to death, but refers to all human actions, holding these to be decreed by God."[4] Other orientalists are inclined to think that because Islam regulates every aspect of the believer's life, a profound sense of fatalism is a natural result: "There is nothing too slight, too personal, too intimate not to stand in need of being arranged by the divine will. This approach, while completely ritualizing life, imparts meaning to the most insignificant act and hallows it as a necessary affirmation of the eternal order. No distinction exists between matters sacred and profane since nothing is religiously irrelevant."[5] Although these theories differ about the extent of fatalism in Islam, both highlight its vital relevance to the lives of the devout. As He wills, and because He wills—to the Muslim, God's will is certain, absolute, irresistible, and inevitable. Hence God's will *is* fate.[6]

The practical implications of the belief in fate have been the subject of conflicting interpretations. On the negative side, the concept provides an easy excuse for absolving one from personal responsibility and shifting it onto an external force. "Fate" is often a label given after the event to explain away one's mistake or failure. It is used as a shelter by the lazy and as a reason for resignation and abnegation by the weak. The result is a lack of readiness to struggle: "Though no good Moslem has ever been a consistent do-nothing fatalist, the spirit of accepting as the will of Allah whatever required much effort to change was sufficiently prevalent to ensure general stagnation. It is not a question of religious doctrine, but of what one *argues* from it. . . . It has not prevented Moslems in past or present from vigorous fighting or from other exertions in directions that allured them."[7] On the positive side, the belief in fate is a source of great comfort: it removes the burden of personal responsibility and associated feelings of guilt; it provides relief from the anxiety and tension that accompany the daily struggle for survival; and it makes a tragedy, hardship, or deprivation easier to bear. As such, the belief in fate amounts to an inestimable psychological asset. In addition, the concept imparts a certain meaning to the human march through time by linking the thread of history from the past through the present to the future and placing it within the framework of a divine design. While fate is inexorable, immutable, and inscrutable, it is personalized in the sense that each human being is assigned an individual lot, thus making it unique and special.

The Arabs are proud of their outlook on life, derived from their religious perspective, which sets their basic disposition apart as "the tranquil soul" (*al-nafs al-muṭma'inna*, Qur'ān 89:27). This designation entails a soul that is at rest, at peace, and in a state of complete satisfaction. In Islamic theology, this stage of the soul represents the final stage of bliss.[8] It is interesting to note that Mikhail Naimy came to the same conclusion through the influence of theosophical and pantheistic beliefs. His sense of serenity is expressed in the poem "Tranquility" ("Al-Ṭuma'nīna"):

The roof of my house is of steel; its pillars, of stone;
Then blow, O winds! moan, O trees!
Swim, O clouds! fall in torrents of rain!
Roar, O thunder! I fear no danger!
The roof of my house is of steel; its pillars, of stone.

From my dim lamp I seek light to see
Whenever the night grows long and darkness spreads,
And even if the dawn dies, and the day ends its life.
Vanish, O stars! put out your light, O moon!
From my dim lamp, I seek light to see.

The door of my heart is made strong for all kinds of sorrow.
So come forward, O woes, at evening or at twilight!
Advance, O misfortunes, with misery and boredom;
Descend in thousands, O mishaps of men!
The door of my heart is made strong for all kinds of sorrow.

Fate is my ally, and destiny is my traveling mate.
So descend with lightnings around my heart, O evils.
Lay siege around my house, O Death!
I fear no torture and I fear no injury!
Fate is my ally; destiny, my traveling mate.[9]

The poem reflects the spiritual confidence of a person who is at one with nature and the forces that govern the universe. This sentiment is in concordance with the Islamic view of life, which encourages people to find contentment in attuning themselves to God's will as it is revealed in the order and harmony of creation.

In the modern period, Arab society has readily availed itself of all the consumer goods produced by the industrially advanced West. The Arab world, however, has been unduly slow in its social, political, economic, and technological development—a fact that has frustrated many Arab intellectuals. Their sense of inadequacy is particularly heightened by the glorious past of the Arab-Muslim civilization, whose achievements were not only material but also spiritual, scientific, philosophical, and cultural. *Li-Mādhā ta'akhkhara al-muslimūn?* ("Why are Muslims backward?") has been a perpetual question among Muslims since Jamāl al-Dīn al-Afghānī.[10] The phenomenal success of Japan in rapidly reconstructing itself after its defeat and massive destruction in World War II—to the extent that the level of technology and modernization attained by this Asian nation has placed it on competitive terms with the West—seemed a relevant model for the Arabs, who hoped to move forward and achieve similar results. This hope has not materialized, and large sections of Arab society have failed to modernize. The sorry state of affairs in most Arab countries and the manifest weakness of the Arab world as a whole have prompted Arab intellectuals to search for the underlying causes of their predicament.

Some scholars put the blame on the long history of Western imperialism and colonialism, which sapped the resources of the Arab world. Others see in the patriarchal structure of traditional Arab society the obstacle to progress and social change. Still others emphasize the subordination of the Arab woman and her absence from public life. Fatima Mernissi, for example, insists that educating women and preparing them to join the labor force is a prerequisite if the East is to rival the West in power and prestige. One of the causes of Arab weakness, she frequently asserts, is the fact that only half of the nation works and produces. The other half—the women—are prevented from taking part in the process of production.[11] Similarly, the French anthropologist Germaine Tillion argues that the subordination of women cripples society and men: "It lowers the active potential of the nation and consequently weakens the State; it paralyzes all forms of collective and individual evolution, male as much as female, and consequently slows down or curbs progress; and it causes multiple and irreparable injuries to children, and hence to the future. As for man, the supposed author and apparent beneficiary of this repression, at every period of his life—as child, as husband, as father—he is a direct victim of it."[12]

There are also Arab intellectuals who are of the opinion that Islam and modernity are incompatible and therefore call for religion to be separated from the state, as was done in Turkey in 1930 by Kemal Atatürk. When Atatürk realized that radical reform within the old Islamic framework, particularly in relation to women, was unlikely, he declared Turkey a secular state, abolished the Islamic family code, and instituted a civil code modeled on that of the Swiss.[13] These Arab intellectuals would like to see Islam relegated to the same position that Christianity occupies in the West—a matter of individual choice. Others make a distinction between true Islam and popular Islam. The true Islam, as al-Afghānī tirelessly reiterated, teaches personal responsibility and activism. Popular Islam, which combines orthodox Islamic dogmas with pagan animistic beliefs, promotes fatalism, passivity, and stagnation.

The pervasive influence of popular Islam figures prominently in the fiction of the Sudanese author al-Ṭayyib Ṣāliḥ, who depicts it as the dominant force in village life and as the major obstacle to change.[14] In his story "The Doum Tree of Wad Ḥāmid" ("Dawmat Wad Ḥāmid"), when the government announces its intention to cut down the sacred tree of Wad Ḥāmid to make a stopping place for a steamer or erect a water pump—in other words, when popular Islam is threatened by modernization—the latter is rejected in favor of the former. Ultimately, the force of popular religious beliefs causes the fall of the government. In Ṣāliḥ's *Season of Migration to the North (Mawsim al-hijra ilā al-shimāl,* 1966), popular Islam, represented by the grandfather as well as the village, is pitted against Western civilization, represented by Muṣṭafā Saʿīd, and again that civilization is rejected when it comes into conflict with popular Islam. In the novella *The Wedding of Zein (ʿUrs al-Zayn,* 1967), a moderate form of modernization is accepted only when it comes under the auspices of popular Islam, that is, the blessing of the holy man al-Ḥanīn.[15] These literary works help to explain why the socialist regimes in Sudan have failed, and why the ideology of Ḥasan al-Turābī, an Islamic radical, has grassroots support.

In recent decades, an increasing number of Arab intellectuals have acknowledged the role of prevailing cultural attitudes in obstructing change and impeding progress. They recognize that the lack of development in Arab society derives in part from a fatalistic value orientation, which is the result of religious indoctrination combined with political subjugation.[16] This view is shared by the distinguished Islamic scholar Gustave E. von Grunebaum, who notes that a belief system that centers life around God's will is bound to prize stability and maintain a static conception of the ideal society: "God is above change and so is His order, revealed once and for all by His Messenger. So change has to be justified as the true interpretation of the divine ordinance finally arrived at, as the reversal from impious innovation to the purity of the beginnings, or else it must be ignored, denied, or fought."[17] Significantly, even in the absence of direct religious influence, the fatalistic attitude seems to prevail, which indicates that this value orientation is internalized to the point where it has become part of the social psychology of the people.

In his article "Shall We Return to Existentialism?" ("Hal naʿūd ilā al-falsafa al-wujūdiyya?" 1990),[18] the Egyptian writer and journalist Anīs Manṣūr suggests that existentialism is the most suitable ideology for the Arabs, given its emphasis on action, freedom of choice, personal responsibility, and the primacy of the present. Manṣūr begins his discussion by expounding the principles of existentialism: "Existentialism is a philosophical and literary theory which is devoted to an interpretation of human existence; namely, that man exists, that he should be aware of his existence, and that he should realize himself as a human being. To be a human being, he must be free. To be free means to be responsible for every opinion and resolution that he adopts for himself and for other people."[19] Thus the first effect of existentialism is that it places the entire responsibility for people's circumstances and experiences squarely upon their own shoulders. There is no determinism, no means of justification, and no excuse to hide behind. Manṣūr reiterates Sartre's principle that people are nothing else but what they make of themselves and that there is no reality except in active involvement. He describes the development of this school of thought in the West and its initial appeal in the Arab world, stressing the overwhelming experience of anguish, abandonment, and despair in the wake of the Six-Day War. On the whole, he sees this philosophy as having helped Europe and Japan move away from the tragedies of the past (i.e., the two world wars), dedicate themselves to the future, and reach new heights. The Arabs, who tend to be culturally oriented toward the past, as reflected in their preoccupation with the glories of the past and its resurrection, must direct their energies toward the future: "Let us look back with anger. Our past certainly contains events that justify our anger, both at them and at ourselves. But after learning what has happened and how, we must adjourn the historical session and shut the ancient files. We must stop the past at its border, so that it will not creep up on our present as the desert creeps up on our cultivated land. We must look ahead with hope."[20] Manṣūr supports his argument with examples from the Bible and classical mythology. He refers to Lot's wife, who ignored the warning not to look back while fleeing Sodom and was turned into a pillar of salt. Likewise, the Greek hero Orpheus, who went to the underworld to get his beloved wife back from the gods, was cautioned not to look at her until they reached home. When he broke his promise and turned to look, his wife faded away into a shade. Manṣūr concludes his discussion with a call for writers, philosophers, and men of religion to help the nation "deliver life from death and the future from the claws of the past. Now is the time. Today, not tomorrow."[21] Thus the rhetorical question with which Manṣūr entitles his article is answered by an affirmation of existentialism as a positive, constructive, and humanistic outlook, well in tune with the pressing needs of Arab society.

The Antireligious Trend

It is pertinent to the present discussion to ascertain whether modern Arabic literature reveals any change of attitudes on the part of writers with regard to the place of faith in modern life in general and the role of Islam in Arab society in particular. The preceding chapters would seem to indicate that the religious frame of reference is no longer satisfactory to all. There are sophisticated and restless minds that are unreconciled to acceptance of divine will. They are critical of the religious answers offered to them and seek more relevant, more rational, and mostly secular solutions.

Antireligious ideas have gained currency in modern Arabic fiction since the turn of the twentieth century. Salih J. Altoma observes three thematic trends: "One is anti-Western and stresses Islam as the foundation of modern society; the second seeks to reconcile Islam with what are regarded as the 'positive values' of the West; and the third rejects Islam both as practiced and as a faith."[22] Altoma points out that the Islam-oriented trend is the least dominant and that the antireligious trend became more pronounced in the period following World War II.

Trevor Le Gassick makes a similar observation: "A new realism developed in which pessimism played an important role. In seeking to display accurately the times of their lives and to reveal the concerns motivating themselves and their society, the writers of this period have also shown that the faith of Islam was undergoing close scrutiny from an orientation that was rationalist and existentialist. Many of the major works of Arabic fiction since written express levels of dissatisfaction with the influence of religion in society and suggest that Islam is irrelevant or even detrimental to the concerns and interests of the fictional characters introduced in their works."[23] Le Gassick cites Yūsuf Idrīs's play *Flipflap and His Master (Al-Farāfīr*, 1963) as an example of the most extreme and outspoken expression of disbelief in the power of God over people's lives. In this innovative work, the world is conceived in terms of a play whose author left it half-finished and disappeared into space, forcing the two actors—the master and the servant—to improvise their parts. In the beginning, the author appears on stage in formal dress; he sets the play in motion, and the actors revolve around him in obedience. Later the author is observed to be without pants, and as the show progresses, the actors start to complain and criticize the play he has written. In the end, both master and servant discover that they are alone on stage (i.e., the universe) and that the author (i.e., God) never really existed.[24]

There are other striking examples of the rejection of religion in modern Arabic fiction. In the story "A Banquet Table from Heaven" ("Ṭabliyya min al-samāʾ"),[25] whose title alludes ironically to Qurʾān 5: 115, Yūsuf Idrīs delivers a biting attack on institutionalized religion while expressing a man's revolt against God. Shaykh ʿAlī is a destitute old man who lives off handouts in a poor Egyptian village. Bad-tempered, bitter, and uncompromising, he finally rebels against his harsh condition and threatens to bring a curse on the village by openly renouncing his faith and blaspheming God, unless he is presented with a table full of food from heaven. Standing bareheaded in public and brandishing his stick at the sky, he furiously addresses his creator:

> What do you want from me? Can you tell me what you want from me? I left al-Azhar because of some shaykhs who appointed themselves the guardians of religion. I divorced my wife. I sold my house. You inflicted poverty on me—only on me. Are there no other people in the world but me? Why don't you pour your wrath, Lord, on Churchill and Eisenhower? Am I the only person you can rule over? What do you want from me now? Before, you let me go hungry for one whole day. I suffered silently, telling myself it's like Ramaḍān, a single day that would pass. This time, I haven't had a bite to eat since the afternoon of the day before yesterday. And I haven't had a cigarette in a whole week. As for hashish, I haven't tasted it in ten days. And you say that in paradise there's the honey of bees and fruit and rivers of milk. Why don't you give me some of that? Are you waiting for me to die of hunger so I can go to paradise and eat of your bounty? No, sir. May God be bountiful unto you. Let me live today, and later you can do with me whatever you want.[26]

In this defiant outcry, Shaykh ʿAlī rejects the idea of a better life after death and emphasizes the primacy of the present. Future reward is no good to him, for he is concerned with the here and now. In the tragicomic ending, the devout villagers, perceiving in the shaykh's threat a danger to their already precarious existence, capitulate to his demands and hasten to bring him whatever food they can find. While the story pokes fun at the superstitious peasant mentality, it also calls into question fundamental Islamic dogmas and the religious leadership.[27]

Another imaginative work that paints a gloomy picture of the role of religion in modern society is Najīb Maḥfūẓ's *Children of Gebelawi (Awlād ḥāratinā,* 1959). In this allegorical novel, which deals with the religious history of humankind, Maḥfūẓ advances the thought that science has defeated God. Not surprisingly, the novel was banned in Egypt, where it met with intense opposition from the conservative religious authorities, and had to be printed in Beirut.

The domain of poetry offers further illustrations. In "The Interrogation" ("Al-Istijwāb") by the Syrian poet Nizār Qabbānī, a man who is being questioned by the police about the murder of an imam makes this confession:

> Masters!
> With this dagger of mine which you now see
> I stabbed him
> In breast and neck.
> I stabbed him
> In his brain, worm-eaten like a log.
> I stabbed him in my own name
> And in the name of the millions of sheep.
> Masters!
> I know that what I am accused of
> Is punishable by death.
> But
> In killing him, I killed
> All the cockroaches that recite in the dark,
> All the idlers on the pavements of dreams.
> In killing him, I killed
> All the parasites in the garden of Islam,
> All who seek a sustenance
> From the shop of Islam.
> In killing him, I killed—
> O worthy masters!—
> All those who for a thousand years
> Have been fornicating in words.[28]

Additional examples of religious criticism have been noted in this work in reference to the novels *The Broken Wings* by Gibran Khalil Gibran, *Egyptian Earth* by ʿAbd al-Raḥmān al-Sharqāwī, *The Seven Days of Man* by ʿAbd al-Ḥakīm Qāsim, and *War in the Land of Egypt* by Yūsuf al-Qaʿīd; the stories "The Village Tale" by Maḥmūd Ṭāhir Lāshīn and "The Beards" by Zakariyyā Tāmir; and the fiction of women writers such as Nawāl al-Saʿdāwī and Ghāda al-Sammān, to mention but a few.

The conclusion that can be drawn from this evidence is intriguing. On the basis of such literary works, it seems plausible to assume that Islam has been a source of contention rather than a fountain of inspiration in Arabic imaginative literature in recent decades.[29] This assumption, however, must be carefully qualified, for the fact remains that devotion to the faith of Islam is a distinctive feature of contemporary Arab society, and the belief in fate still persists among the masses. Modern Arab writers, as well as their readers, come from a small segment of the population of the Arab world. These writers have invariably been exposed to Western ideas and values. While they may have acquired a new view of life, which they aspire to impart to the whole of their society, it does not necessarily follow that that society is ready or willing to accept it. In fact, contemporary folk literature shows that the new values have barely filtered down to the common people, whose loyalty to Islam has never been supplanted by imported ideologies.[30] Thus, though creative writers denounce the pervasive influence of Islam, they acknowledge that it is deeply rooted in the consciousness of the people depicted in their works.

Fatalism, Fundamentalism, and Modernity

The rebellion of modern Arab writers against Islam and religious belief may portend increased secularization in Arab society. Conversely, the rise of Islamic fundamentalism in the Arab world and the apparent success of Iran and Shiism in challenging the power of the West could signal a return to orthodox Islam and the spread of religious extremism. At present, progressive Arab intellectuals appear to put themselves in jeopardy for merely expressing their views. Najīb Maḥfūẓ, the most celebrated Arab author and Nobel Prize laureate, was stabbed and seriously wounded outside his home in Cairo on October 15, 1994. The attack by Muslim militants on the then 82-year-old man was prompted by his allegorical novel *Children of Gebelawi*, in which he suggests that science has superseded God. For this reason, Maḥfūẓ was declared an infidel by Islamic radicals, who put him on their hit list. Another prominent Egyptian, the liberal intellectual and secular writer Faraj Fūda, was assassinated by fundamentalists in 1992. Other public figures, such as the veteran journalist Anīs Manṣūr and the leading feminist Nawāl al-Saʿdāwī, have had to contend with death threats or attempts on their lives throughout their careers. The most dramatic assassination by fundamentalists, which also demonstrates their power, was that of the Egyptian president Anwar Sadat in 1981.

The resurgence of Islamic fundamentalism throughout the Middle East and North Africa is an intriguing phenomenon which is of interest from a literary point of view as well. Historians and political analysts have generally sought an explanation for Islamic fundamentalism in political instability, poverty, social injustice, and cultural confusion. Eric Rouleau, for example, a scholar and journalist, notes: "All radical [Islamic] movements want to replace existing governments, which they consider corrupt and illegitimate. They also want to effect fundamental changes in their societies based on concepts of social justice according to their interpretations of the Qur'ān. Their members are anti-Western, anti-communist, and anti-Israel, and they reject the failed ideologies propagated by successive rulers during the past forty years." He further remarks that Islamic radicals thrive during periods of national crisis and in situations where a political vacuum exists.[31] However, the fact that they are successful in rich as well as in poor countries, among the educated elite as much as among the underprivileged, and among women no less than among men indicates that their movement has far deeper roots.

Modern Arabic literature shows that the belief in fate enhances the appeal of Islamic fundamentalism. Fundamentalists seek a return to the law of the Qur'ān and the traditions of the past. They believe that strict adherence to the early ways of their predecessors will restore their glorious past. In this respect, fundamentalism and preoccupation with the past go hand in hand. The direct corollary of this ideology is a total rejection of modernity. Fatalism, like fundamentalism, is conceptually contradictory to the spirit of liberty and therefore opposed to modernity. Whereas modernity requires freedom of thought and the assimilation of intellectual and scientific principles based on critical analysis and constant questioning, fatalism represents the opposite state of mind. It condemns questioning as blasphemous and heretical. Change is seen not as positive but rather as dangerous, if it originates with human beings and not with God. Moreover, fatalism reinforces the religious dogma of reward and punishment, which is central to fundamentalist thought. Fundamentalists claim that the Arabs' defeat and decline were caused by their failure to comply with God's will as revealed in His laws. Failing to follow the precepts of Islam is interpreted as subversive to God and deserving of punishment. Hence the tendency to fatalism in Arab society is more likely to embrace fundamentalism, with which it shares marked affinities, than modernity, with which it is incompatible. In this way, fatalism creates a mood which is receptive to Islamic fundamentalism.

Fundamentalists thrive on this mood, especially when they declare that they are the instrument of fate to bring the course of Arab history, which has drifted away from its intended path, back to God's divine plan—an argument that strikes a responsive chord in the hearts of the people. On the one hand, the fundamentalists have availed themselves of the technological achievements of modernity; on the other, they have rejected the state of mind that develops them and resorted to the notion of fate to explain the underdeveloped condition of their societies. While fatalism may well lead to passivity, the fundamentalists have seized on the feeling of dissatisfaction among the people to invoke a collective obligation: struggle in the way of God (*jihād*). This call, combined with the doctrine of divine predestination, has the desired effect of mobilizing the will of the people for the accomplishment of a heavenly ordained task. Thus it is at least in part the psychological substratum of the belief in fate that accounts for the remarkable success of the fundamentalist movement, currently the only movement in the Arab world with genuine popular support.

While literature cannot fully explain the appeal of Islamic fundamentalism in the Arab world, it can offer some insight into the dynamic interplay of social and psychological forces at work. A story that depicts the mental and emotional makeup of a member of the Muslim Brotherhood—Egypt's largest and most influential fundamentalist organization—is "Kill Her" ("Uqtulhā") by Yūsuf Idrīs.[32] The story is set in an Egyptian prison and revolves around an encounter between a Muslim Brother, Muṣṭafā, and a female member of the Communist movement, Suzanne. Against the bleak background of physical confinement, love shines out and unites these two political opposites with irresistible power. When Muṣṭafā is ordered by his leader to kill Suzanne in proof of his loyalty and on the grounds that she is an enemy, his faith is put to the test. The murder-by-strangulation scene illustrates the fanatical conviction of the Muslim Brother, who in the heat of religious passion can no longer distinguish between love and hate, life and death.

The concept of fate is the key to understanding this story and the political psychology of Muslim fundamentalists. When Muṣṭafā is instructed by his leader to carry out the assassination act, he is told: "Our will is His; our command is His; whoever disobeys us disobeys Him and becomes our strongest enemy."[33] Significantly, the Muslim Brotherhood is represented by a male and the Communist movement by a female. The ultimate victory and domination belong to the male and hence to the Muslim Brotherhood. In his blind obedience, Muṣṭafā puts aside every moral consideration and throws his arms around Suzanne in a compulsive embrace of both aggression and sexual attraction, which becomes the embrace of death. The ambiguous ending suggests that the protagonists' marriage contract was written in another book, perhaps in the afterlife.

Thus Idrīs skillfully portrays the frame of mind of the fundamentalist leaders and their followers. As condemned prisoners, they are both in jail and in bondage to their ideological convictions. The story demonstrates how difficult it is to argue with religious zealots who think they are acting on behalf of God and interpreting His will and His decrees for His creatures on earth. The challenge presented by the fundamentalist movement to most Arab regimes and to peaceful relations inside and outside the Arab world does not go unnoticed.

Arguably, the most effective mechanism for promoting modernity and reducing the influence of fatalism and fundamentalism lies in the education systems of the Arab states. Many Arab leaders, intellectuals, and common people yearn to join on an equal footing in civilization's march to progress. As noted by one of the greatest poets of Arabic literature, Adonis (b. 1929), in his essay "Poetics and Modernity": "The world today lives in the climate of a single universal civilization, but one which has its own specificities, obvious or hidden, that depend on the level of creative presence in the various peoples."[34] Modern education, which is firmly grounded in science, constitutes a vital tool in unlocking the creative wellspring of the people. Adonis sees science as the main feature of modernity and as the most important sign of power and superiority. The particular relevance of the scientific revolution to the Arabs lies in its ability to transform their consciousness, shifting their focus from the past to the future: "Science makes people open to the idea of a future radically different from anything they have known before, and therefore ready to accept the ending of the past."[35] In the scientific arena, the Arabs will find not only the methods for reforming their societies and building their countries but also the means with which to face future challenges.

The goal of modern education should be to demonstrate that fate is not predetermined to such an extent that personal responsibility and independent activity become superfluous. In this respect, the task of education in shaping a new consciousness is intimately connected with the realm of literature. Literature creates role models for its readers: when these role models are shown not to be bound by predestination but to exercise freedom of choice and individual accountability, they will have a long-lasting effect on the readers' minds. As literature is part of the curriculum of children and young adults, it is within its scope and function to provide ideals, heroes, and patterns of behavior that moderate fatalistic and fundamentalist influences.

A new consciousness, Adonis insists, is crucial in order to achieve growth and development: "I came to believe that the progress of a society is not represented merely by economic and social renewal, but more fundamentally by the liberation of man himself, and the liberation of the suppressed elements beneath and beyond the socioeconomic structure, in such a way that human beings at their freest and most responsive become both the pivot and the goal."[36] Thus social change and modernity require an internal as well as an external process of liberation to ensure enduring success.

Will Islamic fundamentalism reverse the trend set by modern writers, or will Arab intellectuals prove that the humanism, rationalism, and existentialism that they have been expressing for many decades have become essential components of their view of life? Self-conscious writers are constantly exploring, constantly questioning, and deeply wary of prescribed answers handed down to them. The contemporary scene may at times favor one truth or foster another, but the question of human destiny, as confronted by the skeptical minds of gifted individuals, will most likely continue to produce nonconformist views. In the eleventh century, the Syrian poet and philosopher Abū al-ʿAlāʾ al-Maʿarrī was bold enough to articulate heretical sentiments:

Ḥanīfs [Muslims] are stumbling, Christians all astray,
Jews wildered, Magians far on error's way.
We mortals are composed of two great schools—
Enlightened knaves or else religious fools.[37]

Similarly, the Persian Omar Khayyam was outspoken about his metaphysical doubts:

He began my creation with constraint,
By giving me life he added only confusion;
We depart reluctantly still not knowing
The aim of birth, existence, departure.

Heaven's wheel gained nothing from my coming,
Nor did my going augment its dignity;
Nor did my ears hear from anyone
Why I had to come and why I went.

Oh heart you will not arrive at the solving of the riddle,
You will not reach the goal the wise in their subtlety seek;
Make do here with wine and a cup of bliss,
For you may and you may not arrive at bliss hereafter.[38]

These poets confirm that the "flame of questioning" cannot be extinguished in people who are motivated by self-awareness.

The Role of the Writer and the Insights of Literature

The willingness of writers to pit themselves against conventional values and views raises some questions with regard to their position in society. What function do they serve, and what is their relationship with the people on the one hand, and with the authorities on the other? Figuratively speaking, writers can be likened to farmers. Farmers plant, cultivate, and reap crops that are likely to grow in their natural environment. Writers, by analogy, look closely at their society, internalizing its tensions, struggles, and conflicts (they plant); they then establish a continuous dialogue with their community (they cultivate); and finally they gather into literary works the conscious, unconscious, real, and imaginary in their environment (they reap).

Literature is not merely a faithful representation of objective reality—it is a critical exploration into the nature of human beings and society. As a highly creative and sophisticated medium of expression, it offers deep insights into the totality of human life, which it depicts in its most minute and intimate aspects. Works of literature are anchored in situations of human conflict, whose resolution provides both writers and readers with a sense of catharsis and psychological relief. In the main, they present a moral view of life, which affords readers a frame of reference with which to examine the complexity of their own lives and personal experiences.

There is a unique correspondence between writing an imaginative work and conducting a scientific investigation: both processes rely on the method of analysis and deduction to discover the elements and laws of nature, whether physical, social, or psychological. Nawāl al-Saʿdāwī's remark on her dual career as a physician and a writer is illuminating:

> I think that writing is like dissection. When you dissect the body, anatomically, it gives you a lot of insight into the secrets of the body. By studying psychiatry and psychology, I began to understand character. So I don't regret it, because it gave me, as a writer, a lot of insight into the nature of human beings. . . . I don't distinguish very much between art and science. Both of them are searching for the truth. Why do we write? Because we are searching for the truth. What's the end, the aim of science? To know, to know life, to understand the human being. In medicine we dissect the body to understand the nerves, or the liver, and the relationship of each part to the others. It is the same with the community. The human being is a microcosm of the whole society. So when you understand the body, you understand society. And vice versa.[39]

As intellectuals, writers stand on an island somewhere between the people and the authorities. While they provide the authorities with the means to gauge the levels of discontent and criticism among the people, they also attempt to awaken, as much as to shape, the consciousness of the people. The Egyptian author Yūsuf Idrīs once declared: "I am a living vessel [in the tissue] of society. If that society is not alive, I will implore it with my whispers, engage it in skirmishes, or even stab it with my pen in order to resuscitate it."[40] Idrīs, whose literary influence reached throughout the Arab world, perceived his role as a writer primarily as one of service to his country. As a visionary critic, he was wholly committed to unmasking wrongs, pinpointing the ailments of his society, and driving home the message of a vital need for change and reform. He used the medium of the short story as a revolutionary weapon: his realistic, symbolic, and surrealistic stories were largely meant to expose and shock, to inform and provoke, to incite to revolt.[41] Hence, besides being artists, writers are frequently agents of social change, moral awakeners, symbols of the conscience of their society, and representatives of the collective consciousness of their community. Shelley stated: "Poets are the unacknowledged legislators of the world."[42] Amos Oz, a leading Israeli novelist, compared the social function of the writer to that of the prophet: "[In Israel] writers are regarded more or less as representatives of the Prophets and are expected to show the way, to tell a nation where it has gone wrong."[43]

Modern Arabic literature has emphasized the role of the poet as a prophet. This essentially romantic conception is best expressed by the school of Arab-American writers (the Emigrants).[44] In *The Sieve (Al-Ghirbāl,* 1923), Mikhail Naimy defines the poet: "The poet is a prophet, a philosopher, a painter, a musician, and a priest all in one. A prophet, because he can see with his spiritual eye what an ordinary person cannot. A painter, because he is capable of molding what he sees and hears into splendid forms of verbal imagery. A musician, because he can hear harmonious sounds where we hear only discordant noise. Lastly, the poet is a priest because he serves the goddess of Truth and Beauty."[45] Gibran Khalil Gibran elaborates on the social significance of the poet's prophetic gift and mission: "The poet is a messenger who informs the individual what the universal spirit has revealed to him. If there is no message, there is no poet."[46]

An insight into the impulse to produce a work of art is provided by Jabrā Ibrāhīm Jabrā, a versatile writer and artist. Jabrā describes the two oppressive yet essential psychical forces—dream and nightmare—that are at the core of the creative process:

> The artist, as is only natural, dreams. He is a person with an incredible ability to dream, and add dream to dream. How to combine the dream with his reality is the problem that he faces, and the path of his creativity is in fact determined by his skill to do so. . . . As for the nightmare, every person finds himself under terrible pressures which he is unable to resist, however hard he tries, either because they are stronger than he is or because they want to crush him. The intellectual, or writer, succeeds in the end in overcoming the nightmare through the written word, through creative expression. And thus even the nightmare becomes fodder for artistic creativity.[47]

Given that works of literature express people's earnest needs and concerns, their struggles for self-realization, their sorrows and frustrations, as well as their longings and aspirations, it is pertinent to assess the predictive potential of literature. Does literature afford us a window onto the future? Most frequently, the protagonist is an ordinary individual, yet as a microcosm of society, the ordinary man, woman, or child reveals in numerous activities, experiences, and dreams the nature of the entire community. This is analogous to the theory underlying the science of chemistry: one atom or molecule reveals all the characteristics of the element or substance as a whole. The predictive value of literature lies in its ability to get to the heart of the matter by looking at the core issues of existence for the individual in society. The gifted writer keeps a finger on the pulse of society. In portraying the components of reality and the interrelationships between them, the writer penetrates the veil of political and religious ideologies that envelops society and conceals it behind myths and stereotypes. In modern Arabic literature, the writer unravels the mysteries of a closed society and allows readers "the rare privilege of entering a national psychology, in a way that a thousand journalistic articles or television documentaries could not achieve."[48] Literature, therefore, is an invaluable aid in exploring the inner workings and future directions of Arab society.

There is ample evidence to support this conclusion, as illustrated by the recent history of the Middle East. Some of the most important events that have occurred in the Middle East, such as the popular uprising in the territories occupied by Israel after 1967, and the resurgence of Islamic fundamentalism, are seen as the realization of goals and aspirations expressed in Arabic literature years before. With respect to the Palestinian uprising, most of the fictional works of Ghassān Kanafānī call for Palestinians to take upon themselves the struggle to regain their land. Similarly, the poetry of Maḥmūd Darwīsh, Samīḥ al-Qāsim, and Fadwā Ṭūqān abounds with themes of resistance. In a particularly provocative poem entitled "A Wounding Wish" ("Umniyya Jāriḥa"), published by Fadwā Ṭūqān in 1973,[49] Palestinian men are harshly condemned for not standing up to the Israelis as the Vietnamese heroes stood up to American soldiers. About a decade and a half later, in answer to this call, the *intifāḍa* began by Palestinian youths throwing stones. As for the resurgence of Islamic fundamentalism, themes of disillusion with modernity and the values of the West could be detected in the works of poets and prose writers long before these issues were taken up by religious activists and became the driving force of Muslim fundamentalists. The desire to return to Islamic ideology and mysticism, both as a radical reaction to modernization and as an alternative to views derived from the West, was already being articulated in Arabic writing of the turn of the twentieth century. However, such ideas tend to be expressed in the traditional genres rather than in the modern genres—the novel and the short story—which, being of Western origin, are largely boycotted by the fundamentalist leaders and their followers.[50]

While the clouds of war were envisioned in Arabic fiction and poetry, peaceful solutions were also foreseen, though, for obvious reasons, less openly and in much more cautious terms. For example, the peace initiative and historic visit of the late Egyptian president Anwar Sadat to Israel (1977) were predicted in amazing detail in a short story by Yūsuf Idrīs. Written in 1972, "Innocence" ("Al-Barā'a") foreshadows Sadat's assassination, which took place in 1981, in the wake of his signing the peace treaty of 1979 with Israel.[51]

The new, albeit volatile, chapter in the relations between Israelis and Arabs—including the Oslo accords of 1993 between Israel and the Palestinians and the peace treaty of 1994 between Israel and Jordan—was anticipated in works of literature by both Jews and Arabs in Israel in recent decades. As early as 1941, Shmuel Yosef Agnon, the first Hebrew novelist to be awarded the Nobel Prize for literature (1966), in an allegorical story entitled "From Foe to Friend," portrayed the resolution of the conflict between Arabs and Jews and the inevitable evolution of friendly relations.[52] Other Israeli authors such as Aharon Megged, A. B. Yehoshua, Amos Oz, David Grossman, and Yehuda Amichai have expressed in their writings a genuine desire for peaceful coexistence.

On the Palestinian side, many authors who live in the Jewish state—such as Maḥmūd ʿAbbāsī, Muṣṭafā Marār, Tawfīq Muʿammar, Muḥammad Abū Rayyā, ʿAbdallāh ʿAyshān, Muḥammad ʿAlī Ṭāhā, and Zakī Darwīsh—have presented, in contrast to their Arab colleagues elsewhere, a more humane and sympathetic portrayal of the Israeli in their imaginative works.[53] For example, in the story "Tears and Ashes" ("Damʿ waramād") by Muṣṭafā Marār,[54] as well as in "The Angels' Tears" ("Dumūʿ al-malāʾika") by Muḥammad Abū Rayyā,[55] a bereaved Jewish family and a bereaved Arab family are united in their pain and grief over the loss of their loved ones. In the symbolic story "The Bridge" ("Al-Jisr") by Zakī Darwīsh,[56] the brother of the famous poet Maḥmūd Darwīsh, a river separates two warring villages, whose hatred of each other is a legacy bequeathed to them by their forefathers. Eventually, a bridge is constructed over the river, young children cross over to play with each other, and little by little the hostility and hatred are replaced by friendly and loving relations. In the main, both Arab and Jewish authors in Israel deal with similar themes: the existential nightmare (war and siege), the enemy as an individual and as a people, the meeting points (e.g., the neighborhood, the workplace), and the yearning for peace.

Another development that highlights the merit and predictive value of literature is the emergence of Arab writers of Hebrew, whose activity parallels that of Jewish writers of Arabic.[57] This phenomenon is of great significance because there is a process of humanization as well as integration in recognizing each other's languages. There are several prominent figures in this small yet outstanding group, whose members express themselves in Hebrew and in Arabic. The poet and novelist Anṭūn Shammās wrote his widely acclaimed novel *Arabesques* (1986) in Hebrew. Naʿīm ʿArāyidī is a poet and fiction writer who has penned volumes of poetry, a novel, and short stories in Hebrew. The playwright and prose writer Maḥmūd ʿAbbāsī has published literary articles in Hebrew. He is also a cofounder of *Mifgash-Liqāʿ*, a Hebrew-Arabic literary periodical launched in 1964.[58] ʿAṭāllāh Manṣūr, Salmān Nāṭūr, and Muḥammad Ḥamza Ghanāyim are journalists and creative writers of Arabic and Hebrew. Most of these pioneering authors are also engaged in translating masterpieces of Hebrew literature into Arabic. Then again, Samir Naqqash and Yitzhak Bar Moshe are Jewish writers of Iraqi origin who write exclusively in Arabic. Both have several collections of short stories to their names.[59] Other established Jewish writers, such as Sammy Michael, Shimon Ballas, and Nir Shohet, who were born and raised in Arabic-speaking countries, make valuable contributions to the translation of Arabic literature into Hebrew. Even when Arabs and Jews in Israel do not use each other's languages as the medium of expression, the image of the Arab is frequently present in Hebrew fiction, and, conversely, the image of the Israeli is frequently present in Palestinian fiction. Admittedly, the messages conveyed are not always conciliatory, but the fact remains: the identity of the other group has indelibly crept into the consciousness of writers in Israel—be they Arab or Jewish—and has become an integral part of their perception of reality.

In conclusion, modern Arabic literature provides a window through which prevailing trends and attitudes in Arab society can be observed. In accord with the aspirations of people worldwide, Arabs yearn for a just and free society in which they can shape their history and cultivate their identity in the spirit of their own culture and national heritage. Arab intellectuals aspire to a modern society based on rational thought, humanistic values, and democratic ideals. The ordinary people who figure as protagonists in the works of modern Arab writers want to live in a society that protects their human rights and provides them with a dignified way of life, free from the tyranny of poverty, disease, and illiteracy. Arab writers are aware that events and developments in the international community will inevitably affect the future of their countries. They therefore try to stimulate their people to take an active role in the affairs of the world and to keep pace with its advances. Moreover, they insist on their right and duty to make contributions to humanity in every domain, whether spiritual, industrial, scientific, or cultural.

Despite its relatively small readership in the Arab world, the impact of literature is nevertheless significant in that it creates centers of protest which serve as role models for many people, including the uneducated. For the masses, works of literature are often made accessible through adaptations for the stage, cinema, television, and radio. The Arabs' illustrious past serves as a reminder that their contribution to the world hangs primarily on their ability to liberate themselves—namely, "the suppressed elements beneath and beyond the socioeconomic structure"[60]—in order to unlock the vast energies which they possess. Fatalism will inevitably give way to a new value orientation. Modern Arabic literature displays the myriad ways in which the Arabs can take their fate into their own hands.

NOTES

Abbreviations

ER	*Encyclopedia of Religion*, 16 vols. (New York: Macmillan, 1987).
ERE	*Encyclopaedia of Religion and Ethics*, 13 vols. (Edinburgh: T. & T. Clark, 1908–26).
EI1	*First Encyclopaedia of Islam*, 9 vols. (1913–1938; reprint, Leiden: E. J. Brill, 1987).
EI2	*Encyclopaedia of Islam*, new ed., 10 vols. to date (Leiden: E. J. Brill, 1960–).
JAL	*Journal of Arabic Literature.*
JAOS	*Journal of the American Oriental Society.*
MEJ	*Middle East Journal.*

Introduction

1. For the differences between the Islamic and Calvinistic beliefs in predestination, see, for example, Samuel M. Zwemer, *The Moslem Doctrine of God* (London: Darf, 1987), pp. 93–105.

2. Halim Barakat, "Socioeconomic, Cultural, and Personality Forces Determining Development in Arab Society," *Social Praxis* 2, no. 3–4 (1974): 193–95.

3. These definitions are based on John A. Haywood, *Modern Arabic Literature: 1800–1970* (London: Lund Humphries, 1971), pp. 1–2.

4. For a discussion of this overlap, see chapter 2 below, pp. 51–53.

5. These definitions are based on *ER*, s.v. "Fate," "Free Will and Determinism," and "Free Will and Predestination"; and the Oxford English Dictionary.

6. Halim Barakat, *The Arab World: Society, Culture, and State* (Berkeley: University of California Press, 1993), p. 210.

7. Ibid., p. 210; and see also pp. 207–8, 237.

8. Ibid., p. 210.

9. Edward W. Said, *Orientalism* (New York: Vintage, 1979), p. 291.

10. Fred Halliday, " 'Orientalism' and Its Critics," *British Journal of Middle Eastern Studies* 20, no. 2 (1993): 145–63.

11. W. J. Bate, ed., *Criticism: The Major Texts* (New York: Harcourt Brace Jovanovich, 1970), pp. xii–xiii.

12. Ibid., p. xiv.

13. Ibid.

Chapter 1

Unless otherwise stated, all quotations from the Qur'ān are from either N. J. Dawood, trans., *The Koran* (London: Penguin Classics, 1993), or Abdullah Yusuf Ali, *The Holy Qur'ān: Text, Translation, and Commentary* (Washington, D.C.: Khalil al-Rawaf, 1946). Occasionally, there are quotations from Mohammed Marmaduke Pickthall, *The Meaning of the Glorious Koran: An Explanatory Translation* (New York: New American Library, 1953). These different sources have been used for the sake of clarity and economy.

1. Edward FitzGerald, *Rubaiyat of Omar Khayyam*, ed. Nathan Haskell Dole, multi-vorarium edition (Boston: L. C. Page, 1898), 1: 134.

2. *EI2*, s.v. "Lawḥ."

3. Thomas Patrick Hughes, *Notes on Muhammadanism* (Wilmington, Del.: Scholarly Resources, 1976), p. 98. For the Qur'ānic verse, see J. M. Rodwell, trans., *The Koran* (London: Everyman Library, 1994), p. 293. Rodwell notes that *imām mubīn* literally means "the clear prototype"; see ibid., p. 477, n.3.

4. W. Montgomery Watt, *Free Will and Predestination in Early Islam* (London: Luzac, 1948), p. 17. For the pen, see *EI2*, s.v. "Ḳalam."

5. Muslim, *Qadar*, tradition 16. Cited in A. J. Wensinck, *The Muslim Creed* (Cambridge: Cambridge University Press, 1932), p. 54; and in Watt, *Free Will and Predestination*, p. 17.

6. Abū Dāwūd, *Sunna*, b. 16. Cited in Wensinck, *Muslim Creed*, pp. 108–9; cf. similar traditions, pp. 129, 162; and cf. Watt, *Free Will and Predestination*, p. 17.

7. Wensinck, *Muslim Creed*, p. 54.

8. Abū Dāwūd, *Sunna*, b. 16. Cited in ibid., p. 108; and in Watt, *Free Will and Predestination*, p. 19.

9. Muslim, *Qadar*, tradition 3. Cited in Watt, *Free Will and Predestination*, p. 18.

10. Muslim, *Qadar*, tradition 1. Cited in Edward E. Salisbury, "Materials for the History of the Muhammadan Doctrine of Predestination and Free Will: Compiled from Original Sources," *JAOS* 8 (1866): 123.

11. Wensinck, *Muslim Creed*, p. 56.

12. Ibid., p. 51.

13. *EI2*, s.v. "Ḳaḍā'."

14. *EI2*, s.v. "Al-Ḳaḍā' wa'l-Ḳadar."

15. *EI1*, s.v. "Ḳadar."

16. *EI2*, s.v. "Al-Ḳaḍā' wa'l-Ḳadar."

17. Watt, *Free Will and Predestination*, pp. 12–13.

18. Wensinck, *Muslim Creed*, p. 51.

19. W. Montgomery Watt, *Islamic Philosophy and Theology: An Extended Survey* (Edinburgh: Edinburgh University Press, 1985), pp. 25–31.

20. Muḥammad Badr al-Dīn ʿAlawī, *Fatalism, Free Will, and Acquisition as Viewed by Muslim Sects* (Lahore: Orientalia, 1956), pp. 3, 7–9. For the arguments used by each sect, see ibid., pp. 10–24.

21. Ibid., pp. 79–88. See also H. A. R. Gibb, *Mohammedanism* (London: Oxford University Press, 1975), p. 79. The Qur'ānic verse quoted here is from Rodwell's translation.

22. Thomas Patrick Hughes, *Dictionary of Islam* (Chicago: Kazi, 1994), s.v. "Predestination," p. 473. Hughes remarks that the orthodox or Sunni belief is in theory Ashʿarite, but in practice the Sunnis are confirmed Jabrites.

23. Ignaz Goldziher, *Introduction to Islamic Theology and Law*, trans. Andras and Ruth Hamori (Princeton, N.J.: Princeton University Press, 1981), p. 82.

24. W. Montgomery Watt, "Free Will and Predestination (Islamic Concept)," in *ER*, 5: 429.

25. Carra de Vaux, "Fate (Muslim)," in *ERE*, 5: 796.

26. Salisbury, "Materials," p. 182.

27. Goldziher, *Islamic Theology and Law*, pp. 83–84.

28. Ian R. Netton, *Muslim Neoplatonists* (Edinburgh: Edinburgh University Press, 1991), p. 9.

29. Karen Armstrong, *A History of God* (New York: Ballantine, 1993), pp. 36–39, 171.

30. C. A. Qadir, *Philosophy and Science in the Islamic World* (London: Routledge, 1990), p. 81.

31. M. Saeed Sheikh, *Islamic Philosophy* (London: Octagon, 1982), pp. 61, 82, 133.

32. See Reynold A. Nicholson, *The Mystics of Islam* (London: Routledge & Kegan Paul, 1975), pp. 68–101. See also Titus Burckhardt, *Introduction to Sufism*, trans. D. M. Matheson (London: Thorsons, 1995), pp. 21–34, 58–61.

33. Gustave E. von Grunebaum, *Medieval Islam: A Study in Cultural Orientation* (Chicago: University of Chicago Press, 1953), p. 129.

34. *EI1*, s.v. "Al-Ghazālī." See also D. B. Macdonald, *Development of Muslim Theology, Jurisprudence, and Constitutional Theory* (New York: Charles Scribner's Sons, 1903), pp. 238–40.

35. A. J. Arberry, *The Doctrine of the Ṣūfīs*, translated from the Arabic of Abū Bakr al-Kalābādhī (Cambridge: Cambridge University Press, 1977), pp. 28–30.

36. A. J. Arberry, *Avicenna on Theology* (London: John Murray, 1951), p. 38.

37. Ibid.

38. Ibid., p. 39.

39. Shmuel Moreh, "The Shadow Play (*khayāl al-ẓill*) in the Light of Arabic Literature," *JAL* 18 (1987): 48–49.

40. Reynold A. Nicholson, *Studies in Islamic Mysticism* (Richmond, Surrey: Curzon, 1994), p. 260.

41. *EI1*, s.v. "Shaʿbān"; and Gustave E. von Grunebaum, *Muhammadan Festivals* (London: Curzon, 1988), pp. 52–55.

42. Edward William Lane, *Manners and Customs of the Modern Egyptians* (London: East–West, 1989), pp. 465–66.

43. Ibid., p. 466. The prayer is quoted here in part.

44. Shmuel Moreh, ed. and trans., *Al-Jabartī's Chronicle of the First Seven Months of the French Occupation of Egypt* (Leiden: E. J. Brill, 1975), pp. 17–18 of the Arabic text, n. 69. Translation mine.

45. Ibid. On the merit of supplication, see Abū Ḥāmid Muḥammad al-Ghazzālī, *Invocations and Supplications*, trans. K. Nakamura (Cambridge, U.K.: Islamic Texts

Society, 1990), pp. 31–56; on the relation of supplication to the divine decree, see ibid., pp. 90–91.

46. Ṭāhā Ḥusayn, *Shajarat al-bu's* (Cairo: Dār al-maʿarif, 1944), p. 42. Ṭāhā Ḥusayn, *The Tree of Misery*, trans. Mona El-Zayyat (Cairo: Palm, 1997), p. 27.

47. Ibid.

48. Al-Ghazzālī, *Invocations and Supplications*, pp. 90–91.

49. Arberry, *Doctrine of the Ṣūfīs*, pp. 39–42. See also *EI1*, s.v. "Shafāʿa."

50. Lane, *Manners and Customs*, pp. 472–73. For more details, see *EI1*, s.v. "Ramaḍān"; and Grunebaum, *Muhammadan Festivals*, pp. 51–65.

51. Ibid., p. 285.

52. Ibid., p. 278.

53. Ibid., p. 285.

54. Moshe Piamenta, *Islam in Everyday Arabic Speech* (Leiden: E. J. Brill, 1979), pp. 1–3.

55. Ibid., pp. 6, 32–38, 193–95, 203–5. It should be noted that the Qur'ān includes a verse enjoining believers to use the conditional clause *inshāllah*. It reads: "Do not say of anything: 'I will do it tomorrow,' without adding: 'If God wills' " (18:25).

56. Ibid., p. 2.

57. See, for example, Reuben Levy, *The Social Structure of Islam* (Cambridge: Cambridge University Press, 1957), pp. 205–9; von Grunebaum, *Medieval Islam*, pp. 240, 346–47; ʿAbdallāh ʿAlī al-Qaṣīmī, *Hādhī hiya al-aghlāl* (Cairo: Dār Miṣr lil-ṭibāʿa, 1946), p. 241; Isḥāq Mūsā al-Ḥusaynī, *Azmat al-fikr al-ʿarabī* (Beirut: Dār Bayrūt, 1954), pp. 97–98; and Hisham Sharabi, *Muqaddimāt li-dirāsat al-mujtamaʿ al-ʿarabī* (Acre: Dār al-aswār, 1987), pp. 69–81.

58. Raphael Patai, *The Arab Mind* (New York: Charles Scribner's Sons, 1983), p. 153.

59. Ibid.

60. Hilma Granqvist, *Birth and Childhood among the Arabs: Studies in a Muhammadan Village in Palestine* (Helsingfors: Soderstrom, 1947), p. 177.

61. A. Dorner, "Fate (Introductory)," in *ERE*, 5: 774.

62. Charles C. Adams, *Islam and Modernism in Egypt* (London: Oxford University Press, 1933), pp. 4–17, 152–55, 181.

63. Albert Hourani, *Arabic Thought in the Liberal Age: 1798–1939* (Cambridge: Cambridge University Press, 1983), p. 128.

64. Al-Ḥusaynī, *Azmat al-fikr al-ʿarabī*, pp. 97–98. See extracts in Kemal H. Karpat, ed., *Political and Social Thought in the Contemporary Middle East* (New York: Praeger, 1982), pp. 208–14.

65. Halim Barakat, "Socioeconomic, Cultural, and Personality Forces," pp. 194–95.

66. Sania Hamady, *Temperament and Character of the Arabs* (New York: Twayne, 1960), pp. 185, 188–90.

67. Granqvist, *Birth and Childhood*, p. 177.

68. Hamed Ammar, *Growing Up in an Egyptian Village: Silwa, Province of Aswan* (London: Routledge & Kegan Paul, 1954), p. 231.

69. Ibid., p. 36.

70. Barakat, *Arab World*, p. 193.

71. Ibid., p. 194.

72. See Asʿad Abu Khalil, "Al-Jabriyyah in the Political Discourse of Jamāl ʿAbd al-Nāṣir and Ṣaddām Ḥusayn: The Rationalization of Defeat," *The Muslim World* 84, no. 3–4 (1994): 240–57.

73. Ṣādiq Jalāl al-ʿAẓm, *Al-Naqd al-dhātī baʿda al-hazīma* (Beirut: Dār al-ṭalīʿa, 1968), p. 19. Translation mine.

74. Ibid., p. 18. Translation mine.

75. Ibid., p. 20. Translation mine. It should be noted that the term *al-nakba* ("the disaster") designates the 1948 war, and the term *al-naksa* ("the setback") the 1967 war.

76. Aḥmad Amīn, *Ḥayātī* (1950; Beirut: Dār al-kitāb al-ʿarabī, 1971), p. 110; Aḥmad Amīn, *My Life*, trans. Issa J. Boullata (Leiden: E. J. Brill, 1978), p. 59.

77. Ibid.

78. Najīb Maḥfūẓ, *Al-Ḥubb taḥta al-maṭar* (1973; Cairo: Maktabat Miṣr, 1975), pp. 33, 34. Translation mine.

79. Mia I. Gerhardt, *The Art of Story-Telling: A Literary Study of the Thousand and One Nights* (Leiden: E. J. Brill, 1963), pp. 355–58.

80. Helmer Ringgren, *Studies in Arabian Fatalism* (Uppsala: Lundequistska Bokhandeln, 1955), p. 201.

81. Helmer Ringgren, "Islamic Fatalism," in *Fatalistic Beliefs in Religion, Folklore, and Literature* (Stockholm, Almqvist & Wiksell, 1967), pp. 60–61; quoting from *The Thousand and One Nights*, trans. Edward Willis Lane (London: East–West, 1981), 3: 390; 1:160; 1:167.

82. M. M. Badawi, "The Concept of Fate in Modern Egyptian Literature," in *Modern Arabic Literature and the West* (London: Ithaca, 1985), p. 68.

83. Ibid., p. 82.

84. Curt Prüfer, "Drama (Arabic)," in *ERE*, 4: 872. See also von Grunebaum, *Medieval Islam*, p. 287.

85. Georg Jacob, *Geschichte des Schattentheaters* (Berlin: Mayer & Mueller, 1907), p. 93. Cited in Prüfer, "Drama," p. 873.

86. Prüffer, "Drama," p. 873. See also Roger Allen, *The Arabic Literary Heritage: The Development of Its Genres and Criticism* (Cambridge: Cambridge University Press, 1998), pp. 320–21.

87. *EI2*, s.v. "Khayāl al-Ẓill."

88. Farouk Abdel Wahab, ed., *Modern Egyptian Drama: An Anthology* (Minneapolis: Bibliotheca Islamica, 1974), p. 15.

89. M. M. Badawi, "Medieval Arabic Drama: Ibn Dāniyāl," *JAL* 8 (1982): 84.

90. Jacob M. Landau, *Studies in the Arab Theater and Cinema* (Philadelphia: University of Pennsylvania Press, 1958), p. 9.

91. *EI2*, s.v. "Ḳaragöz"; Lane, *Manners and Customs*, p. 385; M. M. Badawi, *Early Arabic Drama* (Cambridge: Cambridge University Press, 1988), pp. 10, 12.

92. Moreh, "Shadow Play," p. 47, citing Ibn Ḥazm, *Kitāb al-akhlāq wa-al-siyar*, ed. and trans. Nada Tomiche (Beirut, 1961), p. 28.

93. Ibid.

94. Ibid., citing al-Ghazzālī, *Iḥyāʾ ʿulūm al-dīn* (Būlāq, 1862), 4: 122.

95. Ibid., p. 51, citing Ibrāhīm Ḥamāda, *Khayāl al-ẓill wa-tamthīliyyāt Ibn Dāniyāl* (Cairo: Al-Muʾassasa al-miṣriyya al-ʿāmma lil-taʾlīf, 1963), p. 45.

96. Ibid.

97. FitzGerald, *Rubaiyat of Omar Khayyam*, 1: 132, 135. The first quatrain is another version of the epigraph included at the beginning of this chapter.

98. See M. M. Badawi, *Early Arabic Drama*, pp. 4–6; Matti Moosa, *The Origins of Modern Arabic Fiction*, 2d ed. (Boulder, Colo.: Lynne Rienner, 1997), pp. 21–22; David Semah, *Four Egyptian Literary Critics* (Leiden: E. J. Brill, 1974), pp. 173–75.

99. Shmuel Moreh, *Live Theater and Dramatic Literature in the Medieval Arab World* (New York: New York University Press, 1992), p. 163.

100. Ṭāhā Ḥusayn, *Duʿāʾ al-karawān* (Cairo: Dār al-maʿārif, 1934), pp. 159–60; Ṭāhā Ḥusayn, *The Call of the Curlew*, trans. A. B. As-Safi (Leiden: E. J. Brill, 1980), pp. 128–30.

101. Yūsuf al-Qaʿīd, *Akhbār ʿizbāt al-Manīsī* (Cairo, 1971). Quoted from al-Qaʿīd, *Al-Aʿmāl al-kāmila*, vol. 4 (Cairo: Al-Hayʾa al-miṣriyya al-ʿāmma lil-kitāb, 1994), pp. 276, 277, 282, 283, 290, 312. Yūsuf al-Qaʿīd, *News from the Meneisi Farm*, trans. Marie-Therese F. Abdel-Messih (Cairo: General Egyptian Book Organization, 1987), pp. 176, 177, 183, 184, 192, 213, respectively.

102. On the motif of the Arab defeat in this novel, see Paul Starkey, "From the City of the Dead to Liberation Square: The Novels of Yūsuf al-Qaʿīd," *JAL* 24, pt. 1 (1993): 65.

103. Fatḥī Ghānim, *Al-Rajul alladhī faqad ẓillahu* (Cairo: Dār al-jumhūriyya lil-ṣiḥāfa, 1962), pt. 1, p. 42; Fatḥī Ghānim, *The Man Who Lost His Shadow*, trans. Desmond Stewart (London: Heinemann, 1980), p. 28. The Arabic text has the expression *wa-amrī li-llāh*, which literally means, "I resign myself to the will of God," or "I confide my cause to God." The translator used the phrase "It's God's will," which conveys a similar idea. For this idiomatic usage, see Piamenta, *Islam in Everyday Arabic Speech*, p. 197.

104. Ghānim, *Al-Rajul alladhī faqad ẓillahu*, pt. 4, pp. 112, 58–59; trans., pp. 288, 264.

105. Yūsuf al-Qaʿīd, *Yaḥduth fī Miṣr al-ān* (Cairo, 1977). Quoted from al-Qaʿīd, *Al-Aʿmāl al-kāmila*, vol. 5 (Cairo: Al-Hayʾa al-miṣriyya al-ʿāmma lil-kitāb, 1995), p. 62. Translation mine.

106. Ibid., pp. 141–42. Translation mine.

107. Ibid., p. 127. Translation mine.

108. Al-Qaʿīd refused to change the title of the novel to "It Happened in Egypt in 1974" when the 4th edition was published in 1985. See al-Qaʿīd's comments on this issue in the introduction to vol. 5 of *Al-Aʿmāl al-kāmila*, pp. 5–8.

109. Muḥammad al-Bisāṭī, *Buyūt warāʾ al-ashjār* (Cairo: Dār al-hilāl, 1993), p. 105. Muḥammad al-Bisāṭī, *Houses behind the Trees*, trans. Denys Jonson-Davies (Cairo: American University in Cairo Press, 1997), p. 81.

110. Ibid., p. 48; trans., p. 36.

111. The title story of Najīb Maḥfūẓ, *Dunyā Allāh* (Cairo: Maktabat Miṣr, 1963), pp. 5–25. Trans. in Najīb Maḥfūẓ, *God's World: An Anthology of Short Stories*, trans. Akef Abadir and Roger Allen (Minneapolis: Bibliotheca Islamica, 1973), pp. 3–18.

112. Ibid., p. 25; trans., p. 17.

113. In Idwār al-Kharrāṭ, *Sāʿāt al-kibriyāʾ* (Beirut: Dār al-ādāb, 1972), pp. 45–55. Trans. Catherine Cobham, *JAL* 15 (1984): 121–31.

114. Ibid., p. 52; trans., p. 128.

115. In ʿAbdallāh ʿAbd, *Māt al-banafsaj* (Damascus: Manshūrāt wizārat al-thaqāfa wa-al-irshād al-qawmī, 1969), pp. 69–83.

116. Ibid., pp. 77, 83. Translation mine.

117. In Khayriyya al-Saqqāf, *An tubḥir naḥwa al-abʿad* (Riyadh: Dār al-ʿulūm lil-ṭibāʿa wa-al-nashr, 1982), pp. 33–44. Trans. in *Assassination of Light: Modern Saudi*

Short Stories, trans. Abu Bakr Bagader and Ava Molnar Heinrichsdorff (Washington D.C.: Three Continents, 1990), pp. 47–51.

118. Ibid., p. 43; trans., p. 51.

119. Cf. Barakat, *Arab World,* pp. 193–94.

120. In al-Ṣāḥib Abī al-Qāsim Ismāʿīl Ibn ʿAbbād, *Al-Amthāl al-sāʾira min shiʿr al-Mutanabbī* (Baghdad: Maktabat al-nahḍa, 1965), p. 63. Translation mine.

121. Author unknown. These lines are cited in the closing statement of *Alf layla wa-layla.* See *The Thousand and One Nights,* trans. Lane, 3: 666.

122. In Aḥmad Shalabī Ibn ʿAbd al-Ghanī, ed., *Awḍāḥ al-ishārāt fī-man tawallā Miṣr al-Qāhira min al-wuzarāʾ wa-al-bāshāt* (Cairo, 1978), p. 387. The poet's name is not mentioned. Translation mine.

123. In Ibrāhīm Nājī, *Layālī al-Qāhira* (Beirut: Dār al-ʿawda, 1979), p. 64. Translation mine.

124. Gibran Khalil Gibran, "The Processions" (Arabic text and English translation), in George Kheirallah, ed. and trans., *The Life of Gibran Khalil Gibran and His Procession* (New York: Arab–American, 1947), p. 45.

125. In Nizār Qabbānī, *Qaṣāʾid* (Beirut: Manshūrāt Nizār Qabbānī, 1967), p. 164. Trans. in Issa J. Boullata, ed. and trans., *Modern Arab Poets: 1950–1975* (Washington, D.C.: Three Continents, 1976), p. 55.

126. In Abū al-Qāsim al-Shābbī, *Aghānī al-ḥayāh* (Cairo: Dār al-kutub al-sharqiyya, 1955), pp. 167–70. Trans. in part, Sargon Boulus and Christopher Middleton, in Salma Khadra Jayyusi, ed., *Modern Arabic Poetry: An Anthology* (New York: Columbia University Press, 1987), p. 97.

127. See Mounah Khouri, "Al-Shābbī as a Romantic,"*Mundus Arabicus* 2 (1982): 3–17.

128. This legal official (*maʾdhūn*), authorized to perform Muslim marriages, is usually a religious leader with some education.

129. The ignorant peasant thinks that the status of a pasha, a high-ranking civil or military official, is below that of a mayor.

130. Cobbling is considered a lowly trade among the peasants, who are deeply attached to the soil.

131. Qurʾān 3:54.

132. Qurʾān 17:37.

133. Sabry Hafez, *The Genesis of Arabic Narrative Discourse: A Study in the Sociology of Modern Arabic Literature* (London: Saqi, 1993), pp. 234, 258. For further reading on Maḥmūd Ṭāhir Lāshīn, see ibid., pp. 215–61.

134. See Mubārak Rabīʿ's psychological study on children's fears and their relation to the social milieu, *Makhāwif al-aṭfāl wa-ʿalāqatuhā bi-al-wasaṭ al-ijtimāʿī* (Rabat: Jāmiʿat Muḥammad al-Khāmis, 1991). For further reading on Mubārak Rabīʿ, see al-ʿArabī Binjallūn, *Al-Naṣṣ al-maftūḥ: dirāsāt fī al-khiṭāb al-qaṣaṣī wa-al-riwāʾī al-maghribī* (Rabat: Maktabat al-maʿārif, 1986), pp. 7–16; and Sayyid Ḥāmid al-Nassāj, *Al-Adab al-ʿarabī al-muʿāṣir fī al-Maghrib al-aqṣā* (Cairo: Al-Hayʾa al-miṣriyya al-ʿāmma lil-kitāb, 1985), pp. 320–65.

Chapter 2

1. A. J. Arberry, *Poems of al-Mutanabbī* (Cambridge: Cambridge University Press, 1967), p. 42, verse 4.

2. W. Montgomery Watt, "Dahr," in *EI2*, 2: 94; and W. Montgomery Watt, *The Formative Period of Islamic Thought* (Oxford: Oneworld, 1998), pp. 88–91.

3. Theodor Nöldeke, "Arabs (Ancient)," in *ERE*, 1: 661. See also Watt, *Free Will and Predestination*, p. 21.

4. Watt, *Free Will and Predestination*, pp. 21–22.

5. Ignaz Goldziher, *Muhammedanische Studien* (Halle: Max Niemeyer, 1889–90), p. 3; cited in ibid., p. 22. On the ideal of *muruwwa*, see W. Montgomery Watt, *Muḥammad at Mecca* (London: Clarendon Press, 1953), pp. 20–22; and Reynold A. Nicholson, *A Literary History of the Arabs* (Cambridge: Cambridge University Press, 1976), pp. 82–85, 178.

6. Nöldeke, "Arabs," p. 661.

7. Salma Khadra Jayyusi, "Contemporary Arabic Poetry: Vision and Attitudes," in R. C. Ostle, ed., *Studies in Modern Arabic Literature* (Warminster: Aris & Phillips, 1975), p. 47.

8. Watt, "Free Will and Predestination," p. 429.

9. Watt, *Islamic Philosophy*, pp. 25–26.

10. L. E. Goodman, "Time in Islam," in Anindita Niyogi Balslev and J. N. Mohanty, eds., *Religion and Time* (Leiden: E. J. Brill, 1993), p. 138.

11. Ibid.

12. Trans. C. J. Lyall, in James Kritzeck, ed., *Anthology of Islamic Literature* (New York: Meridian, 1964), p. 62. The exact dates of birth and death of this poet are unknown. He is assumed to have lived during the period of Nuʿmān Ibn Mundhir, who reigned *c.* 580–602 C.E.

13. Ringgren, *Studies in Arabian Fatalism*, p. 31.

14. Ibid., p. 32.

15. Ḥātim al-Ṭāʾī, a pre-Islamic Arab poet who died *c.* 605 C.E. Cited in ibid., p. 33. For further comments on time as the agent of destiny in pre-Islamic Arabic poetry, see ibid., pp. 30–46.

16. Nicholson, *Literary History*, pp. 135–36.

17. Ibid., p. 136, quoting from Abū Tammām's *Ḥamāsa*.

18. See W. Montgomery Watt, *Bell's Introduction to the Qurʾān* (Edinburgh: Edinburgh University Press, 1970), pp. 122, 148.

19. See Albert Arazi, *La Réalité et la fiction dans la poésie arabe ancienne* (Paris: Maisonneuve & Larose, 1989), pp. 94–103.

20. Ali, *Holy Qurʾān*, p. 1783.

21. Ignaz Goldziher, *Die Zahiriten* (Leipzig, 1884), p. 153; cited in Watt, *Free Will and Predestination*, p. 31, n. 23. See also Edward William Lane, *An Arabic–English Lexicon* (Beirut: Librairie du Liban, 1980), 3: 923, under *al-dahr*.

22. See Ignaz Goldziher, *Muslim Studies*, ed. S. M. Stern, trans. C. R. Barber and S. M. Stern (London: Allen and Unwin, 1967), 1: 230; and Ignaz Goldziher, *The Ẓāhirīs: Their Doctrine and Their History*, trans. and ed. Wolfgang Behn (Leiden: E. J. Brill, 1971), pp. 142, 144, n. 1. This point is also mentioned in Goodman, "Time in Islam," p. 138.

23. Watt, *Free Will and Predestination*, p. 25; and Watt, *Muḥammad at Mecca*, pp. 24, 77.

24. Ringgren, *Studies in Arabian Fatalism*, p. 199.

25. Ibid., p. 203, quoting from *The Book of the Thousand Nights and a Night*, trans. Richard F. Burton (Benares, 1885), 4: 220.

26. Ibid.

27. Ibid., p. 202, quoting from *The Book of the Thousand Nights and a Night*, trans. Burton, 1: 56.

28. Ibid.

29. Ringgren, "Islamic Fatalism," in *Fatalistic Beliefs in Religion, Folklore, and Literature*, p. 60.

30. Jayyusi, "Contemporary Arabic Poetry," p. 47.

31. Nicholson, *Literary History*, p. 299.

32. Arberry, *Poems of al-Mutanabbī*, p. 42, verse 4; p. 56, verse 5; p. 36, verse 1; and p. 50, verses 13–14, respectively.

33. Badawi, *Modern Arabic Literature and the West*, p. 68.

34. Abū al-ʿAlāʾ al-Maʿarrī, *The Quatrains of Abu'l-Ala*, trans. Ameen F. Rihani (New York: Doubleday, Page, 1903), p. 54.

35. Nicholson, *Literary History*, p. 316.

36. Ibid., pp. 321–22.

37. Watt, "Dahr," p. 95.

38. Goodman, "Time in Islam," p. 161.

39. Jayyusi, "Contemporary Arabic Poetry," p. 56.

40. Ismāʿīl Ṣabrī, "Shakwā al-ḥayāh," in Najīb Tawfīq, *Ismāʿīl Ṣabrī Bāshā: Shaykh al-Shuʿarāʾ* (Cairo: Al-Hayʾa al-miṣriyya al-ʿāmma lil-kitāb, 1985), p. 138. Translation mine.

41. In Kheirallah, *Life of Gibran*, pp. 17, 21, 30.

42. Jayyusi, "Contemporary Arabic Poetry," pp. 47–48.

43. Ibid., p. 48.

44. In Badr Shākir al-Sayyāb, *Dīwān Badr Shākir al-Sayyāb* (Beirut: Dār al-ʿawda, 1986), 1: 474–81. Trans. Lena Jayyusi and Christopher Middleton, in Jayyusi, ed., *Modern Arabic Poetry*, p. 430.

45. In Adonis, *Al-Āthār al-kāmila* (Beirut: Dār al-ʿawda, 1971), 1: 263. Trans. in Issa J. Boullata, *Modern Arab Poets*, p. 69.

46. In Adonis, *Al-Āthār al-kāmila*, 1: 375. Trans. in Adonis, *The Pages of Day and Night*, trans., Samuel Hazo (Marlboro, Vt.: Marlboro, 1994), p. 24.

47. In the introduction to Najīb Maḥfūẓ, *Wedding Song*, trans. Olive E. Kenny, ed. and rev. Mursi Saad El Din and John Rodenbeck (Cairo: American University in Cairo Press, 1984), p. x.

48. Ibid.

49. Najīb Maḥfūẓ, *Aṣdāʾ al-sīra al-dhātiyya* (Cairo: Maktabat Miṣr, 1995), p. 150. Translation mine.

50. Rasheed El-Enany, *Naguib Mahfouz: The Pursuit of Meaning* (London: Routledge, 1993), p. 71.

51. Ibid., p. 70, citing Najīb Maḥfūẓ, *Ataḥaddath Ilaykum*, ed. Ṣabrī Ḥafiẓ (Beirut: Dār al-ʿawda, 1977), pp. 150–51.

52. Ibid., p. 71, citing Maḥfūẓ, *Ataḥaddath Ilaykum*, p. 46. For further comments on the topic of time and human beings in Maḥfūẓ's work, see ibid., pp. 70–98.

53. Sasson Somekh, *The Changing Rhythm: A Study of Najīb Maḥfūẓ's Novels* (Leiden: E. J. Brill, 1973), pp. 106–12.

54. See also Fatma Moussa-Mahmoud, *The Arabic Novel in Egypt: 1914–1970* (Cairo: General Egyptian Book Organization, 1973), pp. 71–78.

55. Jabrā Ibrāhīm Jabrā, *Al-Safīna* (Beirut: Dār al-nahār lil-nashr, 1970), p. 22. Jabrā Ibrāhīm Jabrā, *The Ship*, trans. Adnan Haydar and Roger Allen (Washington, D.C.: Three Continents, 1985), p. 21. For further comments on the treatment of

time in this novel, see Roger Allen, *The Arabic Novel: An Historical and Critical Introduction*, 2d ed. (Syracuse, N.Y.: Syracuse University Press, 1995), pp. 177–83.

56. Yūsuf Idrīs, *Al-Ḥarām* (Cairo: Dār al-hilāl, 1959), p. 143. Yūsuf Idrīs, *The Sinners*, trans. Kristin Peterson-Ishaq (Washington, D.C.: Three Continents, 1984), p. 112.

57. Ṭāhā Ḥusayn, *Al-Ayyām*, vol. 1 (1929; reprint, 3 vols. in 1, Cairo: Markaz al-Ahrām lil-tarjama wa-al-nashr, 1992), p. 98. Ṭāhā Ḥusayn, *An Egyptian Childhood*, trans. E. H. Paxton (1932; London: Heinemann, 1981), p. 62.

58. A reference to the unilateral Declaration of the British government to Egypt on 28 February 1922, offering to recognize Egypt's independence on condition that the defense of Egypt, protection of communications, protection of foreign and minority interests, and the administration of Sudan are left to the discretion of the British government.

59. A reference to the agrarian reform of 1952, passed by Nasser's revolutionary regime, which limited land ownership to 200 feddans (1 feddan equals 1.038 acres) per landowner. The surplus was expropriated and distributed among landless farmers. In 1961, a new law set the ceiling for a single owner at 100 feddans, and in 1964 it was reduced to 50 feddans.

60. A reference to the despotic leader Ismāʿīl Ṣidqī (1875–1950), who served as Egypt's interior minister in 1924–25 and as prime minister in 1930–33. His unpopular policies provoked strikes and protests by laborers and students and culminated in repression and bloodshed.

61. See, for example, the story "Al-Ṣūra," in Najīb Maḥfūẓ, *Khammārat al-qiṭṭ al-aswad* (Cairo: Maktabat Miṣr, 1968), pp. 214–23. See also "Al-Ṣuwar al-mutaḥarrika," in Maḥfūẓ, *Aṣdā' al-sīra al-dhātiyya*, p. 17.

62. For Maḥfūẓ's tendency toward Ṣūfism, see chapter 7 below, p. 199.

63. There are many critical studies of the fiction of Najīb Maḥfūẓ. See the bibliography for further references.

64. For further reading on Ghassān Kanafānī, see Fayḥā' ʿAbd al-Hādī, *Ghassān Kanafānī: Al-riwāya wa-al-qiṣṣa al-qaṣīra* (East Jerusalem: Al-Jamʿiyya al-filasṭīniyya lil-shu'ūn al-dawliyya, 1990).

65. Najīb Maḥfūẓ, *Zuqāq al-Midaq* (1947; Cairo: Maktabat Miṣr, 1961), p. 10. Najīb Maḥfūẓ, *Midaq Alley*, trans. Trevor Le Gassick (Washington, D.C.: Three Continents, 1977), p. 6.

Chapter 3

1. Al-Maʿarrī, *Quatrains*, p. 33.

2. John Morley, "Robespierre," in *Critical Miscellanies* (London: Macmillan, 1904), 1: 93.

3. Edgar Pierce, *The Philosophy of Character* (Cambridge: Harvard University Press, 1924), pp. 11–12.

4. I. F. Stone, *The Trial of Socrates* (New York: Doubleday, 1989), p. 63.

5. Ibid.

6. See al-Ḥakīm's postscript to his play *Al-Malik Ūdīb* (Cairo: Maktabat al-ādāb, 1949), p. 216; and Badawi, *Modern Arabic Literature and the West*, p. 72.

7. Sigmund Freud, *The Psychopathology of Everyday Life* (Harmondsworth: Penguin, 1975), p. 300.

8. Sigmund Freud, *Introductory Lectures on Psychoanalysis* (Harmondsworth: Penguin, 1979), pp. 46–47, 138–39.

9. Freud, *Psychopathology*, p. 316.

10. See also A. A. Roback, *The Psychology of Character* (New York: Harcourt, Brace, 1931), pp. 285–89.

11. James W. Daley, "Freud and Determinism," *Journal of Southern Philosophy* 9, no. 2 (1971): 180.

12. M. J. L. Young, "Arabic Biographical Writing," in M. J. L. Young, J. D. Latham, and R. B. Serjeant, eds., *Religion, Learning and Science in the ʿAbbasid Period* (Cambridge: Cambridge University Press, 1990), pp. 180, 183; See also von Grunebaum, *Medieval Islam*, pp. 270, 276; and C. Nijland, *Mikhāʾīl Nuʿaymah: Promoter of the Arabic Literary Revival* (Istanbul: Nederlands Historisch-Archaeologisch Instituut, 1975), pp. 64–67.

13. See W. Montgomery Watt, trans., *The Faith and Practice of al-Ghazālī* (Oxford: Oneworld Publications, 1994), pp. 9–10.

14. Gustave E. von Grunebaum, "The Hero in Medieval Arabic Prose," in N. T. Burns and C. J. Reagan, eds., *Concepts of the Hero in the Middle Ages and the Renaissance* (Albany: State University of New York Press, 1975), p. 90.

15. Ibid.

16. Al-Ḥakīm, *Al-Malik Ūdīb*, pp. 216–17; Tawfīq al-Ḥakīm, *Plays, Prefaces, and Postscripts*, trans. William M. Hutchins (Washington, D.C.: Three Continents, 1981), 1: 292–93.

17. Ibid., p. 216; trans., p. 292.

18. Kritzeck, *Anthology of Islamic Literature*, p. 138. For a study of Ibn Ḥazm, *Kitāb al-akhlāq wa-al-siyar*, with a complete translation of his book, see Muhammad Abu Laylah, *In Pursuit of Virtue: The Moral Theology and Psychology of Ibn Ḥazm al-Andalusi* (London: TaHa, 1990).

19. ʿAlī Ibn Ahmad Ibn Ḥazm, *Al-Akhlāq wa-al-siyar fī mudāwāt al-nufūs*, ed. al-Ṭāhir Aḥmad al-Makkī (Cairo: Dār al-maʿārif, 1981), pp. 90–91. Trans. of chapter 1, Kritzeck, in *Anthology of Islamic Literature*, p. 139.

20. Ibid., p. 92; trans. pp. 139–40.

21. *EI2*, s.v. "Fiṭra"; and Fazlur Rahman, *Major Themes of the Qurʾān* (Minneapolis: Bibliotheca Islamica, 1994), p. 18.

22. Hans Wehr, *A Dictionary of Modern Written Arabic*, ed. J. Milton Cowan, 4th ed. (Ithaca, N.Y.: Spoken Language Services, 1994).

23. Watt, *The Formative Period of Islamic Thought*, pp. 104–7. It should be noted that three of the canonical collections of traditions include a special chapter on *qadar*. These are: Bukhārī, Muslim, and Tirmidhī. Abū Dāwūd has a *bāb* in the chapter on *sunna*.

24. Salisbury, "Materials," p. 125.

25. Ibid., p. 128.

26. Ibid.; cf. parallel traditions, pp. 126, 127.

27. Ibid., p. 139; cf. parallel traditions, pp. 140–41.

28. Ibid., p. 150.

29. For the meaning of the "tablet" and the "pen," see chapter 1 above, pp. 4–5.

30. Omar Khayyam, *The Ruba'iyat of Omar Khayyam*, trans. Peter Avery and John Heath-Stubbs (Harmondsworth: Penguin, 1981), p. 52.

31. In Nicholson, *Literary History*, p. 302.

32. Trans. Herbert Howarth and Ibrahim Shukrallah, in Kritzeck, *Anthology of Islamic Literature*, p. 88.

33. See Barakat, *Arab World*, pp. 181–90.

34. L. Carl Brown and Norman Itzkowitz, eds., *Psychological Dimensions of Near Eastern Studies* (Princeton, N.J.: Darwin, 1977), p. 11.

35. Hisham Sharabi, in collaboration with Mukhtar Ani, "Impact of Class and Culture on Social Behavior: The Feudal-Bourgeois Family in Arab Society," in Brown and Itzkowitz, eds., *Psychological Dimensions*, pp. 240–56.

36. Hisham Sharabi, *Muqaddimāt li-dirāsat al-mujtamaʿ al-ʿarabī* (Acre: Dār al-aswār, 1987), pp. 59, 69, 71. Translation mine.

37. Muḥammad Shukrī, *Al-Khubz al-ḥāfī* (London: Saqi, 1982), pp. 12, 89. Muḥammad Shukrī, *For Bread Alone*, trans. Paul Bowles (1973; San Francisco: City Lights, 1987), pp. 9, 56.

38. See, for example, the stories "Al-Ṣaqr" and "Al-Raʿd" in Zakariyyā Tāmir, *Al-Raʿd* (Damascus: Manshūrāt ittiḥād al-kuttāb al-ʿarab, 1970), pp. 13–16, 93–94 respectively, and the title story in Zakariyyā Tāmir, *Al-Numūr fī al-yawm al-ʿāshir* (Beirut: Dār al-ādāb, 1978), pp. 54–58.

39. Ṭāhā Ḥusayn, *Al-Ayyām*, vol. 2 (1939; reprint, 3 vols. in 1, Cairo: Markaz al-Ahrām lil-tarjama wa-al-nashr, 1992), p. 274. Ṭāhā Ḥusayn, *The Stream of Days*, trans. Hilary Wayment (Cairo: Dar al-maʿārif, 1943), p. 172.

40. Amīn, *Ḥayātī*, p. 119; trans., p. 67.

41. See also Elizabeth Warnock Fernea, ed., *Children in the Muslim Middle East* (Austin: University of Texas Press, 1995), pp. 269–71.

42. See Barakat, *Arab World*, pp. 11, 43, 118, 203.

43. For critical analyses of these stories, see Dalya Cohen-Mor, *Yūsuf Idrīs: Changing Visions* (Potomac, Md.: Sheba, 1992).

44. Tawfīq al-Ḥakīm, *Sijn al-ʿumr* (1964; Cairo: Dār Miṣr lil-ṭibāʿa, 1990), p. 11. Tawfīq al-Ḥakīm, *The Prison of Life*, trans. Pierre Cachia (Cairo: American University in Cairo Press, 1992), p. 3.

45. Ibid., pp. 59–60; trans., p. 49.

46. Ibid., pp. 84, 129; trans., pp. 73, 116–17.

47. Ibid., pp. 218–19; trans., p. 200.

48. Ibid., p. 219; trans., pp. 200-201.

49. Ibid., p. 220; trans., p. 201.

50. In Yūsuf Idrīs, *Uqtulhā* (Cairo: Maktabat Miṣr, 1982), pp. 18–48. Trans. in Yūsuf Idrīs, *The Piper Dies and Other Stories*, trans. Dalya Cohen-Mor (Potomac, Md.: Sheba, 1992), pp. 143–78.

51. Ibid., p. 48; trans., p. 175.

52. Ibid., p. 50; trans., p. 177.

53. Ibid., p. 51; trans., p. 178.

54. Amīn, *Ḥayāī*, p. 53; trans., p. 9.

55. Ibid., pp. 53–54; trans., pp. 9–10.

56. Ibid., p. 286; trans., p. 224.

57. Zaydān's memoirs (*Sīrat Ḥayātī*, 1908) were published posthumously as *Mudhakkirāt Jurjī Zaydān*, ed. Ṣalāḥ al-Dīn al-Munajjid (Beirut, 1966); reprinted in *Mu'allafāt Jurjī Zaydān al-kāmila*, vol. 20 (Beirut: Dār al-jīl, 1982). Regretfully, the passage quoted here from the English translation is not included in the latter

edition. Jurjī Zaydān, *The Autobiography of Jurji Zaidan*, ed. and trans. Thomas Philipp (Washington, D.C.: Three Continents, 1990), pp. 48–49.

58. M. H. Bakalla, *Arabic Culture through Its Language and Literature* (London: Kegan Paul, 1984), pp. 248–53.

59. Ammar, *Growing Up in an Egyptian Village*, p. 142. See also Granqvist, *Birth and Childhood*, p. 166.

60. For further reading on Maḥmūd Taymūr, see Sabry Hafez, *The Genesis of Arabic Narrative Discourse*, pp. 199–214. See also Hamza Muḥammad Buqārī, *Al-Qiṣṣa al-qaṣīra fī Miṣr wa-Maḥmūd Taymūr* (Riyadh: Dār al-Rifāʿī, 1984), pp. 111–91.

61. This translation was first published in Yūsuf Idrīs, *The Piper Dies*, pp. 93–94. The analysis of this story first appeared in Cohen-Mor, *Yūsuf Idrīs: Changing Visions*, pp. 94–97.

62. See Barakat, *Arab World*, pp. 102–3.

63. Ali, *Holy Qurʾān*, p. 730.

64. There are many critical studies of Yūsuf Idrīs's art of storytelling. See the bibliography for further references.

Chapter 4

1. ʿAbd al-Raḥmān Ibn Muḥammad Ibn Khaldūn, *Muqaddimat Ibn Khaldūn*, ed. ʿAlī ʿAbd al-Wāḥid Wāfī (Cairo: Lajnat al-bayān al-ʿarabī, 1960), 3: 900. Ibn Khaldūn, *The Muqaddimah: An Introduction to History*, trans. Franz Rosenthal, ed. and abridged by N. J. Dawood (Princeton, N.J.: Princeton University Press, 1969), p. 300.

2. Edward Burnett Tylor, *The Origins of Culture* (Gloucester, Mass.: Peter Smith, 1970), p. 1.

3. Leslie A. White, "The Concept of Culture," *American Anthropologist* 61, no. 2 (1959): 228.

4. See Dawood's introduction to Ibn Khaldūn, *The Muqaddimah*, p. ix.

5. Ibn Khaldūn, *Muqaddimat Ibn Khaldūn*, 2: 419; trans., p. 95.

6. Ibid., 2: 693–94; trans., p. 245.

7. Wilhelm Max Wundt, *Ethics: An Investigation of the Facts and Laws of the Moral Life* (London: Swan Sonnenschein, 1908), 1: 156–57. Cited in Louis H. Gray, "Custom," in *ERE*, 4: 374.

8. Edward Westermarck, *The Origin and Development of the Moral Ideas* (London: Macmillan, 1906–8), 1: 160. Cited in Gray, "Custom," pp. 376–77.

9. C. Kluckhohn and H. A. Murray, eds., *Personality and Culture* (New York: Alfred A. Knopf, 1967), pp. 58–59.

10. Gray, "Custom," p. 375.

11. Ibid., citing David Leslie, *Among the Zulus and Amatongas* (Edinburgh, 1875), p. 146.

12. Ibid., citing Wundt, *Ethics*, 1: 139.

13. *EI1*, s.v. "ʿUrf."

14. *EI2*, s.v. "ʿĀda."

15. Reuben Levy, *The Social Structure of Islam* (Cambridge: Cambridge University Press, 1957), p. 248.

16. Ibid., p. 243.

17. A marriage contracted for a limited period and for a certain sum of money payable to the woman. Exclusively for the purpose of sex for men traveling on business or posted away from their homes, temporary marriage is frequently criticized as legalized prostitution.

18. Levy, *Social Structure of Islam*, pp. 243–47.

19. Edward Westermarck, *Pagan Survivals in Mohammedan Civilisation* (Amsterdam: Philo, 1973).

20. Hamady, *Temperament and Character*, p. 152.

21. John L. Esposito, *Women in Muslim Family Law* (Syracuse, N.Y.: Syracuse University Press, 1982), p. 103.

22. *EI2*, s.v. "Taḳlīd."

23. *EI1*, s.v. "Taḳlīd."

24. Hava Lazarus-Yafeh, *Studies in al-Ghazzālī* (Jerusalem: Magnes, Hebrew University, 1975), pp. 488–89.

25. Cited in ibid., p. 57. Translation mine.

26. H. A. R. Gibb and Harold Bowen, *Islamic Society and the West* (London: Oxford University Press, 1950), vol. 1, pt. 1, p. 214. See also Hamady, *Temperament and Character*, p. 153.

27. Raphael Patai, "The Middle East as a Culture Area," *MEJ* 6, no. 1 (1952): 19.

28. Adonis, "Language, Culture, and Reality," in Ferial J. Ghazoul and Barbara Harlow, eds., *The View from Within: Writers and Critics on Contemporary Arabic Literature* (Cairo: American University in Cairo Press, 1994), pp. 27–33.

29. John Stuart Mill, *On Liberty and Other Essays*, ed. John Gray (London: Oxford University Press, 1991), p. 78.

30. Ibid., pp. 78–79.

31. Ibid., p. 65.

32. Barakat, *Arab World*, pp. 97–118.

33. Ibid., pp. 49–60, 201–2.

34. Patai, *Arab Mind*, p. 383.

35. In Yūsuf Idrīs, *Lughat al-āy āy* (1965; Beirut: Dār al-ʿawda, 1977), pp. 9–17. Trans. in Idrīs, *The Piper Dies*, pp. 55–70.

36. Ibid., p. 9; trans., p. 55.

37. Ibid., p. 15; trans., pp. 64–65.

38. Ibid., p. 17; trans., pp. 68–69.

39. Patai, *Arab Mind*, pp. 90–91.

40. Ibid., p. 95.

41. In Yaḥyā al-Ṭāhir ʿAbdallāh, *Al-Kitābāt al-Kāmila* (Cairo: Dār al-mustaqbal al-ʿarabī, 1983), pp. 224–33. Trans. in Yaḥyā al-Ṭāhir ʿAbdallāh, *The Mountain of Green Tea: Short Stories*, trans. Denys Johnson-Davies (London: Heinemann, 1984), pp. 10–18.

42. Ibid., p. 230; trans., p. 16.

43. Ibid., p. 231; trans., p. 17.

44. In the introduction to ʿAbdallāh, *Mountain of Green tea*, pp. viii–ix.

45. Patai, *Arab Mind*, p. 209.

46. Ibid.

47. In Yūsuf al-Shārūnī, *Al-Umm wa-al-waḥsh* (Cairo: Dār Majīd lil-ṭibāʿa, 1982), pp. 26–44. Trans. in Yūsuf al-Shārūnī, *Blood Feud: Short Stories*, trans. Denys Johnson-Davies (London: Heinemann, 1984), pp. 120–37.

48. Ibid., p. 26; trans., p. 120.

49. This parenthetical comment does not appear in the Arabic text of the edition cited above. The translation, however, includes it; see ibid., p. 129.

50. Ghālib Halasā, "Al-Bashʿa," in *Wadīʿ wa-al-qiddīsa Mīlādah wa-ākharūn* (Cairo: Dār al-thaqāfa al-jadīda, 1971), pp. 3–26. Translated as "Trial by Ordeal" in Mahmoud Manzalaoui, ed., *Arabic Writing Today: The Short Story* (Cairo: American Research Center in Cairo, 1968), pp. 256–68. For a description of this ritual, see Austin Kennett, *Bedouin Justice* (London: Frank Cass, 1968), pp. 107–14.

51. Al-Shārūnī, "Al-Tha'r," p. 41; trans., p. 134.

52. Ibid., p. 43; trans., p. 136.

53. Yaḥyā Ḥaqqī, *Qindīl Umm Hāshim* (1944; Cairo: Dār al-maʿārif, 1984), pp. 29–30, 32. Yaḥyā Ḥaqqī, *The Saint's Lamp and Other Stories*, trans. M. M. Badawi (Leiden: E. J. Brill, 1973), pp. 19–20.

54. ʿAbd al-Ḥakīm Qāsim, *Ayyām al-insān al-sabʿa* (Cairo: Dār al-kātib al-ʿarabī lil-ṭibāʿa wa-al-nashr, 1969), p. 36. ʿAbd al-Ḥakīm Qāsim, *The Seven Days of Man*, trans. Joseph Norment Bell (Evanston, Ill.: Northwestern University Press, 1996), p. 29.

55. The word "sun" in Arabic is grammatically feminine, whereas "crescent moon" is masculine. The girl implies that the sun (and hence the feminine gender) is more important because there is no life without it.

56. In eastern Libya.

57. *Al-Ḥabl ʿalā al-jarrār*, a proverb referring to a continuous chain of events in which one event triggers the next.

58. A district in southern Syria.

59. The aunt is Fāris's own mother. As she was killed in the bombing of Damascus by the French, and Fāris was an officer in the French army, it is implied that he was responsible for her death.

60. Patai, *Arab Mind*, pp. 73–75.

61. For further reading on Ḥabīb Jāmātī, see Yūsuf Asʿad Dāghir, *Maṣādir al-dirāsa al-adabiyya* (Beirut: Al-Maktaba al-sharqiyya, 1972), vol. 3, pt. 1, pp. 244–45. See also Khayr al-Dīn al-Ziriklī, *Al-Aʿlām: qāmūs tarājim li-ashhar al-rijāl wa-al-nisāʾ min al-ʿarab wa-al-mustaʿribīn wa-al-mustashriqīn* (Beirut: Dār al-ʿilm lil-malāyīn, 1998), 2: 165.

62. Also known as Timur and Timur Lang (1336–1404). A great but ruthless leader of Turkish-Mongolian origin, he conquered much of central Asia and eastern Europe. In 1400–1401, Tamerlane's forces raided Syria and destroyed Damascus.

63. Lane, *Manners and Customs*, pp. 37–38, 278, and p. 561, n. 4. In the novel *Egyptian Earth* by ʿAbd al-Raḥmān al-Sharqāwī, for example, the authorities punish the rebel peasant Muḥammad Abū Suwaylim (and his fellow rebels) in several harsh ways, among them by shaving his mustache in front of other villagers and then forcing him to say "I am a woman." See ʿAbd al-Raḥmān al-Sharqāwī, *Al-Arḍ* (Cairo: Dār al-shaʿb, 1970), pp. 202, 210. These details have been omitted in the English translation of the novel.

64. Moshe Ma'oz, *Asad, the Sphinx of Damascus: A Political Biography* (New York: Grove Weidenfeld, 1988), pp. 149–58.

65. Ibid., pp. 159–63.

66. *EI1*, s.v. "Timur Lang."

67. See, for example, the story "Genghis Khan" in Zakariyyā Tāmir, *Rabīʿ fī al-ramād* (Damascus: Wizārat al-thaqāfa wa-al-irshād al-qawmī, 1973), pp. 103–9; and the story "Yawma raḍiba Genghis Khan" in Zakariyyā Tāmir, *Nidāʾ Nūḥ* (London: Riad El-Rayyes, 1994), pp. 279–85. For further reading on Zakariyyā Tāmir, see ʿAbd al-Razzāq ʿĪd, *Al-ʿĀlam al-qaṣaṣī li-Zakariyyā Tāmir* (Beirut: Dār al-Fārābī, 1989); for some comments on this particular story, see ibid., pp. 86–92.

Chapter 5

1. Umm Gad is one of the women interviewed in Nayra Atiya, *Khul-Khaal: Five Egyptian Women Tell Their Stories* (Syracuse, N.Y.: Syracuse University Press, 1982), pp. 17–18.

2. Maḥmūd ʿĪsā al-Mashhādī, "A Woman for Sale," in Bagader and Heinrichsdorff, trans., *Assassination of Light*, p. 34.

3. Evelyne Accad, *Veil of Shame* (Sherbrooke, Quebec: Editions Naaman, 1978), p. 20.

4. In Alīfa Rifʿat, *Distant View of a Minaret and Other Stories*, trans. Denys Johnson-Davies (London: Heinemann, 1987), pp. 5–11. Regretfully, I have not been able to obtain a copy of the Arabic text and thus cannot provide equivalent pagination.

5. The title story of Alīfa Rifʿat, *Fī layl al-shitāʾ al-ṭawīl* (Cairo: Maṭbaʿat al-ʿāṣima, 1985), p 10. Trans. in Rifʿat, *Distant View of a Minaret*, pp. 57–58.

6. Nawāl al-Saʿdāwī, *Mudhakkirāt ṭabība* (Cairo: Dār al-maʿārif, 1965), pp. 5–6. Nawāl al-Saʿdāwī, *Memoirs of a Woman Doctor*, trans. Catherine Cobham (San Francisco: City Lights, 1989), pp. 9–10.

7. See, for example, Juliette Minces, *Veiled: Women in Islam*, trans. S. M. Berrett (Watertown, Mass.: Blue Crane, 1994); Fatima Mernissi, *Doing Daily Battle: Interviews with Moroccan Women*, trans. Mary Jo Lakeland (New Brunswick, N.J.: Rutgers University Press, 1989); and John L. Esposito, *Women in Muslim Family Law* (Syracuse, N.Y.: Syracuse University Press, 1982).

8. Barakat, *Arab World*, pp. 102–3.

9. Patai, *Arab Mind*, p. 120.

10. Ibid., p. 119.

11. Accad, *Veil of Shame*, p. 23.

12. Fatima Mernissi, "Virginity and Patriarchy," in Azizah al-Hibri, ed., *Women and Islam* (Oxford: Pergamon, 1982), p. 183.

13. Amīn, *Ḥayātī*, p. 239; trans., p. 181.

14. Accad, *Veil of Shame*, p. 23.

15. Ibid., p. 24.

16. Fatima Mernissi, *Beyond the Veil: Male-Female Dynamics in a Modern Muslim Society* (Cambridge, Mass.: Schenkman, 1975), pp. 75–79.

17. Germaine Tillion, *The Republic of Cousins: Women's Oppression in Mediterranean Society*, trans. Quintin Hoare (London: Saqi, 1983), p. 166.

18. Accad, *Veil of Shame*, p. 31.

19. Khālida Saʿīd, "Al-Marʾa al-ʿarabiyya: kāʾin bi-ghayrihi am bi-dhātihi?" in Khālida Saʿīd, *Al-Marʾa, al-taḥarrur, al-ibdāʿ* (Casablanca: Nashr al-fanak, 1991), pp. 67–81. See also Barakat, *Arab World*, p. 105.

20. In Nāzik al-Malāʾika, *Shaẓāyā wa-ramād* (Baghdad: Maṭbaʿat al-maʿārif, 1949), pp. 97–100. Trans. in Kamal Boullata, ed. and trans., *Women of the Fertile*

Crescent: An Anthology of Modern Poetry by Arab Women (Washington D.C.: Three Continents, 1978), p. 17.

21. In Nāzik al-Malā'ika, *Shajarat al-qamar* (Beirut: Dār al-ʿilm lil-malāyīn, 1968), pp. 145–48. Translated as "My Silence" in Boullata, *Women of the Fertile Crescent*, p. 19.

22. In Nāzik al-Malā'ika, *Qarārat al-mawja* (Beirut: Dār al-ādāb, 1957), pp. 145–48. Trans. in Boullata, *Women of the Fertile Crescent*, pp. 20–21.

23. Nawāl al-Saʿdāwī, *Imra'a ʿinda nuqṭat al-ṣifr* (Beirut: Dār al-ādāb, 1975), p. 77. Nawāl al-Saʿdāwī, *Woman at Point Zero*, trans. Sherif Hetata (London: Zed, 1983), p. 68.

24. On the theme of freedom in the fiction of Arab women writers, see ʿAfīf Farraj, *Al-Ḥurriyya fī adab al-mar'a* (Beirut: Dār al-Fārābī, 1977).

25. See Evelyne Accad, *Sexuality and War: Literary Masks of the Middle East* (New York: New York University Press, 1990), p. 62. See also Roger Allen, *The Arabic Novel*, pp. 231–44.

26. In Fadwā Ṭūqān, *Dīwān Fadwā Ṭūqān* (Beirut: Dār al-ʿawda, 1978), pp. 434–35. Translated as "Captivity" in *Selected Poems of Fadwā Ṭūqān*, trans, Ibrahim Dawood (Irbid, Jordan: Yarmouk University Publications, 1994), pp. 68–69.

27. Elizabeth Warnock Fernea, ed., *Women and the Family in the Middle East* (Austin: University of Texas Press, 1985), pp. 1–3.

28. A common Egyptian dish consisting of a patty made from crushed beans, onion, garlic, and parsley.

29. For a critique of Nawāl al-Saʿdāwī, with her own response, see Georges Tarabishi, *Woman against Her Sex*, trans. Basil Hatim and Elizabeth Orsini (London: Saqi, 1988). For further reading, see Fedwa Malti-Douglas, *Men, Women, and God(s): Nawal El Saadawi and Arab Feminist Poetics* (Berkeley: University of California Press, 1995).

30. Translated by Yasir Suleiman and first published in *JAL* 19, pt. 2 (1988): 142–48.

31. For a reference to this story, see chapter 1 above, p. 28.

32. See Nawāl al-Saʿdāwī, *The Hidden Face of Eve: Women in the Arab World*, trans. Sherif Hetata (Boston: Beacon, 1982), pp. 165–66.

33. For a study of the image of the male protagonist in the fiction of Arab women writers, see Sawsan Nājī, *Ṣūrat al-rajul fī al-qaṣaṣ al-nisā'ī* (Cairo: Wikālat al-Ahrām lil-nashr wa-al-tawzīʿ, 1995).

34. For further reading on Samīra ʿAzzām, see Kathyanne Piselli, *A Daughter of Palestine: The Short Fiction of Samirah Azzam* (Ann Arbor, Mich.: University Microfilms, 1986).

Chapter 6

1. J. L. Burckhardt, *Arabic Proverbs* (Richmond, Surrey: Curzon, 1984), p. 240. This popular saying is attributed to the pre-Islamic Arab king of Ḥīra, Nuʿmān Ibn Mundhir, who reigned from 580 to 602 or from 585 to 607 C.E.

2. This includes a prohibition on gambling and alcohol consumption.

3. Max Weber, *The Sociology of Religion*, trans. Ephraim Fischoff (Boston: Beacon, 1993), p. 263.

4. Afzalur Rahman, *Economic Doctrines of Islam* (Lahore: Islamic Publications, 1974), 1: 11–13.

5. Hughes, *Dictionary of Islam*, s.v. "Ṣūfī," pp. 611–12.

6. Von Grunebaum, *Medieval Islam*, pp. 127–28.

7. Robert Roberts, *The Social Laws of the Qur'ān* (London: Curzon, 1990), pp. 70–74.

8. Ibid., p. 73.

9. *EI2*, s.v. "Māl."

10. Afzalur Rahman, *Economic Doctrines of Islam*, 1: 2–9.

11. Ali E. Hillal Dessouki, "The Resurgence of Islamic Organizations in Egypt: An Interpretation," in Alexander S. Cudsi and Ali E. Hillal Dessouki, eds., *Islam and Power* (Baltimore: Johns Hopkins University Press, 1981), pp. 115–16.

12. Ali, *Holy Qur'ān*, p. 1308.

13. Raphael Patai, "The Dynamics of Westernization in the Middle East," *MEJ* 9, no. 1 (1955): 12.

14. Thomas Sowell, *Marxism: Philosophy and Economics* (New York: William Morrow, 1985), p. 53.

15. Karl Marx, *A Contribution to the Critique of Political Economy* (New York: International Publishers, 1970), pp. 20–21.

16. Tom Bottomore, ed., *A Dictionary of Marxist Thought*, 2d ed. (Cambridge, Mass.: Basil Blackwell, 1991), pp. 84–85.

17. Karl Marx and Friedrich Engels, *The German Ideology* (New York: International Publishers, 1947), p. 39. Cited in Sowell, *Marxism*, p. 67.

18. Bottomore, *Marxist Thought*, p. 143.

19. Karl Marx, *The Communist Manifesto*, ed. F. L. Bender (New York: W. W. Norton, 1988), pp. 55–75.

20. Kenneth Cragg, "The Intellectual Impact of Communism upon Contemporary Islam," *MEJ* 8, no. 2 (1954): 129.

21. Walter Z. Laqueur, "The Appeal of Communism in the Middle East," *MEJ* 9, no. 1 (1955): 21, 24.

22. Bernard Lewis, "Communism and Islam," *International Affairs* 30, no. 1 (1954): 12.

23. Ibid., p. 9.

24. Ibid., pp. 9–10, 12.

25. Cragg, "Intellectual Impact of Communism," pp. 136, 137.

26. ʿAbd al-Raḥmān al-Sharqāwī, *Al-Arḍ* (1954; Cairo: Dār al-shaʿb, 1970), p. 67. ʿAbd al-Raḥmān al-Sharqāwī, *Egyptian Earth*, trans. Desmond Stewart (London: Heinemann, 1962), pp. 64–65.

27. In ʿAbd al-Raḥmān al-Sharqāwī, *Aḥlām ṣaghīra* (Cairo: Hay'at al-kuttāb, 1956). Quoted from *Mu'allafāt ʿAbd al-Raḥmān al-Sharqāwī*, vol. 1 (Cairo: Al-Hay'a al-miṣriyya al-ʿāmma lil-kitāb, 1978), pp. 266–81. Trans. David Bishai, rev. Ronald Ewart, in Mahmoud Manzalaoui, ed., *Arabic Writing Today: The Short Story*, pp. 180–92.

28. Ibid., p. 266; trans., pp. 180–81.

29. Ibid., p. 274; trans., p. 187.

30. In Ghā'ib Ṭuʿma Firmān, *Mawlūd ākhar* (Baghdad: Maṭbaʿat al-nujūm, 1959). Quoted from ʿAlī Jawād al-Ṭāhir, ed., *Fī al-qaṣaṣ al-ʿirāqī al-muʿāṣir: naqd wa-mukhtārāt* (Beirut: Manshūrāt dār al-maktaba al-ʿaṣriyya, 1967), pp. 101–9.

31. Ibid., p. 108. Translation mine.

32. Shukrī, *Al-Khubz al-ḥāfī*, p. 15; trans., p. 11.

33. Ibid., p. 16; trans., p. 12.

34. Starkey, "The Novels of Yūsuf al-Qaʿīd," p. 68.

35. Yūsuf al-Qaʿīd, *Al-Ḥarb fī barr Miṣr* (1978; Cairo: Dār al-Qāhira lil-nashr wa-al-tawzīʿ, 1985), p. 92. Yūsuf al-Qaʿīd, *War in the Land of Egypt*, trans. Olive and Lorne Kenny and Christopher Tingley (London: Saqi, 1986), p. 110.

36. Ibid., pp. 106–7; trans., pp. 126–27.

37. Yūsuf Idrīs, *Jumhūriyyat Faraḥāt* (Cairo: Dār Rūz al-Yūsuf, 1956). Quoted from Yūsuf Idrīs, *Al-Riwāyāt* (Beirut: Dār al-shurūq, 1987), pp. 818–40. Trans. in *Modern Arabic Short Stories*, ed. and trans. Denys Jonson-Davies (London: Heinemann, 1981), pp. 1–19.

38. Ibid., p. 837; trans., p. 15.

39. A casino is a restaurant or nightclub, without the Western component of gambling, located especially alongside the Nile in Cairo and the Mediterranean coast in Alexandria.

40. Idrīs, *Jumhūriyyat Faraḥāt*, pp. 837, 839; trans., pp. 15, 17.

41. Dessouki, "Resurgence of Islamic Organizations," p. 112. See also Barakat, *Arab World*, pp. 245–51.

42. Donald M. Reid, *The Odyssey of Faraḥ Anṭūn* (Minneapolis: Bibliotheca Islamica, 1975), pp. 114–15.

43. Badawi, *Modern Arabic Literature and the West*, pp. 61–63.

44. M. M. Badawi, ed., *An Anthology of Modern Arabic Verse* (London: Oxford University Press, 1970), p. xvi.

45. Badawi, *Modern Arabic Literature and the West*, p. 10.

46. In Ṣalāḥ ʿAbd al-Ṣabūr, *Dīwān Ṣalāḥ ʿAbd al-Ṣabūr* (Beirut: Dār al-ʿawda, 1972), pp. 29–32. Trans. Lena Jayyusi and John Heath-Stubbs, in Salma Khadra Jayyusi, ed., *Modern Arabic Poetry*, pp. 123–25.

47. Badawi presents this poem as an example of the rebellion against the belief in fate in modern Egyptian literature. See Badawi, *Modern Arabic Literature and the West*, pp. 74–76. See also his critical analysis of this poem, "ʿAwda ilā al-nās fī bilādī," *Fuṣūl* 2, no. 1 (1981): 76–78.

48. The turban is the typical headdress worn by Muslim scholars and men of religion. The different methods of arranging it on the head denote religious distinctions, social standing, and peculiarities of disposition.

49. For further reading on ʿAbd al-Raḥmān al-Sharqāwī, see Kamāl Muḥammad ʿAlī, ed., *ʿAbd al-Raḥmān al-Sharqāwī: al-fallāḥ al-thāʾir* (Cairo: Al-Hayʾa al-miṣriyya al-ʿāmma lil-kitāb, 1990). See also Thurayyā al-ʿUsaylī, *Adab ʿAbd al-Raḥmān al-Sharqāwī* (Cairo: Al-Hayʾa al-miṣriyya al-ʿāmma lil-kitāb, 1995).

50. See Suhayl Idrīs's introduction to *Aqāṣīṣ ūlā* (Beirut: Dār al-ādāb, 1977), p. 6.

51. For further reading on Suhayl Idrīs, see Jūrj Azwaṭ, *Suhayl Idrīs fī-qiṣaṣihi wa-mawāqifihi al-adabiyya* (Beirut: Dār al-ādāb, 1989).

Chapter 7

1. Ghāda al-Sammān, "Fazzāʿ ṭuyūr ākhar," in *Layl al-ghurabāʾ* (Beirut: Dār al-ādāb, 1966), p. 13. A complete translation of this story is included at the end of this chapter.

2. Michiko Yusa, "Chance," in *ER*, 3: 192.

3. Ibid.

4. Leonard W. Doob, *Inevitability: Determinism, Fatalism, and Destiny* (New York: Greenwood, 1988), p. 17.

5. Yusa, "Chance," p. 194.

6. David F. Bell, *Circumstances: Chance in the Literary Text* (Lincoln: University of Nebraska Press, 1993), p. 203.

7. Doob, *Inevitability*, pp. 17, 20.

8. Bell, *Circumstances*, pp. 12–13.

9. Yusa, "Chance," pp. 195–96.

10. Ali, *Holy Qur'ān*, p. 1462.

11. Ibid., p. 605.

12. Rahman, *Major Themes of the Qur'ān*, p. 8.

13. Ibid.

14. Afzalur Rahman, *Economic Doctrines of Islam*, 4: 115–32.

15. Samuel M. Zwemer, *The Influence of Animism on Islam* (New York: Macmillan, 1920), pp. 178–79.

16. For more on the word *naṣīb*, see Piamenta, *Islam in Everyday Arabic Speech*, pp. 188, 190.

17. In Najīb Mahfūz, *Khammārat al-giṭṭ al-aswad*, pp. 199–212. Trans. in Maḥfūẓ, *God's World*, pp. 75–84.

18. In Yūsuf Idrīs, *Lughat al-āy āy*, pp. 127–33. Trans. Trevor Le Gassick, in Roger Allen, ed., *In the Eye of the Beholder: Tales of Egyptian Life from the Writings of Yūsuf Idrīs* (Minneapolis: Bibliotheca Islamica, 1978), pp. 11–18.

19. For a critical analysis of this story, see Cohen-Mor, *Yūsuf Idrīs: Changing Visions*, pp. 97–100.

20. Ghānim, *Al-Rajul alladhī faqad ẓillahu*, pt. 4, pp. 57–58; trans., p. 263.

21. Ibid., pp. 58–59, 60; trans., pp. 264, 265.

22. In Nawāl al-Saʿdāwī, *Kānat hiya al-aḍʿaf* (Beirut: Dār al-ādāb, 1979), pp. 47–54. Trans. in Dalya Cohen-Mor, ed. and trans., *An Arabian Mosaic: Short Stories by Arab Women Writers* (Potomac, Md.: Sheba, 1993), pp. 57–64.

23. In Ḥasan Naṣr, *Layālī al-maṭar* (Tunis: Al-Dār al-tunisiyya lil-nashr, 1968), pp. 101–3. Translation mine.

24. In Yaḥyā Ṭāhir ʿAbdallāh, *Al-Kitābāt al-kāmila*, p. 325. Trans. in ʿAbdallāh, *Mountain of Green Tea*, p. 65.

25. Al-Ḥakīm, *Sijn al-ʿumr*, p. 23; trans., p. 14.

26. Jabrā Ibrāhīm Jabrā, "Modern Arabic Literature and the West," *JAL* 2 (1971): 87.

27. Ibid., pp. 87–88.

28. Ibid.

29. Ibid.

30. Ibid., pp. 89–90.

31. Ibid., p. 90.

32. Jean-Paul Sartre, "Existentialism Is Humanism," in Walter Kaufmann, ed., *Existentialism from Dostoevsky to Sartre* (New York: New American Library, 1975), p. 352.

33. Hyden Carruth, in the introduction to Jean-Paul Sartre, *Nausea*, trans. Lloyd Alexander (New York: New Directions, 1964), p. ix.

34. Kaufmann, in the title article of his *Existentialism from Dostoevsky to Sartre*, pp. 46–47.

35. Ibid., p. 47.

36. The title story of Najīb Maḥfūẓ, *Taḥta al-miẓalla* (Cairo: Maktabat Miṣr, 1969), pp. 5–14.

37. Jacques Berque, "L'inquiétude arabe des temps modernes," *Revue des Études Islamiques* 26 (1958): 87–107.

38. Ibid., pp. 100–101. See also Vincent Monteil, ed., *Anthologie bilingue de la littérature arabe contemporaine* (Beirut: Imprimerie Catholique, 1961), p. xxxiii.

39. Sasson Somekh, "Zaʿbalāwī: Author, Theme, Technique," *JAL* 1 (1970): 31. See also Ḥamdī Sakkūt, "Naguib Mahfouz and the Sufi Way," in Ferial J. Ghazoul and Barbara Harlow, eds., *The View from Within*, pp. 90–98.

40. The translation of this story first appeared in Cohen-Mor, *An Arabian Mosaic*, pp. 141–54. This is a slightly revised version.

41. An exclusive neighborhood in Beirut, with villas surrounded by spacious gardens.

42. See Ghāda al-Sammān, "The Sexual Revolution and the Total Revolution," in Elizabeth Warnock Fernea and Basima Qattan Bezirgan, eds., *Middle Eastern Muslim Women Speak* (Austin: University of Texas Press, 1977), pp. 392–99.

43. For further reading on Ghāda al-Sammān, see Ghālī Shukrī, *Ghāda al-Sammān bi-lā ajniḥa* (Beirut: Dār al-ṭalīʿa, 1977); Hanan Ahmad Awwad, *Arab Causes in the Fiction of Ghādah al-Sammān (1961–1975)* (Sherbrooke, Quebec: Editions Naaman, 1983); and Najlā Naṣīb al-Ikhtiyār, *Taḥarrur al-marʾa ʿabra aʿmāl Sīmūn dū Būfwār wa-Ghāda al-Sammān, 1965–1986* (Beirut: Dār al-ṭalīʿa, 1991).

44. For further reading on Fuʾād al-Takarlī, see ʿAlī Jawār al-Ṭāhir, *Fī al-qaṣaṣ al-ʿirāqī al-muʿāṣir*, pp. 11–35; and Roger Allen, *A Library of Literary Criticism: Modern Arabic Literature* (New York: Ungar, 1987), pp. 323–26.

Chapter 8

1. These lines appear in the closing statement of *Alf layla wa-layla*. See *The Thousand and One Nights*, trans. Lane, 3: 666.

2. The story of Adam's fall is narrated in several places in the Qurʾān, including Sūra 2 and Sūra 7.

3. Rahman, *Major Themes of the Qurʾān*, pp. 25–26, 124.

4. Ibid., p. 25.

5. Abū Ḥāmid Muḥammad al-Ghazzālī, *Iḥyāʾ ʿulūm al-dīn*, ed. ʿAbd al-Raḥīm Ibn al-Ḥusayn al-ʿIrāqī (Cairo: Al-Maktaba al-tijāriyya al-kubrā, n.d.), 1: 57. Al-Ghazzālī, *The Book of Knowledge*, trans. Nabih Amin Faris (Lahore: Sh. Muhammad Ashraf, 1962), p. 149.

6. Author unknown. The Arabic lines run: *yatamannā al-marʾu fī al-sayfi al-shitāʾ/ fa-idhā jāʾa al-shitāʾ ankarah/ fa-hwa lā yaṣbiru ʿalā ḥalātin/ qutila al-insānu mā akfarah.* The last line contains a verse from the Qurʾān (80:17). Translation mine.

7. George Bernard Shaw, *Man and Superman* (New York: Dodd, Mead, 1947), act 4.

8. James Russell Lowell, "Two Scenes from the Life of Blondel," in *The Poetical Works of James Russell Lowell* (Boston: Houghton, Mifflin, 1886), p. 381.

9. In Kheirallah, *Life of Gibran*, p. 34.

10. In Yaḥyā Ḥaqqī, *Qindīl Umm Ḥāshim*, pp. 87–103. Translated as "A Game of Cards," in Ḥaqqī, *The Saint's Lamp*, pp. 59–69.

11. Ibid., pp. 91, 103; trans., pp. 62, 69.

12. Samuel Johnson, *The History of Rasselas: Prince of Abissinia*, ed. Geoffrey Tillotson and Brian Jenkins (London: Oxford University Press, 1971), p. 47.

13. Mikhail Naimy, "Dhammuka al-ayyām," in *Hams al-jufūn* (1945; Beirut: Dār Ṣādir, 1962), pp. 81–82. Translated as "To Rail at Fate," in Mikhail Naimy, *A New Year: Stories, Autobiography, and Poems*, ed. and trans. J. R. Perry (Leiden: E. J. Brill, 1974), p. 64.

14. Cited in Piamenta, *Islam in Everyday Arabic Speech*, p. 188.

15. Muhammad Abul Quasem, *The Ethics of al-Ghazālī* (Delmar, N.Y.: Caravan, 1978), p. 188.

16. Ibid., pp. 128–29.

17. Abū Ḥāmid Muḥammad al-Ghazzālī, *The Alchemy of Happiness*, trans. Claud Field, rev. and annotated by Elton L. Daniel (Armonk, N.Y.: M. E. Sharpe, 1991), p. 30.

18. Cited in Ammar, *Growing Up in an Egyptian Village*, p. 36.

19. Cited in Lane, *An Arabic–English Lexicon*, 5: 1881.

20. Cited in ibid., 5: 1882.

21. Mikhail Naimy's "Al-ʿĀqir" appears in *Kāna ma kāna* (Beirut: Maṭbaʿat al-ittiḥād, 1937). Yūsuf Idrīs's "Alif al-aḥrār" appears in *Ākhir al-dunyā* (Cairo: Dār Rūz al-Yūsuf, 1961). Yūsuf al-Shārunī's "Al-Ziḥām" appears in *Muṭāradat muntaṣaf al-layl* (Cairo: Dār al-maʿārif, 1973).

22. In Iḥsān Kamāl, *Saṭr maghlūṭ wa-qiṣaṣ ukhrā* (Cairo: Al-Hay'a al-miṣriyya al-ʿāmma lil-ta'līf wa-al-nashr, 1971), p. 47. Trans. in Cohen-Mor, *An Arabian Mosaic*, p. 14.

23. Al-Saʿdāwī, *Mudhakkirāt ṭabība*, pp. 20–21, 22–23; trans., pp. 22, 23–24.

24. Ibid., p. 84; trans., p. 79.

25. Ibid., p. 41; trans., p. 39.

26. Barakat, *Arab World*, pp. 216–21.

27. Ibid., pp. 216–17.

28. Najīb Maḥfūẓ, *Al-Shaḥḥādh* (1965; Cairo: Maktabat Miṣr, 1976), p. 121. Najīb Maḥfūẓ, *The Beggar*, trans. Kristin Walker Henry and Nariman Khales Naili al-Warraki (New York: Anchor, 1990), p. 108. See also Barakat, *Arab World*, p. 218.

29. Maḥfūẓ, *Al-Ḥubb taḥta al-maṭar*, p. 31. Translation mine.

30. Maḥfūẓ, *Zuqāq al-Midaqq*, p. 55; trans., p. 44. See also Barakat, *Arab World*, p. 217.

31. Ibid., pp. 56–57; trans; p. 45. See also Barakat, *Arab World*, p. 219.

32. See Ulfat al-Idilbī's collection of articles on the customs and traditions of old Damascene quarters, entitled *ʿĀdāt wa-taqālīd al-ḥārāt al-dimashqiyya al-qadīma* (Damascus: Ishbīlīyya lil-dirāsāt wa-al-nashr wa-al-tawzīʿ, 1996), pp. 7–58.

33. For further reading on Ulfat al-Idilbī, see Mārūn ʿAbbūd, *Naqadāt ʿābir* (Beirut: Dār al-thaqāfa, 1967), pp. 204–8; and Yūsuf al-Shārūnī, *Maʿa al-qiṣṣa al-qaṣīra* (Cairo: Al-Hay'a al-miṣriyya al-ʿāmma lil-kitāb, 1985), pp. 140–44.

34. The translation of this story first appeared in Cohen-Mor, *An Arabian Mosaic*, pp. 95–99. This is a slightly revised version.

35. J. E. Cirlot, *A Dictionary of Symbols* (New York: Philosophical Library, 1971), p. 137.

36. Westermarck, *Pagan Survivals*, pp. 27–38, 117–18. See also William Cruickshank, "Numbers (Semitic)," in *ERE*, 9: 416.

37. For further reading on Laylā Bin Māmī, see Evelyne Accad, "Women's Voices from the Maghreb," *Mundus Arabicus* 2 (1982): 28–30. See also Jean Fon-

taine, *Ecrivaines Tunisiennes* (Tunis: Gai Savior, 1990), pp. 18–20, 32; and Svetozar Pantuček, *Tunesische Literaturgeschichte* (Wiesbaden: Otto Harrassowitz, 1974), pp. 108–10.

Chapter 9

1. Adonis, *Al-Shiʿriyya al-ʿarabiyya* (Beirut: Dār al-ādāb, 1985), p. 99. Adonis, *An Introduction to Arab Poetics*, trans. Catherine Cobham (London: Saqi, 1990), p. 90.

2. For an interpretation of this verse, see Abū Jaʿfar Muḥammad Ibn Jarīr al-Ṭabarī, *Jāmiʿ al-bayān ʿan taʾwīl āy al-Qurʾān*, 2d ed. (Cairo: Maktabat Muṣṭafā al-Bābī al-Ḥalabī, 1954), 23: 5–6. See also Jalāl al-Dīn Muḥammad Ibn Aḥmad al-Maḥallī and Jalāl al-Dīn ʿAbd al-Raḥmān Ibn Abī Bakr al-Suyūṭī, *Tafsīr al-Jalālayn*, ed. Marwān Sawwār (Beirut: Dār al-maʿrifa, n.d.), p. 582.

3. See chapter 1 above, pp. 3–9; and chapter 2 above, pp. 47–49, 51–53.

4. De Vaux, "Fate (Muslim)," p. 794.

5. Gustave E. von Grunebaum, *Islam: Essays in the Nature and Growth of a Cultural Tradition* (Westport, Conn.: Greenwood, 1981), p. 67.

6. Zwemer, *The Moslem Doctrine of God*, pp. 98–99.

7. William Earnest Hocking, *The Spirit of World Politics* (New York: Macmillan, 1932), p. 441. My emphasis.

8. Ali, *Holy Qurʾān*, p. 1735.

9. In Mikhail Naimy, *Hams al-jufūn*, pp. 73–74. Trans. in Mounah A. Khouri and Hamid Algar, eds. and trans., *An Anthology of Modern Arabic Poetry* (Berkeley: University of California Press, 1974), p. 33.

10. Hourani, *Arabic Thought in the Liberal Age*, p. 228; and Cragg, "Intellectual Impact of Communism," p. 136.

11. Mernissi, *Beyond the Veil*, p. xi.

12. Tillion, *Republic of Cousins*, pp. 166–67.

13. Leila Ahmed, "Feminism and Feminist Movements in the Middle East: A Preliminary Exploration," in al-Hibri, *Women and Islam*, pp. 156–57.

14. Ahmad A. Nasr, "Popular Islam in al-Ṭayyib Ṣāliḥ," *JAL* 11 (1980): 88–104.

15. Ibid., p. 103.

16. See chapter 1 above, pp. 16, 17, 26, 29–30, 40.

17. Von Grunebaum, *Islam*, p. 67; and von Grunebaum, *Medieval Islam*, p. 346.

18. Anīs Manṣūr, "Hal naʿūd ilā al-falsafa al-wujūdiyya?" *Al-Sharq* (Shfaram, Israel) 20, no. 2 (1990): 51–59.

19. Ibid., p. 51. Translation mine.

20. Ibid., p. 58. Translation mine.

21. Ibid., p. 59. Translation mine.

22. Salih J. Altoma, "Westernization and Islam in Modern Arabic Fiction," in *Yearbook of Comparative and General Literature* 20 (1971): 81.

23. Trevor Le Gassick, "The Faith of Islam in Modern Arabic Fiction," *Religion and Literature* 20, no. 1 (1988): 100.

24. This play was translated by Trevor Le Gassick in Mahmoud Manzalaoui, ed., *Arabic Writing Today: The Drama* (Cairo: American Research Center in Egypt, 1977), pp. 335–454.

25. In Yūsuf Idrīs, *Ḥādithat sharaf* (Beirut: Dār al-ādāb, 1958), pp. 40–51.

26. Ibid., pp. 45–46. Translation mine.

27. See also Mona N. Mikhail, *Studies in the Short Fiction of Mahfouz and Idris* (New York: New York University Press, 1992), pp. 64–69.

28. In Nizār Qabbānī, *Al-Aʿmāl al-kāmila* (Beirut: Manshūrāt Nizār Qabbānī, 1993), 3: 134–36. Translated and cited as an example of religious criticism in Pierre Cachia, *An Overview of Modern Arabic Literature* (Edinburgh: Edinburgh University Press, 1990), pp. 211–12.

29. Cf. Le Gassick, "Faith of Islam," p. 108; and Cachia, *Overview*, p. 207. This issue is further discussed in Badawi, *Modern Arabic Literature and the West*, pp. 44–65; and Pierre Cachia, "Freedom from Clerical Control: The Portrayal of Men of religion in Modern Arabic Literature," *JAL* 26 (1995): 175–85.

30. Cachia, *Overview*, pp. 201–2, 212–13. For values prevailing in folk literature, see Pierre Cachia, "Social Values Reflected in Egyptian Popular Ballads," in R. C. Ostle, ed., *Studies in Modern Arabic Literature*, pp. 86–98; and Pierre Cachia, *Popular Narrative Ballads of Contemporary Egypt* (Oxford: Clarendon, 1989), pp. 65–67.

31. Eric Rouleau, "Islamic Fundamentalism in the Middle East," *Middle East Institute Newsletter* (Washington D.C.), July 1993.

32. The title story of Yūsuf Idrīs, *Uqtulhā*, pp. 83–100. Trans. in Idrīs, *The Piper Dies*, pp. 95–112.

33. Ibid., p. 94; trans., p. 107.

34. Adonis, *Al-Shiʿriyya al-ʿarabiyya*, p. 100; trans., pp. 91–92.

35. Ibid., p. 102; trans., p. 93.

36. Ibid., p. 105; trans, p. 96.

37. These verses appear in al-Maʿarrī, *Risālat al-ghufrān*. Trans. in Nicholson, *Literary History*, p. 318.

38. Khayyam, *Ruba'iyat of Omar Khayyam*, p. 47.

39. Nawāl al-Saʿdāwī, "Reflections of a Feminist," in Margot Badran and Miriam Cooke, eds., *Opening the Gates: A Century of Arab Feminist Writing* (Bloomington: Indiana University Press, 1990), pp. 397–98.

40. P. M. Kurpershoek, *The Short Stories of Yūsuf Idrīs: A Modern Egyptian Author* (Leiden: E. J. Brill, 1981), p. 47.

41. Cohen-Mor, *Yūsuf Idrīs: Changing Visions*, pp. 167–71.

42. Percy Bysshe Shelley, *A Defence of Poetry* (1821). Quoted from H. F. B. Brett-Smith, ed., *Peacock's Four Ages of Poetry*, (Oxford: Basil Blackwell, 1937), p. 59.

43. Interview with Amos Oz, *Washington Jewish Week* 18, December 11, 1986. A similar statement appears in Amos Oz, *Israel, Palestine, and Peace: Essays* (London: Vintage, 1994), p. 72.

44. M. M. Badawi, *A Short History of Modern Arabic Literature* (Oxford: Clarendon, 1993), p. 44. See also Roger Allen, *The Arabic Literary Heritage*, pp. 107–14.

45. Mikhail Naimy, *Al-Ghirbāl* (1923; Beirut: Dār Ṣādir, 1964), pp. 84–85. Translation mine.

46. In Muḥyī al-Dīn Riḍā, ed., *Balāghat al-ʿarab fī al-qarn al-ʿishrīn* (Cairo, 1920–21), p. 55. Translation mine.

47. Jabrā Ibrāhīm Jabrā, "Min al-ḥulm ilā al-kābūs," *Al-Sharq* (Shfaram, Israel) 22, no. 4 (1992): 20. Translation mine.

48. John Fowles, in the introduction to Najīb Maḥfūẓ, *Miramar*, trans. Fatma Moussa-Mahmoud (Washington, D.C.: Three Continents, 1983), p. xv.

49. In Ṭūqān, *Dīwān Fadwā Ṭūqān*, pp. 624–25.

50. Cachia, *Overview*, p. 213; Shmuel Moreh, "Arab Poets Dreamed about the Palestinian Uprising" (in Hebrew), *Maariv* (Tel Aviv, Israel), July 12, 1990. See also Halim Barakat, "Arabic Novels and Social Transformation," in R. C. Ostle, ed., *Studies in Modern Arabic Literature*, pp. 126–39.

51. Yūsuf Idrīs, "Al-Barā'a," in *Anā sulṭān qānūn al-wujūd* (Cairo: Maktabat Gharīb, 1980), pp. 53–63. Trans. in Idrīs, *The Piper Dies*, pp. 71–82. For a critical analysis of this story, see Cohen-Mor, *Yūsuf Idrīs: Changing Visions*, pp. 126–34.

52. Shmuel Yosef Agnon, "Me-Oyev le-ohev," in *Eilu ve-eilu* (Tel Aviv: Schocken, 1953); trans. Joel Blocker and first published in *The Jerusalem Post* in 1958; reprinted in Ehud Ben-Ezer, ed., *Sleepwalkers and Other Stories: The Arab in Hebrew Fiction* (Boulder, Colo.: Lynne Rienner, 1999), pp. 53–56.

53. Maḥmūd ʿAbbāsī, "Al-ʿAlāqāt al-yahūdiyya–al-ʿarabiyya fī al-qiṣṣa al-ʿarabiyya fī Isrāʾīl" (Jewish–Arab Relations in the Arabic Short Story in Israel), *Mifgash-Liqāʾ* 1 (5) (1984): 48–54.

54. The title story of Muṣṭafā Marār, *Damʿ wa-ramād* (Jerusalem: Majallat al-sharq, 1972), pp. 11–37.

55. In Muḥammad Abū Rayyā, *Arḍ lā tunbit al-mawt* (Jerusalem: Majallat al-sharq, 1974), pp. 97–102.

56. In Zakī Darwīsh, *Al-Jisr wa-al-ṭūfān* (Jerusalem: Majallat al-sharq, 1972), pp. 103–11.

57. See ʿAṭāllāh Manṣūr, "ʿArab yaktubūn bi-al-ʿibriyya: al-wuṣūl ilā al-jār" (Reach Thy Neighbor: Arabs Writing Hebrew), *Bulletin of the Israeli Academic Center in Cairo* 16 (1992): 66–72.

58. Owing to financial difficulties, this periodical has appeared irregularly in recent years.

59. See Nancy E. Berg, *Exile from Exile: Israeli Writers from Iraq* (Albany: State University of New York Press, 1996).

60. Adonis, *Al-Shiʿriyya al-ʿarabiyya*, p. 105; trans., p. 96. Cited in full earlier in this chapter p. 251.

GLOSSARY

abū: father of, used with the name of a man's eldest son as a respectful substitute for his own name.

ʿamm: uncle, also a form of address for any older man.

al-Azhar: a great mosque and university in Cairo, founded in 972 C.E. Regarded as Egypt's and Islam's supreme theological school, it has long been the seat of Muslim authority and orthodoxy.

bey: formerly the title of the governor of a small Ottoman province. It went out of official use in Egypt after the 1952 revolution and is now used loosely to indicate respect or to flatter.

bint: girl; daughter of.

casino: a restaurant or a nightclub, without the Western component of gambling, located especially alongside the Nile in Cairo and the Mediterranean coast in Alexandria.

effendi: sir, gentleman (when referring to an Egyptian man in Western clothes); also a title of respect.

fatwā: a formal religious opinion or ruling issued by Muslim authorities.

feddan: a measure of land, a little over an acre.

Ḥadīth: the corpus of traditions of the sayings and doings of the prophet Muḥammad; a *ḥadīth* (with small initial) is such a tradition.

ḥājj/ḥājja: an honorific title bestowed on a person (male or female, respectively) who has made the pilgrimage to Mecca.

ibn: son of.

ijtihād: the exercise of human reason to ascertain a rule of Sharīʿa law.

imam: leader, especially religious leader; also leader in communal prayer.

intifāḍa: derived from a verb meaning "to be shaken off," this is the name given to the Palestinian uprising that began in 1987 in the territories occupied by Israel after the 1967 war.

jinn: spiritual beings of the middle kind between angels and devils. Created from fire and not, like humans, from clay, they include good and evil spirits.

kaffiyyah: the headdress worn by Arab men.

lalla: madame or lady in Moroccan Arabic.

Laylat al-Oadr: the Night of Power, or of the Divine Decree. This is the night when, according to Sūra 97, the Qur'ān was first revealed to the prophet Muḥammad. It is celebrated during the night between the twenty-sixth and twenty-seventh of Ramaḍān. Tradition holds that prayers made to God during this night will be answered.

madhāhib (sing. *madhhab*): the four orthodox schools of law or rites in Islam.

Mahjar: the term used of Arab writers who emigrated to the Americas during the late nineteenth and early twentieth centuries. They formed a distinct literary school which introduced a new set of concepts into modern Arabic poetry and prose.

Mu'tazila: name of a theological school which introduced speculative dogmatics into Islam.

pasha: title of high civil or military rank used in the Ottoman Empire and adopted in Egypt until the 1952 revolution. It is now used as a polite or respectful form of address.

qāḍī: a judge who administers Islamic law (Sharī'a).

Ramaḍān: the ninth month of the Muslim lunar calendar. It is passed in fasting every day from sunrise to sunset.

sharī'a: the canonical law of Islam.

shaykh: village, clan, or tribal leader; also a title of respect for an older man, and the title or form of address for a man who is of the Islamic professions (e.g., Qur'ān reciter, head of a Ṣūfī order) and to whom some religious status is attributed.

sitt: Mrs, woman.

Ṣūfī: Muslim mystic.

Ṣūfism: Islamic mysticism.

sūra: a chapter of the Qur'ān.

tawakkul: complete trust in God.

turban: the typical headdress worn by Muslim scholars and men of religion. The different methods of arranging it on the head denote religious distinctions, social standing, and peculiarities of disposition.

'ulamā' (sing. *'ālim*): scholars, especially those learned in the Islamic sciences; also religious leaders.

'umda: village mayor in Egypt and Sudan.

umm: mother, used with the name of a woman's eldest son as a respectful substitute for her own name.

SELECT BIBLIOGRAPHY

ʿAbbūd, Mārūn. *Naqadāt ʿābir*. Beirut: Dār al-thaqāfa, 1967.

ʿAbd, ʿAbdallāh. *Māt al-banafsaj*. Damascus: Manshūrāt wizārat al-thaqāfa wa-al-irshād al-qawmī, 1969.

ʿAbd al-Bāqī, Muḥammad ʿAbd al-Ḥakam. *Al-Simāt al-fanniyya fī al-qiṣṣa al-qaṣīra ʿinda Najīb Maḥfūẓ*. Cairo: Sharikat al-ṣafā, 1990.

ʿAbd al-Hādī, Fayḥāʾ. *Ghassān Kanafānī: al-riwāya wa-al-qiṣṣa al-qaṣīra*. East Jerusalem: Al-Jamʿiyya al-filasṭīniyya lil-shuʾūn al-dawliyya, 1990.

ʿAbdallāh, Yaḥyā al-Ṭāhir. *Al-Kitābāt al-kāmila*. Cairo: Dār al-mustaqbal al-ʿarabī, 1983.

———. *The Mountain of Green Tea: Short Stories*. Translated by Denys Johnson-Davies. London: Heinemann, 1984.

ʿAbd al-Muʿṭī, Fārūq. *Yūsuf Idrīs bayna al-qiṣṣa al-qaṣīra wa-al-ibdāʿ al-adabī*. Beirut: Dār al-kutub al-ʿilmiyya, 1994.

ʿAbd al-Ṣabūr, Ṣalāḥ. *Dīwān Ṣalāḥ ʿAbd al-Ṣabūr*. Beirut: Dār al-ʿawda, 1972.

Abdel-Malek, Anouar, ed. *Anthologie de la littérature arabe contemporaine: Les essais*. Paris: Editions du Seuil, 1965.

Abdel Wahab, Farouk, ed. *Modern Egyptian Drama: An Anthology*. Minneapolis: Bibliotheca Islamica, 1974.

Abū ʿAwf, ʿAbd al-Raḥmān. *Yūsuf Idrīs wa-ʿālamuhu al-qaṣaṣī wa-al-riwāʾī*. Cairo: Dār al-ghad, 1991.

Abu Khalil, Asʿad. "Al-Jabriyyah in the Political Discourse of Jamāl ʿAbd al-Nāṣir and Ṣaddām Ḥusayn: The Rationalization of Defeat." *The Muslim World* 84, no. 3–4 (1994): 240–57.

Abu Laylah, Muhammad. *In Pursuit of Virtue: The Moral Theology and Psychology of Ibn Ḥazm al-Andalusi*, with a translation of his book *Al-Akhlāq wa'l-siyar*. London: TaHa, 1990.

Abul Quasem, Muhammad. *The Ethics of al-Ghazālī*. Delmar, N.Y.: Caravan, 1978.

Abū Rayyā, Muḥammad. *Arḍ lā tunbit al-mawt*. Jerusalem: Majallat al-sharq, 1974.

Accad, Evelyne. *Veil of Shame*. Sherbrooke, Quebec: Editions Naaman, 1978.

———. "Women's Voices from the Maghreb." *Mundus Arabicus* 2 (1982): 18–34.

———. *Sexuality and War: Literary Masks of the Middle East*. New York: New York University Press, 1990.
———. "Rebellion, Maturity, and the Social Context: Arab Women's Special Contribution to Literature." In *Arab Women: Old Boundaries, New Frontiers*, edited by Judith E. Tucker. Bloomington: Indiana University Press, *c.* 1993.
———, and Rose Ghurayyib. *Contemporary Women Writers and Poets*. Beirut: Beirut University College, 1985.
Adams, Charles C. *Islam and Modernism in Egypt*. London: Oxford University Press, 1933.
Adonis (ʿAlī Aḥmad Saʿīd). *Al-Āthār al-kāmila*. 2 vols. Beirut: Dār al-ʿawda, 1971.
———. *Al-Shiʿriyya al-ʿarabiyya*. Beirut: Dār al-ādāb, 1985. *An Introduction to Arab Poetics*. Translated by Catherine Cobham. London: Saqi, 1990.
———. "Language, Culture, and Reality." In *The View from Within: Writers and Critics on Contemporary Arabic Literature*, edited by Ferial J. Ghazoul and Barbara Harlow. Cairo: American University in Cairo Press, 1994.
———. *The Pages of Day and Night*. Translated by Samuel Hazo. Marlboro, Vt.: Marlboro, 1994.
El-Affendi, Abdelwahab. *Turābī's Revolution: Islam and Power in Sudan*. London: Gray Seal, 1991.
Ahmed, Leila. *Women and Gender in Islam*. New Haven: Yale University Press, 1992.
Ajami, Fouad. *The Arab Predicament: Arabic Political Thought and Practice since 1967*. Cambridge: Cambridge University Press, 1982.
ʿAlawī, Muḥammad Badr al-Dīn. *Fatalism, Free Will, and Acquisition as Viewed by Muslim Sects*. Lahore: Orientalia, 1956.
Ali, Abdullah Yusuf. *The Holy Qurʾān: Text, Translation, and Commentary*. Washington, D.C.: Khalil al-Rawaf, 1946.
ʿAlī, Kamāl Muḥammad, ed. *ʿAbd al-Raḥmān al-Sharqāwī: al-fallāḥ al-thāʾir*. Cairo: Al-Hayʾa al-miṣriyya al-ʿāmma lil-kitāb, 1990.
Allen, Roger. *The Arabic Novel: An Historical and Critical Introduction*. 2d ed. Syracuse, N.Y.: Syracuse University Press, 1995.
———. *The Arabic Literary Heritage: The Development of Its Genres and Criticism*. Cambridge: Cambridge University Press, 1998.
———, ed. *In the Eye of the Beholder: Tales of Egyptian Life from the Writings of Yūsuf Idrīs*. Minneapolis: Bibliotheca Islamica, 1978.
———, ed. *A Library of Literary Criticism: Modern Arabic Literature*. New York: Ungar, 1987.
———, ed. *Critical Perspectives on Yūsuf Idrīs*. Washington D.C.: Three Continents, 1994.
Altoma, Salih J. "Westernization and Islam in Modern Arabic Fiction." In *Yearbook of Comparative and General Literature* 20 (1971): 81–88.
Amīn, Aḥmad. *Ḥayātī*. 1950. Beirut: Dār al-kitāb al-ʿarabī, 1971. *My Life*. Translated by Issa J. Boullata. Leiden: E. J. Brill, 1978.
Ammar, Hamed. *Growing Up in an Egyptian Village: Silwa, Province of Aswan*. London: Routledge & Kegan Paul, 1954.
Amyuni, Mona Takieddine, ed. *Tayeb Salih's Season of Migration to the North: A Casebook*. Beirut: American University of Beirut Press, 1985.
Arazi, Albert. *La Réalité et la fiction dans la poésie arabe ancienne*. Paris: Maisonneuve & Larose, 1989.
Arberry, A. J. *Avicenna on Theology*. London: John Murray, 1951.

———. *Poems of al-Mutanabbī*. Cambridge: Cambridge University Press, 1967.
———, trans. *The Doctrine of the Ṣūfīs*. Cambridge: Cambridge University Press, 1977.
———. *Ṣūfism: An Account of the Mystics of Islam*. London: Allen & Unwin, 1979.
Armstrong, Karen. *A History of God*. New York: Ballantine, 1993.
Atiya, Nayra. *Khul-Khaal: Five Egyptian Women Tell Their Stories*. Syracuse, N.Y.: Syracuse University Press, 1982.
Awad, Louis, ed. *The Literature of Ideas in Egypt*. Atlanta: Scholars, 1986.
Awwad, Hanan Ahmad. *Arab Causes in the Fiction of Ghādah al-Sammān (1961–1975)*. Sherbrooke, Quebec: Editions Naaman, 1983.
Ayrout, Henry Habib. *The Fellaheen*. Translated by Hilary Weyment. Cairo: R. Schindler, 1945.
al-ʿAẓm, Ṣādiq Jalāl. *Al-Naqd al-dhātī baʿda al-hazīma*. Beirut: Dār al-ṭalīʿa, 1968.
Azwaṭ, Jūrj. *Suhayl Idrīs fī qiṣaṣihi wa-mawāqifihi al-adabiyya*. Beirut: Dār al-ādāb, 1989.
ʿAzzām, Samīra. *Al-Ẓill al-kabīr*. Beirut: Dār al-sharq al-jadīd, 1956.
Badawi, ʿAbd al-Raḥmān. *Al-Zamān al-wujūdī*. Cairo: Maktabat al-nahḍa al-miṣriyya, 1945.
———. *Al-Insāniyya wa-al-wujūdiyya fī al-fikr al-ʿarabī*. Cairo: Maktabat al-nahḍa al-miṣriyya, 1947.
———. *Dirāsāt fī al-falsafa al-wujūdiyya*. Cairo: Maktabat al-nahḍa al-miṣriyya, 1966.
Badawi, M. M. *A Critical Introduction to Modern Arabic Poetry*. Cambridge: Cambridge University Press, 1975.
———. "Medieval Arabic Drama: Ibn Dāniyāl." *Journal of Arabic Literature* 8 (1982) : 83–107.
———. *Modern Arabic Literature and the West*. London: Ithaca, 1985.
———. *Modern Arabic Drama*. Cambridge: Cambridge University Press, 1987.
———. *Early Arabic Drama*. Cambridge: Cambridge University Press, 1988.
———. *A Short History of Modern Arabic Literature*. Oxford: Clarendon, 1993.
———, ed. *An Anthology of Modern Arabic Verse*. London: Oxford University Press, 1970.
———, ed. *Modern Arabic Literature*. Cambridge: Cambridge University Press, 1992.
Badran, Margot, and Miriam Cooke, eds. *Opening the Gates: A Century of Arab Feminist Writing*. Bloomington: Indiana University Press, 1990.
Baer, Gabriel. *Population and Society in the Middle East*. Translated by Hanna Szoke. Westport, Conn.: Greenwood, 1976.
Baerlein, Henry. *The Diwan of Abu'l-Ala*. London: John Murray, 1948.
Bagader, Abu Bakr, and Ava M. Heinrichsdorff, trans. *Assassination of Light: Modern Saudi Short Stories*. Washington, D.C.: Three Continents, 1990.
Bakalla, M. H. *Arabic Culture through Its Language and Literature*. London: Kegan Paul, 1984.
Baʿlabakkī, Laylā. *Anā aḥyā*. Beirut: Dār majallat shiʿr, 1958.
———. *Al-Āliha al-mamsūkha*. Beirut: Dār majallat shiʿr, 1960.
———. *Safīnat ḥanān ilā al-qamar*. Beirut: Al-Muʿassasa al-waṭaniyya lil-ṭibā ʿa wa-al-nashr, 1963.
Balslev, Anindita Niyogi, and J. N. Mohanty, eds. *Religion and Time*. Leiden: E. J. Brill, 1993.

Barakat, Halim. "Socioeconomic, Cultural, and Personality Forces Determining Development in Arab Society." *Social Praxis* 2, no. 3–4 (1974): 179–204.

———. *Visions of Social Reality in the Contemporary Arab Novel.* Washington D.C.: Center for Arab Studies, Georgetown University, 1977.

———. *The Arab World: Society, Culture, and State.* Berkeley: University of California Press, 1993.

Bell, David F. *Circumstances: Chance in the Literary Text.* Lincoln: University of Nebraska Press, 1993.

Berger, Morroe. *The Arab World Today.* New York: Doubleday, 1962.

Berque, Jacques. "L'inquiétude arabe des temps modernes." *Revue des Études Islamiques* 26 (1958) : 87–107.

———. *The Arabs: Their History and Future.* Translated by Jean Stewart. London: Faber and Faber, 1964.

———. *Cultural Expression in Arab Society Today.* Translated by Robert W. Stookey. Austin: University of Texas Press, 1978.

Binjallūn, al-ʿArabī. *Al-Naṣṣ al-maftūḥ: dirāsāt fī al-khiṭāb al-qaṣaṣī wa-al-riwāʾī al-maghribī.* Rabat: Maktabat al-maʿārif, 1986.

———. *Abʿād al-naṣṣ: qirāʾāt fī al-adab al-maghribī al-ḥadīth.* Rabat: Maṭbaʿat al-risāla, 1986.

Bin Māmī, Laylā. *Ṣawmaʿa taḥtariq.* Tunis: Qāsim al-ʿArabī, 1968.

Binmasʿūd, Rashīda. *Al-Marʾa wa-al-kitāba: suʾāl al-khuṣūṣiyya/balāghat al-ikhtilāf.* Casablanca: Afrīqiyā al-sharq, 1994.

al-Bisāṭī, Muḥammad. *Buyūt warāʾ al-ashjār.* Cairo: Dār al-hilāl, 1993. *Houses behind the Trees.* Translated by Denys Johnson-Davies. Cairo: American University in Cairo Press, 1997.

Bottomore, Tom, ed. *A Dictionary of Marxist Thought.* 2d ed. Cambridge, Mass.: Basil Blackwell, 1991.

Boullata, Issa J. *Trends and Issues in Contemporary Arabic Thought.* Albany: State University of New York Press, 1990.

———, ed. and trans. *Modern Arab Poets: 1950–1975.* Washington, D.C.: Three Continents, 1976.

———, ed. *Critical Perspectives on Modern Arabic Literature: 1945–1980.* Washington, D.C.: Three Continents, 1980.

———, and Terry De Young, eds. *Tradition and Modernity in Arabic Literature.* Fayetteville: University of Arkansas Press, 1997.

Boullata, Kamal, ed. and trans. *Women of the Fertile Crescent: An Anthology of Modern Poetry by Arab Women.* Washington, D.C.: Three Continents, 1978.

Brockelmann, Carl. *Geschichte der arabischen Litteratur.* 3 vols. Leiden: Brill, 1937–42.

Brown, L. Carl, and Norman Itzkowitz, eds. *Psychological Dimensions of Near Eastern Studies.* Princeton, N.J.: Darwin, 1977.

Brugman, J. *An Introduction to the History of Modern Arabic Literature in Egypt.* Leiden: Brill, 1984.

Buqārī, Ḥamza Muḥammad. *Al-Qiṣṣa al-qaṣīra fī Miṣr wa-Maḥmūd Taymūr.* Riyadh: Dār al-Rifāʿī, 1984.

Burckhardt, J. L. *Arabic Proverbs.* Richmond, Surrey: Curzon, 1984.

Burckhardt, Titus. *Introduction to Sufism.* Translated by D. M. Matheson. London: Thorsons, 1995.

Burns, N. T., and C. J. Reagan, eds. *Concepts of the Hero in the Middle Ages and the Renaissance*. Albany: State University of New York Press, 1975.

Burrell, David B. *Freedom and Creation in Three Traditions*. Notre Dame, Ind.: University of Notre Dame Press, 1993.

Cachia, Pierre. *Ṭāhā Ḥusayn: His Place in the Modern Arab Literary Renaissance*. London: Luzac, 1956.

———. *Popular Narrative Ballads of Contemporary Egypt*. Oxford: Clarendon, 1989.

———. *An Overview of Modern Arabic Literature*. Edinburgh: Edinburgh University Press, 1990.

———. "Freedom from Clerical Control: The Portrayal of Men of Religion in Modern Arabic Literature." *Journal of Arabic Literature* 26 (1995): 175–85.

Cahn, Steven M. *Fate, Logic, and Time*. New Haven: Yale University Press, 1967.

Campbell, Robert B., ed. *Aʿlām al-adab al-ʿarabī al-muʿāṣir: siyar wa-siyar dhātiyya*. Beirut: Al-Maʿhad al-almānī lil-abḥāth al-sharqiyya, 1996.

Cirlot, J. E. *A Dictionary of Symbols*. New York: Philosophical Library, 1971.

Cleveland, William L. *A History of the Modern Middle East*. Boulder, Colo.: Westview, 1994.

Cohen-Mor, Dalya. *Yūsuf Idrīs: Changing Visions*. Potomac, Md.: Sheba, 1992.

———, ed. and trans. *An Arabian Mosaic: Short Stories by Arab Women Writers*. Potomac, Md.: Sheba, 1993.

Cooke, Miriam. *The Anatomy of an Egyptian Intellectual: Yaḥyā Ḥaqqī*. Washington, D.C.: Three Continents, 1984.

———. *War's Other Voices: Women Writers on the Lebanese Civil War*. Cambridge: Cambridge University Press, 1988.

———. "Arab Women Writers." In *Modern Arabic Literature*, edited by M. M. Badawi. Cambridge: Cambridge University Press, 1992.

Cragg, Kenneth. "The Intellectual Impact of Communism upon Contemporary Islam." *The Middle East Journal* 8, no. 2 (1954): 127–38.

Cromer, Evelyn Baring, Earl of. *Modern Egypt*. 2 vols. London: Macmillan, 1908.

Cudsi, Alexander S., and Ali E. Hillal Dessouki, eds. *Islam and Power*. Baltimore: Johns Hopkins University Press, 1981.

Dāghir, Yūsuf Asʿad. *Maṣādir al-dirāsa al-adabiyya*. 4 vols. Beirut: Al-Maktaba al-sharqiyya, 1972.

Daley, James W. "Freud and Determinism." *The Journal of Southern Philosophy* 9, no. 2 (1971): 179–88.

Darwīsh, Zakī. *Al-Jisr wa-al-ṭūfān*. Jerusalem: Majallat al-sharq, 1972.

Dawood, N. J., trans. *The Koran*. London: Penguin Classics, 1993.

Voogd, Lourina de, ed. *Literatuur in Marokko en andere Arabische landen*. Den Haag: Nederlands Bibliotheek en Lektuur Centrum, 1984.

Disūqī, Fārūq. *Ḥurriyyat al-insān fī al-fikr al-islamī: baḥth fī al-qaḍā' wa-al-qadar wa-al-jabr wa-al-ikhtiyār*. Alexandria: Dār al-daʿwa, 1982.

———. *Al-Qaḍā' wa-al-qadar fī al-islām*. 3 vols. Alexandria: Dār al-daʿwa, 1982–84.

Doob, Leonard W. *Inevitability: Determinism, Fatalism, and Destiny*. New York: Greenwood, 1988.

Dorner, A. "Fate (Introductory)." In *Encyclopaedia of Religion and Ethics*. Edinburgh: T. & T. Clark, 1908–26.

Elkhadem, Saad. *Old Arab Sayings, Similes, and Metaphors*. Fredericton, New Brunswick: York, 1991.

Elster, Jon. *Making Sense of Marx*. Cambridge: Cambridge University Press, 1985.
El-Enany, Rasheed. *Naguib Mahfouz: The Persuit of Meaning*. London: Routledge, 1993.
Esposito, John L. *Women in Muslim Family Law*. Syracuse, N.Y.: Syracuse University Press, 1982.
———. *The Islamic Threat: Myth or Reality?* New York: Oxford University Press, 1999.
Fakhry, Majid. *A History of Islamic Philosophy*. New York: Columbia University Press, 1983.
al-Fākhūrī, Ḥannā. *Ta'rīkh al-adab fī al-Maghrib al-ʿarabī*. Beirut: Dār al-jīl, 1996.
Faraḥ, Anṭūn. *Al-Dīn wa-al-ʿilm wa-al-māl*. Alexandria: Al-Mudun al-thalāth, 1903.
Farrāj, ʿAfīf. *Al-Ḥurriyya fī adab al-mar'a*. Beirut: Dār al-Fārābī, 1975.
Farsoun, Samih K., ed. *Arab Society: Continuity and Change*. London: Croom Helm, 1985.
Fernea, Elizabeth Warnock, ed. *Women and the Family in the Middle East: New Voices of Change*. Austin: University of Texas Press, 1985.
———, ed. *Children in the Muslim Middle East*. Austin: University of Texas Press, 1995.
———, and Basima Qattan Bezirgan, eds. *Middle Eastern Muslim Women Speak*. Austin: University of Texas Press, 1977.
Firmān, Ghā'ib Ṭuʿma. *Mawlūd ākhar*. Baghdad: Maṭbaʿat al-nujūm, 1959.
FitzGerald, Edward. *Rubaiyat of Omar Khayyam*. Edited by Nathan Haskell Dole. Multi-variorum edition. 2 vols. Boston: L. C. Page, 1898.
Flew, Anthony Garrard. "Psychoanalysis and the Philosophical Problems of Free Will." In *Psychoanalysis and Philosophy*, edited by Charles Hanly and Morris Lazerowitz. New York: International Universities, 1970.
Fontaine, Jean. *Al-Adab al-tūnisī al-muʿāṣir*. Tunis: Al-Dār al-tūnisiyya lil-nashr, 1989.
———. *Ecrivaines Tunisiennes*. Tunis: Gai Savior, 1990.
Freud, Sigmund. *The Psychopathology of Everyday Life*. Harmondsworth: Penguin, 1975.
———. *Introductory Lectures on Psychoanalysis*. Harmondsworth: Penguin, 1979.
Freyha, Anis. *A Dictionary of Modern Lebanese Proverbs*. Beirut: Librairie du Liban, 1974.
Gardet, L. "Al-Ḳaḍā' wa'l-Ḳadar." In *The Encyclopaedia of Islam*. New ed. Leiden: E. J. Brill, 1960–.
Gerhardt, Mia I. *The Art of Story-Telling: A Literary Study of the Thousand and One Nights*. Leiden: E. J. Brill, 1963.
Ghānim, Fatḥī. *Al-Rajul alladhī faqad ẓillahu*. Cairo: Dār al-jumhūriyya lil-ṣiḥāfa, 1962. *The Man Who Lost His Shadow*. Translated by Desmond Stewart. London: Heinemann, 1980.
Ghazoul, Ferial J., and Barbara Harlow, eds. *The View from Within: Writers and Critics on Contemporary Arabic Literature*. Cairo: American University in Cairo Press, 1994.
al-Ghazzālī, Abū Ḥāmid Muḥammad. *Iḥyā' ʿulūm al-dīn*. Edited by ʿAbd al-Raḥīm Ibn al-Ḥusayn al-ʿIrāqī. Cairo: Al-Maktaba al-tijāriyya al-kubrā, n.d.
———. *The Book of Knowledge*. Book 1 of *Iḥyā' ʿulūm al-dīn*. Translated by Nabih Amin Faris. Lahore: Sh. Muhammad Ashraf, 1962.

———. *Invocations and Supplications.* Book 9 of *Iḥyāʾ ʿulūm al-dīn.* Translated by K. Nakamura. Cambridge, U.K.: Islamic Texts Society, 1990.

———. *The Alchemy of Happiness.* Translated by Claud Field. Revised and annotated by Elton L. Daniel. Armonk, N.Y.: M. E. Sharpe, 1991.

———. *The Ninety-Nine Beautiful Names of God.* Translated with notes by David B. Burrell and Nazih Daher. Cambridge, U.K.: Islamic Texts Society, 1992.

Gibb, H. A. R. *Arabic Literature: An Introduction.* London: Oxford University Press, 1963.

———. *Mohammedanism.* London: Oxford University Press, 1975.

———, and Harold Bowen. *Islamic Society and the West.* 2 vols. London: Oxford University Press, 1950.

Gibran, Gibran Khalil. *Al-Ajniḥa al-mutakassira.* New York: Mirʾāt al-gharb, 1912. *The Broken Wings.* Translated by Anthony R. Ferris. New York: Citadel, 1965.

———. "Al-Mawākib." New York: Mirʾāt al-gharb al-yawmiyya, 1918.

Goldschmidt, Arthur Jr. *Historical Dictionary of Egypt.* Metuchen, N.J.: Scarecrow, 1994.

———. *A Concise History of the Middle East.* Boulder, Colo.: Westview, 1998.

Goldziher, Ignaz. *A Short History of Classical Arabic Literature.* Translated by Joseph Desomogyi. Hildesheim: Georg Olms, 1966.

———. *Muslim Studies.* 2 vols. Edited by S. M. Stern. Translated by C. R. Barber and S. M. Stern. London: Allen and Unwin, 1967.

———. *The Ẓāhirīs: Their Doctrine and Their History.* Translated and edited by Wolfgang Behn. Leiden: E. J. Brill, 1971.

———. *Introduction to Islamic Theology and Law.* Translated by Andras and Ruth Hamori. Princeton, N.J.: Princeton University Press, 1981.

Goodman, L. E. "Time in Islam." In *Religion and Time,* edited by Anindita Niyogi Balslev and J. N. Mohanty. Leiden: E. J. Brill, 1993.

Granqvist, Hilma. *Birth and Childhood among the Arabs: Studies in a Muhammadan Village in Palestine.* Helsingfors: Soderstrom, 1947.

Gray, Louis H. "Custom." In *Encyclopaedia of Religion and Ethics.* Edinburgh: T. & T. Clark, 1908–26.

Grunebaum, Gustave E. von. *Medieval Islam: A Study in Cultural Orientation.* Chicago: University of Chicago Press, 1953.

———. *Modern Islam: The Search for Cultural Identity.* Berkeley: University of California Press, 1962.

———. "The Hero in Medieval Arabic Prose." In *Concepts of the Hero in the Middle Ages and the Renaissance,* edited by N. T. Burns and C. J. Reagan. Albany: State University of New York Press, 1975.

———. *Islam: Essays in the Nature and Growth of a Cultural Tradition.* Westport, Conn.: Greenwood, 1981.

———. *Muhammadan Festivals.* London: Curzon, 1988.

Hafez, Sabry (Ḥāfiẓ, Ṣabrī). "The Modern Arabic Short Story." In *Modern Arabic Literature,* edited by M. M. Badawi. Cambridge: Cambridge University Press, 1992.

———. *The Genesis of Arabic Narrative Discourse: A Study in the Sociology of Modern Arabic Literature.* London: Saqi, 1993.

al-Ḥakīm, Tawfīq. *Al-Malik Ūdīb.* Cairo: Maktabat al-ādāb, 1949.

———. *Sijn al-ʿumr*. 1964. Cairo: Dār Miṣr lil-ṭibāʿa, 1990. *The Prison of Life*. Translated by Pierre Cachia. Cairo: American University in Cairo Press, 1992.

———. *Plays, Prefaces, and Postscripts of Tawfiq al-Ḥakīm*. 2 vols. Translated by William M. Hutchins. Washington, D.C.: Three Continents, 1981.

Halasā, Ghālib. *Wadīʿ wa-al-qiddīsa Mīlādah wa-ākharūn*. Cairo: Dār al-thaqāfa al-jadīda, 1971.

Halliday, Fred. " 'Orientalism' and Its Critics." *British Journal of Middle Eastern Studies* 20, no. 2 (1993) : 145–63.

Ḥamāda, Ibrāhīm. *Khayāl al-ẓill wa-tamthīliyyāt Ibn Dāniyāl*. Cairo: Al-Mu'assasa al-miṣriyya al-ʿāmma lil-ta'līf, 1963.

al-Hamadhānī, Badīʿ al-Zamān. *The Maqāmāt of Badīʿ al-Zamān al-Hamadhānī*. Translated by J. Prendergast. London: Curzon, 1973.

Hamady, Sania. *Temperament and Character of the Arabs*. New York: Twayne, 1960.

Ḥaqqī, Yaḥyā. *Qindīl Umm Hāshim*. 1944. Cairo: Dār al-maʿārif, 1984.

———. *The Saint's Lamp and Other Stories*. Translated by M. M. Badawi. Leiden: E. J. Brill, 1973.

Haykal, Muhammad Ḥusayn. *Zaynab*. Cairo: Maṭbaʿat al-jarīda, 1913. *Zaynab: The First Egyptian Novel*. Translated by John Mohammed Grinsted. London: Darf, 1989.

Haywood, John A. *Modern Arabic Literature: 1800–1970*. London: Lund Humphries, 1971.

al-Hibri, Azizah, ed. *Women and Islam*. Oxford: Pergamon, 1982.

Hinds, Martin, and El-Said Badawi. *A Dictionary of Egyptian Arabic*. Beirut: Librairie du Liban, 1986.

Hocking, William Ernest. *The Spirit of World Politics*. New York: Macmillan, 1932.

Hopwood, Derek. *Egypt: Politics and Society 1945–1984*. London: Allen & Unwin, 1985.

Hospers, John. "Free-Will and Psychoanalysis." In *Readings in Ethical Theory*, edited by Wilfrid Sellars and John Hospers. New York: Appleton-Century-Crofts, 1952.

Hourani, Albert. *Arabic Thought in the Liberal Age: 1798–1939*. Cambridge: Cambridge University Press, 1983.

———. *A History of the Arab Peoples*. Cambridge, Mass.: Harvard University Press, 1991.

Hughes, Thomas Patrick. *Notes on Muhammadanism*. Wilmington, Del.: Scholarly Resources, 1976.

———. *Dictionary of Islam*. Chicago: Kazi, 1994.

Ḥusayn, Tāhā. *Al-Ayyām*. 3 vols. Cairo: 1929, 1939, 1972. Reprint (3 vols. in 1), Cairo: Markaz al-Ahrām lil-tarjama wa-al-nashr, 1992.

———. *An Egyptian Childhood*. Vol. 1 of *Al-Ayyām*. Translated by E. H. Paxton. 1932. London: Heinemann, 1981.

———. *The Stream of Days*. Vol. 2 of *Al-Ayyām*. Translated by Hilary Wayment. Cairo: Dar al-maʿārif, 1943.

———. *A Passage to France*. Vol. 3 of *Al-Ayyām*. Translated by Kenneth Cragg. Leiden: E. J. Brill, 1976.

———. *Duʿā' al-karawān*. Cairo: Dār al-maʿārif, 1934. *The Call of the Curlew*. Translated by A. B. As-Safi. Leiden: E. J. Brill, 1980.

———. *Shajarat al-bu's*. Cairo: Dār al-maʿārif, 1944. *The Tree of Misery*. Translated by Mona El-Zayyat. Cairo: Palm, 1997.

al-Ḥusaynī, Isḥāq Mūsā. *Azmat al-fikr al-ʿarabī*. Beirut: Dār Bayrūt, 1954.
Ibn Ḥazm, ʿAlī Ibn Aḥmad. *Al-Akhlāq wa-al-siyar fī mudāwāt al-nufūs*. Edited by al-Ṭāhir Aḥmad Makkī. Cairo: Dār al-maʿārif, 1981.
Ibn Khaldūn, ʿAbd al-Raḥmān Ibn Muḥammad. *Muqaddimat Ibn Khaldūn*. 4 vols. Edited by ʿAlī ʿAbd al-Wāḥid Wāfī. Cairo: Lajnat al-bayān al-ʿarabī, 1957–62.
———. *The Muqaddimah: An Introduction to History*. Translated by Franz Rosenthal. Edited and abridged by N. J. Dawood. Princeton, N.J.: Princeton University Press, 1969.
ʿĪd, ʿAbd al-Razzāq. *Al-ʿĀlam al-qaṣaṣī li-Zakariyyā Tāmir*. Beirut: Dār al-Fārābī, 1989.
al-Idilbī, Ulfat. *Qiṣaṣ shāmiyya*. Damascus: Dār al-yaqẓa al-ʿarabiyya, 1954.
———. *Dimashq yā basmat al-ḥuzn*. Damascus: Wizārat al-thaqāfa wa-al-irshād al-qawmī, 1980. *Sabriya: Damascus Bitter Sweet*. Translated by Peter Clark. New York: Interlink, 1997.
———. *ʿĀdāt wa-taqālīd al-ḥārāt al-dimashqiyya al-qadīma: muḥāḍarāt wa-maqālāt*. Damascus: Ishbīliyya lil-dirāsāt wa-al-nashr wa-al-tawzīʿ, 1996.
Idrīs, Suhayl. *Aqāṣīṣ thāniya*. Beirut: Dār al-ādāb, 1977.
———. *Mawāqif wa-qaḍāyā adabiyya*. Beirut: Dār al-ādāb, 1977.
Idrīs, Yūsuf. *Arkhaṣ layālī*. Cairo: Dār Rūz al-Yūsuf, 1954.
———. *Jumhūriyyat Faraḥāt*. Cairo: Dār Rūz al-Yūsuf, 1956.
———. *Qiṣṣat Ḥubb*. First published in *Jumhūriyyat Faraḥāt*. Reprinted under its own title, Cairo: Dār al-kātib al-ʿarabī, 1967.
———. *Ḥādithat sharaf*. Beirut: Dār-al-ādāb, 1958.
———. *Al-Ḥarām*. Cairo: Dār al-hilāl, 1959. *The Sinners*. Translated by Kristin Peterson-Ishaq. Washington, D.C.: Three Continents, 1984.
———. *Ākhir al-dunyā*. Cairo: Dār Rūz al-Yūsuf, 1961.
———. *Al-Farāfīr*. Cairo: Dār al-taḥrīr, 1964. *Flipflap and His Master*. Translated by Trevor Le Gassick. In *Arabic Writing Today: The Drama*, edited by Mahmoud Manzalaoui. Cairo: American Research Center in Egypt, 1977.
———. *Lughat al-āy āy*. 1965. Beirut: Dār al-ʿawda, 1977.
———. *Al-Naddāha*. Cairo: Dār al-hilāl, 1969.
———. *Anā sulṭān qānūn al-wujūd*. Cairo: Maktabat Gharīb, 1980.
———. *Uqtulhā*. Cairo: Maktabat Miṣr, 1982.
———. *The Cheapest Nights and Other Stories*. Translated by Wadida Wassef. Washington, D.C.: Three Continents, 1978.
———. *Al-Riwāyāt*. Beirut: Dār al-shurūq, 1987.
———. *Al-Qiṣaṣ al-qaṣīra*. 2 vols. Beirut: Dār al-shurūq, 1990–91.
———. *The Piper Dies and Other Stories*. Translated by Dalya Cohen-Mor. Potomac, Md.: Sheba, 1992.
al-Ikhtiyār, Najlā Naṣīb. *Taḥarrur al-marʾa ʿabra aʿmāl Sīmūn dū Būfwār wa-Ghāda al-Sammān*. Beirut: Dār al-ṭalīʿa, 1991.
ʿImāra, Muḥammad. *Tayyārāt al fikr al-islamī*. Cairo: Dār al-hilāl, 1982.
———. *Al-Muʿtazila wa-mushkilat al-ḥurriyya al-insāniyya*. Cairo: Dār al-shurūq, 1988.
Jabrā, Jabrā Ibrāhīm. *Al-Safīna*. Beirut: Dār al-nahār lil-nashr, 1970. *The Ship*. Translated by Adnan Haydar and Roger Allen. Washington, D.C.: Three Continents, 1985.
———. "Modern Arabic Literature and the West." *Journal of Arabic Literature* 2 (1971): 76–91.

———. "Min al-ḥulm ilā al-kābūs." *Al-Sharq* (Shfaram, Israel) 22, no. 4 (1992) : 20.
Jāmātī, Ḥabīb. *Ta'rīkh mā ahmalahu al-ta'rīkh*. A series of *c*. 15 vols. Cairo: Al-Dār al-qawmiyya lil-ṭibāʿa wa-al-nashr. Last publication *c*. 1964.
———. "Qātil wa-qatīl." *Qāfilat al-zayt* 7, no. 12 (1960): 23–25.
Jayyusi, Salma Khadra. "Contemporary Arabic Poetry: Vision and Attitudes." In *Studies in Modern Arabic Literature*, edited by R. C. Ostle. Warminster: Aris & Phillips, 1975.
———. *Trends and Movements in Modern Arabic Poetry*. Leiden: E. J. Brill, 1977.
———, ed. *Modern Arabic Poetry: An Anthology*. New York: Columbia University Press, 1987.
———, ed. *The Literature of Modern Arabia: An Anthology*. London: Kegan Paul International. 1988.
———, ed. *Anthology of Modern Palestinian Literature*. New York: Columbia University Press, 1992.
———, and Roger Allen, eds. *Modern Arabic Drama: An Anthology*. Bloomington: Indiana University Press, 1995.
Johnson, Samuel. *The History of Rasselas: Prince of Abissinia*. Edited by Geoffrey Tillotson and Brian Jenkins. London: Oxford University Press, 1971.
Johnson-Davies, Denys, ed. and trans. *Modern Arabic Short Stories*. London: Heinemann, 1981.
Kamāl, Iḥsān. *Saṭr maghlūṭ wa-qiṣaṣ ukhrā*. Cairo: Al-Hay'a al-miṣriyya al-ʿāmma lil-ta'līf wa-al-nashr, 1971.
Kanafānī, Ghassān. *ʿĀlam laysa lanā*. Beirut: Dār al-ṭalīʿa, 1965.
Kannūn, ʿAbdallāh. *Aḥādīth ʿan al-adab al-maghribī al-ḥadīth*. Cairo: Dār al-rā'id lil-ṭibāʿa, 1964.
Kardiner, Abram. *The Psychological Frontiers of Society*. New York: Columbia University Press, 1945.
———. *The Individual and His Society*. Westport, Conn.: Greenwood, 1974.
Karpat, Kemal H., ed. *Political and Social Thought in the Contemporary Middle East*. New York: Praeger, 1982.
Kassem, Ceza, and Malak Hashem, eds. *Flights of Fantasy: Arabic Short Stories*. Cairo: Elias, 1985.
Kassis, Hanna E. *A Concordance of the Qur'ān*. Berkeley: University of California Press, 1983.
Kaufmann, Walter, ed. *Existentialism from Dostoevsky to Sartre*. New York: New American Library, 1975.
Khadduri, Majid. *Political Trends in the Arab World*. Baltimore: The Johns Hopkins Press, 1970.
al-Kharrāṭ, Idwār. *Sāʿāt al-kibriyā'*. Beirut: Dār al-ādāb, 1972.
al-Khaṭīb, ʿAbd al-Karīm. *Al-Qaḍā' wa-al-qadar bayna al-falsafa wa-al-dīn*. Cairo: Dār al-fikr al-ʿarabī, 1979.
———. *Mashī'at Allāh wa-mashī'at al-ʿibād*. Riyadh: Dār al-liwā', 1980.
Khayyam, Omar. *The Ruba'iyat of Omar Khayyam*. Translated by Peter Avery and John Heath-Stubbs. Harmondsworth: Penguin, 1981.
Kheirallah, George, ed. and trans. *The Life of Gibran Khalil Gibran and His Procession*. New York: Arab–American, 1947.
Khouri, Mounah. "Al-Shābbī as a Romantic." *Mundus Arabicus* 2 (1982): 3–17.

———, and Hamid Algar, eds. and trans. *An Anthology of Modern Arabic Poetry*. Berkeley: University of California Press, 1974.

al-Kīlānī, Taysīr, and Naʿīm ʿĀshūr. *Muʿjam al-amthāl al-muqārana inklīzī–ʿarabī*. Beirut: Librairie du Liban, 1991.

Kluckhohn C., and H. A. Murray, eds. *Personality and Culture*. New York: Alfred A. Knopf, 1967.

Kritzeck, James, ed. *Anthology of Islamic Literature*. New York: Meridian, 1964.

Kupperman, Joel J. *Character*. London: Oxford University Press, 1991.

Kurpershoek, P. M. *The Short Stories of Yūsuf Idrīs: A Modern Egyptian Author*. Leiden: E. J. Brill, 1981.

Lammens, Henry. *Islam: Beliefs and Institutions*. Translated by E. Denison Ross. London: Frank Cass, 1968.

Landau, Jacob M. *Studies in the Arab Theater and Cinema*. Philadelphia: University of Pennsylvania Press, 1958.

Lane, Edward William. *An Arabic–English Lexicon*. 8 vols. Beirut: Librairie du Liban, 1980.

———, trans. *The Thousand and One Nights*. 3 vols. London: East–West, 1981.

———. *Manners and Customs of the Modern Eygptians*. London: East–West, 1989.

Laqueur, Walter Z. "The Appeal of Communism in the Middle East." *The Middle East Journal* 9, no. 1 (1955): 17–27.

Lāshīn, Maḥmūd Ṭāhir. *Yuḥkā anna*. Cairo: Maṭbaʿat al-ʿuṣūr, 1929.

Lazarus-Yafeh, Hava. *Studies in al-Ghazzālī*. Jerusalem: Magnes, Hebrew University, 1975.

Le Gassick, Trevor. "The Faith of Islam in Modern Arabic Fiction." *Religion and Literature* 20, no. 1 (1988): 97–109.

———, ed. *Critical Perspectives on Naguib Mahfouz*. Washington, D.C.: Three Continents, 1991.

Levy, Reuben. *The Social Structure of Islam*. Cambridge: Cambridge University Press, 1957.

Lewis, Bernard. "Communism and Islam." *International Affairs* 30, no. 1 (1954): 1–12.

———. *The Arabs in History*. New York: Harper & Row, 1967.

———. *The Political Language of Islam*. Chicago: University of Chicago Press, 1988.

———. *Islam in History: Ideas, People, and Events in the Middle East*. 2d ed. Chicago: Open Court, 1993.

———. *Islam and the West*. New York: Oxford University Press, 1993.

Lichtheim, George. "Freud and Marx." In *Freud: The Man, His World, His Influence*, edited by Jonathan Miller. Boston: Little, Brown, 1972.

al-Maʿarrī, Abū al-ʿAlāʾ. *The Quatrains of Abu'l-Ala*. Selected and translated by Ameen F. Rihani. New York: Doubleday, Page, 1903.

Macdonald, D. B. *Development of Muslim Theology, Jurisprudence, and Constitutional Theory*. New York: Charles Scribner's Sons, 1903.

———. *The Religious Attitude and Life in Islam*. Beirut: Khayats, 1965.

———. "Ḳadar." In *First Encyclopaedia of Islam*. 1913–1938. Reprint, Leiden: E. J. Brill, 1987.

al-Maḥallī, Jalāl al-Dīn Muḥammad Ibn Aḥmad, and Jalāl al-Dīn ʿAbd al-Raḥmān Ibn Abī Bakr al-Suyūṭī. *Tafsīr al-Jalālayan*. Edited by Marwān Sawwār. Beirut: Dār al-maʿrifa, n.d.

Maḥfūẓ, Najīb. *Zuqāq al-Midaqq*. 1947. Cairo: Maktabat Miṣr, 1961. *Midaq Alley*. Translated by Trevor Le Gassick. Washington, D.C.: Three Continents, 1977.

———. *Bidāya wa-nihāya*. Cairo: Maktabat Miṣr, 1949. *The Beginning and the End*. Translated by Ramses Hanna Awad. Edited by Mason Rossiter Smith. Cairo: American University in Cairo Press, 1985.

———. *Al-Thulāthiyya*. 3 vols. Vol. 1, *Bayna al-qaṣrayn*. Cairo: Maktabat Miṣr, 1956. Vol. 2, *Qaṣr al-shawq*. Cairo: Maktabat Miṣr, 1957. Vol. 3, *Al-Sukkariyya*. Cairo: Maktabat Miṣr, 1957.

———. *The Trilogy*. Vol. 1, *Palace Walk*. Translated by William Maynard Hutchins and Olive E. Kenny. New York: Doubleday, 1990. Vol. 2, *Palace of Desire*. Translated by William Maynard Hutchins, Lorne M. Kenny, and Olive E. Kenny. New York: Doubleday, 1991. Vol. 3, *Sugar Street*. Translated by William Maynard Hutchins and Angele Botros Samaan. New York: Doubleday, 1992.

———. *Awlād ḥāratinā*. Serialized in *al-Ahrām* in 1959. Published in book form, Beirut: Dār al-ādāb, 1967. *Children of Gebelawi*. Translated by Philip Stewart. London: Heinemann, 1981.

———. *Al-Liṣṣ wa-al-kilāb*. Cairo: Maktabat Miṣr, 1961. *The Thief and the Dogs*. Translated by Trevor Le Gassick and M. M. Badawi. Revised by John Rodenbeck. Cairo: American University in Cairo Press, 1984.

———. *Al-Summān wa-al-kharīf*. Cairo: Maktabat Miṣr, 1962. *Autumn Quail*. Translated by Roger Allen. Revised by John Rodenbeck. Cairo: American University in Cairo Press, 1985.

———. *Dunyā Allāh*. Cairo: Maktabat Miṣr, 1963.

———. *Al-Shaḥḥādh*. 1965. Cairo: Maktabat Miṣr, 1976. *The Beggar*. Translated by Kristin Walker Henry and Nariman Khales Naili al-Warraki. New York: Anchor, 1990.

———. *Mīrāmār*. Cairo: Maktabat Miṣr, 1967. *Miramar*. Translated by Fatma Moussa-Mahmoud. Introduced by John Fowles. Washington, D.C.: Three Continents, 1983.

———. *Khammārat al-qiṭṭ al-aswad*. Cairo: Maktabat Miṣr, 1968.

———. *Taḥta al-miẓalla*. Cairo: Maktabat Miṣr, 1969.

———. *Al-Ḥubb taḥta al-maṭar*. 1973. Cairo: Maktabat Miṣr, 1975.

———. *God's World: An Anthology of Short Stories*. Translated by Akef Abadir and Roger Allen. Minneapolis: Bibliotheca Islamica, 1973.

———. *Ataḥaddath Ilaykum*. Edited by Ṣabrī Ḥāfiẓ. Beirut: Dār al-ʿawda, 1977.

———. *Afrāḥ al-qubba*. Cairo: Maktabat Miṣr, 1981. *Wedding Song*. Translated by Olive E. Kenny. Edited and revised by Mursi Saad El Din and John Rodenbeck. Cairo: American University in Cairo Press, 1984.

———. *Aṣdā' al-sīra al-dhātiyya*. Cairo: Maktabat Miṣr, 1995. *Echoes of an Autobiography*. Translated by Denys Johnson-Davies. American University in Cairo Press, 1997.

Makarius, Raoul. *Anthologie de la littérature arabe contemporaine: Le roman et la nouvelle*. Préface de Jacques Berque. Paris: Editions du Seuil, 1964.

al-Malā'ika, Nāzik. *Shaẓāyā wa-rāmad*. Baghdad: Maṭbaʿat al-maʿrif, 1949.

———. *Qarārat al-mawja*. Beirut: Dār al-ādāb, 1957.

———. *Shajarat al-qamar*. Beirut: Dār al-ʿilm lil-malāyīn,1968.

Malti-Douglas, Fedwa. *Blindness and Autobiography: Al-Ayyām of Ṭāhā Ḥusayn*. Princeton, N.J.: Princeton University Press, 1988.

———. *Woman's Body, Woman's Word: Gender and Discourse in Arabo-Islamic Writing*. Princeton, N.J.: Princeton University Press, 1991.

———. *Men, Women, and God(s): Nawal El Saadawi and Arab Feminist Poetics*. Berkeley: University of California Press, 1995.

Manṣūr, Anīs. "Hal naʿūd ila al-falsafa al-wujūdiyya?" *Al-Sharq* (Shfaram, Israel) 20, no. 2 (1990): 51–59.

Manzalaoui, Mahmoud, ed. *Arabic Writing Today: The Short Story*. Cairo: American Research Center in Egypt, 1968.

———, ed. *Arabic Writing Today: The Drama*. Cairo: American Research Center in Egypt, 1977.

Ma'oz, Moshe. *Asad, the Sphinx of Damascus: A Political Biography*. New York: Grove Weidenfeld, 1988.

Marār, Muṣṭafā. *Damʿ wa-ramād*. Jerusalem: Majallat al-sharq, 1974.

Martin, A. S. "Predestination." In *Enyclopaedia of Religion and Ethics*. Edinburgh: T. & T. Clark, 1808–26.

Marx, Karl. *Capital*. Edited by Friedrich Engels. New York: International Publishers, 1967.

———. *A Contribution to the Critique of Political Economy*. New York: International Publishers, 1970.

———. *The Communist Manifesto*. Edited by F. L. Bender. New York: W. W. Norton, 1988.

al-Maydānī, Aḥmad Ibn Ibrāhīm. *Majmaʿ al-amthāl*. Edited by Naʿīm Ḥusayn Zarzūr. Beirut: Dār al-kutub al-ʿilmiyya, 1988.

Mernissi, Fatima. *Beyond the Veil: Male-Female Dynamics in a Modern Muslim Society*. Cambridge, Mass.: Schenkman, 1975.

———. "Virginity and Patriarchy." In *Women and Islam*, edited by Azizah al-Hibri. Oxford: Pergamon, 1982.

———. *Doing Daily Battle: Interviews with Moroccan Women*. Translated by Mary Jo Lakeland. New Brunswick, N.J.: Rutgers University Press, 1989.

———. *The Veil and The Male Elite*. Translated by Mary Jo Lakeland. Reading, Mass.: Addison-Wesley, 1991.

———. *Women's Rebellion and Islamic Memory*. London: Zed, 1996.

Mikhail, Mona N. *Studies in the Short Fiction of Mahfouz and Idris*. New York: New York University Press, 1992.

Mill, John Stuart. *On Liberty and Other Essays*. Edited by John Gray. London: Oxford University Press, 1991.

Milson, Menahem. *Najīb Maḥfūẓ: The Novelist-Philosopher of Cairo*. New York: St. Martin's, 1998.

Minces, Juliette. *Veiled: Women in Islam*. Translated by S. M. Berrett. Watertown, Mass.: Blue Crane, 1994.

Mitchell, Richard P. *The Society of the Muslim Brothers*. New York: Oxford University Press, 1993.

Monteil, Vincent, ed. *Anthologie bilingue de la littérature arabe contemporaine*. Beirut: Imprimerie Catholique, 1961.

Moosa, Matti. *The Origins of Modern Arabic Fiction*. 2d ed. Boulder, Colo.: Lynne Rienner, 1997.

Moreh, Shmuel. *Modern Arabic Poetry: 1800–1970*. Leiden: E. J. Brill, 1976.

———. "The Shadow Play (*khayāl al-ẓill*) in the Light of Arabic Literature." *Journal of Arabic Literature* 18 (1987): 46–61.

———. *Live Theater and Dramatic Literature in the Medieval Arab World.* New York: New York University Press, 1992.

———, ed. and trans. *Al-Jabartī's Chronicle of the First Seven Months of the French Occupation of Egypt.* Leiden: E. J. Brill, 1975.

Moughrabi, Fouad M. "The Arab Basic Personality: A Critical Survey of the Literature." *International Journal of Middle East Studies* 9 (1978): 99–112.

Moussalli, Ahmad S. *Radical Islamic Fundamentalism: The Ideological and Political Discourse of Sayyid Quṭb.* Beirut: American University of Beirut Press, 1992.

Moussa-Mahmoud, Fatma. *The Arabic Novel in Egypt: 1914–1970.* Cairo: General Egyptian Book Organization, 1973.

Nagy, Gy. Kaldy. "Ḳaḍāʾ." In *The Encyclopaedia of Islam.* New ed. Leiden: E. J. Brill, 1960–.

Naimy, Mikhail. *Al-Ghirbāl.* 1923. Beirut: Dār Sādir, 1964.

———. *Kāna mā kāna.* Beirut: Maṭbaʿat al-ittiḥād, 1937.

———. *Hams al-jufūn.* 1945. Beirut: Dār Ṣādir, 1962.

———. *A New Year: Stories, Autobiography, and Poems.* Edited and translated by J. R. Perry. Leiden: E. J. Brill, 1974.

Nājī, Ibrāhīm. *Layālī al-Qāhira.* Beirut: Dār al-ʿawda, 1979.

Nājī, Sawsan. *Ṣūrat al-rajul fī al-qaṣaṣ al-nisāʾī.* Cairo: Wikālat al-Ahrām lil-nashr wa-al-tawzīʿ, 1995.

Nasr, Ahmad A. "Popular Islam in al-Ṭayyib Ṣāliḥ." *Journal of Arabic Literature* 11 (1980): 88–104.

Naṣr, Ḥasan. *Layālī al-maṭar.* Tunis: Al-Dār al-tūnisiyya lil-nashr, 1968.

al-Nassāj, Sayyid Ḥāmid. *Al-Adab al-ʿarabī al-muʿāṣir fī al-Maghrib al-aqṣā.* Cairo: Al-Hayʾa al-miṣriyya al-ʿāmma lil-kitāb, 1985.

Netton, Ian R. *Muslim Neoplatonists.* Edinburgh: Edinburgh University Press, 1991.

Nicholson, Reynold A. *The Mystics of Islam.* London: Routledge & Kegan Paul, 1975.

———. *A Literary History of the Arabs.* Cambridge: Cambridge University Press, 1976.

———. *Studies in Islamic Mysticism.* Richmond, Surrey: Curzon, 1994.

Nijland, C. *Mikhāʾīl Nuʿaymah: Promoter of the Arabic Literary Revival.* Istanbul: Nederlands Historisch-Archaeologisch Instituut, 1975.

Nöldeke, Theodor. "Arabs (Ancient)." In *Encyclopaedia of Religion and Ethics.* Edinburgh: T. & T. Clark, 1908–26.

Ostle, R. C., ed. *Studies in Modern Arabic Literature.* Warminster, U.K.: Aris & Phillips, 1975.

———, ed. *Modern Literature in the Near and Middle East: 1850–1970.* London: Routledge, 1991.

Pantuček, Svetozar. *Tunesische Literaturgeschichte.* Wiesbaden: Otto Harrassowitz, 1974.

Patai, Raphael. "The Middle East as a Culture Area." *The Middle East Journal* 6, no. 1 (1952): 1–21.

———. "The Dynamics of Westernization in the Middle East." *The Middle East Journal* 9, no. 1 (1955): 1–16.

———. *The Arab Mind.* New York: Charles Scribner's Sons, 1983.

Peled, Mattityahu. *Religion, My Own: The Literary Works of Najīb Maḥfūẓ.* New Brunswick, N.J.: Transaction, 1983.

———. *Aspects of Modern Arabic Literature*. Louvain: Peeters, 1988.

Peristiany, Jean G., ed. *Honor and Shame: The Values of Mediterranean Society*. Chicago: University of Chicago Press, 1966.

Philipp, Thomas. *Gurgī Zaidān: His Life and Thought*. Beirut: Orient-Institut der Deutschen Morgenlandischen Gesellschaft, 1979.

———, ed. and trans. *The Autobiography of Jurjī Zaidān*. Washington, D.C.: Three Continents, 1990.

Piamenta, Moshe. *Islam in Everyday Arabic Speech*. Leiden: E. J. Brill, 1979.

Pickthall, Mohammed Marmaduke. *The Meaning of the Glorious Koran: An Explanatory Translation*. New York: New American Library, 1953.

Pierce, Edgar. *The Philosophy of Character*. Cambridge, Mass.: Harvard University Press, 1924.

Piselli, Kathyanne. *A Daughter of Palestine: The Short Fiction of Samirah Azzam*. Ann Arbor, Mich.: University Microfilms, 1986.

Prüfer, Curt. "Drama (Arabic)." In *Encyclopaedia of Religion and Ethics*. Edinburgh: T. & T. Clark, 1908–26.

Pryce-Jones, David. *The Closed Circle: An Interpretation of the Arabs*. New York: Harper & Row, 1989.

———. *At War with Modernity: Islam's Challenge to the West*. London: Alliance Publishers for the Institute for European Defence and Strategic Studies, 1992.

Qabbānī, Nizār. *Qaṣā'id*. Beirut: Manshūrāt Nizār Qabbānī, 1967.

———. *Al-A'māl al-kāmila*. 8 vols. Beirut: Manshūrāt Nizār Qabbānī, 1993.

Qadir, C. A. *Philosophy and Science in the Islamic World*. London: Routledge, 1990.

al-Qa'īd, Yūsuf. *Akhbār 'izbat al-Manīsī*. Cairo: Al-Hay'a al-miṣriyya al-'āmma lil-kitāb, 1971. *News from the Meneisi Farm*. Translated by Marie-Therese F. Abdel-Messih. Cairo: General Egyptian Book Organization, 1987.

———. *Yaḥduth fī Miṣr al-ān*. Cairo: Maṭba'at dār Usāma, 1977.

———. *Al-Ḥarb fī barr Miṣr*. 1978. Cairo: Dār al-Qāhira lil-nashr wa-al-tawzī', 1985. *War in the Land of Egypt*. Translated by Olive and Lorne Kenny and Christopher Tingley. London: Saqi, 1986.

———. *Al-A'māl al-kāmila*. 6 vols. Cairo: Al-Hay'a al-miṣriyya al-'āmma lil-kitāb, 1990–95.

Qāsim, 'Adb al-Ḥakīm. *Ayyām al-insān al-sab'a*. Cairo: Dār al-kātib al-'arabī lil-ṭibā'a wa-al-nashr, 1969. *The Seven Days of Man*. Translated by Joseph Norment Bell. Evanston, Ill.: Northwestern University Press, 1996.

al-Qaṣīmī, 'Abdallāh 'Alī. *Hādhī hiya al-aghlāl*. Cairo: Dār Miṣr lil-ṭibā'a, 1994.

Quṭb, Sayyid. *Fī ẓilāl al-Qur'ān*. Beirut: Dār iḥyā' al-turāth al-'arabī, 1961.

———. *Social Justice in Islam*. Translated by John B. Hardie. New York: Octagon, 1970.

———. *Milestones*. Translated by S. Badrul Hasan. Karachi: International Islamic, 1981.

al-Quṭṭ, 'Abd al-Ḥāmid 'Abd al-'Aẓīm. *Yūsuf Idrīs wa-al-fann al qaṣaṣī*. Cairo: Dār al-ma'ārif, 1980.

Rabī', Mubārak. *Sayyidunā Qadr*. Rabat: Maktabat al-ma'ārif, 1969.

———. *Makhāwif al-atfāl wa-'alāqatuhā bi-al-wasaṭ al-ijtimā'ī*. Rabat: Jāmi'at Muḥammad al-Khāmis, 1991.

Rahman, Afzalur. *Economic Doctrines of Islam*. Vols. 1-3. Lahore: Islamic Publications, 1974. Vol. 4. London: Muslim Schools Trust, 1979.

Rahman, Fazlur. *Major Themes of the Qur'ān*. Minneapolis: Bibliotheca Islamica, 1994.

Reid, Donald M. *The Odyssey of Faraḥ Anṭūn*. Minneapolis: Bibliotheca Islamica, 1975.

Rifʿat, Alīfa. *Man yakūn al-rajul?* Cairo: Al-Markaz al-qawmī lil-funūn wa-al-ādāb, 1981.

———. *Fī layl al-shitā' al-ṭawīl*. Cairo: Maṭbaʿat al-ʿāṣima, 1985.

———. *Distant View of a Minaret and Other Stories*. Translated by Denys Johnson-Davies. London: Heinemann, 1987.

Ringgren, Helmer. *Studies in Arabian Fatalism*. Uppsala: Lundequistska Bokhandeln, 1955.

———, ed. *Fatalistic Beliefs in Religion, Folklore, and Literature*. Stockholm: Almqvist & Wiksells, 1967.

Roback, A. A. *The Psychology of Character*. New York: Harcourt, Brace, 1931.

Roberts, Robert. *The Social Laws of the Qur'ān*. London: Curzon, 1990.

Rodwell, J. M., trans. *The Koran*. London: Everyman Library, 1994.

Ṣabrī, Ismāʿīl. *Dīwān Ismāʿīl Ṣabrī Bāshā*. Edited by Aḥmad al-Zayn and Ḥasan Rifʿat Bey. Cairo: Maṭbaʿat lajnat al-ta'līf wa-al-tarjama wa-al-nashr, 1938.

al-Saʿdāwī, Nawāl. *Ḥanān qalīl*. Cairo: Dār Rūz al-Yūsuf, 1962.

———. *Mudhakkirāt ṭabība*. Cairo: Dār al-maʿārif, 1965. *Memoirs of a Woman Doctor*. Translated by Catherine Cobham. San Francisco: City Lights, 1989.

———. *Al-Mar'a wa-al-jins*. Beirut: Al-Mu'assasa al-ʿarabiyya lil-dirāsāt wa-al-nashr, 1971.

———. *Imra'atān fī imra'a*. Beirut: Dār al-ādāb, 1975. *Two Women in One*. Translated by Osman Nusairi and Jana Gough. London: Saqi, 1985.

———. *Mawt al-rajul al-waḥīd ʿalā al-arḍ*. Beirut: Dār al-ādāb, 1976. *God Dies by the Nile*. Translated by Sherif Hetata. London: Zed, 1985.

———. *Imra'a ʿinda nuqṭat al-ṣifr*. Beirut: Dār al-ādāb, 1977. *Woman at Point Zero*. Translated by Sherif Hetata. London: Zed, 1983.

——. *Al-Wajh al-ʿārī lil-mar'a al-ʿarabiyya*. Beirut: Al-Mu'assasa al-ʿarabiyya lil-dirāsāt wa-al-nashr, 1977. *The Hidden Face of Eve: Women in the Arab World*. Translated by Sherif Hetata. Boston: Beacon, 1982.

———. *Kānat hiya al-aḍʿaf*. Beirut: Dār al-ādāb, 1979.

Said, Edward W. *Orientalism*. New York: Vintage, 1979.

Saʿīd, Khālida. *Al-Mar'a, al-taḥarrur, al-ibdāʿ*. Casablanca: Nashr al-fanak, 1991.

Sakkūt, Ḥamdī. *The Egptian Novel and Its Main Trends 1913–1952*. Cairo: American University in Cairo Press, 1971.

———. "Naguib Mahfouz and the Sufi Way." In *The View from Within: Writers and Critics on Contemporary Arabic Literature*, edited by Ferial J. Ghazoul and Barbara Harlow. Cairo: American University in Cairo Press, 1994.

Ṣāliḥ, al-Ṭayyib. *Mawsim al-hijra ilā al-shimāl*. Beirut: Dār al-ʿawda, 1966. *Season of Migration to the North*. Translated by Denys Johnson-Davies. London: Heinemann, 1969.

———. *ʿUrs al-Zayn*. Beirut: Dār al-ʿawda, 1967.

———. *Dawmat Wad Ḥāmid*. Beirut: Dār al-ʿawda, 1967.

———. *The Wedding of Zein and Other Stories*. Translated by Denys Johnson-Davies. London: Heinemann, 1968.

Salisbury, Edward E. "Materials for the History of the Muhammadan Doctrine of

Predestination and Free Will: Compiled from Original Sources." *Journal of the American Oriental Society* 8 (1866): 105–82.
al-Sammān, Ghāda. *Layl al-ghurabā'*. Beirut: Dār al-ādāb, 1966.
———. "Al-Thawra al-jinsiyya wa-al-thawra al-kāmila." *Mawāqif* 2, no. 12 (1970): 68–73.
al-Saqqāf, Khayriyya. *An tubḥir naḥwa al-ab'ad*. Riyadh: Dār al-'ulūm lil-ṭibā'a wa-al-nashr, 1982.
al-Sayyāb, Badr Shākir. *Dīwān Badr Shākir al-Sayyāb*. 2 vols. Beirut: Dār al-'awda, 1986.
Schacht, Joseph, and C. E. Bosworth, eds. *The Legacy of Islam*. Oxford: Oxford University Press, 1979.
Schacht, Richard. *Alienation*. Lanham, Md.: University Press of America, 1984.
Schimmel, Annemarie. *Mystical Dimensions of Islam*. Chapel Hill: University of North Carolina Press, 1975.
Semah, David. *Four Egyptian Literary Critics*. Leiden: Brill, 1974.
Shaaban, Bouthaina. *Both Right and Left-Handed: Arab Women Talk about Their Lives*. London: Women's Press, 1988.
al-Shābbī, Abū al-Qāsim. *Aghānī al-ḥayāh*. Cairo: Dār al-kutub al-sharqiyya, 1955.
Shaheen, Mohammad. *The Modern Arabic Short Story: Shahrazad Returns*. London: Macmillan, 1989.
Sharabi, Hisham. *Arab Intellectuals and the West: The Formative Years 1875–1914*. Baltimore: Johns Hopkins University Press, 1970.
———. *Muqaddimāt li-dirāsat al-mujtama' al-'arabī*. Acre: Dār al-aswār, 1987.
———. *Neopatriarchy: A Theory of Distorted Change in Arab Society*. New York: Oxford University Press, 1988.
———, in collaboration with Mukhtar Ani. "Impact of Class and Culture on Social Behavior: The Feudal-Bourgeois Family in Arab Society." In *Psychological Dimensions of Near Eastern Studies*, edited by L. Carl Brown and Norman Itzkowitz. Princeton, N.J.: Darwin, 1977.
al-Sharqāwī, 'Abd al-Raḥmān. *Al-Arḍ*. 1954. Cairo: Dār al-sha'b, 1970. *Egyptian Earth*. Translated by Desmond Stewart. London: Heinemann, 1962.
———. *Aḥlām ṣaghīra*. Cairo: Hay'at al-kuttāb, 1956. Reprinted in *Mu'allafāt 'Abd al-Raḥmān al-Sharqāwī*. Vol. 1. Cairo: Al-Hay'a al-miṣriyya al-'āmma lil-kitāb, 1978.
———. *Muḥammad rasūl al-ḥurriyya*. Cairo: 'Ālam al-kutub, 1962.
al-Shārūnī, Yūsuf. *Muṭāradat muntaṣaf al-layl*. Cairo: Dār al-ma'ārif, 1973.
———. *Al-Umm wa-al-waḥsh*. Cairo: Dār Mājid lil-ṭibā'a, 1982.
———. *Blood Feud: Short Stories*. Translated by Denys Johnson-Davies. London: Heinemann, 1984.
——. *Ma'a al-qiṣṣa al-qaṣīra*. Cairo: Al-Hay'a al-miṣriyya al-'āmma lil-kitāb, 1985.
al-Shaykh, Ḥanān. *Ḥikāyat Zahra*. Beirut: Dār al-nahār, 1980. *The Story of Zahra*. Translated by Peter Ford. London: Quartet, 1986.
Sheikh, M. Saeed. *Islamic Philosophy*. London: Octagon, 1982.
Sherif, Mohamed Ahmed. *Ghazālī's Theory of Virtue*. Albany: State University of New York Press, 1975.
Shubayl, 'Abd al-'Azīz. *Al-Fann al-riwā'ī 'inda Ghāda al-Sammān*. Tunis: Dār al-ma'ārif, 1987.

Shukrī, Ghālī. *Ghāda al-Sammān bi-lā ajniḥa*. Beirut: Dār al-ṭalīʿa, 1977.
Shukrī, Muḥammad. *Al-khubz al-ḥāfī*. London: Saqi, 1982. *For Bread Alone*. Translated by Paul Bowles. 1973. 2d ed. San Francisco: City Lights, 1987.
Siddiq, Muhammad. *Man Is a Cause: Political Consciousness and the Fiction of Ghassān Kanafānī*. Seattle: University of Washington Press, 1984.
Sivan, Emmanuel. *Interpretations of Islam: Past and Present*. Princeton, N.J.: Darwin, 1985.
———. *Radical Islam: Medieval Theology and Modern Politics*. New Haven: Yale University Press, 1985.
———, and Menachem Friedman, eds. *Religious Radicalism and Politics in the Middle East*. Albany: State University of New York Press, 1990.
Somekh, Sasson. "Zaʿbalāwī: Author, Theme, Technique." *Journal of Arabic Literature* 1 (1970): 24–35.
———. *The Changing Rhythm: A Study of Najīb Maḥfūẓ's Novels*. Leiden: E. J. Brill, 1973.
———. *Mabnā al-qiṣṣa wa-mabnā al-masraḥiyya fī adab Yūsuf Idrīs*. Acre: Maṭbaʿat al-Sarūjī, 1981.
———. *Genre and Language in Modern Arabic Literature*. Wiesbaden: Otto Harrassowitz, 1991.
Sowell, Thomas. *Marxism: Philosophy and Economics*. New York: William Morrow, 1985.
Starkey, Paul. *From the Ivory Tower: A Critical Study of Tawfīq al-Ḥakīm*. London: Ithaca, 1987.
———. "From the City of the Dead to Liberation Square: The Novels of Yūsuf al-Qaʿīd." *Journal of Arabic Literature* 24, pt. 1 (1993): 62–74.
———, and Julie Scott Meisami, eds. *Encyclopedia of Arabic Literature*. New York: Routledge, 1998.
Stone, I. F. *The Trial of Socrates*. New York: Doubleday, 1989.
Stowasser, Barbara Freyer. *Women in the Qurʾān, Traditions, and Interpretation*. New York: Oxford University Press, 1994.
al-Suhrawardy, Abdullah al-Mamun. *The Sayings of Muhammad*. New York: Carol, 1990.
al-Ṭabarī, Abū Jaʿfar Muḥammad Ibn Jarīr. *Jāmiʿ al-bayān ʿan taʾwīl āy al-Ourʾān*, 2d ed. 30 vols. Cairo: Maktabat Muṣṭafā al-Bābī al-Ḥalabī, 1954.
al-Ṭāhir, ʿAlī Jawād. *Fī al-qaṣaṣ al-ʿirāqī al-muʿāṣir: naqd wa-mukhtārāt*. Beirut: Manshūrāt dār al-maktaba al-ʿaṣriyya, 1967.
al-Takarlī, Fuʾād. *Al-Wajh al-ākhar*. 2d ed. Baghdad: Manshūrāt wizārat al-thaqāfa wa-al-iʿlām, 1982.
Tāmir, Zakariyyā. *Al-Raʿd*. Damascus: Manshūrāt ittiḥād al-kuttāb al-ʿarab, 1970.
———. *Rabīʿ fī al-ramād*. Damascus: Wizārat al-thaqāfa wa-al-irshād al-qawmī, 1973.
———. *Al-Numūr fī al-yawm al-ʿāshir*. Beirut: Dār al-ādāb, 1978.
———. *Tigers on the Tenth Day and Other Stories*. Translated by Denys Johnson-Davies. London: Quartet, 1985.
———. *Nidāʾ Nūḥ*. London: Riad El-Rayyes, 1994.
Tarabishi, Georges. *Woman against Her Sex: A Critique of Nawal el-Saadawi with a Reply by Nawal el-Saadawi*. Translated by Basil Hatim and Elizabeth Orsini. London: Saqi, 1988.

Tawfīq, Najīb. *Ismāʿīl Ṣabrī Bāshā: Shaykh al-shuʿarāʾ.* Cairo: Al-Hayʾa al-miṣriyya al-ʿāmma lil-kitāb, 1985.

Taymūr, Aḥmad. *Al-Amthāl al-ʿāmmiyya.* 4th ed. Cairo: Markaz al-Ahrām lil-tarjama wa-al-nashr, 1986.

Taymūr, Maḥmūd. *Al-Shaykh Jumʿa wa-qiṣaṣ ukhrā.* Cairo: Al-Maṭbaʿa al-salafiyya, 1925.

Tillion, Germaine. *The Republic of Cousins: Women's Oppression in Mediterranean Society.* Translated by Quintin Hoare. London: Saqi, 1983.

Tucker, Judith E., ed. *Arab Women: Old Boundaries, New Frontiers.* Bloomington: Indiana University Press, *c.* 1993.

Ṭūqān, Fadwā. *Dīwān Fadwā Ṭūqān.* Beirut: Dār al-ʿawda, 1978.

———. *Selected Poems of Fadwā Ṭūqān.* Translated by Ibrahim Dawood. Irbid, Jordan: Yarmouk University Publications, 1994.

Tylor, Edward Burnett. *The Origins of Culture.* Gloucester, Mass.: Peter Smith, 1970.

al-ʿUsaylī, Thurayyā. *Adab ʿAbd al-Raḥmān al-Sharqāwī.* Cairo: Al-Hayʾa al-miṣriyya al-ʿāmma lil-kitāb, 1995.

ʿUthmān, Iʿtidāl, ed. *Yūsuf Idrīs: 1927–1991.* Cairo: Al-Hayʾa al-miṣriyya al-ʿāmma lil-kitāb, 1991.

Vatikiotis, P. J. *The History of Modern Egypt: From Muhammad Ali to Mubarak.* Baltimore: Johns Hopkins University Press, 1991.

Vaux, Carra de. "Fate (Muslim)." In *Encyclopaedia of Religion and Ethics.* Edinburgh: T. & T. Clark, 1908–26.

Voogd, Lourina de, ed. *Literatuur in Marokko en andere Arabische landen.* Den Haag: Nederlands Bibliotheek en Lektuur Centrum, 1984.

Walzer, Richard. *Greek into Arabic: Essays on Islamic Philosophy.* Cambridge, Mass.: Harvard University Press, 1962.

Watt, W. Montgomery. *Free Will and Predestination in Early Islam.* London: Luzac, 1948.

———. *Muḥammad at Mecca.* London: Clarendon, 1953.

——. "Dahr." In *The Encyclopaedia of Islam.* New ed. Leiden: E. J. Brill, 1960–.

——. *Bell's Introduction to the Qurʾān.* Edinburgh: Edinburgh University Press, 1970.

——. *Islamic Philosophy and Theology: An Extended Survey.* Edinburgh: Edinburgh University Press, 1985.

——. "Free Will and Predestination (Islamic Concept)." In *The Encyclopedia of Religion.* New York: Macmillan, 1987.

——. *Islamic Fundamentalism and Modernity.* London: Routledge, 1988.

——, trans. *The Faith and Practice of al-Ghazālī.* Oxford: Oneworld, 1994.

——. *The Formative Period of Islamic Thought.* Oxford: Oneworld, 1998.

Weber, Max. *The Sociology of Religion.* Translated by Ephraim Fischoff. Boston: Beacon, 1993.

Wehr, Hans. *A Dictionary of Modern Written Arabic.* Edited by J. Milton Cowan. 4th ed. Ithaca, N.Y.: Spoken Languages Services, 1994.

Wensinck, A. J. *The Muslim Creed.* Cambridge: Cambridge University Press, 1932.

Westermarck, Edward. *The Origin and Development of the Moral Ideas.* 2 vols. London: Macmillan, 1906–8.

——. *Pagan Survivals in Mohammedan Civilisation.* Amsterdam: Philo, 1973.

White, Leslie A. "The Concept of Culture." *American Anthropologist* 61, no. 2 (1959): 227–51.

Wundt, Wilhelm Max. *Ethics: An Investigation of the Facts and Laws of the Moral Life*. 3 vols. London: Swan Sonnenschein, 1908.

Young, M. J. L., J. D. Latham, and R. B. Serjeant, eds. *Religion, Learning and Science in the ʿAbbasid period*. Cambridge: Cambridge University Press, 1990.

Yusa, Michiko. "Chance." In *The Encyclopedia of Religion*. New York: Macmillan, 1987.

Zaydān, Jurjī. *Mudhakkirāt Jurjī Zaydān*. Edited by Ṣalāḥ al-Dīn al-Munajjid. Beirut, 1966.

——. *Muʾallafāt Jurjī Zaydān al-kāmila*. 20 vols. Beirut: Dār al-jīl, 1982.

——. *The Autobiography of Jurji Zaidan*. Edited and translated by Thomas Philipp. Washington, D.C.: Three Continents, 1990.

Zeidan, Joseph T. *Arab Women Novelists: The Formative Years and Beyond*. Albany: State University of New York Press, 1995.

———. *Maṣādir al-adab al-nisāʾī fī al-ʿālam al-ʿarabī al-ḥadīth 1800–1996*. Beirut: Al-Muʾassasa al-ʿarabiyya lil-dirāsāt wa-al-nashr, 1999.

al-Ziriklī, Khayr al-Dīn. *Al-Aʿlām: qāmūs tarājim li-ashhar al-rijāl wa-al-nisāʾ min al-ʿarab wa-al-mustaʿribīn wa-al-mustashriqīn*. 8 vols. Beirut: Dār al-ʿilm lil-malāyīn, 1998.

Zwemer, Samuel M. *The Moslem Doctrine of God*. 1905. London: Darf, 1987.

——. *The Influence of Animism on Islam*. New York: Macmillan, 1920.

PERMISSIONS

Maḥmūd Ṭāhir Lāshīn, "The Village Tale," from *Yuḥkā anna*. Cairo: Maṭbaʿat al-ʿuṣūr, 1929. Permission to translate granted by the publisher.

Mubārak Rabīʿ, "Our Lord Qadr," from *Sayyidunā Qadr*. Rabat: Maktabat al-maʿārif, 1969. Permission to translate granted by the author.

Najīb Maḥfūẓ, "An Old Picture," from *Dunyā Allāh*. Cairo: Maktabat Miṣr, 1963. Permission to translate granted by the American University in Cairo Press.

Ghassān Kanafānī, "The Viper Is Thirsty," from *ʿĀlam laysa lanā*. Beirut: Dār al-ṭalīʿa, 1965. Permission to translate granted by the publisher.

Maḥmūd Taymūr, "The Would-Be Traveler," from *Al-Shaykh Jumʿa wa-qiṣaṣ ukhrā*. Cairo: Al-Maṭbaʿa al-salafiyya, 1925. Permission to translate granted by the publisher.

Yūsuf Idrīs, "The Sunken Mattress," from *Al-Naddāha*. Cairo: Dār al-hilāl, 1969. Permission to translate granted by the author.

Ḥabīb Jāmātī, "Blood Feud," from *Qāfilat al-zayt* 7, no. 12 (1960). Permission to translate granted by the publisher.

Zakariyyā Tāmir, "The Beards," from *Al-Raʿd*. Damascus: Manshūrāt ittiḥād al-kuttāb al-ʿarab, 1970. Permission to translate granted by the author.

Nawāl al-Saʿdāwī, "She Is Not a Virgin," from *Ḥanān qalīl*. Cairo: Dār Rūz al-Yūsuf, 1962. Permission to translate granted by the author.

Samīra ʿAzzām, "Fate," from *Al-Ẓill al-kabīr*. Beirut: Dār al-sharq al-jadīd, 1956. Translated by Yasir Suleiman and first published in *Journal of Arabic Literature* 19, pt. 2 (1988). Reprinted by permission of E. J. Brill Publishing House in Leiden.

ʿAbd al-Raḥmān al-Sharqāwī, "Little Dreams," from *Aḥlām ṣaghīra*. Cairo: Hay'at al-kuttāb, 1956. Reprinted in *Mu'allafāt ʿAbd al-Raḥmān al-Sharqāwī*, vol. 1. Cairo: Al-Hay'a al-miṣriyya al-ʿāmma lil-kitāb, 1978. Permission to translate granted by the General Egyptian Book Organization.

Suhayl Idrīs, "The Yellow Cotton Bird," from *Aqāṣīṣ thāniya*. Beirut: Dār al-ādāb, 1977. Permission to translate granted by the author.

Ghāda al-Sammān, "Another Scarecrow," from *Layl al-ghurabā'*. Beirut: Dār al-ādāb, 1966. Permission to translate granted by the author.

Fu'ād al-Takarlī, "The Boil," from *Al-Wajh al-ākhar*. 2d ed. Baghdad: Manshūrāt wizārat al-thaqāfa wa-al-iʿlām, 1982. Permission to translate granted by the publisher.

Ulfat al-Idilbī, "Hard Luck," from *Qiṣaṣ shāmiyya*. Damascus: Dār al-yaqẓa al-ʿarabiyya, 1954. Permission to translate granted by the author.

Laylā Bin Māmī, "I Want Him to Be Free," from *Ṣawmaʿa taḥtariq*. Tunis: Qāsim al-ʿArabī, 1968. Permission to translate granted by the publisher.

INDEX